Jewish Stars in Texas

NUMBER EIGHTY-FOUR
The Centennial Series
of the Association of Former Students
Texas A&M University

Jewish Stars
in Texas

Rabbis and Their Work

HOLLACE AVA WEINER

Foreword by Rabbi Jimmy Kessler

Texas A&M University Press
COLLEGE STATION

The paper used in this book meets the minimum requirements
of the American National Standard for Permanence
of Paper for Printed Library Materials, z39.48-1984.
Binding materials have been chosen for durability.

*Publication of this volume
is made possible in part by a grant
from the Texas Jewish Historical Society.*

Parts of the preface and chapters 1, 2, 3, 4, and 6 of the present work
appeared in "The Mixers: The Role of Rabbis Deep in the Heart of
Texas," by Hollace Ava Weiner, *American Jewish History* 85 (September, 1997): 289–332, © The Johns Hopkins University Press. Parts of
chapter 8 appeared in "A Reverence for Art in Lubbock," August 22,
1993, by Hollace Ava Weiner, © *Fort Worth Star-Telegram*. Parts of
chapter 5 appeared in "KKK Skeletons," February 25, 1990; "A Question of Principle," February 19, 1995; and "Trailblazing Texas Rabbi,"
January 25, 1997, all by Hollace Ava Weiner, © *Fort Worth Star-Telegram*.

Library of Congress Cataloging-in-Publication Data

Weiner, Hollace Ava, 1946–
    Jewish stars in Texas : rabbis and their work / Hollace Ava
Weiner ; foreword by Jimmy Kesler.
       p.   cm. — (The Centennial series of the Association of
Former Students, Texas A&M University ; no. 84)
    Includes bibliographical references and index.
    ISBN 0-89096-900-0 (c)
    1. Rabbis—Texas—Biography.   2. Jews—Texas—Social
life and customs.   3. Reform Judaism—Texas.   4. Texas—
Biography.   5. Texas—Ethnic relations.   I. Title   II. Series.
BM750.W33   1999
296′.092′2764—dc21   99-30317
[B]   CIP

Contents

Illustrations

Foreword

The teachers of Israel have historically reflected in their lives the history of the Jews of their generation. Texas is no exception. The rabbis of the Lone Star State, whether newcomers or natives, have faithfully responded to the calling of their people. Moreover, they have embodied the hopes and expectations of those who sought to preserve their heritage while contributing to their communities. Their stories are the fruition of the dreams of many. These rabbis truly shined in Texas and had a significant role in shaping the Texas Jewish experience.

Hollace Ava Weiner has given us a major link in the recorded history of Texas Jewry by compiling, and thereby preserving, this rich heritage. Her selection of rabbis provides the reader with an overview of some of the most well-known members of the Texas Jewish community, as well as some of the lesser known. The lives of these rabbis help convey an understanding of Jewish life in Texas. Passing on such stories is a key to keeping a people alive.

Hollace's volume, *Jewish Stars in Texas: Rabbis and Their Work,* joins a limited number of books on the Jews of Texas. Although the presence of Jews in the region stretches back to the conquistadors, until recently little has been written about them. Jews came to *Nueva España* in the early 1500s as the property of those who searched for wealth in the New World. These Jews were record keepers who provided administrative skills lacking in the average Spaniard. Although they were literate, we know little of them. Unfortunately the only extant records of their presence are those of the Inquisition, the source of their persecution.

Fortunately for students of history, Weiner has preserved an important record of experiences. Moreover, she has not shied away from recording controversy as well as convention. Her writing clearly conveys the laughter, tears, feelings, and thinking of these notable teachers. Her experience and persistence as a journalist have meshed well with the requirements for a writer of history, for she has unearthed previously unpublished personal journals and letters. The resulting narratives, descriptive of their respective communities, add immeasurably to our understanding of life in Texas by Jews and non-Jews.

Weiner has also gathered comments from those who knew the subjects. Inasmuch as many of the rabbis were placed in the paths of the most influential, her book introduces us to such luminaries as Stanley Marcus, Robert Strauss, and federal judge Reynaldo Garza. As a result, we have a unique perspective on historical events.

As a native Texan, a Texas rabbi for the past three decades, and founder of the Texas Jewish Historical Society, I have personally known several of the rabbis in this book and had the opportunity to consider their activities in light of the Texas Jewish experience. *Jewish Stars in Texas* gives us insight that might otherwise be lost. Having written the first doctorate on Texas Jewish history, I am aware of the rich, untapped resources available. This book provides a wonderful example of what can be produced from these materials. Hollace Weiner is to be congratulated for this outstanding effort.

RABBI JIMMY KESSLER, D.H.L.
CONGREGATION B'NAI ISRAEL
GALVESTON, TEXAS

Preface

When I arrived in Texas the summer of 1977, my Dallas cousins, Irene and Joe, had an old issue of *D: The Magazine of Dallas* propped on their mantel like some favorite family portrait. The cover pictured Rabbi Levi Olan, a local icon with a countenance guaranteed to sell magazines.[1] Nine months later, I moved to Fort Worth, a city of half a million, where Rabbi Robert Schur's name was a household word. He was a civil rights leader and humanitarian with a reputation disproportionate to his 350-member Reform congregation. The city's Orthodox rabbi, Isadore Garsek, was likewise a giant in the public eye. A scholarly entertainer and educator, Garsek drew busloads of Jews and non-Jews to his book reviews, where he breathed expression into characters from best-selling novels.

The prominence of these rabbis gave me culture shock. I was born in Washington, D.C., where 5 percent of the populace is Jewish and rabbis are too numerous to gain much notice. In Texas, where Jews are a minuscule portion of the population—six-tenths of 1 percent—rabbis had evolved into public personalities, precious resources recruited for a variety of roles. Their scarcity guaranteed their visibility and entrée to leadership circles. In a Bible Belt state that historically prized individuality over conformity, rabbis were objects of curiosity and respect who brought erudition and an exotic element to the Western mix. Their Old Testament roots engendered deference, while their educational training outside the region elevated them to a lofty intellectual plane. Moreover, a rabbi's keen sense of social justice, honed through centuries of Talmudic commentary, gave him moral clout, particularly in Texas where other ministers stressed salvation in the next world rather than justice on earth. The reason a rabbi was on a magazine cover became clear.

Fast-forward to 1991. I was a veteran reporter with the *Fort Worth Star-Telegram,* interviewing an Israeli at the home of Fay Brachman, president of the Texas Jewish Historical Society. In persuasive, Jewish-mother style, Fay pulled me aside and practically ordered me to write a book about the Lone Star State's Jewish past. So much has occurred; so little is recorded.

Her directive echoed in my soul. Although I was a news reporter rather than a religion writer, stories of Jewish interest often carried my byline. Recording my heritage comes naturally. Still, a book topic eluded me for a year. Then I found myself at a banquet, seated next to a grandmother from Lubbock who had a crucifix dangling from her neck and a twang to rival LBJ's. "Ah knew a Jew once," Emily Finnell told me. "He was Rabbi Alex Kline. He brought art and culture to Lubbock, Texas." So great was this rabbi's reputation that when he died, the local museum named a room in his honor.

Click! Then and there I decided to examine Texas history through the eyes of its rabbis. Stories about their careers and their communities could provide a new window on Texas' past and the American Jewish experience. So many nearly forgotten rabbis have left imprints on twentieth-century Texas. As civic leaders they founded hospitals, symphonies, and charities. As moral leaders, they confronted the Ku Klux Klan and championed racial minorities. Appointed to state boards, rabbis worked for academic freedom and prison reform. Within the Jewish world, they were instrumental in resettling ten thousand refugees who entered the United States through Galveston and eight thousand penniless Jews who arrived in North America via Mexico's port of Veracruz. Outside the Jewish community, they delivered invocations at rodeos and instinctively formed ecumenical alliances with Texans of all creeds. The names of Lone Star rabbis appear on state documents, on cornerstones, and in Texas and Mexican history books.

Elsewhere they might not have been as proactive or prominent. Rabbis who accepted a call to the Lone Star State, especially when it was still a far corner of the Diaspora, often did so as a last resort. Several were never ordained. Others had no better pulpit offers. Those from Europe were often rebelling against traditional religious practices. These maverick rabbis were drawn to places with little Jewish history or hierarchy, communities where they could create their own religious blueprint. Texas provided ample room.

Mixers, mavericks, and motivators, the eleven rabbis profiled in this study are a varied lot, selected mainly for their impact beyond their congregations. All of them were foreign-born (although five grew up in the United States), an indication that they were amenable to change. Nine of the rabbis were raised within a framework of Orthodox Judaism—the denomination that stresses rituals and traditions—yet none remained as observant into adulthood or old age. Ten of these rabbis led congregations that affiliated with Judaism's Reform movement—the denomination that interprets the faith in light of Western culture and stresses social justice and community service. One of the rabbis was affiliated with both the Reform and the Conservative branch of Judaism, which seeks to balance tradition with modernity. Not surprisingly, Reform rabbis best fit the book's selection criteria of rabbinical figures who became civic leaders. Texas history, however, includes many Orthodox and Conservative rabbis who became well-known municipal leaders. Traditional rabbis mentioned in the book and who merit further study in this regard include Isadore Garsek of Fort Worth, Abraham Schechter of Houston, and Joseph Roth of El Paso.

The breadth and shape of Texas made geography another selection criteria for this study of influential rabbis. A vast state, Texas stretches 800 miles, north to south, from the Panhandle to the Gulf of Mexico, and 770 miles, east to west, from the forests bordering the Deep South to the deserts of the Southwest. Surely the Jewish community in Lubbock—an arid, agricultural hub on the edge of the Great Plains—developed with a different profile than Brownsville's congregation on the Gulf Coast's Mexican border. The dynamics of Houston—with its population explosions—seemed evident in the recurrent schisms within its Jewish congregations. Dallas, a more stable city, historically resolved its frictions behind the scenes. Fort Worth, although only forty miles west of Dallas, developed a Jewish community a world apart—smaller, less organized, more indifferent, and less munificent toward Jewish causes. When rabbis stepped up to pulpits across Texas, the interaction of place and personality shaped their careers.

Scattered Jews have been part of the Texas landscape since before its founding as a republic. Jewish soldiers of fortune and land developers came as single men into what was a Catholic province of Mexico. When Texas gained its independence in 1836, the republic's thirty-nine thousand inhabitants included two hundred Jews, among them at least a dozen veterans of the Texas Revolution.[2] A decade later, when Texas attained statehood, it had one Jewish institution—a Hebrew cemetery consecrated in Houston in 1844 by a visiting rabbi.

The first concentrated wave of Jewish settlers to Texas came in the 1870s, with the completion of railroad lines. Texas was often a place of second settlement for these entrepreneurs. Many were merchants from Germany (meaning Alsace and Prussia) who had previously lived in the Midwest or the Deep South. A second wave of Jewish immigrants began arriving in the 1880s, driven from Eastern Europe by pogroms—Russian government-

The eleven cities profiled in this book are designated by six-pointed Jewish stars. Austin, the Texas state capital, has a five-pointed star. Other cities shown on the map are among the places mentioned in the text. Map by Frank Pontari.

sponsored massacres. These refugees had led insulated lives and clung to past religious rituals, leading to tension between them and the old-guard Jews, who seemed more Texan than Jewish. A third wave of Jews came to Texas between 1907 and 1914, drawn by the Galveston movement, an effort to steer refugees away from the crowded northeastern cities and into the hinterland. From this wave of ten thousand refugees, three thousand settled in Texas, eventually sending for relatives.

The first rabbi in this case study, Heinrich Schwarz, was an immigrant from the first wave, an old-fashioned figure, more of a family rabbi than a communal leader. Research indicates that he was Texas' first ordained rabbi. His 1873 migration to Hempstead, a rail depot fifty miles beyond Houston, illustrates why Jews initially came to Texas and how they proliferated and culturally assimilated. The rabbi's great-grandson, politician Robert Schwarz Strauss, became chairman of the National Democratic Party and United States ambassador to Russia.

Rabbi Samuel Rosinger, a younger, more adaptable religious figure than Schwarz, was jobless in 1910 when he answered a want ad from a Beaumont synagogue seeking a "mixer." The ad demonstrated the congregation's need of an "ethnic broker," a diplomat who could "bridge the gap between different cultures," an ambassador to the gentiles equipped to take a seat at the communal table in a city where Jews were a prominent minority and everyone was awash in oil.[3]

As rabbis "mixed" they took the lead in communal projects and gained secular notice. Tyler's Maurice Faber served on the University of Texas Board of Regents, making front-page news in 1916 when he tangled with the governor over academic freedom. Galveston's Henry Cohen, who spearheaded state prison reform, lobbied and befriended mayors, governors, and presidents. Cohen's name has become synonymous with *West of Hester Street* (Mondell Productions, 1983), the docu-drama that reenacts the arrival of Jews through Galveston.

Fort Worth's Rabbi G. George Fox provides some counterpoint to Cohen. While bold and humanitarian, Fox had a less than positive attitude toward the refugee movement that Cohen championed; Fox had Jewish prostitutes deported, while Cohen delivered funeral rites over a harlot's grave; Fox minimized the influence of the Ku Klux Klan, while Cohen confronted it. Fox's twelve years in Texas spotlight the uneasy collisions and accommodations between cultures. His career also contrasts the far-reaching impact of a Texas pulpit with the unheralded ministry of a big city rabbi.

The theme of refugee resettlement picks up in El Paso with Rabbi Martin Zielonka, who helped resolve an international dilemma when illegal Jewish refugees slipped across the border in 1921. Zielonka's efforts led to the twentieth century's largest Jewish migration to Mexico. Despite his refugee relief work, Zielonka fell into disfavor with much of El Paso Jewry because of his ideological stance against Zionism—another theme that runs through the Jewish history of the region.

A better consensus builder was Sam Perl, a lay rabbi whose Brownsville congregation provides a close-up of small-town life along the Texas-Mexican border. A consummate "ethnic broker," Perl was neither a scholar nor a theologian. He was a haberdasher with the personality, civic pride, chutzpah, conciliatory skills, and deep religious attachment sought in a Texas rabbi. His heartwarming career illustrates how, in the absence of a trained rabbi, the community anointed one.

Lubbock's Rabbi Alex Kline also became a leading citizen in a remote town with a dearth of Jews. Refined, intellectual, and at the end of a disappointing career, Kline expected to retire to obscurity. Instead, his West Texas years turned into his zenith. Audiences thrilled to his cut-and-pasted collection of artistic prints. At a time when Dallasites tried to outlaw abstract art, Kline taught Lubbock residents to appreciate it. Through the medium of art, Alex Kline, along with his wife and partner Eleanore, built bridges of tolerance and understanding.

Not all rabbis achieved popular success. Ephraim Frisch—like Kline an intellectual who shared his professional life with his wife—was forced to retire from his San Antonio pulpit in 1942. Still, he is revered for his support of labor unions, his focus upon poor Mexican Americans, and his sentiments against Francisco Franco's tyranny in Spain. A visionary, he inspired a generation of idealistic young adults, but alienated many establishment Jews and gentiles by his lack of tact. In San Antonio, he remains controversial.

World War II set off a tinderbox of emotions among Jews over whether or not to champion the creation of Israel. Houston's most prestigious congregation, Beth Israel, ruptured over political Zionism. The drama that unfolded has rarely been explored in print, although it directly affected the careers of three rabbis—Henry Barnston, Robert I. Kahn, and Hyman Judah Schachtel. The narrative focuses on Schachtel, a friend to LBJ and George Bush, a rabbi who reflected Houston's love of the limelight.

This study closes with another postwar pulpit, that of Dallas's Rabbi Levi Olan. A heavyweight thinker, arresting speaker, and community activist, Olan roasted the right wing, championed African Americans, and became a media star via his Sunday radio sermons. His career invites comparison with Schachtel. Both were prominent in major metropolitan areas; both built national reputations; both delivered weekly radio sermons. Olan, however, dared make audiences and public officials uncomfortable. He never soothed, but challenged and changed attitudes. His arrival and his impact are evidence of the growth and maturity of the Texas rabbinate.

Before embarking on this research, I made a pilgrimage to Cincinnati to run my ideas by the late Rabbi Jacob Rader Marcus, founder of the American Jewish Archives and blunt authority on Jewish American history.[4] Professor Marcus, then ninety-seven years old, cautioned me that rabbis who went to Texas, particularly before the Second World War, were not the best and the brightest. The motion picture, *The Frisco Kid* (Warner Brothers, 1979), which chronicles the pratfalls of a young rabbi exiled from Europe to the Far West, was not far off the mark. Texas, Marcus recalled, was a *"loch,"* a hole, a landscape incapable of retaining polished or accomplished rabbis. He allowed that most rabbis who ventured to Texas were "decent fellows," but not the caliber sought by prestigious pulpits in New York, Chicago, or Cincinnati.

In light of his remarks, the professor was surprised to learn that Maurice Faber, a lackluster member of the Central Conference of American Rabbis, had pulled the charter of a Masonic Lodge allied with the Klan. He was unaware that Rabbi Sidney Wolf, his former student, had founded the Corpus Christi Symphony and integrated the municipal golf course. He was fascinated with Martin Zielonka's refugee work in Mexico and insisted that all my files on the subject be copied, at his expense, and sent to the American Jewish Archives.

Still, the Cincinnati-based historian remained irreverent toward Rabbi Henry Cohen, describing him as "something of a poseur," a man with "pizzazz," but without a rabbinical diploma. The only Texas rabbi Marcus praised wholeheartedly was Levi Olan, the theologian whose portrait had graced the cover of *D* magazine. Marcus, I subsequently learned, had urged Levi Olan to accept the Dallas pulpit.

As the guru of American Jewish history, Marcus seemed intrigued that so many "average" rabbis had mastered the Texas environment and made a difference far beyond their pulpits. He postulated that Texas' needs had served as a catalyst to their careers, turning these religious leaders into "men for all seasons." Marcus cautioned that I not treat Texas rabbis as saints, but he acknowledged that our conversation had revealed the Lone Star State as an untapped vein of rabbinical research and Jewish scholarship.

Acknowledgments

The first interview was December 13, 1992, with the irreverent Jacob Rader Marcus in Cincinnati; the last was June 22, 1998, with a misty-eyed Sadye Maye Garsek in Fort Worth. In between, I traveled thousand of miles in the air and on the road, reminisced with hundreds of people, used up reams of paper, acquired two new library cards, and lost two library books. I met new colleagues, made dozens of friends, and drew support and expertise from those who have always been there for me.

Completing this book would have been impossible without the patience and support of my husband, Bruce, to whom I am indebted for his unconditional love and for persuading me to flee the land of bagels and lox for the domain of boots and barbecue. Additional thanks to my children, Mark and Dawn, whose eyes lit up at the idea that I would write a book about Lone Star rabbis; and to my big sister and kindred spirit, Judie Mopsik, for her empathy and her advice to call Mary Holdcroft, the career counselor who helped focus my resolve.

At the *Fort Worth Star-Telegram,* book editor Larry Swindell gave counsel on writing a prospectus; computer whizzes Jim Brady, Mike Gerst, and Josh Romonek set up my software; Carolyn Bauman turned old photos and documents into illustrations; Frank Pontari illustrated the first rabbinical profile I wrote for the paper in 1993, and he came through with my final request for a Jewish-starred map; Carmelita Bevill saved me with her copyediting eye; Cathy Frisinger double-checked for typos.

Marcie Cohen Ferris, formerly with the Museum of the Southern Jewish Experience, counseled me to gather an informal advisory committee of academicians. She steered me to Bobbie Malone, who brainstormed and line-edited, off and on, for six years; and Juliet George, a soul mate who loaned me reference books that I kept for the duration. When Berkley Kalin and Mark Bauman planned an anthology called *Quiet Voices: Southern Rabbis and Black Civil Rights* (University of Alabama Press, 1997), Juliet referred them to me for a profile of Corpus Christi rabbi Sidney Wolf. Mark Bauman, working with Bobbie Malone, decreed that my next project would be an essay in *American Jewish History* (September, 1997) examining the phenomenon of "The Mixers." A master teacher and editor, it was Bauman who began turning me from journalist into historian through his searing critiques. My virtual committee also includes *Hell's Half Acre* historian Richard Selcer, who suggested that I query Texas A&M University Press.

Without the archivists who placed a smorgasbord of material before me, this research would have been impossible. I am indebted to Kevin Proffitt and his incomparable staff at the American Jewish Archives; Carol Roark at the Dallas Public Library's Texas/Dallas History and Archives Division; Carrie Hoffman, at Houston's Beth Israel Library; Paige Thomas, at Southern Methodist University's posh Bridwell Library; Kinga Perzynska at the Catholic Archives of Texas; Casey Greene and Shelly Henley Keller at the Rosenberg Library's Galveston and Texas History Center; Judy Linsley and Jonathan Gerland at Beaumont's Tyrrell Historical Library; Gary Mack and Marian Ann Montgomery at the Sixth Floor Museum; and Norma Spungeon, at Spertus Institute's Chicago Jewish Archives. Norma gave my number to a New York grad student who told me about the American Jewish Archives' four-week, $1,000 fellowships. I applied, and a year later was awarded the Rabbi Frederic A. Doppelt Memorial Fellowship in American Jewish Studies.

A couple of two-week stints at the American Jewish Archives, in the fall of 1996 and the spring of 1997, turned this project from pastime to obsession. Mike Meyer sat with me at a picnic table and discussed the outline. Alex Rofé, my dinner and walking companion from Hebrew University, translated Rabbi Heinrich Schwarz's nineteenth-century Hebrew ramblings. Tobias Brinkmann deciphered Schwarz's German penmanship and filled gaps in my reading list. I became joined at the hips with Linda Borish and Holly Snyder, forming a triumvirate we dubbed "the three fellows." Rabbi Shelly Zimmerman, Hebrew Union College president and a Texan in exile, suggested asking Jonathan Sarna at Brandeis University to review my work. Sarna read the rough drafts and responded with suggested articles, corrections, insights, encouragement, and upbeat e-mail. Zimmerman also directed me to A. Stanley Dreyfus, another ex-Texan who, with wife Marianne, welcomed me to their Brooklyn room with a view. Another Rock of Gibraltar has been Philadelphia rabbi Henry Cohen, grandson of the famous Galveston rabbi.

The librarians who went the extra mile include Don Jacobs at the underfunded Fort Worth Public Library, Dan Sharon at Spertus's Asher Library, Pradeep Lele at Lamar University, and Maureen Reister of the Weisberg Library at Dallas Temple Emanu-El. The Southern Jewish Historical Society endorsed my project with a grant to assist with photos and indexing. The Texas Jewish Historical Society provided a grant as well as moral support and contacts from El Paso to Beaumont.

In his book, *The Art and Craft of Feature Writing* (New American Library, 1988), author William Blundell advises biographers to latch onto a "rabbi"—a wise, knowledgeable, unselfish source, willing to give background data and entrée to other sources. I was blessed with many such "rabbis"—in Brownsville, Bruce Aiken and Simon Rubinsky; in Beaumont, Lawrence Blum; in Lubbock, Pauline Bean and Norma Skibell; in Corpus Christi, Helen Wilk; in San Antonio, Allen Goldsmith; in Austin, Decherd and Margaret Ann Turner. James Wilkins led me to folks who recalled Maurice Faber. Rosalind and Herman Horwitz arranged dinner with Sam Rosinger's surrogate daughters. Bill Roddy shared Heinrich Schwarz's journals. The incomparable Frances Kallison shared anecdotes and expertise. Betty Kyle staged the first Schwarz reunion. Members of the Journalism and Women Symposium gave me fortitude—particularly ex-Texan Celia Morris, who opened up her little black book with phone numbers for Dave McComb and Mimi Gladstein. Mimi became part of my virtual committee.

For bed-and-breakfasts, thanks to Aunt Genell and Uncle Sanford; Margie and Glen Meyer of Cincinnati, who put up a stranger; Susy and Zay Smith of Chicago, who kept me the week Yitzhak Rabin was assassinated; Marina and Dominick Pisano in San Antonio; Mary and Rick Clark in Kentucky; Rose and Dick Rubin in Memphis; Cyvia and Melvin Wolff of Houston, who shared observations over a home-cooked meal; Charlotte Lee, who made pancakes for breakfast in San Antonio; and Joe Cutbirth, who extended an invitation to sleep on his couch whenever I was in Austin. I did, often.

For reading chapters in various stages, *todah rabah* (thank you) to Bruce Rutherford, Rachel Heimovics, Norman Schwartz, Seth Wolitz, Corinne Krause, Rolly Schur, Bob LaRocca, Mark Murphy, Sandra Lubarsky, Amrita Shlachter, Marianne and Harvey Plaut—who double-checked names and population figures and identified the basketball players in a 1917 photo. Batya Brand remained on call for Hebrew translations. Jimmy Kessler read over my shoulder the past year. My final editor was *my* rabbi, Ralph Mecklenburger, whose clear thinking helped me draw conclusions from this wealth of stories.

In memoriam, I cannot forget those who shared their recollections and did not live to read the completed manuscript: Yvonne Ewell, Edwin Gale, Leonard Goodman Sr., Leonard Goodman Jr., Doris Kivel, Lewis Lee, Jacob Rader Marcus, Bill Rips, Sally Rosen, Marion Weil, and Bébé Wolf. Their passing underscores the importance of the memories in this book.

Jewish Stars in Texas

1

From the Prussian Provinces to the Texas Frontier

HEINRICH (CHAYIM) SCHWARZ, HEMPSTEAD

Yis-ga-dal v'-yis-ka-dash sh'-may rah-baw.
Let God's glory be extolled, let God's great name
be hallowed in the world.

THE MOURNERS MURMURED the ancient Hebrew lines as they stood in prayer, crowded into a backyard chapel across the road from a Texas county courthouse. Swaying forward and back, they chanted the *Kaddish* in memory of Rabbi Heinrich Schwarz. The seventy-six-year-old scholar from Prussia had immigrated to Hempstead twenty-seven years before in 1873 and gained notice as the first ordained rabbi to settle in the Lone Star State.[1] To the Jewish men, women, and children gathered at the funeral, the rabbi was simply "Chayim." He was recalled as a husband, brother, uncle, father of nine, and grandfather of thirty-five, a spiritual leader so immersed in Jewish learning that he penned Hebraic elegies and had packed a Torah scroll for his journey to America. To the gentiles paying respects, the rabbi was mourned as a pastor, linguist, poet, and pious neighbor, highly regarded among the two thousand souls scattered throughout this farm-and-ranch community, a watermelon capital fifty miles northwest of Houston.[2]

Conducting the funeral was Rabbi Aron Suhler from Waco, son-in-law of the deceased, also an ordained rabbi, but a part-time clergyman with letterhead stationery from Massachusetts Mutual Life Insurance Company.[3] Among the pallbearers was Gabriel Schwarz, seventy, an itinerant optometrist who had hurried home from Indian Territory for his eldest brother's funeral.[4] Hard of hearing, Gabriel clutched a horn to his ear. He grieved alongside his youngest brother, Sam, fifty-nine, who, despite declaring bankruptcy the year before, was among Hempstead's leading public servants—a Mason, a charter school board member, and a Confederate veteran with two bullets lodged in his body.[5] Sam Schwarz had helped design this white clapboard synagogue. He constructed it in 1880 with his nephew Benno, the rabbi's eldest son, a merchandising whiz who operated Hempstead's leading store—the Big Store. The family's quaint Gothic chapel, with its arched windows, sharply peaked roof, and yellow stained glass, could have been mistaken for a Baptist church. It graced Benno's backyard. The Schwarzes named their synagogue the Hempstead Hebrew Congregation, although many called it *Heychal Chayim,* a Hebrew name with dual meaning—Temple of Life and Heinrich's Palace.[6]

This morning, October 19, 1900, the deceased rabbi's offspring shared the front-row pews. Leo was in from Lockhart, a railroad stop thirty miles south of the state capital. He had moved from Hempstead several years before after a falling-out with brother Benno, a rift still evident in his wife Selma's cool demeanor. A successful merchant, Leo was full of details of his latest buying trips to New York and Hamburg, Germany. Near Leo, veiled in black, was his sister Valeria Schwarz Lissner, also of Lockhart. Similarly dressed for mourning were the departed's two other daughters: Frances Schwarz Simmons, the family bookworm who inherited her father's diaries and notebooks; and Clara Schwarz Suhler, the officiating rabbi's wife, a mother of nine, who enjoyed smoking little black cigars. Both sisters had made the 136-mile journey by train from Waco. Near them sat their brother Alfred, the ne'er-do-well of the family, a profligate with wives on both sides of the ocean—Hulda, in Hempstead with an infant; and Lina, in Europe raising four youngsters. Also among the pallbearers were two more Schwarz brothers—George, a dutiful son and dependable dry-goods clerk; and Marks, the youngest son, a Houston slumlord who squirreled away his profits in dozens of banks around the state.

The Hempstead Hebrew Congregation, also called Heychal Chayim *(Heinrich's Palace), served the Jews of Hempstead from the 1880s until 1939.*
From Edwin M. Gale Papers.

Behind the immediate family stood the Galewsky brothers—Morris, Jake, and Haiman—childhood friends of the Schwarzes who had followed their lead to Texas, opened dry-goods stores in Hempstead, and married into the extended family tree of Rabbi Heinrich Schwarz.[7]

From the Prussian provinces to the Texas frontier, the Schwarzes had ventured to Texas one by one and in family clusters. Though part of a large, ongoing wave of German Jews coming to America, they were typical of a smaller stream that trickled into the Lone Star State post–Civil War. Their family history illuminates the reasons German-speaking Jews left Europe for the United States, the paths they took to the Southwest, and the evolution—as well as the dilution—of Judaism on Texas soil. The small-town experience Americanized the Schwarzes and prepared their children and grandchildren to move into larger cities and social spheres. Like many settlers arriving in frontier Texas, the Schwarzes had never been big-city people. Rather, they were small-town folks following new rail lines in search of economic opportunities. Although their passports identified the Schwarzes as Prussian Jews, there was nothing of Prussia in their hearts. The Texas terrain—where few people were native-born—gave them a regional identity and a cultural pride that quickly became entwined in their religious heritage.

THE NEW WORLD AND THE OLD

The presence of a rabbi among the Schwarzes distinguished their clan from all others. For a rabbi to venture to Texas was rare. Rabbi Heinrich Schwarz had come to Hempstead reluctantly, skeptically, after years of entreaties from his brothers. He was the last of the Schwarzes to immigrate, and no wonder. Texas was a wilderness in the 1870s with fewer than three thousand scattered Jews—a mere two-tenths of a percent of its population.[8] Worship was no priority in Texas, and neither was education. Jewish scholars spoke of Texas as exile.[9] Even Baptists termed Texas a "theological dumping ground."[10] What was fertile field for merchants appeared to be a wasteland to clergy, a place where guns were more plentiful than Bibles and acts of God materialized in tornadoes and hurricanes. Before the turn of the century, only the most zealous or adventurous clergy came. Heinrich Schwarz, a timid man and a gentle scholar, was neither. The pull of family, rather than a call from God, propelled him to this backwater.[11]

Initially a part of Mexico, Texas had begun as a territory where only

Catholic worship was permitted. After its 1836 independence, Texas became missionary territory for preachers seeking the salvation of souls and
the prohibition of spirits.[12] Texas had no resident rabbis in 1844, when
Texas' first Jewish cemetery was consecrated in Houston; or in 1852, when
a visiting New Orleans rabbi dedicated a second Jewish cemetery in Galveston. The handful of so-called rabbis who followed were largely free-
lancers, wandering scholars, jobless émigrés, even impostors who lacked
religious credentials. They found employment by answering want ads
placed in the Jewish press by remote communities seeking kosher butchers, Hebrew readers, cantors, and circumcisers to whom they gave the
honorary and affectionate title of "rev." Houston Jewry saw five such religious leaders come and go between 1859 and 1876.[13] Texarkana Jews settled
for less, sharing with Protestants the services of a Polish Jew—the Rev.
Charles Goldberg—who had converted to Christianity.[14] Galveston's energetic rabbi, Dr. Abraham Blum, had studied at an Alsatian seminary but
was no doctor of divinity. His title came from the local medical college,
and most of his medical experience, from circumcisions.[15]

Rabbi Heinrich Schwarz had *s'mikhah,* a Hebrew term for ordination.
A rabbinical sage had lain his hands on Heinrich's head and confirmed his
student's knowledge of Judaic precepts and rabbinical law. Heinrich's
teacher was Rabbi Meir Loeb ben Jehiel Michael, a man so revered among
Jewish scholars that he was called the Malbim, an acronym taken from his
Hebrew initials. He was also called "der Kempener," after the years he
spent in Heinrich Schwarz's hometown.[16]

The Schwarzes traced their roots to Kempen, a village in the duchy of
Posen, a forested region that Prussia annexed from Poland during the
1790s. Outsiders referred to Poseners as "country Jews" and *"Hinterberlin-
ers"* because they lived beyond the cultured capital of Berlin. Of Kempen's
twelve thousand residents, three thousand were Jewish—as many Jews as
in all of Texas. Despite their numbers and their literacy, the Jews of Kempen were minority-status souls, blackballed from craft guilds, denied civil
service jobs, and restricted to housing in the city's Jewish quarter. They
could attend but not teach at universities. Centuries-old Church restrictions against Jewish land ownership kept them from becoming farmers.
They were, however, eligible for the army, which inducted soldiers for up
to twenty years and did not promote Jews.[17]

The Schwarz family patriarch of old was Baruch Benjamin, an impoverished merchant, private Hebrew teacher, and freelance writer. Stricken
with cholera on December 20, 1848, the fifty-year-old scholar died within

twelve hours. He left behind his wife, Helene, and six children, among them, three sons—Chayim, Gabriel, and Sam—who were close in spirit yet distant in outlook.[18]

Chayim—better known by his German name, Heinrich—was the eldest, a scholar teaching elementary school in the nearby town of Rawicz while studying for the rabbinate. After the customary year of mourning, he married Julia (Gittel) Nathan, one of his students, then embarked on a rabbinical career filled with more frustrations than rewards. His calling took him to dots on the map such as Reichenbach, Allenstein, and Gumbinnen—Prussian towns that Jews were deserting for the capitals of Europe and America.[19] He yearned for the life of a full-time scholar and spiritual leader. However, his struggling congregations could neither afford a *shochet* to slaughter geese and cattle in the kosher manner nor a teacher to tutor bar mitzvah students. These demeaning duties fell to him. In his private journal, Heinrich complained of constantly "soiling" his hands with the blood of "sheep and goats" and teaching Hebrew to insolent children who boarded in his home. "So that I will not become a mockery, . . . I need to find another way to help myself," he confided in a letter to a colleague.[20]

WESTWARD, HO! ONE BY ONE

While Heinrich struggled professionally, his brother Gabriel had turned into the epitome of a wandering Jew. To escape conscription, Gabriel had fled to the United States in 1848. In New York, he married Jeanette Koppel, a stylish immigrant girl, and together they worked their way down the Atlantic seaboard. Gabriel failed to contact his family for a decade, and when he finally wrote home, he was raising a family in Charleston, South Carolina, and doing well enough to send money for others to join him.

His youngest brother, Sam, followed. Sam Schwarz was a resourceful fellow, fluent in a number of languages and trades, with work experience as a foreign-language tutor and stock clerk. He had attended Breslau's Jewish Theological Seminary until his money ran out. After receiving Gabriel's letter, Sam embarked on a seven-week voyage to Charleston, where he went to work hauling pine-log firewood for a dollar a day. He felt instant allegiance to his surroundings, and in 1860, before the first shots of the Civil War were fired at nearby Fort Sumter, Sam enlisted for the Confederate cause. He fought at Manassas, was wounded in battle along the

Rappahannock River, and suffered another injury at Jacksonville, Florida, where he was taken prisoner.[21] Released in New York after the South's surrender, Sam gravitated to an enclave of Posen immigrants. Despite Sam's Confederate ties, these fellow Jews welcomed him as a *landsman,* a fellow countryman, and introduced him to seventeen-year-old Minna Hirsch, his future bride.

The newlyweds first settled in Charleston, then contemplated a move out West because each of them had a brother in Texas. Gabriel, who somehow eluded service during the Civil War, wrote that he and Jeanette had journeyed to Hempstead, Texas, by Conestoga wagon, along with their daughter, who played with an apronful of worthless Confederate currency.[22] Minna's older brother, Adolph Harris, a dry-goods merchant who immigrated to Texas via Galveston in 1859, operated a flourishing Houston store.[23] With encouragement and a few dollars from both sides of the family, Sam and Minna saved for the journey and by 1868 planted their hopes and their stakes in Hempstead.[24]

A day's travel by stagecoach from Houston, Hempstead was a railhead town, a destination for farmers who carted cotton and watermelons to the depot. It was also a lawless locale, dubbed "Six Shooter Junction," a county seat where outspoken newspaper editors were "shot or forced to move on."[25] Commercially, Hempstead showed promise with its three hotels, bookstore, iron foundry, cotton gins, and shops making soap, brooms, plows, and furniture. White clay beneath the topsoil produced crockery that held a glaze. Berries grew wild in the timbered bottomlands of the Brazos where unfenced cattle grazed. Although a young town, established in 1857, Hempstead heralded the region's past. Thirty-two of Stephen F. Austin's "Old Three-Hundred" Texas settlers had land grants in the vicinity. At Liendo Plantation, five miles from town, General Sam Houston had camped with the ragtag army of the Republic of Texas. During Reconstruction, Major General George Custer, later of Little Bighorn fame, based his Union troops at Liendo Plantation.[26]

Sam, Minna, and their two-year-old daughter arrived in Hempstead two years before the federal troops' departure. Sam opened a dry-goods store, joined veterans' groups, and was tapped for membership in the local fraternal order of the Chosen Friend Lodge Knights, signaling his acceptance into Waller County's inner circle. Already, Sam's southern identity was more evident than his Prussian past. He wrote letters home that extolled Hempstead's blessings and urged others to join him.

Heinrich showed no interest in the United States, but his children were eager. The rabbi's eldest son, eighteen-year-old Benno, arrived in Hempstead early in 1870 and opened a shop a block from the railroad station. Alfred, an incorrigible boy of fifteen, followed the next year. When Leo turned eighteen in 1872, he too left Europe, traveling steerage and slipping the crew a few extra coins for sour pickles that calmed his seasickness. Leo kept a travel diary, recording his amazement at flying fish and rainbows that embraced the sky. When his ship docked in Havana, Cuba, the lad bought a dollar's worth of cigars at four cents apiece—one-fifth the Texas price. If Heinrich expected any of his sons to follow him into the rabbinate, it was Leo. But the youth was less intrigued with biblical lore than becoming part of the B. Schwarz & Brothers store in Texas. The rabbi's next son, George, followed suit.[27]

Rabbi Heinrich had his doubts about America. By 1872 he had moved to Lyck, an East Prussian mecca of Hebrew publishing and progressive ideas.[28] The rabbi was drawn there by the intellectual reformation stirring in Jewish circles. He studied the writings of Moses Mendelssohn, a Jewish philosopher and an icon of the German Enlightenment. He became an advocate of *Jüdische Wissenschaft*—literally Jewish Science, the analytical movement that systematically surveyed the breadth of Jewish history.[29] Comprehensive study of the past uncovered countless ways that Jewish observances had changed in response to surrounding cultures. Reformers, trying to coax European Jews from medieval into modern times, argued that the Jewish faith need not have static rituals but could bend and adapt. In concert with the intellectual movement, Heinrich translated the works of Jewish poets from fifteenth-century Spain and annotated these verses for discussion. He traced popular fables to their Mosaic sources and sold his writings to periodicals at the forefront of Jewish thought. One of those journals, called *Ha-Maggid,* revived biblical Hebrew to write about science, literature, and current events. Another publication he wrote for was *Der Israelit,* a German Jewish weekly whose editor advanced the rabbi money and maintained a personal correspondence.[30]

Heinrich also read the *American Israelite,* mailed to him by his brothers, who dared hope its want ads would prompt Heinrich to apply for an American pulpit. Heinrich was deeply troubled by what he read in this American Jewish tabloid. The *Israelite* preached a flexible strain of Judaism that dropped the dietary code laid out in Leviticus and discarded the skullcap—like the yarmulke Rabbi Schwarz wore at all times out of respect for the Almighty. This was too radical for Heinrich. The American Reform school of thinking abandoned the dream of returning to Zion, categorizing Judaism as simply another faith, comparable to Methodism. The *Israelite*'s publisher was Bohemian-born Isaac Mayer Wise, founder of the American Reform Jewish movement. Summing up his disapproval, Heinrich paraphrased a line from Isaiah and wrote in his journal, "I do not trust the plot of the Wise."[31]

What did impress the rabbi was the abundant opportunity in America, particularly Texas. Although Texas' Jews were few, they encountered scant anti-Semitism. Few Texans were native born, and the frontier judged men and women by their work ethic, not their worship practices. Christians showed more curiosity than animosity toward Jews, who mingled easily. In Houston, the Hebrew Benevolent Association took a secular turn by marching in the Fourth of July parade. Such social mixing was unheard of in Europe, where centuries of prejudice and legal discrimination blocked Jews from the mainstream.[32] Perpetual outsiders in Europe, Jews were insiders in Texas, influential civic figures elected and appointed to public office.

Yet Rabbi Heinrich's upbringing made him suspicious of non-Jews. Although Christians often preached "love thy neighbor"—a phrase taken from the Hebrew Bible—the Catholics and Protestants of Europe had historically libeled and persecuted the Jews. "A look into the pages of history fails to verify this . . . '—love thy neighbor'. . . . claim," Heinrich wrote.[33] The rabbi's mistrust of non-Jews—whom he collectively called "Canaanites"—played a large role in his reluctance to come to America. In Europe, he circulated within a Jewish universe and enjoyed the intellectual tug-of-war among his colleagues. In Texas he expected little, if any, Jewish scholarship. Still, he felt an emotional pull toward America. His brothers had wives and children whom he had never met, and his Texas kin lived far more comfortably than he.

Should he leave Europe or stay? The creation of the German Reich in 1871 had led to more freedom for Jews, but a stock market crash in early 1873 made scapegoats of Jewish bankers. Heinrich had saved enough money for tickets across the Atlantic. Would Germany's financial problems deflate his savings? If he moved to Texas, would he receive the same deferential nods a rabbi received in Kempen or Lyck? If he stayed in Europe, who would be left to marry his daughters? As he mulled over his future, the conflicted rabbi wrote in his notebook, *"Lech lecha,"* the same words God spoke to Abraham in Genesis: "Go forth from your country to a land that I will show you." He quoted another biblical verse, this time in a letter to his editor friend, a rhetorical question posed in 2 Kings 7:3: "Why should we sit here waiting for death?" The answer to Heinrich's dilemma was in the Bible. He would emigrate.[34]

For the final move of his life, the rabbi packed a trunk full of books—from the poetry of Heinrich Heine to the plays of Euripides in Greek. Tenderly, he wrapped a silver chalice inscribed as a remembrance from his congregation in Reichenbach—*H. Schwarz, z. Andenken v. seiner Gemeinde i. Reichenbach 1859*. The most precious possession the rabbi packed was a Torah, the handwritten parchment scroll with the Five Books of Moses. This scroll was rolled between two ornately carved wooden poles. With this treasure, the Hempstead Jewish community would become a congregation.

The rabbi also gathered the personal notebooks he had written in since the start of his rabbinical training. In these he had copied letters to matchmakers, requests to money lenders, drafts of sermons, and notations of births and deaths. There were pages of poetic epitaphs—Hebrew acrostics that spelled out names and attributes of scores of people he had buried. Some journal entries were written in calligraphic Hebrew print, others in the slanted German script taught in grade school. There was a smattering of French, Latin, Greek, Yiddish, and Aramaic. Occasionally, he had copied newspaper articles, among them his father's obituary. These notebooks told the story of Heinrich's adulthood. Blank pages remained for the next chapter in Texas.

THE ADJUSTMENT

Heinrich was forty-eight and Julia forty-five when they arrived in America in May, 1873, along with five remaining children—Clara, age twenty-two; Flora, twenty; Valeria, fifteen; Frances, seven; and Marks, five. The family received a celebrity welcome. The *Houston Telegraph* noted their arrival: "The Rev. H. Schwartz [*sic*], a Hebrew Rabbi . . . is about to locate in Hempstead, where he has a brother."[35] The *Brenham Weekly Banner* made mention.[36] Within days, Houston's Congregation Beth Israel invited Schwarz to conduct a service. "He delivered a fine speech in German and acted as *chazzan,* [reading and chanting in Hebrew] throughout the service," the *American Israelite* reported.[37]

*Rabbi Heinrich (Chayim) Schwarz, came to Hempstead, Texas, from Prussia in
1873, with the handwritten notebooks he had compiled during his rabbinical career.
This page includes epitaphs written in acrostic form for two children, Aryeh and
Menashe.* Photo composition by Carolyn Bauman. Portrait from Texas Jewry
Collections, the Texas Collection, Baylor University, Waco, Texas. Rabbi's
journal courtesy descendants of Frances Schwarz Simmons.

The following year, Rabbi Schwarz officiated in Dallas during the High
Holy Days of Rosh Hashanah and Yom Kippur. Two years later, Dallas's
Temple Emanu-El invited him back for the dedication of the city's first
synagogue.[38] Schwarz had by then established a scholarly rapport with
Dallas's first rabbi, Aron Suhler, a thirty-two-year-old widower and an
honors graduate of Wurzburg's Jewish seminary. Turning matchmaker,

Schwarz arranged for his eldest daughter, Clara, to accompany him to the May 30, 1876, dedication ceremony.[39] Three months later, the family announced Clara and Aron's upcoming wedding. "The felicitous event takes place on the 10th of next month when we will be on hand to congratulate the happy couple if business will permit a trip to Hempstead where the ceremony will take place," reported the editor of the *Dallas Weekly Herald*.[40]

Rabbi Schwarz encountered more scholarship than he expected in Hempstead. He acquired a gifted pupil, Jacob Voorsanger, the self-trained rabbi at Houston's Congregation Beth Israel. Voorsanger, a Dutch immigrant who had begun his pulpit career as a Philadelphia cantor, later became one of San Francisco's leading rabbis. While in Texas, from 1878 to 1886, Voorsanger made regular pilgrimages to Hempstead to engage in dialogue with Schwarz over the laws of the Torah. Calling himself Schwarz's "disciple," Voorsanger wrote the *American Israelite*: "The Rabbi H. Schwarz is, in your correspondent's humble opinion, one of the best Jewish scholars in the country, and were it not for his comparative ignorance of the English, would grace the highest position in the land. The constant flow of wisdom that proceeds from his lips is of exceeding benefit."[41]

Rabbi Schwarz began his days in prayer and study. At noon, he joined his brother Sam on the balcony of his store for lunch and conversation with Dr. Edmund Montgomery, a Scotsman. The physician had retired to Liendo Plantation and was married to Elisabet Ney, the sculptor commissioned to create statues of Texas heroes for the state capitol. The artist, the physician, the rabbi, and his brother were all fluent in German as well as the philosophy of Immanuel Kant.[42]

There were few language barriers for the rabbi and his wife, who mixed with the German- and Polish-speaking dairy farmers in nearby Brenham, then home to fourteen Jewish families.[43] Occasionally, surprise visitors disembarked from the train. During Passover of 1879, Charles Wessolowsky, associate editor of the *Jewish South*, visited Hempstead while on a regional tour to drum up subscriptions and support for B'nai B'rith, the Jewish fraternal organization. "We met the learned Rev. Mr. Schwartz [*sic*], with whom we spent a few hours, and found him very agreeable," the journalist reported.[44] Annually, on the second night of Passover, the rabbi and Julia invited all Hempstead Jews to their table for a seder, the holiday meal accompanied by a service commemorating the Exodus from Egypt. From forty to sixty people crowded around their extended table.[45]

Julia Nathan Schwarz, circa 1880. From Texas Jewry Collections,
the Texas Collection, Baylor University, Waco.

When a local Jewish photographer snapped portraits of Heinrich and
Julia in the 1880s, the rabbi looked Old World with his fez-shaped cap and
triangular beard, a wiry man with a long face, a bump below the bridge of
his nose, and an inquiring crease between thick, angled eyebrows. He
walked with a gold-headed cane, a gift from the Hempstead Hebrew Benevolent Society. Julia's portrait reveals a somber countenance and the
modest dress of a pious Jewish woman. Her long hair is parted in the
middle, then pulled back and hidden beneath a hat with a veil extending
down her back. A collar pin pinches her dark dress at the neck, and puffed
sleeves conceal her arms.[46]

Julia wrote poetry and kept busy in her domestic role, tending to grandchildren. Each Schwarz household had domestic help, something taken
for granted in a Confederate region where cotton plantations were once
the norm. Rather than work in the family stores, the Schwarz women were

homemakers who joined educational clubs and auxiliaries, adapting to the American way of life. An exception was Jeanette, Gabriel's wife, who ran the popular Millinery Bazaar in Brenham.[47] For special occasions, the Schwarzes set their family table with linen napkins, sterling silverware, and hollow-stemmed champagne glasses. Hearing such stories of grandeur, Leo's German bride, Selma Weinbaum, wore white gloves for her first meeting with the family in 1884 and was disappointed to find the rest of the women in aprons.[48]

Selma wrote home to her family that Rabbi Heinrich kept kosher, slaughtered meat and fowl for the family table, and read *Die Deborah,* a German Jewish weekly published by Rabbi Isaac Mayer Wise. Overcoming his initial disdain for the Cincinnati publisher, Schwarz submitted articles to *Die Deborah,* which printed his annual Jewish New Year's poems and his translations, fables, and homilies. These essays were filled with metaphors from nature: the wind offered a hymn of praise; silver dewdrops taught a lesson in the value of giving; the Torah, a gurgling brook of knowledge, never dried up.[49]

Heinrich Schwarz had carved out a niche in Texas as a family rabbi and a full-time scholar. Surrounded by relatives, many a landsman, and new acquaintances, he drew respect in a community that cherished freedom of religion. His articles in the Jewish press signaled to outsiders that there was at least one iota of Jewish scholarship on the Texas frontier.

CHANGING CURRENTS

The rabbi's presence served to anchor the family to its ancient religion, for they were rapidly incorporating their new surroundings into their ancient faith. Few members of his family rested on the Sabbath, because Saturday was the best business day of the week. The Schwarzes added Christmas to the family calendar—not as a religious holiday, but as an occasion when they could count on closing their stores and converging for a family meal. When all the cousins arrived on Christmas Day, they gathered under a giant pecan tree where Leo shook loose the ripe nuts—a treat as tasty as candy. In America, up-to-date retailers like Sam, Benno, and Leo set the customs more so than a rabbi like Heinrich, a remnant of the Old World. Even Heinrich began making concessions. When he dressed up in a vest and tailored suit, he removed his yarmulke, although he still wore it for worship.

As the family tree branched across Texas, Schwarzes opened retail stores at remote railroad junctions in Spur, Haskell, Bracketville, Stamford, Rosenberg, and Del Rio. In these towns with few Jews, the families closed their stores for the High Holidays—often their only outward show of Judaism. Otherwise, they blended in. Schwarz merchants built floats for rodeo parades. Their children competed as Bluebonnet Belles, Goddesses of West Texas, and varsity ballplayers. Jewish youngsters attended evangelical revivals with non-Jewish playmates. "We knew we were Jewish," recalled Felicia Joy Zeidenfeld, one of Rabbi Schwarz's great-granddaughters. "We never pretended to be anything else. No one tried to convert us."[50]

Robert Schwarz Strauss, one of Heinrich's great-grandsons in the Leo Schwarz line, grew up in Stamford (pop. 4,000) cognizant of two things about being a Jew: his father griped about closing the store for the High Holidays, because it always seemed to land on a Saturday; and his mother drilled into him the mantra that Jews are the Chosen People. "I felt sorry for all those other kids in school, because they weren't chosen," recalled Strauss, who became president of Dallas Temple Emanu-El, chairman of the National Democratic Committee, U.S. trade negotiator, and U.S. ambassador to Russia. His Jewish identity translated into his quest to excel, while his Texas persona predominated.[51] Life in the boondocks, far from sheltering Strauss, equipped him with the skills to fit in.

Cultural assimilation was a fact of life, more threatening to traditional Judaism than proselytization or persecution. Among the generation of Schwarzes who migrated to America, all married within the faith. Among the first generation born in Texas, there were several intermarriages. Two of Clara's sons married non-Jewish women and raised their children as Christian Scientists and Episcopalians.[52] The relatives were shocked and ashamed. In each generation, interfaith marriages increased. The shock wore off; the shame turned to regret at losing a member of the tribe. Sometimes the non-Jewish partner converted to Judaism and became active in synagogue affairs. Sometimes not.

As religious rituals waned, Jewish identity became less spiritual, more secular and social. By the second generation, some of the youngsters were more familiar with Jewish summer camps than synagogues. In many a household, the Passover seder became a big meal with little ceremony. Most of the Schwarzes graduated from small-town high schools to the University of Texas, where the campus's Jewish fraternities and sororities replaced matchmakers of old. As Jews took on Texan identities, their most significant Jewish networks became Greek social organizations such as Phi

Sigma Delta, Sigma Alpha Mu, Alpha Epsilon Phi, and Sigma Delta Tau—secular Jewish groups that maintained active alumni ties.[53]

Despite slackened ritual, the Schwarz family's second- and third-generation descendants felt a strong identity as Jews. From their ranks came presidents of congregations in Houston, Beaumont, Dallas, and Fort Worth. From succeeding generations have come fund-raisers, philanthropists, and writers for Jewish causes ranging from Judaic studies to Zionism. The ancient heritage took on new shapes. In a changing world, where Jews had the freedom to live next door to gentiles, religious observance and ethnic identity were bound to undergo transformations.

Two of the Galewsky cousins—Lawrence in Beaumont and Sol in Fort Worth—shortened their surnames to Gale during World War II. Fort Worth acquaintances privately chuckled over the way the Galewskys had "chopped their name in half," perhaps to sound less ethnic. The family maintained that the name change was not an attempt to hide their heritage, for Sol Galewsky/Gale was president of Fort Worth's Temple Beth-El at the time. The switch to a short, easily pronounced name ended confusion, particularly when placing overseas phone calls. The Gales supported Jewish causes philanthropically, and the war effort, physically on Normandy Beach. They viewed World War II as America's fight to stop Hitler's persecution of the Jews. By any name, the cousins felt their religious identity compatible with their national pride.

Generations of Gales and Galewskys are entwined on the Schwarz family tree—an elaborate computer printout that encompasses six generations and 781 offspring. Members of the current generation, mobilized by the "roots" phenomenon, embarked on genealogical research that led to a family reunion in Santa Fe, New Mexico, in 1997. Examination of the Schwarz family tree shows that the three brothers who immigrated to Texas did not spawn a dynasty, but rather a scattered family that multiplied and dispersed, becoming part of the Diaspora across Texas and the American West.

HEIRLOOMS AND LEGACIES

When Rabbi Heinrich Schwarz died at the turn of the century, he was the last of his scholarly breed. The *Houston Post* eulogized him as a "Hebrew Litterateur." The *American Israelite* praised his "intimacy with classical Hebrew." After the rabbi's passing, his brother Sam conducted services at the Hempstead Hebrew Congregation, which in 1916 adopted the Reform prayer book. When Sam passed away in 1918, he was mourned as Texas' oldest Confederate veteran, as well as a civic figure and the lay leader of Hempstead Jewry.[54] Sam Schwarz, the adaptable brother, was the role model for the future, the immigrant who best demonstrated that being Texan and southern were compatible with being an American Jew.

Weekly worship continued at Hempstead's backyard synagogue until 1939, when the town no longer had a minyan—the ten Jewish men necessary for a prayer service.[55] The backyard chapel was converted to rental housing, and its altar chairs presented to the Catholic parish church. Eventually, the erstwhile house of worship was moved or torn down; no one knows for certain. The house next door, the house that Benno built and where the rabbi resided, still stands, but lamentably is boxed in by a McDonald's fast-food restaurant and used-car lots. The landmark house remains in the family, occupied by Edis Schwarz, widow of one of the rabbi's great-grandsons and honorary guide to Hempstead's Jewish sights. The Hempstead Hebrew Cemetery, eerie and picturesque with Spanish moss filtering the view of family plots, remains hidden at the end of a country road. Gone from the cemetery is an obelisk in which was chiseled the Hebrew phrase, "Lech lecha."

Each branch of Heinrich, Sam, and Gabriel Schwarz's family still passes to the next generation some remnant of their possessions, whether a photo, a letter, a family Bible, or a ritual object. The rabbi's handwritten notebooks and manuscripts went to his daughter Frances, then to her children and grandchildren in Waco. His silver chalice was inherited by son Leo, whose Dallas descendants sip from it at wedding ceremonies. His gold-headed cane, inscribed by the Hempstead Hebrew Benevolent Society, is in Scarsdale, New York, a relic cherished by descendants of the wayward son, Alfred. The rabbi's pocket calendar, scribbled with birth dates of Jewish philosophers, poets, and family members, is in the collection of a California great-great-granddaughter. The marble Ten Commandments tablets that adorned the altar of the backyard chapel grace the mantel of Benno's great-grandson, H. D. "Trey" Schwarz III, who operates Hempstead's Schwarz store, the Big Store, which now competes with a Wal-Mart.

The Torah scroll that Rabbi Heinrich carried from the Old World to the New was safeguarded for years by his son Marks. When Houston's Reform Jews acrimoniously split in 1943, Marks sided with the breakaway faction forming Congregation Emanu El, and the Schwarz Torah became the new congregation's first scroll.[56] A majestic object of Judaica, the Schwarz Torah dates to the 1840s and, with its five-foot poles, is taller than some bar mitzvah students.[57] Yet this religious heirloom is lighter than other Torahs the synagogue later acquired. Its carved wooden poles were fashioned from lightweight wood. Its calfskin parchment was stretched and scraped paper-thin, reducing its bulk and leaving a surface with space for large, clear Hebrew lettering. Two of Heinrich's great-grandsons read from that Torah for their bar mitzvah ceremonies when they turned thirteen.

During *Simchat Torah,* a holiday when the Torahs are paraded around the synagogue, the majestic Schwarz scroll leads the procession because of its size and significance. More than an object to gaze upon, it provides an object lesson for the tiniest tots at the temple. The rabbi lifts each preschooler into the holy ark and measures his or her height against the towering object. A two-year-old may be as tall as the Torah's breast plate; a three-year-old a few inches higher. Physically, the children grasp how much they have grown in relation to the Torah, the story of their people. The lesson also measures the continuity of a rabbi who reluctantly journeyed from the provinces of Prussia to the Texas frontier.

2

The Mixer

SAMUEL ROSINGER, BEAUMONT

Wanted: Rabbi. Young man, native of America or England, that is a good lecturer who can make himself agreeable with either Orthodox or Reform Congregation. In other words, we want a MIXER.
We pay $1,500 a year.

—*AMERICAN ISRAELITE*, APRIL 7, 1910

RABBI SAMUEL ROSINGER was uncertain whether Beaumont's Temple Emanuel wanted a rabbi or a bartender. Intrigued by the Texas mystique and charmed by the colloquial ad, the Midwest rabbi was among eight clergymen to respond to the synagogue's search in 1910. Other rabbis who answered the call were more seasoned than Rosinger, a thirty-two-year-old with two years of pulpit experience. Yet only Rosinger was sent a train ticket and an invitation to deliver a weekend of trial sermons in the Texas oil town. Preach he did, in his Hungarian accent. Inspired by the rabbi's fervor and touched by the tender way he handled the Torah scrolls, the congregation voted unanimously to offer the darkly handsome Rosinger a two-year contract that stretched into a lifetime.[1]

Months after he was hired, the rabbi asked temple President Hyman Perlstein, "What made you decide to invite me?" Perlstein, a Russian-born blacksmith who forged his reputation in real estate and oil, responded, "I liked your beautiful handwriting."[2]

WANTED, RABBI,

(REFORM)

By CONGREGATION EMANUEL,

Of BEAUMONT, TEXAS.

Young man, a native of America or England, that is a good lecturer who can make himself agreeable with either Orthodox or Reform Congregation. In other words, we want a MIXER. We pay $1,500.00 a year. Address

H. A. PEARLSTEIN,

Pres't of Emanuel Congregation, Beaumont, Tex.

This advertisement in the American Israelite, *April 7, 1910, seeking a "mixer," lured Rabbi Samuel Rosinger to Texas. Temple President Hyman Asher Perlstein's name is misspelled in the ad.* From Klau Library, Hebrew Union College, Cincinnati, Ohio.

Forget theology. Forget ideology. Forget philosophy. This remote corner of the Diaspora, with three hundred Jews among its 20,640 residents, sought a rabbi who would mix and blend, a master of human relations as polished as the Catholic priests in the diocese and the minister at the Magnolia Baptist Church. Beaumont Jewry desired a spiritual leader and an educated role model to serve as good-will ambassador to the town. Although Temple Emanuel had advertised for a native English speaker, this congregation of immigrants was comfortable with Rosinger's educated, Old World accent. They, too, spoke with the guttural sounds and rhythms of Europe, although their children chattered with a soft Gulf Coast drawl. Unlike Jewish communities elsewhere in the United States, Beaumont had not advertised for a combination *shochet* (kosher animal slaughterer), *mohel* (circumciser), and *hazzan* (cantor). Beaumont wanted a rabbi of the twentieth century, not some bearded figure from the past.

Beaumont was focused on the future. The week after the rabbi's debut, the city hosted an exhibition baseball game, a doubleheader that pitted the Galveston Sand Crabs against the Waco Navigators. The strong turnout guaranteed the city a Texas League team of its own, and Beaumont yearned to become a minor-league town. Founded during Texas' war for independence in 1835, Beaumont was initially little more than a crossroads of marsh and mosquitoes. Ninety miles from Houston and twenty-seven miles from the Louisiana line, Beaumont was an out-of-the-way place where lumberjacks floated logs down the Neches River to the Gulf of Mexico.

The backwater soared from obscurity into history January 10, 1901, when a geyser of oil erupted that could not be capped for a week. As seventy-five thousand barrels a day gushed from the depths of the Spindletop field, the city burgeoned from a few thousand inhabitants into a boom town that doubled in population and multiplied its economic output a hundredfold. Business deals matured into international oil companies, among them Gulf, Mobil, and Texaco.[3] A forest of derricks sprouted. Gas fumes filtered through the air. A town once scented with sawdust now smelled of money. Hyman Perlstein, the immigrant who began his Beaumont career as a blacksmith, constructed the city's first high-rise, a six-story landmark that was for years the tallest building between Houston and New Orleans.[4] Sam Solinsky, another immigrant businessman, turned his initials into dollar signs and stipulated that his distinctive signature be chiseled onto his tombstone at Hebrew Rest Cemetery. It reads: $am $olinsky.[5]

The town's minuscule Jewish congregation—begun as a minyan of ten men in 1887, named Emanuel (God is with us) Congregation in 1895, and officially chartered in 1900—erected its first building the same year the oil boom began. Previously, Jewish weddings had been performed at City Hall or St. Mark's Episcopal Church. Previously, Beaumont had been home to five dozen Jewish families, many of them German immigrants who reached Beaumont via St. Louis and New Orleans. After the oil strike, however, scores more Hebrew merchants followed. Jewish-owned businesses flourished. What child didn't plead to romp through the fourth floor of J. J. Nathan's department store, a wonderland stocked exclusively with toys? What lady didn't keep cool with a plumed straw hat from Rosenthal's, run by brothers Joe and Leon? What gent didn't linger in Morris J. Loeb's cigar shop?[6] Most Beaumont residents considered Loeb the city's first Jew; he had arrived in 1878. Technically, he was the second.

A Polish-born Jew, merchant Simon Wiess, had come to Beaumont in 1838 with his Scots-Presbyterian wife but had nothing more to do with Judaism. His descendants later controlled Humble Oil.[7]

FROM BUDAPEST TO BEAUMONT

Beaumont seemed an unlikely locale for a worldly yet traditional Jew like Samuel Rosinger. Born in the foothills of Hungary's Carpathian Mountains December 21, 1877, he was one of eight siblings raised in a thatched-roof cottage with an earthen floor. An eager student, the lad left his native village of Tibold-Darocz at age nine to study religion under a series of Hungarian scholars. Educational opportunities drew him to universities in Budapest, Bern, and finally to Berlin, where he received an undergraduate degree in philosophy and German literature.

In 1904, Rosinger migrated to New York, where he simultaneously studied for a master's degree at Columbia University and ordination from the Jewish Theological Seminary. Rosinger's spiritual mentor was Solomon Schechter, seminary president and founder of Judaism's Conservative movement, which stresses tradition with a modicum of change. His academic mentor was Joseph Jacobs, an Australian-born Jewish historian and folklorist who taught English to foreign-born rabbinical students. Jacobs encouraged Rosinger's journalistic bent by publishing an essay of his in the *American Hebrew,* a sophisticated New York weekly with nationwide Jewish circulation.[8]

Rosinger's first pulpit was Temple Sholom in Toledo, Ohio. He arrived there in the summer of 1908 with his bride, New Yorker Gertrude Kaelter. Although the Toledo synagogue had roomy facilities, congregants who kept kosher, and a qualified religious school staff, the rabbi lamented, "I could not breathe life into the dry bones of my congregation." Members bickered over a multitude of issues, and few attended Sabbath services. Faced with empty pews, the rabbi quit in the spring of 1910. For the next five months, faith sustained Samuel and Gertrude Rosinger, who by then had a year-old son and a second child due in October.[9]

The call to Beaumont seemed heaven-sent. Texas, twelve hundred miles south, reawakened Rosinger's wanderlust. He was already a fan of the new movie genre, the Western, which was gaining popularity with the release of Texan Tom Mix's first cowboy film. The discovery of oil, headlined na-

Samuel Rosinger, the rabbi who responded to the "mixer" ad, served as Beaumont's rabbi from 1910 to 1965. From Kallah, Volume II, [1928] Year Book, 5689.

tionwide, also fueled the Texas mystique. Beaumont had the raw ingredients and the potential for adventure and growth.

Rosinger's first journey to Beaumont, the third week of August, turned into an arduous trek. From Toledo to Texas, the climate changed from temperate to torrid. Newspapers reported three deaths from Texas' 103-degree heat.[10] Travel-weary, Rosinger missed a train connection in New Orleans, delaying his Beaumont arrival a day.[11] When his train pulled into the depot just past 9 P.M., a greeting committee whisked him by car to Temple Emanuel, where 120 congregants awaited the belated start of Sabbath evening services. Sweaty, exhausted, and plagued with mosquito bites, Rosinger bowed his head and prayed for inspiration: "Heavenly

Father, open the gates of heaven to our prayer, and give thy faint servant strength to endure this trial."[12]

Temple Emanuel did not disappoint Rosinger, although it was full of surprises. Beaumont's Jews radiated the "glow of their faith," yet were lax in its rituals.[13] Some congregants thought that a *tallis*—the traditional, fringed prayer shawl—was for warmth and found no need for it.[14] Merchants were too busy at work to gather for daily morning prayers. Congregants looked upon America as the Jews' new Promised Land, while Rosinger was a Zionist who believed in reestablishing the Promised Land of old. On the Zionist issue, Rosinger converted his flock by pointing out that the nation's most prominent Jew, Supreme Court Justice Louis Brandeis, was also an international Zionist leader. On matters of religious ritual, however, the rabbi persuaded few fellow Jews to reverse course, for they were assimilating into the Texas milieu at too rapid a pace.[15]

A master of prose, Rosinger lamented the loss of Jewish traditions through his column in the *Texas Jewish Herald,* a Houston weekly. From his paper pulpit, the rabbi delivered a three-part series against intermarriage, a "cancer" that he termed "tantamount to religious suicide."[16] He deplored a trend among Texas Jews to name children after "heroes of the Middle Ages" and "pagan celebrities." His central European Jewish tradition dictated that babies' names commemorate a "departed one," never a living person. Yet the *Herald*'s social columns showed that "Milton, Mortimer, and Marion" were more popular names than Moses. "Alfred, Alton, and Aubrey" had upstaged Aaron. Naming a son after his father and nicknaming the boy "Bubba" or "Junior" was also contrary to the rabbi's upbringing. His own name, Samuel, was in memory of his paternal grandfather as well as the biblical judge.[17]

Rosinger endorsed the Jewish dietary laws that banned pork and the mixing of milk with meat. He encouraged keeping kosher, arguing that the dietary code was centuries ahead of America's "pure food laws" and also put a "Jewish impress upon the home."[18] But to keep kosher in Beaumont meant waiting in line at "Rev." Lazar Yellen's house on Saturdays after sundown while Yellen, who lived above his butcher shop, carved calves' livers and chuck roasts to order. Keeping kosher entailed selecting a live chicken at Mr. Nelson's Fish and Poultry Market, then carrying the flapping fowl to "Rev." Sol Zabludosky, a shochet whose place of work smelled foul to begin with. Keeping kosher excluded shellfish from the diet and therefore gumbo, the soupy Gulf Coast medley of crab, chicken, okra, onions, tomatoes, and spices ladled over sticky rice. Keeping kosher ruled out the ham salad sandwiches that the local section of the National Council of Jewish Women sold as a temple fund-raiser at the Jefferson County Fair.[19]

As the years passed, the Rosinger household gradually began to patronize non-kosher markets that appeared more hygienic than the premises of the local shochets. The Rosingers' housekeeper, Odeliah Bowser, an African American woman raised in Cajun country, simmered pots of gumbo for the family. The rabbi passed up the specialty dish, but he never criticized his family for slurping it down. Flexibility became part of his theology. He inched from Judaism's Conservative school toward its Reform movement, which put less emphasis on tradition and more on adaptation to current surroundings.[20] "Piety and pastry" are not always synonymous, he preached, nor is Judaism a "petrified creed," but rather a "way of life" open to "interpretation and application."[21]

The rabbi's religious views relaxed, but his ethics did not. Racial segregation of water fountains, restrooms, hospitals, and schools troubled him. He spoke before black audiences, being introduced as a man whose "skin may be white, but [whose] heart is as black as ours."[22] He joined the Rotary and served as the community service organization's president and longtime newsletter editor. He joined the Masons, a fraternal group that his father had mistakenly warned him was atheistic. He launched Beaumont's Red Cross chapter. After a visit to Memphis, Tennessee, he brought home the concept of the Community Chest, which consolidated charitable donations into one central organization. Beaumont adopted the idea. Reflecting upon his multiple roles, Rosinger told the *Beaumont Enterprise,* "The rabbis of olden times were studious, quiet men who perhaps held themselves aloof from activity other than theological. We [modern rabbis] . . . do not make recluses of ourselves. The world is our workshop."[23]

Modest about his achievements and persistent in his goals, the rabbi was a soft-spoken advocate and preacher, a gentle person whom colleagues characterized as sweet and sincere. When his ire was aroused on issues such as Zionism or intermarriage, he raised and waved his arms, bent at the elbows. When peeved with insubordinate Sabbath School students, he shook a crooked middle finger in their faces. A man of medium height and build, with arched brows and softly lit brown eyes, Rosinger remained attentive and concerned when engaged in one-on-one conversation. Unlike the more fashionable men of the day, who sported waxed and twirled mustaches, the rabbi trimmed his mustache into a no-nonsense rectangle. Beneath that thick mustache, the rabbi's pursed lips often fell into a lopsided smile that crinkled the corners of his eyes and warmed the community.

THE MELTING POT

Beaumont's populace was an amalgam of creeds, the metaphorical "melting pot" popularized in playwright Israel Zangwill's 1909 Broadway hit. Catholic settlers of Acadian ancestry had migrated to Beaumont from Louisiana's bayous. Freed slaves had also come west from Louisiana, particularly during the cattle drive era of the 1880s. Because of their mixed heritage of Choctaw, Spanish, French, and African, Beaumont's black residents joked that they were "gumbos."[24] The men worked as cowboys, then laborers. Black women knocked on back doors to offer their services as cooks and housekeepers for white families. By day, ethnic groups mixed in business dealings. They bought their rice from the Broussards, a family of French extraction, and their groceries from the Phelans, whose ancestors had fled the Irish potato famine. They tipped their hats to Mr. Gatze Jans Rienstra, leader of the Dutch farming community in nearby Nederland.[25] They crowded into Jewish entrepreneur Sol Gordon's movie theaters: the Tivoli, the Liberty, the Jefferson, and the People. They cheered the Beaumont Exporters, the Texas League baseball team whose players took to the field in red woolen uniforms.

For religious worship, ethnic groups separated. The Sicilian Catholics prayed in Italian, the Greek Orthodox in Greek. Black Catholics had a church of their own. The Jews, in addition to Temple Emanuel, supported a small Orthodox congregation, Kol Israel, voice of Israel, where the liturgy was in Hebrew and women prayed in a balcony apart from the men. Kol Israel had no religious school, so all the Jewish children frequented Rosinger's temple for lessons, worship, and socializing. All of Beaumont's Jewish youngsters grew up equating Judaism with Samuel Rosinger. On Yom Kippur, the most solemn day on the Hebrew calendar, the congregation collectively held its breath when the rabbi, weak from twenty-four hours of fasting and resplendent in white satin robe, knelt before the Torah and touched his forehead to the floor as he chanted the *Aleynu*. How devoutly he prayed.

PRIDE AND PREJUDICE

Although America guaranteed freedom of worship, Rosinger detected prejudice beneath the surface. On his eldest son Leonard's first day of school in 1914, classmates taunted the six-year-old with shouts of "Jew-baby."[26] The rabbi noticed that whenever a Christian and a Jewish child had a "falling out," the "first epithet" the non-Jew spit out was "Christ-killer."[27] Reflecting on such incidents, the rabbi wrote in the *Texas Jewish Herald:* "I thought that the scholastic career of a Jewish child runs smoothly until the snobbery of college, but now I see that he is labeled with the Jew's badge on the very threshold of the primary grade."[28]

The rabbi's response to schoolyard prejudice was to become active in the public schools and eventually serve as PTA president. His advice to Jews was to meet taunts with dignified silence. "Never boast of birth or religious affiliation. Simply live it and derive comfort from it." He lectured Christians that the crucifixion story was a needless source of anti-Semitism. "The account of his death ought to . . . spread . . . the sentiment of love and not the gall of hatred."[29]

Such preaching was to little avail. Beaumont's amiable ethnic balance toppled in 1921 with the emergence of the Ku Klux Klan. The city was then home to forty thousand residents. It was also home to Klavern No. 7, one of Texas earliest Klan chapters, which were numbered consecutively by founding date and grew to exceed one hundred. Neighboring Port Arthur, fifteen miles south, formed Jefferson County's second chapter.[30] The masked Kluxers, whose white cloaks and hoods supposedly symbolized racial purity, termed themselves moral watchdogs.

The Beaumont Klan made its public debut May 7, 1921, with the abduction of Dr. J. S. Paul, a physician accused of performing abortions. The doctor was whipped, tarred, feathered, and warned to leave town within seventy-two hours. He departed in two.[31] Another victim of masked terrorism was Harry Sams, a Port Arthur hotel clerk accused of procuring prostitutes. Tarred and feathered, Sams was tossed into the Plaza Hotel lobby amid revelers at an American Legion dance.[32] At least a dozen acts of brutality and intimidation were reported in Jefferson County. Police apprehended no culprits for these crimes, nor for fifty similar Klan atrocities reported across the state during the first eight months of 1921.[33] Few involved Jews. The Texas Klan's chief targets were bootleggers, abortionists, womanizers, Catholics, and African Americans.

Emboldened, in March, 1922, Beaumont's hooded fraternity targeted Sacred Heart Catholic Church, where parishioners were black and the priest was white. A warning glued to the sanctuary door threatened that the Klan would dynamite the premises unless the church shut down and its priest, Father A. A. LaPlante, left town. The defiant priest refused, and gun-toting Knights of Columbus guarded Sacred Heart. A dozen white Catholics prominent in Beaumont's business community sent a protest letter to the mayor and sheriff denouncing the "cowardly anarchists." Referring to the Klan's terror, the mayor responded, "It is as bad as Bolshevism and it has got to stop." The county sheriff did not respond, for he was a charter member of the Beaumont Klan.[34]

Only one civic group—the Rotary, of which the rabbi was a mainstay—followed the Catholics' lead. The membership passed a resolution supporting the mayor and denouncing the Klan. Rotarians, including Rosinger, on March 25, 1922, circulated a petition that gathered one hundred signatures condemning mob violence. The petition led to an anti-Klan rally at the American Legion Hall attended by sixteen hundred people and to the formation of a Citizens Executive Committee Against the Ku Klux Klan.[35]

Within days, an attorney in the Kiwanis Club proposed that his group, too, condemn the Klan. The lawyer, however, was silenced, ruled out of order by a fellow member, the Rev. Walter Rogers of Magnolia Avenue Baptist Church. Rogers was not the only minister in sympathy with the Klan. The Rev. A. D. Ellis, rector of St. Mark's Episcopal, served as exalted cyclops of the Beaumont Klan and grand dragon of the Texas Knights. The Rev. Caleb A. Ridley, former minister at Beaumont's Magnolia Avenue Baptist Church, was the Invisible Empire's imperial klud—Klan terminology for national chaplain.[36]

Who else was under those white robes? Grand jury investigations led to the trial, conviction, and ouster of the sheriff, but did little to unmask the culprits. Elections in 1922 and 1924 returned the sheriff to office, along with a Klan-endorsed slate of county officials. Candidates backed by the Citizens Executive Committee lost. The rabbi felt an unseasonable chill. "Clouds of strife and dissension," he wrote, "obscured the skies of our community."[37]

The hooded fraternity paraded down Pearl Street, a haunting procession so long it took twenty-two minutes for participants to pass one corner.[38] Jewish parents warned children to hide if they spotted Klansmen in cars or on street corners, where they set fire to whiskey stills. Herman Horwitz, a Port Arthur preschooler during the Klan era, recalled, "My mother told me they hated Jews and they did terrible things. They made fires and sometimes burned places. My mother didn't want me out when the Klan was around." One day when he was playing outside his father's store on Proctor Street, the boy heard the clip-clop of Klansmen's horses. "I hid behind something. It was scary. These guys were wearing these big masks and hats. You couldn't see their faces."[39]

A Klansman telephoned the rabbi's friend Hyman Perlstein with an invitation to join, which he, of course, declined.[40] Ignorant of Judaism, a number of Klansmen asked their leaders why the KKK was closed to Jews. At a barbecue on the county fairgrounds attended by thirty thousand Klan families, the KKK's imperial emperor explained the reasons: "Why not take the Jew? It would not be fair to . . . take in the Jew and take his money when the Jew cannot, following the beliefs of his fathers, accept Christ as the example as the Ku Klux Klan does. I have some of my best friends in the Jews."[41]

Rosinger did not let the burgeoning Klan stand in the way of his agenda. He practiced what he preached: live Judaism and derive comfort from it; meet taunts with dignified silence. At the height of Klan power, he proceeded with plans to construct a synagogue, a $110,000 landmark at 848 Broadway Street. The building, with seating for six hundred, had as its centerpiece a copper-domed sanctuary with sparkling stained-glass windows designed at Jerusalem's renowned Bezalel School of Arts and Crafts.[42] Completed in 1923, the building was planned with a finished basement, an ambitiously designed floor with classrooms, auditorium, kitchen, and meeting rooms. However, because of Beaumont's swampy subsoil, moisture seeped into these subterranean rooms. The basement, to this day, perennially floods.[43]

The gravest need Rosinger perceived in Jefferson County was health care. Tuberculosis victims lived quarantined in tents, camped out in Magnolia Park for months until they recovered or perished. Rosinger spearheaded a $50,000 county bond election in October, 1922—during the height of Ku Klux Klan fever—that financed construction of the Jefferson County Tuberculosis Hospital.[44] The institution treated both whites and blacks—albeit in facilities eight miles apart. Earmarking bond money for African Americans was a feat seldom attempted along the Texas-Louisiana line. The rabbi's efforts did not end with construction of the stucco buildings. For two decades he was president of the Jefferson County Tuberculosis Association. He pushed to consolidate and integrate the hospital, to no avail. He championed subsequent bond measures that enlarged both facilities.

To entertain patients, he escorted Sunday School classes to the sanitarium to perform cantatas and skits. "I was a bit germ-conscious, and I used to hold my breath," one of those youngsters recalled decades later. The rabbi also visited the hospital with his daughters, Doris and Ruth, and their three best friends—Adele Feinberg, Helen Goldstien, and her little sister Lee—who entertained patients with musical recitals. Doris played violin; Ruth and Helen, the piano; Lee danced, while Adele serenaded as vocalist.

A FULL HOUSE

Doris and Ruth's trio of friends were integral members of the Rosinger household at 1520 Broadway. Adele, who lived three doors away, practically moved in. Her father had died in 1919 when she was two years old, leaving her mother with six children. Gertrude Rosinger, herself orphaned at an early age, automatically looked after Adele who was the same age as Doris and two years older than Ruth. "The three of us were just like sisters," Adele recalled. "Samuel Rosinger became like a father to me. He was always watching over me while he was watching over his two daughters."

When the rabbi was home, he gardened, read, repaired the bindings of old books, and listened to Saturday radio broadcasts from the Metropolitan Opera. He began each weekday in solitude with a morning prayer. Facing east toward Jerusalem, the rabbi whispered in Hebrew, "Hear O Israel, the Lord is our God, the Lord is One." While praying, he wrapped his left arm and his forehead with *tefillin,* two long leather straps and two small leather cubes containing passages from Exodus and Deuteronomy. The ritual, a daily reminder to keep the words of the Torah foremost in one's mind, is a biblical commandment Rosinger observed throughout his life.[45]

The rabbi's unfulfilled passion was to play the violin, a quest that led to daily practice and ear-splitting squeaks that drove the youngsters outdoors.[46] In Beaumont's tropical heat, they wandered barefoot from house to house oblivious to the sun, thanks to the shade of the sycamores. Next door lived a Jewish family, the Sampsons, who operated the scrap iron yard. Next door to them was a Syrian family, the Kojaks. Across the street lived temple members Hippolyte and Dora Uhry, school superintendent Dr. Moore, and an Italian family, the Generos.[47] The rabbi's modest two-story house, with its mahogany paneling, was dark and cool inside with a breezy sleeping porch where Doris, Ruth, Adele, Helen, and Lee often slept on summer nights, giggling after the shades were rolled down.

"Everyday things were special and fun," according to Adele. "Once, we were allowed to stay in the living room for a wedding—if we were very quiet. How thrilled we were." Another thrill came the day the rabbi drove the girls to the oilfields to witness roughnecks capping the latest gusher. Geysers of oil and flares of fire were integral memories of a Beaumont childhood.

The local heartthrob was Hank Greenberg, a home-run hitter and future Hall of Famer who played for the Exporters. The muscular six-footer caused heads to turn at the temple when he and a teammate, pitcher Izzy Goldstein, slipped into a back row to pray during Yom Kippur of 1932. "Our hearts were all aflutter," Adele recalled.

In the Rosinger household, Odeliah the housekeeper baby-sat Friday nights when the rabbi, Gertrude, and their two older sons attended services. Leonard, born in 1908, was the eldest. A clever youngster who excelled in school, he became a successful advertising agent, salesman, and founder of *Magnolia Hall,* a Victorian furniture catalog. His brother Marvin, born in 1912, almost died from a childhood illness that slowed his mental development. Kind and considerate like his father, Marvin was a plodder destined for vocational school, not college. Another child, born October 8, 1910, died before the age of four after suffering what her death certificate called "acute indigestion."[48] The Rosingers rarely discussed the details of her sudden death, referring to it as a "terrible" event. Just glimpsing the child's tombstone at Hebrew Rest Cemetery was a shock, because her name was Doris, the same as the Rosingers' next daughter, born in 1917. The name also honored the memory of Gertrude's mother, Dorothea.[49]

Gertrude Rosinger, who taught Sunday School, prided herself on being the rabbi's "partner, not his echo or shadow." He facetiously called her the severest critic in his "kitchen cabinet."[50] One of Gertrude's sisters married the rabbi's youngest brother, Benjamin, an immigrant to New York who waited tables at a Hungarian restaurant. The marriages of two sisters to two brothers led to a host of "double cousins." Among them was Lawrence

The Rosingers at home in Beaumont at 1520 Broadway, ca. 1935.
From left: Leonard, Ruth, Rabbi Samuel, Gertrude, Doris, and Marvin.
Courtesy Adele F. Silverberg, Beaumont.

Kaelter Rosinger, a political scientist, author, and China expert blacklisted from academia during the Red Scare. The McCarthy-era episode was a painful blow to a family that subscribed to the American dream.[51]

TEMPLE TIDINGS

Saturdays were special. The entire Rosinger household dressed up for Sabbath morning services, during which Doris, Ruth, Adele, Helen, and Lee sang in the junior choir. The rabbi dubbed the young singers his "spiritual angels." Ever the wordsmith, he called the core group of Sabbath worshipers his "faithful remnant." His appellation for Adele was "pomegranate queen" after a favorite tree in his garden. Miriam Brookner, a graceful teen who delighted the town with her nimble dancing, was to the rabbi a "floral offering."

Appropriately, the rabbi selected Miriam Brookner to lay flowers upon the altar during the confirmation ceremony set for the holiday of *Shavuos* in May, 1937. Tragedy intervened. Returning from a glee club trip to Palestine, Texas, on April 4, the sixteen-year-old dancer died in a car crash. All Beaumont mourned. Tearful schoolmates gathered in the Brookner family parlor. Nuns knelt at her coffin. With bowed head, the rabbi delivered a eulogy that conveyed the town's sorrow, a tribute so poignant that it ran verbatim in the afternoon paper. Adele clipped the newspaper article and kept it folded up in her wallet for decades: "Darling child, the apple of your parents' eye, the joy of your teachers, the favorite of your classmates, and the pet of the public, fare thee well, but not forever. . . . The Lord . . . has transferred the scene of your confirmation from our humble synagogue into the sanctuary of Heaven, and chosen you, the living flower, as the floral offering upon his holy altar."[52]

A premature death such as Miriam's loomed large in a close-knit community like Beaumont where children and grandchildren often followed their elders into family businesses. When Hitler's shadow and the threat of the Second World War dominated the front pages, the young men at Temple Emanuel could not help but recall Sam Lewis, the twenty-year-old Jewish youth killed in World War I just three weeks before the armistice. How could they forget? The first stained-glass window to the right of the pulpit was inscribed in his memory. The words on the window haunted Lawrence Blum. He, and other boys of draft age, knew the inscription by heart: *In loving memory of Sam Lewis. Died in defense of his country. October 21, 1918. Veaux Champagne, France.* "We didn't want to get killed in the last week of a war," he recalled.[53]

Death drew congregants close and sometimes asunder. When Edgar Jones, a gentile married to temple member Cipora Jones, died in 1934, the congregation's executive board insisted that he be buried in Hebrew Rest Cemetery. The rabbi was adamant that the burial take place elsewhere. Edgar Jones, although an active temple participant, had never converted to Judaism. According to tradition, only Jews may be interred in a Hebrew cemetery. Faced with the board's wrath and the rare threat of resignations, Rosinger prayed for the wisdom of Solomon. His solution: string a length of wire fencing inside the perimeters of Edgar Jones' grave. Technically, the deceased was laid to rest in a separate cemetery.[54] Some rules the rabbi could bend but not break.

The town grew, and Rosinger's religious school students grew up. He was proud of his temple offspring. Irving Goldberg, a Port Arthur boy, left the Gulf Coast for the University of Texas and Harvard Law. When he married a pharmacist's daughter from the central Texas town of Taylor,

Rabbi Rosinger pronounced their vows in the bride's living room. Gold-berg later became a national board member for Jewish refugee relief orga-nizations and, in 1966, a judge on the Fifth U.S. Circuit Court of Appeals.[55] During World War II another former Beaumont boy, Lloyd Friedman, who had moved to Houston, was touched to receive a letter of prayer and support from the rabbi just days before he reported for active duty. "I hadn't been to that temple since confirmation," Friedman recalled.[56] Rabbi Rosinger somehow kept abreast of his congregants' milestones and achievements. When a 1958 grand jury recommended desegregation of Beaumont's TB hospital, Rosinger sent a note of thanks to a Jew on the panel, a young man who grew up with Temple Emanuel. Hospital integra-tion, still controversial, did not occur until 1963 and the civil rights era, two years before the rabbi's death.

Odeliah, the Rosingers' capable housekeeper, married, raised a daugh-ter, and remained a lifelong family friend. Born and raised along Louisi-ana's bayous, Odeliah had no birth certificate and no schooling. She never learned to read. In her old age, she lacked the know-how and the docu-mentation to apply for the Social Security and Medicare benefits due her. Government assistance seemed out of the question until the rabbi's son-in-law, a lawyer married to Doris, cut through the red tape, verified her eligibility, and overcame all bureaucratic roadblocks.

Rosinger's contributions to Beaumont took center stage in 1960, the year he turned eighty-three and the city's population reached 119,000. The local Exchange Club, which bestowed an annual Golden Deeds Award on one exemplary citizen, singled out the rabbi for the prize. At a banquet in Rosinger's honor, four of his six grandchildren and more than 275 of his friends lauded his accomplishments, great and small. Even more signifi-cant than the Community Chest, the Red Cross, and the TB hospital were the rabbi's personal contacts throughout the years: the blind woman to whom he had read aloud; the elderly African American educator for whom Rosinger pulled up a chair in a crowded auditorium when no one else would; the breast cancer patient who had embarrassed the rabbi by uncovering the Star of David pendant resting on her bosom. The rabbi with the beautiful handwriting had not only fulfilled his original mission as communal mixer. Through personal courage he had achieved much more, becoming a spiritual anchor and moral leader.[57]

Rosinger was content with his life and legacy. He had never thought of Beaumont, or Texas for that matter, as a remote corner of the Diaspora. Nor had he contemplated leaving for greener pastures. He believed that serving one community for more than fifty years was a privilege. At the Golden Deeds banquet in his honor, the rabbi ate little, for the appetizer was shrimp cocktail and the main course, milk-fed chicken, foods outside his kosher regimen. The menu did not matter. Rosinger felt as full and fulfilled as the verse in the twenty-third Psalm: "My cup runneth over." At the end of an evening of tributes, the rabbi's response to those assembled was not a speech or a sermon, but a public prayer.

3

Faber versus Ferguson

A Fight for Academic Freedom

MAURICE FABER, TYLER

Unless I may be assured of your full and complete cooperation . . .
send . . . me at once your resignation
as a member of the Board of Regents.

—GOV. JAMES FERGUSON, SEPTEMBER 11, 1916

THE ULTIMATUM WAS FROM the governor of Texas. The subject was politics at the state university; the recipient was a rural Texas rabbi who prized principle above politics or position. Responding with defiance, the rabbi wrote, "I respectfully decline to concede to your wishes. . . . I never dreamed that . . . an appointee is expected to be a . . . marionette to move and act . . . when the Chief Executive pushes the button or pulls the string."[1]

The testy correspondence between the governor and the rabbi evolved into a skirmish of words and wills. Governor James E. Ferguson—"Farmer Jim" to the voters—was determined to pull the strings and force Rabbi Maurice Faber to help oust seven educators from the University of Texas. One of the objectionable professors owned a newspaper that "skinned the governor from hell to breakfast."[2] Another lecturer published cowboy ballads that the governor derided. ("When I die, don't bury me at all. Just pickle my bones, in alcohol."[3]) A third academician crusaded against the state capital's bars and brothels, a threat to Ferguson's financial backers, who were brewers.[4] The chief executive wanted those "butterfly chasers," "day dreamers," "two-bit thieves," and "educated fools" off the state payroll.[5] Academic freedom be damned; the governor expected his state employees and appointees to "stand hitched."[6]

The Democratic governor had appointed Rabbi Faber to the University of Texas Board of Regents on March 3, 1915, distinguishing him as the first clergyman and the second Jew to serve on the panel. The rabbi's six-year term had more than four years remaining on September 11, 1916, when the chief executive wrote demanding his backing or his departure: "The time has come when I must know who is for me and who is against me."[7]

The governor's words stunned the rabbi. The letter arrived on the eve of the Jewish High Holy Days, a period of introspection when Faber laid aside secular concerns and focused on services and sermons for his Tyler congregation of fifty families. The governor's missive required a response, but the rabbi needed time to consult his conscience, alert his colleagues on the board, and craft a reply. With a four-line note mailed two days later, the rabbi put off the governor, promising a "complete and full reply" within ten days.[8] Thus began a behind-the-scenes struggle that thrust the small-town rabbi into the headlines, the governor into disrepute, and turned the university into a "football of politics."[9] Faber versus Ferguson had commenced.

Rabbi Faber was already legendary in Tyler, a fashionable East Texas town, when the governor's ultimatum arrived. "You could hear his voice —and his opinion—clear across the street," recalled a congregant.[10] One rabbinical colleague observed: "He was never neutral. Few men whose lives count for anything are."[11] Short, fast-talking, and fast-walking, the pipe-smoking rabbi was an unmistakable figure who carried a gold-headed cane that he used not as a crutch but as a pointer or gavel to bring an unruly meeting to order. Garrulous and determined, the rabbi often strode into the Mayer and Schmidt department store and yelled, "Jake," interrupting the vice president, Jake Wolf, no matter what the merchant was doing.[12]

The bald, mustachioed rabbi with fan-shaped ears and blue eyes had arrived in East Texas at the turn of the century, invited by a congregation impressed with reports of his patriotic 1898 speech on the U.S. Constitution. Faber often remarked that "he was more of an American than those who chanced to be born here, because he was an 'an American by choice.'"[13] Long before his move to Texas, he had opted to leave behind the autocracy of the Austro-Hungarian Empire. Freedom of religion, educational opportunity, and democracy in government were to him more than platitudes. They were convictions. He winced when he heard the governor's remark that "too many Texans" were going "hog-wild over higher education."[14] He steeled his spine when the governor warned audiences that his dispute with the university could turn into "the biggest bear fight that has ever taken place in the state of Texas."[15] The weary rabbi set aside the governor's letter and allowed himself time for prayer and reflection.

THE OLD COUNTRY AND THE NEW

Born December 30, 1854, in Sinska, a Hungarian village later incorporated into Czechoslovakia, Maurice Faber retained scant trace of the Old Country in his diction or religious practice. He hailed from an unbroken line of rabbis: his grandfather, father, uncle, and brother were rabbinical scholars. Steered from birth toward the pulpit, Maurice Faber's given name was Mosheh—Hebrew for Moses. He received his education and training in Hungary and was ordained in 1873, but he rejected the orthodoxy of his forebears. Instead, the young rabbi embraced Reform Judaism, the movement that arose in early nineteenth-century Germany and sought to adapt the ancient Hebrew faith to Western civilization. The contemporary movement, fast gaining adherents in the United States, regarded Judaism's moral laws as far more binding than its Mosaic rituals. It gave prophetic ethics more weight than daily prayers. Faber's father, Leon, had only scorn for the reformation. The ideological break between father and son proved irreparable. For his "unfilial" rebellion, the son was disinherited. With his wife Regina, the twenty-four-year-old rabbi emigrated in 1878, relinquishing his ties to the past.[16]

America was everything this young rabbi had imagined—a land receptive to new ideas, religious and political. He found freedom of religion and an abundance of job opportunities for an educated immigrant. In 1884, as quickly as the law allowed, he took his oath as a United States citizen.[17] His first years in the United States were spent in Wilmington, Delaware, where his wife blessed him with a daughter, Fannie (1881), named after his mother; a son, Harry (1883); and then, sadly, left him a young widower.[18] He remarried, taking as his bride his wife's half-sister, Johannah Lion, a woman seven years his junior. The couple moved to northwestern Pennsylvania in February, 1889, and Faber performed double duty as public school teacher and rabbi. In the forested town of Titusville—where America's first oil well had been drilled in 1859—he taught high school history and German literature and served as part-time rabbi at Congregation B'nai Zion, a synagogue with ten families.[19] He often visited Cincinnati, the seat of the Reform Jewish movement, and attended an 1889 organizational meeting of his denomination's Central Conference of American Rabbis.[20] During nearly a decade in Titusville, Johannah gave birth to three children: Arthur (1889), Gertrude (1891), and Edwin (1896). Faber pronounced wedding vows for twelve couples, buried fourteen congregants, confirmed twenty-two teenagers, and set his sights on a larger Jewish community.[21]

Ambition and the opportunity to serve a more visible congregation led him in 1898 to the Midwest town of Keokuk, Iowa, a Mississippi River port with an antebellum congregation dating to 1856. Congregation B'nai Israel's two-story synagogue had stained-glass windows and an ornate row of spires rising along the roof's edge. Faber expected to serve a thriving community, but Keokuk's golden age had peaked three years before. Steamboat traffic was on the decline and railroads bypassed the town.[22] In two years' time, Faber blessed two births and six marriages. He buried seven congregants, confirmed five, and kept alert for a more viable pulpit.[23]

When an opening in Tyler, Texas, was advertised in the Jewish press, Faber applied. He fit the first two criteria—"middle aged, married man"—but not the last stipulation, which was for a "Conservative" rabbi.[24] Faber was no Conservative Jew. That term applied to a branch of Judaism begun in America in 1883, a denomination midway between the Orthodox traditions of Faber's forebears and the modernism of the Reform movement he embraced.[25] Still, Faber applied and turned out to be exactly what Tyler sought—a contemporary thinker with Old World roots. The immigrant shopkeepers who ran the Tyler temple took an immediate liking to this rabbi who bellowed out his trial sermon in August, 1900. He mixed rabbinic folktales with his prophetic message. He understood where the more observant members in the congregation were coming from. He indicated that he could span the differences. Also important, he shared their passion for the card game of bridge—and they often needed a fourth.

For the rabbi and his family, Tyler opened a new world: a forested landscape laced with dogwood, a prosperous county seat with a skyline of church spires and a southern perspective. Located seventy-five miles from Shreveport, Louisiana, Tyler possessed a heritage more Deep South than Southwestern. During the war between the states, the Confederate Army's largest prisoner-of-war camp west of the Mississippi was near Tyler. By virtue of its woods and farmland, Tyler had served as a supply depot for the Confederacy, maintaining an ordnance plant, an armory, and a commissary stocked with locally grown corn, wheat, peaches, and strawberries. When ruin ravaged neighboring states, Tyler received a flood of refugees.[26] Post–Civil War, Tyler became the hub of East Texas—a commercial center and a force in state politics. By the end of the century, three Texas governors had hailed from Tyler, each of them a rambunctious sort. Tyler politicians spoke their minds, and Faber fit into that mix.

The first clusters of Jews to gravitate to Tyler had been Germans who hailed from Rogasen, a Prussian town east of Berlin. Many were kin to one another. Some had previously lived in Mississippi and moved to Texas in the aftermath of the war. The Lipstates opened a clothing store. The Jacobses ran a saloon. The Wadels sold horse collars and shotgun shells. Most of the Jewish merchants had storefronts on the busy streets radiating from the county courthouse.

After 1881, a second wave of Jewish immigrants began filtering into Tyler and the rest of America. These newcomers, largely from Russia and Eastern Europe, were not as worldly or sophisticated as the German-born Jews. Their lives had been confined by law and prejudice to small Jewish enclaves, and Judaism was to them both a culture and a religion. They sought to transplant their customs to Texas soil.

By 1884, Tyler Jewry totaled fifty families—about 1 percent of the town's population—and local Jews consecrated a portion of the Oakwood Cemetery. The next year, the Jewish community organized a Sabbath school that met on Saturdays. By Passover in the spring of 1887, fifty-three Jewish families chartered Congregation Beth El, Hebrew for house of God. They conducted worship services at the Odd Fellows Hall, in the same building on the courthouse square that housed Isaac and Annie Jacobs' saloon.[27] In 1889 a synagogue was erected, where lay leaders and itinerant rabbis officiated through the turn of the century. A favorite among them was "Rabbi" William Levy—an army major by rank and a "rabbi by courtesy."[28]

Inside the Tyler congregation, bickering and divisiveness were the rule, uneasy compromises the norm. Congregants who married outside the faith—not uncommon on the frontier—forfeited their five-dollar mem-

Rabbi Maurice Faber with confirmation class at Congregation Beth El, Tyler, May, 1915. Standing: Ruth Friedlander, Rae Liebreich, Leonard Bruck, Helen Wadel, Beatrice Goldstucker. Seated: Dorothy Goldstein, Rabbi Faber, Mildred Bruck.
Courtesy Congregation Beth El, Tyler.

bership fees. During the High Holy Days of Rosh Hashanah and Yom Kippur, the Hebrew prayer book *Minhag Yastrov* was used. The balance of the year, the new *Union Prayer Book*, with its abbreviated worship services and English translations, was read. Few were appeased by these arrangements. Orthodox worshipers, appalled by "theological breaches," broke away and in 1897 celebrated Sabbath on the premises of the Woodmen of the World Lodge.[29]

When Faber stepped into the pulpit at Tyler's Congregation Beth El, change inevitably followed: The men's skullcap worn during prayer was banned within the next year. The Sabbath School moved from Saturdays to Sundays. The bar mitzvah, a coming-of-age ceremony for thirteen-year-old boys, was phased out in favor of confirmation, a graduation exercise for boys and girls. All services were conducted out of the Americanized prayer book. Shortly before Faber's arrival, the temple board repealed the banishment of Jews who intermarried. Faber concurred with the change.[30]

By the summer of 1903, the breakaway Orthodox faction gained enough defectors to charter Congregation Ahavath Achim, Hebrew for brotherly love. Members recruited a religious leader from Poland, Rev. Samuel Isaac Greenberg, to serve as *hazzan, shochet,* and *mohel.* Although Greenberg was not an ordained rabbi, his time was filled with religious duties—two worship services a day, rest and prayer on the Sabbath, the kosher slaughtering of fowl and livestock on his farm on the city's outskirts. As an alternative to ham, Greenberg's wife, Jenny, perfected a smoked-turkey recipe that their descendants still market today.[31]

Although both congregations grew, Faber carried the mantle in the larger community, presiding as the more worldly rabbi and the public representative of Tyler's Jews. The Fabers lived near the center of town in a parsonage built for them adjacent to the temple. Beth El's house of worship was a Tyler landmark—a rectangular wooden building with an onion-domed entry tower, a dozen slender, arched, stained-glass windows, and a leaky roof. Surrounded by a white picket fence, the temple on South College Avenue was across the street from the high school. Whenever the temple was closed, the parsonage was open for tutoring, confirmation class discussions, weddings, and communal cooking of hot tamales in Johannah Faber's kitchen.

The rabbi's forty-nine-year-old wife complained of medical problems and internal pain. Despite a trip to New York for surgery, she passed away April 22, 1910. Mourners filled the parsonage to console the rabbi, a widower for the second time. A few years later, his daughter Gertrude moved into the parsonage with her husband and three young sons. In due time the house on College Avenue again became a lively center for cooking, card playing, and kibitzing.

Rabbi Faber declared that a town the size of Tyler needed a library, and then followed through. He directed the Lipstates to assemble a group to donate land, then he negotiated with the Carnegie Foundation for the money. The result was a furnished, two-story library with an upstairs stage and meeting room crowned with an arched ceiling. The rabbi did not stop with bricks and mortar but remained on the board for eighteen years as the library built a collection of twelve thousand books. Faber also moderated town hall meetings and directed the Associated Charities and Welfare Committee for the city and county. In Europe, these were roles rabbis assumed within the Jewish community. In Tyler, Faber spread Judaism's tenets of learning and charity beyond his temple.

Tyler's five-hundred-member St. John's Masonic Lodge courted Rabbi Faber, and he joined. His service to the Masons included seven years as a high priest. But during the 1920s, the rabbi detected a menacing shift as the

Ku Klux Klan infiltrated the state. Applicants to the lodge were required to apply simultaneously for membership in the Klan. From his insider's perch, the rabbi condemned the policy as anathema, inconsistent with Masonic principles. When the practice continued, the rabbi gathered fifty-four allies, and in the spring of 1925 they lodged a complaint with Masonic headquarters in Austin. The result was a ten-month suspension of the St. John's Masonic Lodge charter—a document dating to 1849. During the intervening months, a secessionist lodge of sixty-five men formed, with Rabbi Faber installed as a board member and chaplain. On February 1, 1926, the two lodges pledged to function in peace, and the grand master restored the old St. John's Lodge charter.[32] The rabbi could not rid Tyler of the Klan, but he had defied it. This, then, was the conviction and stature of the man whom the governor of Texas sought to bend in a battle over academic freedom.

THE CHIEF EXECUTIVE

When Faber was tapped to serve as a regent, he was already familiar with the Austin campus as a visiting classroom lecturer and a frequent guest speaker at dinners for the university's Jewish students.[33] He was acquainted with the other Jewish regent, Alex Sanger, a leading Dallas retailer and a former president at Dallas Temple Emanu-El. However, he knew Governor Ferguson only by reputation.

The governor had been elected in 1914 on a tide of votes from tenant farmers who lived at the "forks of the creeks" and endorsed his campaign promise to freeze sharecroppers' rents, fight Prohibition, and attack women's suffrage.[34] A native of Salado Creek, Texas, Ferguson was a country boy with a backwoods education who married into money, became a lawyer, a banker, and a rancher, and ascended to the governor's mansion in his first bid for public office. Ferguson's colloquialisms and shenanigans became frequent fodder for humorists—particularly years later when his wife, Miriam Amanda "Ma" Ferguson, ran for governor and won. ("He is the only governor in the world by marriage," quipped columnist Will Rogers.[35]) During "Pa" Ferguson's inaugural year as governor, the controversy that caused the biggest flap stemmed from platters of chicken salad the governor's mansion had ordered from Austin's Driskill Hotel and charged to the state tab.[36] The grocery bill ruffled the legislature, which was reimbursed after appealing the dispute to the state supreme court.

Such was Texas politics. Indigestion spurred lawsuits. Indiscretions could apparently be overlooked, for with little stir, the governor deposited state money in his bank to bail it out of trouble and directed civil servants to buy cattle for his family farm. He figured he could have his way with the "big boys" at the state university as well.[37]

The governor had long mistrusted the campus in Austin. He found the faculty smug. Ferguson himself had quit school as a teenager when a teacher ordered him to chop wood. He had stomped out of the school-house and headed west, graduating to adulthood as a vagabond who hitched rides on trains and tramp steamers, picked grapes, harnessed mules at a lumber camp, dug for ore, and joined railroad gangs building bridges across the Texas Trans Pecos. He liked to say his diploma was from the "University of Hard Knocks." Returning home to Bell County, he was determined to become an attorney by reading up on the law. He ultimately passed the bar in 1897 by sharing a quart of Four Roses whiskey with the judges administering the oral test. The jurists never asked the aspiring attorney a question.[38]

Ferguson dabbled in several political campaigns and entered the governor's mansion bearing a grudge against the University of Texas. Years earlier, he had been ignored when he recommended his brother, a botany instructor at Texas Agricultural and Mechanical College, for a teaching position in Austin.[39] Now that he was in charge, Ferguson contended that the state university, founded in 1883, was run by elitists solely for the benefit of rich fraternity and sorority members who belittled the rest of the students as "barbs"—his lingo for barbarians.[40] In a state with 4.46 million people, the privileged few—2,900 students—attended the university, which operated on an $820,000 budget.[41] Yet, Ferguson complained, folks living "at the forks of the creeks" had few "little red schoolhouses."[42] While the state spent $282 per college student, it expended only $4.50 per pupil for the public schools to educate the "poor children who picked cotton and made the crops."[43] (Ferguson neglected to mention that Texas spent less per capita for its state university than forty-three other states: seventeen cents per resident compared with Michigan's seventy-eight cents.[44]) The governor proposed adjusting the disparity between rich and poor Texans by spending three times as much on rural education as on higher education. "When higher education . . . wants to rule with a college diploma alone, then I am against higher education, and I consider it book learnin' gone to seed."[45]

Certificate appointing Maurice Faber to the University of Texas Board of Regents in 1915 refers to the rabbi as "Father Faber." Certificate from Eugene Lipstate, Lafayette, La. Photo by Carolyn Bauman.

The battle lines in his mind were clear when, after his inauguration in January, 1915, the governor asked his aides for nominees to fill two vacancies on the University of Texas Board of Regents. Lieutenant Colonel John Durst, a Tyler politician, recommended the rabbi—a veritable high priest in his home town. Durst, whose military rank reflected nothing more than his position on the governor's "staff of colonels," vouched for the rabbi's loyalty to state and nation.[46] The forty-three-year-old governor was impressed. Rabbi Maurice Faber, age sixty, seemed to possess the common touch the governor sought: immigrant stock, a widower, a Mason, and, despite his rabbinical credentials, no university degree on his résumé.[47]

Still, the appointment was surprising. The governor, the son of a Methodist preacher, harbored stereotypes against Jews and was not averse to declaring that a "mob" of Israelites had "lynched the Savior."[48] Furthermore, Judaism was so unfamiliar to Ferguson and his staff that the certificate naming the rabbi a regent twice identified the appointee as "Father Faber."[49]

HOSTILITY AND HIGHER EDUCATION

At the time of Faber's appointment to the Board of Regents, fiscal tension was escalating between the governor and the university. The campus auditor had recently died, and the post of university president was vacant. Acting president William J. Battle was an academician, not a politician. The governor accosted him with questions about the university budget, particularly the "dead men on the payroll." Versed in classical languages but not the nuances of numbers, Battle acknowledged that the budget was padded with unfilled positions. Nor was the university interviewing to fill the slots. It diverted the money to needy areas. Dissecting the budget further, the governor learned that during the previous four years, two dozen professors had drawn partial pay while on semester leaves of absence to teach at northern universities. Although assured this was a "common practice" at "first class institutions," the governor did not equate prestige with partial pay.[50]

The more the governor probed the budget, the more confounded he became. He learned that some full-time professors taught less than fifteen hours a week—part-time status so far as a former construction worker like Ferguson was concerned. Some professors who traveled around the state to lecture brought along their wives and children, who dined at university expense. Some of those same professors tallied their travel expenses at three cents per mile—a half-cent higher than the customary rate.[51] Such chicanery riled the governor, who declared, "I have found more corruption in the affairs at the University of Texas than in all of the other departments of state government. . . . I have found far more disloyalty in the State University at Austin than among the Germans or the people of any other nationality."[52] Ferguson was prepared to purge the faculty and reshuffle the Board of Regents, if that was what it took for the campus to conform to his way of thinking.

Targeting seven employees, including the acting president and the faculty secretary, the governor picked apart their expense accounts, their political views, and their peccadilloes.[53] Among the seven was folklorist John A. Lomax, a Harvard-educated Texan whose 1910 volume of frontier ballads salvaged from obscurity such favorites as "Home on the Range."[54] Also targeted for dismissal was Lomax's friend Charles S. Potts, a political science and law professor who later became a founding member of the *Texas Law Review* and dean of Southern Methodist University's law school. The governor sought to blacklist physicist William T. Mather, a reformer who headed a decency league in Austin and an athlete who played a role in the formation of the Southwest Conference. Also on the governor's hit list were psychology professor A. Caswell Ellis and journalism department head William H. Mayes, who edited the feisty *Brownwood Bulletin.* Ferguson was bullying some of the best.[55]

Rabbi Faber shuddered. One principle at stake was due process for faculty members under fire. Each deserved a personnel hearing. But to lawyerly Ferguson, due process was relevant only "when you are going to hang somebody."[56] Another concern was interference in the day-to-day operations of the university. How could a backwater state like Texas build a prestigious university if its regents were to kowtow to an unlettered politician?[57] How could it hire top professors if faculty members, esteemed at out-of-state colleges, were subject to the arbitrary will of Farmer Jim?

The governor's complaints were petty. His bid for control was not. The regents balked with their own power play. In April, 1916, the board announced a surprise selection as university president: Dr. Robert E. Vinson, a theologian and president of nearby Austin Presbyterian Theological Seminary. The governor, still culling his list of nominees, was incensed. His authority usurped, Ferguson termed the reverend doctor "a silver-tongued ex-minister . . . not big enough for the job."[58] During a face-to-face meeting, Ferguson demanded that Vinson fire the seven educators, branding them phonies, critics, and thieves. The new president refused to yield but promised to hold personnel hearings if specific charges were filed. Summarizing the meeting in a letter mailed to the governor September 5, Vinson asked the exact grounds for dismissal.

Ferguson's response was terse: "I am the governor of Texas; I don't have to give reasons."[59]

Six days later, the governor wrote Rabbi Maurice Faber demanding his resignation or his vote. The stunned rabbi never doubted the governor's authority to remove him from the board. Nor was Faber's support for the university in question. To the rabbi, the university's autonomy was at stake. Expecting his own imminent removal from the regents, Faber contemplated how much time and room he had to maneuver.

By mail, the rabbi learned that the board's other Ferguson appointee, S. J. Jones, had received a similar gubernatorial demand—oust the faculty or step aside. Jones, a political crony from the governor's home county, found Ferguson's interference distasteful. In private correspondence, he accused the governor of turning "animosity" into "policy." He felt trapped as he weighed "the humiliation of being summarily dismissed [against] . . . moral cowardice at the bar of conscience."[60] However, Jones told Faber he felt compelled to give in, because he had promised the governor that "he could have my resignation at any time that he wished." Nonetheless, Jones counseled the rabbi to do the opposite. "As your position is somewhat different, I advise you to remain on the board."[61]

Alex Sanger, Faber's co-religionist, was ambivalent about the rabbi's course. "Since he is persona non grata with the governor, . . . I don't know whether I could advise Dr. Faber to disregard the governor's request— much as I would like to have him stay," Sanger wrote to regent David Harrell.[62] But Harrell, an Austin retail merchant, was incensed at the governor's demands. Urging the rabbi to stay and fight, he wrote, "I would hate to see you resign, when it would all be under a misapprehension of existing conditions, and I believe when the matter is viewed in the light of actual facts and not suspicion, a different phase [sic] will be put on the matter. . . . I do not think it fair or just to yourself to surrender your commission. . . . The welfare of this great Institution certainly needs your services now."[63]

The rabbi agreed to stand firm and clarify his position to the governor. On September 20, eleven days after receipt of the governor's ultimatum, the rabbi typed a two-page reply, a letter that would ultimately be praised for its candor and moral force: "When, at the solicitations of my friends, you saw fit to confer upon me the distinction and honor of appointing me one of the Regents of the University of Texas, I took the oath of Office to serve the State . . . to the best of my abilities and according to the dictates of my own conscience. I never dreamed that such an appointee is expected to be a mere marionette to move and act as and when the Chief Executive pushes the button or pulls the string. I was of the opinion that in the selection of the men who . . . serve the State without remuneration you were moved by the single purpose of securing men who are the best fitted to render good service to our Commonwealth without fear and dread of any influence."[64]

The rabbi conceded that his position as a regent "flattered" his "vanity" but said that "in all due modesty" he believed he had "faithfully discharged" his duties. Denying the governor's conspiracy allegations, the rabbi defended his fellow regents. "They are men of integrity, [and] highest moral character, who have earned their golden spurs in the arena of Public Service and in the Republic of letters." He added:

I cannot pledge myself to follow the arbitrary will of any person, no matter how high and exalted, without being convinced of the justice of his demands. In my humble opinion, such course will disorganize and disrupt the University, the just pride of the people of Texas. It will produce untold harm to the cause of Higher Education and practically destroy the labors of a generation to bring up the University of Texas to the high rank it now occupies among the universities of the land. With all due respect to you, my dear Governor, I do not concede to you the right or authority to interfere in the internal management of the University of Texas. That is the sole business of the board of Regents and for that purpose they are created. I would by far rather return to my honorable obscurity than stand in the limelight of public glamour purchased at the cost of manhood and conscience. . . . I respectfully decline to concede to your wishes.[65]

The rabbi was resolute. The governor, expecting obeisance and not defiance from his appointee, was dumbfounded. Five days later, the governor wrote the rabbi a second missive accusing him of insolence, neglect, and fiscal extravagance:

I do not care to bandy words with you further, but . . . I shall not hesitate to repair the wrong which I have done in appointing you. . . . If you want to force me to remove you, you can rest assured that I shall not shirk from the task. . . . You are . . . alligning [*sic*] yourself with a political ring in the University who, if permitted to continue, will cause the people sooner or later to rise up and disown the whole affair. Your bold statement that the governor of the State has no right or authority to interfere or inquire into the management of the University proves conclusively the arrogance which has attained to a marked degree in the institution, and shows how far the idea has gained credence that the people are to have nothing to do with this institution except to shoulder and pay high appropriations to be turned over to a set of men to continue their unholy spree of establishing an educational hierarchy.[66]

A week later, the rabbi sent a terse response to the governor "emphatically" denying disloyalty to university or state. With the backing of the regents, but not the governor, the rabbi joined in preparations for a personnel hearing on behalf of the faculty members who had so irked Ferguson. The hearings would be private, with the governor present and the transcript ultimately printed in pamphlet form and disseminated.

BEYOND THE BOARD ROOM

Few of the behind-the-scenes maneuvers remained private. Regents vice chairman Will Hogg—a powerful attorney, public servant, business leader, philanthropist, and son of an ex-governor—surreptitiously distributed copies of the Faber-Ferguson correspondence to influential politicians and alumni.[67] The prickly exchange of letters was just the vehicle to marshal public opinion against the governor and to keep future chief executives from tampering with the university's affairs. Two previous Texas governors—Thomas Campbell (1907–11) and Oscar Branch Colquitt (1911–15)—had also tried to curtail the terms of uncooperative regents. Hogg spotted a meddlesome trend and was determined to dethrone the governor rather than any regents or faculty members. He wrote Faber, "I think all publicity should be given [the governor's] rotten attitude in this matter and at such time your classical communication will be of great service."[68]

To Hogg's way of thinking, the controversy could help energize the lethargic University Ex-Students Association. The alumni organization, housed on campus and dependent on the university for its $1,250 publications budget, was a sleeping giant. The college had twenty thousand "exes," an inclusive term meant to encompass graduates and dropouts. But the Ex-Students Association had a mere three thousand members— many in arrears on their dues. If more paid up, the association could become an independent political force.[69]

In letters to key alumni, Hogg urged Longhorns to "fight all over the state before submitting to the downfall of the board of regents." Alumni had been planning to amass in Austin during Homecoming celebrations on Thanksgiving. Hogg maneuvered to pair that date with the inauguration of university president Vinson. The regent envisioned a symbolic showdown with thousands of ex-students parading across campus, waving orange banners in support of their alma mater and the regents. Daily headlines in the *Austin American* escalated the controversy. "Shakeup in U. of T. to Be Discussed by the Regents." "Board Meeting Tuesday to Have Full Stenographic Record; No Resignations Expected." "More than 5,000

Will March at Inauguration with Orange Pennants . . . Red Fire and Elaborate Display to Mark Homecoming."[70]

While Hogg stirred up headlines and alumni, Vinson ventured into the countryside to court rural public opinion. The educator assured voters that the university was egalitarian—it enrolled five hundred sons and daughters of farmers and ranchers and two hundred students with widowed mothers. It was no "rich man's school." Forty-two percent of UT students worked to pay their own tuition. "I plead with you for a greater amount of intelligent sympathy," the university president implored audiences.[71]

The governor, too, stumped the state, characterizing the controversy as class war. Mispronouncing Greek letters, he maintained that 439 fraternity men and 107 sorority women ran the campus through bloc voting in student elections. The same sort of elitists dominated the Ex-Students Association, the governor said.[72]

Throughout the public posturing, Faber kept a low profile. His diligence focused on the regents' meeting room. During a month-long period, the regents heard evidence for and against the targeted faculty members. None of the seven educators accused of corruption denied a single allegation hurled by the governor. They maintained there was "no wrongdoing whatever involved" but rather "conflicting opinions . . . as to the proper administration of the university's affairs."[73] The Texas attorney general weighed in with the opinion that the university's business practices were permissible: campus administrators could indeed shuffle funds from one department to another; professors could travel with families if their expense accounts were not out of line; mileage reimbursement formulas varied among academic disciplines. Free-speech guarantees protected the journalism teacher who operated a newspaper and the faculty secretary who published cowboy poetry.

By a five-to-three vote among the regents, all seven faculty members were exonerated. A relieved Rabbi Faber boarded the train back home to Tyler, convinced that his mission was accomplished. On November 20, ten days before the UT Homecoming, the rabbi mailed the governor a polite letter of resignation.[74] He was ready to return to "honorable obscurity."

Obscurity was not to be his lot. The rabbi's resignation turned into front-page news in Dallas and Austin. His timing was opportune, falling at the moment when Homecoming fans were gathering in Austin. The press clamored to know why the rabbi had resigned. The governor told the

Austin American he welcomed the rabbi's exit—"belated though it was."[75]
The rabbi responded that he felt his duty done. The episode prompting his
defiance had passed. Moreover, the rabbi refused to "bind" himself "to
follow the dictates of any man unless convinced of the justness of his demands." He added that "it is distasteful to anyone to serve where he is persona non grata."[76]

The rabbi's resignation piqued the public's curiosity until the struggle
burst into the open. A month later, the regents' full investigative record
was released with the distribution of three thousand transcripts. Included
in the text was the exchange of letters between the rabbi and the governor.
Their clash of words helped shape public opinion. "Ferguson-Faber Communication Peppery," headlined the *San Antonio Express,* which characterized Ferguson's prose as a self-indictment.[77] Now readers perceived the
context of the rabbi's resignation and applauded his diplomatic rhetoric.
Fan mail filled the rabbi's mail box. Wrote one South Texas rancher, "If
Furgeson [*sic*] had the brains of an ass or sense of chivalry, he would re-
tract his letter and beseech U to remain upon the board." Fort Worth attorney Hal Lattimore, a Texas Law School graduate and confidant of Will
Hogg's, concurred: "When your opponent is making an ass of himself, it
is very difficult sometimes to keep from attempting to bray, even though
you know that it is foreign to your nature. . . . To read of your action gives
me a genuine thrill of pleasure on knowing that all sturdy independence is
not gone from us in our political body yet."[78]

Other letter writers pondered the governor's political future. San Antonio attorney John M. Duncan predicted that the governor's behavior would "darken and impair" his electoral prospects. Austin broker William G. Bell lamented: "Dirty politics should not be allowed to creep into
the university. If Ferguson and his gang keep on, we will have no university." Regents chairman Frederick W. Cook of San Antonio expressed
regret that Faber, a man with "fearless moral character," felt "the battle
is over."[79]

The rabbi may have exiled himself to East Texas, but an alert was in
force across the state. Within a month, three other regents' terms expired
—Sanger, Harrell, and Hogg, all Faber allies and Ferguson foes. A majority of the board would soon be Ferguson appointees. Hogg created a
new position for himself—secretary of the central committee of the University Ex-Students Association, with headquarters in the Driskill Hotel
of chicken-salad fame. Well managed and financed, the Ex-Students Association launched an offensive.[80] It joined other Ferguson foes in double-

checking allegations, raised during Ferguson's 1916 campaign, of bank fraud, misapplication of public money, embezzlement, diversion of special funds, and receipt of $156,000 from a secret source. The ex-students obtained a court injunction to restrain the Board of Regents from firing a growing list of professors under gubernatorial attack. State senator Offa "O. S." Shivers Lattimore, father and law partner of Hal Lattimore, requested a legislative investigation into the controversy at the university. The inquiry was to discern whether new nominees to the Board of Regents had promised to oust faculty members on the governor's whim. Faber, on his own volition, journeyed to the North Texas town of Sherman to meet banker W. R. Brents, the regent appointed to replace him. The rabbi wrote his allies that Brents seemed a man of "independent action," strong enough to stand up to the governor's bullying. His assumption proved correct.[81]

The governor was shocked at the mounting opposition, for which there was "no precedent" in his experience. Previously, when Ferguson had ordered a staffer at Prairie View A&M College dismissed, opposition was minimal. When he had demanded the removal of three employees at a state hospital, their termination was swift. Perhaps Ferguson needed to raise the ante at the university.[82]

In May, 1917, the governor retaliated with a threat to veto the university's $820,000 appropriation. That threat merely spread the opposition from regents and ex-students to current students, who marched en masse past the governor's office singing "The Eyes of Texas" and hoisting placards that compared Ferguson to the German Kaiser. Ferguson followed through with his veto, but the attorney general quibbled over its validity. Controversy and animosity ballooned, spurring to action a host of politicians suspicious of the governor's manipulations.[83]

Ferguson appeared before a Travis County grand jury during July, 1917, and within days was indicted on nine charges.[84] Seven related to misuse of public money, one to embezzlement, and one to diversion of a special fund. After posting $13,000 bond, the unrepentant governor announced plans to run for a third term. Days later, the speaker of the Texas house called for Ferguson's removal. Twenty-one articles of impeachment were drawn up—five related to Ferguson's feud with the university, including his attempt to bully and remove regents such as Faber without cause. Another charge involved an unpaid $156,000 loan from the Texas Brewers' Association, bolstering rumors that the governor had made a fortune from the "beer trust."[85]

The rabbi returned to Austin, this time subpoenaed to the senate impeachment proceedings where the prosecutor read the rabbi's correspondence into the trial record.[86] Faber was not called as a witnesses, but his replacement, W. R. Brents, affirmed the governor's bullying tactics. On September 25, 1917, the Texas senate took the extreme step of removing the governor from office and barring him—but not his spouse—from future state positions.

POST-IMPEACHMENT

Although Faber's duel of words with the chief executive had helped marshal public opinion, the rabbi never trumpeted his role in the downfall of the governor. It saddened Faber to see a democratic leader resort to chicanery and elected legislators implement the machinery of impeachment. He saw the governor as a demagogue without convictions, save promotion of his ego and the beer industry.

The winds of politics had also wearied the professors under attack. Linguist William J. Battle resigned at the end of the spring semester to take a post at the University of Cincinnati. Political science professor Charles Potts left Austin for the U.S. Department of Agriculture. The talented folklorist John Lomax was among six other faculty members fired when Ferguson reshuffled the Board of Regents. Although invited back after the impeachment trial, Lomax had already taken a job as a Chicago bond trader, hardly a vocation that suited his muse. The political fight had left the university with the task of rebuilding its faculty and its stability.[87]

Expulsion did not end Ferguson's political career. No "honorable obscurity" for him. Lusting for redemption and a public platform, the impeached politician ran for president of the United States—on his own party ticket, a losing proposition that kept him in the limelight. He vied for the U.S. Senate in 1922, losing to a Ku Klux Klan nominee. In the next election cycle, he ran his wife for governor. "Ma" Ferguson won in a runoff, with "Pa" Ferguson pulling the strings. Their victory led Will Rogers to remark: "The hardest thing Jim had to do after the last election was to learn to sign 'Mrs.' or 'Miriam' in front of his own name."[88]

Although the Fergusons' victory kept the Klan out of the governor's mansion, the rabbi and many other Jews remained wary of "Farmer Jim." They sensed that his beef with the Klan had more to do with his stand against Prohibition then any aversion to prejudice. In the heat of battle,

Ferguson had once penned a column, "The Cloven Foot of the Dallas Jews," that damned Dallas merchants for refusing to advertise in his weekly paper. "You Israelites can boycott me if you want to," he editorialized in the *Ferguson Forum*. "As between the Dallas Jews and the Dallas Ku Klux, I want to say that the Ku Klux is the better of the two."[89]

Despite such venom, Pa and Ma Ferguson worked with the legislature to unmask the Invisible Empire. Their weapon was an Anti-Mask Law, passed in 1925, making it a crime to parade in disguise or engage in masked attacks.[90] Klan parades disappeared. Membership waned. The Texas Klan receded from view, retreating to Masonic lodges and fraternal organizations, where men like Faber quietly continued the fight.

Rabbi Faber spent his final years in Tyler, where he was regarded as an honored, colorful statesman. Gradually, he grew into the role of Smith County's senior minister and Texas' senior rabbi. Homage came his way. He accepted honorary membership in the University of Texas Ex-Students Association and organized "The Squabblers," a discussion group for young Jewish adults. He remained an inveterate bridge player, insisting on foursomes after Friday night services. He became a friendly adversary of Tyler's Conservative rabbi, Aaron Moskovits, a colleague with whom he argued spiritual and philosophical matters. Although Faber never repaired the breach with his father, he corresponded in Yiddish with his brother in Czechoslovakia and annually raised money for a poverty-stricken rabbinical academy in Prague.[91] When he became blind in his later years, the rabbi's Orthodox co-religionists read aloud to him from Hebrew texts, and relatives read him the daily Tyler papers. On September 16, 1934, the seventy-nine-year-old rabbi quietly passed away.

Memorial plaudits poured in—statewide from politicians and nationwide from rabbis. Over and over, the tributes noted that Maurice Faber was a man of principle who, no matter the controversy, articulated his views and acted upon them.[92] In his break with his father, Faber had argued his beliefs, then moved to a country where he could practice religion as he saw fit. In his correspondence with the governor, he articulated the ideals of an immigrant and the promises of state-supported education. Eulogizing the rabbi, a local school superintendent recounted the Board of Regents episode and observed that Maurice Faber was a minister who stood for righteousness in religion and government. The rabbi gave Jews a standing in Tyler, and Tyler a standing in Texas.[93]

4

The Quintessential Texas Rabbi

HENRY COHEN, GALVESTON

*In all the state of Texas
from Fort Worth to San Anton'
There's not a man who hasn't heard
of Rabbi Henry Cohen*

—IRVE TUNICK, "BALLAD OF RABBI HENRY COHEN"

HE WAS THE DEAN of Lone Star rabbis. The ultimate Jewish star. The chief rabbi of Texas. Not that such a position exists, but during six decades in Galveston, Rabbi Henry Cohen grew into that role. More than seniority earned him his status. Texas shaped and seasoned his style. Serving in Galveston from 1888 to 1952, this Londoner with a puckish flair and an unshakable faith in God became the epitome of a twentieth-century Lone Star rabbi—a pastor to all the people (he saved a Greek Catholic from deportation); a defender of Judaism (he banished Shakespeare's Shylock from the Galveston public schools); a partner to the Christian clergy (his best friend was a priest); and a lobbyist from city hall to Capitol Hill.[1]

He was not "too" Jewish: No beard. No prayer shawl. No guttural accent—just a nervous stutter that he overcame. He was never a Zionist—a taboo among the socially assimilated Jews of the South. Rather than rabbinical, he looked Episcopal, wearing a Prince Albert frock coat that he called a "Prince Isaac." Although he abstained from eating pork, shellfish, and his wife's homemade gumbo, he never imposed his kosher habits on others. His scholarship extended beyond the parochial to encompass medicine, literature; Texas history, and a dozen foreign tongues.

In a remote harbor of the Diaspora, the world came to him. During the Gay Nineties, he befriended a papal emissary from Rome. In the thirties, *Reader's Digest* ran an unforgettable profile. In the forties, NBC radio turned his biography, *The Man Who Stayed in Texas,* into a half-hour broadcast. And in every decade, novice Texas rabbis emulated and confided in him.[2]

In a state that prized mavericks over conformists, idiosyncrasies marked Cohen's style. He rode a bicycle, rather than a carriage, a trolley, or a car. He soiled his starched white shirt cuffs with penciled lists of tasks to be done. He left a trail of cigar ash as well as good deeds when he made his hospital rounds. A spiritual giant but no saint, he was quick with a naughty limerick, thankful for a midday shot of scotch, and flattered when lipsticked ladies kissed him "good *Shabbos.*"[3] When he wandered into an orphanage, he yelled "ice cream" to attract a crowd, and when a priggish woman spent the night at his house, he dressed up a broom as a man and tucked it into her bed.[4]

More concerned with individuals than ivory-tower causes, this rabbi succeeded at both. He pressed for admission of an African American student to the local medical school.[5] He administered Christian funeral rites to a whore.[6] He extended a handshake to ten thousand unscrubbed Jewish refugees who disembarked in Galveston during the years before the First World War. A people's lobbyist, he convinced the Texas legislature to raise the age of consent in rape cases from ten to eighteen, and during three decades on the state prison board he instituted vocational training, parole reforms, and separation of first offenders from seasoned criminals.[7] Although he came of age in an era of oratory and elocution, his sermons were short and direct. Henry Cohen's entire life was a homily that blended humanitarianism and individualism, the ethics of Judaism with the ethos of Texas.

GALVESTON, OH GALVESTON

Location had something to do with Cohen's clerical prominence. Galveston in 1888 was the South's second-largest city, after New Orleans. Locals compared it to Manhattan—an island that boasted the state's wealthiest banks and most fashionable stores. Located two miles off the Texas mainland and fifty miles south of swampy Houston, Galveston was the vacation destination for tourists who craved a beach, a boardwalk, and the relief of a Gulf breeze. Plaguing the island were hurricanes, yellow fever outbreaks, and soupy fog reminiscent of Henry Cohen's British homeland. Blessing the thirty-mile-long barrier isle was the state's deepest harbor, which turned the city into an international port that shipped homegrown pecans and cotton around the globe. By the turn of the century, this Texas gateway was the nation's fifth-largest cotton exporter at 2.2 million bales per year. The city raised one-eighth of the state's tax revenue. Awash in money, merchant princes outdid one another building gargoyled Victorian homes. Commercial success, foreign consular offices, and a flourishing vice district made Galveston the state's most cosmopolitan city. And with one thousand Jews among its twenty-two thousand residents, it was Texas' Jewish capital for decades. Its rabbi automatically stepped into the limelight.[8]

Jews were never strangers to Galveston. Pirate Jean Laffite, a buccaneer of Jewish ancestry, used Galveston as his base camp from 1817 to 1821. When the island's first parcels of land were sold in 1838, a Dutch-born Jew, Joseph Osterman, and his Baltimore bride, Rosanna Dyer, bought a corner lot and built a two-story dwelling. She later willed part of their Texas fortune to local Jewish institutions. Another Dutch-born Jew, Michael Seeligson, served as an early alderman and mayor. Galveston's Jews consecrated a cemetery in 1852 but were slow to form a congregation. They were more civically than religiously attuned.[9]

The creation of a congregation did not come until after the Civil War and a push from the *Galveston Daily News,* which in 1866 posed the question: "Why don't the Israelites of our city build or rent a suitable hall for the purpose of exercising the peculiar rites of their religion? . . . We believe emphatically in religious toleration, and as churches among the Christians are the means of improving the morals of any community . . . so we suppose the Jews will be improved by the erection of a synagogue."[10] Two years later, Galveston's Jews chartered Congregation B'nai Israel. To launch a building fund, they hosted a communitywide gala at which revelers toasted the future with $72 worth of wine and cleared a $900 profit.[11]

By Cohen's arrival, Congregation B'nai Israel had a landmark synagogue, with elegant gas-lit fixtures, and a prominent place in community affairs. At the congregation's core was a generation of wealthy Texans,

among them lawyers, financiers, Confederate veterans, and aggressive entrepreneurs. These were dynastic Jewish families with a sense of noblesse
oblige. Chief among them were the Kempners—millionaire cotton factors and later founders of the Imperial Sugar Company—who gave the
rabbi an open-ended line of credit to underwrite his charitable deeds.[12] Attorney Leo Napoleon Levi, a future president of the International Order of
B'nai B'rith, was temple president. With congregants well known in international business and religious circles, Galveston's Jewish leaders under-
standably sought a rabbi with a personal and universal touch.

The congregation had experienced three previous spiritual leaders and
in 1888 was shopping for a fourth. Its last young rabbi had gone north as
a guest speaker and been hired away by a New York congregation.[13] Needless to say, when B'nai Israel searched for its next rabbi, eloquence was
not to be a key criterion. Four candidates auditioned. Most intriguing was
twenty-five-year-old Cohen. Worldly, well traveled, and warm, he possessed a passion for justice, enough religious credentials for the temple's
wayward Jews, and a contagious laugh.

FROM WHENCE HE CAME

The joie de vivre and savoir faire that made Cohen such a good fit for Galveston were ironically rooted in his lower-middle-class London upbringing. The youngest of seven children—five daughters and two sons—he
was born April 7, 1863, to Polish immigrants Josephine and David Cohen.
His father, a tinsmith and factory worker, crafted Jewish ceremonial objects from scrap metal. His mother maintained a strictly kosher kitchen,
growing upset if the youngsters mixed up dishes designated for dairy and
meat. His father winked at his wife's tirades. The Cohens' piety was evident
enough from their tiny backyard chapel, a neighborhood shul where fellow Jews *davened*—or prayed—daily.

With few pence to spare, the family enrolled Henry at a free Jewish
boarding school for the poor. For six years he studied and lived at *N'veh
Tzedek* (house of righteousness), a turreted four-story building also called
Jews Hospital. At school, Henry studied religious and secular subjects,
acquired a taste for cold fried fish, and got in a potato fight with village
toughs who chanted anti-Semitic rhymes. He graduated at age fifteen to a
full-time job with the Board of Guardians for the Relief of the Jewish Poor.
The agency hired him as an "almoner"—a social worker who distributes

charitable gifts. Over cobblestoned streets, he ran errands, giving bread tickets to the needy and paying sick calls to the poor. His superiors noted his zest for scurrying from one appointment to the next. The only assignments he disliked involved sitting behind a desk.

After work, Cohen rode the trolley to night classes at Jews College, where he began his rabbinical studies. Among his classmates was Israel Zangwill, a budding playwright whose path would cross Cohen's later in life. At Jews College, rabbinical students like Cohen graduated with the title of "minister," not "rabbi." The difference: a minister was a Torah reader, a Hebrew teacher, a *shochet* (trained in the ritual slaughter of livestock), and a *mohel* (trained to circumcise infant boys); a "rabbi" was a more prestigious position, an arbiter and interpreter of Jewish law, a title that followed ordination from Europe's Talmudic academies. Henry Cohen never went through the requisite academic steps, although in practice he covered more ground.[14]

Cohen's alter ego was his older brother Mark, a footloose fellow who hung around music halls and dreamed of journeying to "the Cape," shorthand for Cape Town, South Africa. He persuaded Henry to interrupt his rabbinical studies and accompany him on the adventure of a lifetime. By the time Mark was twenty-five and Henry eighteen, the pair had saved and borrowed and embarked on a three-year escapade to the tip of Africa. Mark worked as a bookkeeper in lively Cape Town. Henry became an interpreter for Her Majesty's government. His ear easily sorted out the jangle of languages in the marketplace—Dutch, Arabic, Chinese, and an assortment of tribal tongues that enabled him to communicate with Zulus, Hottentots, and Basutos. Most fun was the "click" language of the Xhosa people, who rolled the tongue across the palate to interject a clip-clop sound in their speech. Cohen's linguistic talent led to an assignment in a remote garrison town where the basic-training component of the job gave him skills as a sharpshooter. When Zulus went on a rampage one night, a warrior knocked Cohen unconscious with the butt of a rifle, leaving him with a permanent scar and an enduring tale.[15]

Three years in Africa did not diminish Cohen's dream of becoming a rabbi. (One Rosh Hashanah, he hiked thirty miles to reach a synagogue.) The African experience did fuel his wanderlust. When he returned to London to finish up at Jews College, he was able to view England from an outsider's perspective. Judaism was practiced so narrowly there. The new wave of Reform Judaism was making headway elsewhere, but not in Great Britain, where the chief rabbi of England interpreted Judaic law and graduates of Jews College administered it. For example, the chief rabbi decreed that the Fourth Commandment—"Remember the Sabbath day and keep it holy"—restricted Jews from all exertion between sundown Friday and sunset Saturday. Henry was chided for taking a Saturday afternoon trolley ride and relaxing with a cigarette. To him, such leisure pursuits constituted neither work nor disrespect for the Sabbath. He followed the ethics inherent in Judaism but believed its traditions subject to wide interpretation. If he ministered in England, he would be forever under the yoke of the chief rabbi. He was ready for change. Through contacts at the Board of Guardians, Cohen was called to a Caribbean pulpit.[16]

THE NEW WORLD

At the Kingston Synagogue of Amalgamated Israelites in Jamaica, Cohen filled a number of roles. He was "assistant reader" of Torah as well as the island's mohel and part-time shochet. He researched the island's history, picked up the Spanish language, and once passed out on Jamaican rum. The tropical environs, scented with hibiscus and framed by blue mountains, were paradise. But the congregation Cohen administered was pandemonium. The aristocrats of the synagogue were Sephardic Jews of Spanish descent. They bickered with the Ashkenazic Jews of Polish origin. Minor differences in ritual and Hebrew pronunciation sparked major flares. Cohen, himself of Ashkenazic heritage, could foresee no peace or compromise. One year in Jamaica was plenty.[17] He resigned in 1885 with plans to return to England by way of New York. While awaiting a transatlantic ship, Cohen received a message from Isaac T. Hart, a Mississippi lawyer born in Jamaica and eager to recruit him to a pulpit in the Deep South. With little to lose, Henry Cohen headed to Congregation Beth Israel in Woodville, Mississippi.[18]

MISSISSIPPI TRANSITION

Thirty miles inland from the Mississippi River's antebellum port of Natchez lay Woodville, a town of twelve hundred people proud of their aristocratic heritage. Jefferson Davis, the Confederacy's ex-president, owned nearby Rosemont mansion and wrote letters to the local paper defending his reputation.[19] Former plantation owners carted wagonloads of cotton and lumber to the West Feliciana Railroad office on the courthouse square. Cohen ministered to a congregation of eighteen families who reminisced about the days when Woodville had so many Jews it was called "Little Jerusalem."[20]

The pace was peaceful and the people cordial. Cohen, however, was outraged over his congregants' disregard for the Fourth Commandment. Jewish merchants opened their shops on Saturday, conducting commerce while he conducted Sabbath worship. The rabbi threatened to quit until a compromise was reached: Jews agreed to keep their stores closed until Saturday morning services ended, and the rabbi kept the services short. Cohen had asserted his rabbinical authority in a manner not unlike that of the chief rabbi of England. Christian shopkeepers also began closing their stores on Saturday mornings, for unless the Jewish merchants were open for business, few customers bothered coming to town.[21]

With time on his hands, Cohen turned the synagogue into a weekday private school and advertised plans to teach "all the branches of a thorough English education (including) foreign languages and shorthand." The school apparently folded, for within a short time, Cohen was teaching Romance languages at the Woodville Female Seminary.[22]

These were quiet but pivotal years for Cohen, whose window on America was the front page of the *Woodville Republican*. Headlines cheered the career of Irish American John L. Sullivan, who reigned as world heavyweight boxing champion. A little Alabama girl named Helen Keller, who was blind and deaf, astounded the world by learning to read. An African American passenger refused to leave the whites-only section of a train, the type of incident that eventually led to "separate but equal" facilities across the South.[23] In Jewish affairs, the *Woodville Republican* reported that a group of "progressive" rabbis, meeting in Pittsburgh, Pennsylvania, had published a platform delineating how "to Americanize the Jew."[24] Cohen took note. Eager to slip back into the mainstream, he began to look beyond Mississippi for a region more focused on the future than the past. When Galveston's largest synagogue put out a call for a rabbi, confident Henry Cohen auditioned.

On Cohen's first visit to Galveston, he realized how homesick he had become for the sights, sounds, and even the squalor of a bustling city. Galveston radiated energy, and Cohen felt reawakened and alert. Just as in Africa, opportunity seemed unlimited. Entrepreneurs quickly made millions and spent money just as fast. Gunslingers shot on sight. Theater marquees promoted vaudeville and opera. "He was in young country again," his son and daughter-in-law wrote years later, "country that you could see growing—vigorous and a little rowdy . . . a city looking ahead, not backward."[25]

Cohen was enthralled. Yet he hardly overwhelmed listeners at Congregation B'nai Israel with his trial sermon, a speech spiced with tales of Africa. Two young women giggled because the rabbi with the clipped British accent stuttered. Scolding skeptical congregants, temple president Leo N. Levi advised, "He'll get over it, and if he doesn't, we'll get used to it."[26] So what if this well-traveled rabbi had a speech impediment? He could stutter comfortably in a dozen languages, and the port of Galveston was a Tower of Babel.

THE ROLE OF THE RABBI DEEP IN THE HEART

Galveston was a big step up from rural Mississippi, and Cohen had adjustments to make. The vast Lone Star State had but five rabbis, compared with seven or eight in Mississippi. None of Texas' rabbis were of long tenure, except for Hempstead's Heinrich Schwarz, who was more a family rabbi than a congregational leader. With no one to consult, Cohen reinvented the role of rabbi. It seemed insufficient in Texas to lead services, teach in a classroom, or study the fine points of Jewish law, which few frontier people concerned themselves with. It was impossible to be an autocrat like the chief rabbi of England. An ultimatum such as Cohen had issued in Mississippi would not be heeded. In Galveston, a clergyman lacked the clout to alter the business pace. (Only labor unrest could do that.) The island's Jews were honest and philanthropic but focused on commercial pursuits and scarcely educated in Judaic matters. Because Jews worked on Saturday, Cohen's Sabbath-morning flock was meager. Friday night services drew a respectable crowd, so he delivered his weightiest sermons on Sabbath eve.

B'nai Israel's Sunday School was open to all Jewish youngsters, whether or not their parents belonged to the congregation—and most did not. Many a student was raised in a home where immigrant parents spoke Yiddish and davened at the Orthodox shul that evolved from the Young Men's Hebrew Association.[27] Cohen saw his Sunday School as an opportunity for instilling children with the traditions and ethics of Judaism. His mandatory curriculum included memorization of the Ten Commandments; recitation of biblical passages that illustrated each one; Hebrew reading; and forty-five verbatim principles of Judaism. Cohen's catechism of faith included the "belief in the existence, eternity, unity, omnipotence, and infinite wisdom of God."[28] The Jewish education drilled into Galveston youngsters turned them into premier religious school teachers when they left the island for college in Austin or new lives in remote Texas towns. The only controversial aspect of the curriculum was Cohen's insistence on Hebrew, which the influential Lasker banking family objected to.[29]

Galveston's Jews were mainstream. That gave Cohen license to take his pulpit to all the island's people and tackle this role as he had his very first job as an almoner, visiting everyone and learning their talents and travails. He chose not to restrict his ministry to Jews or Anglos. "In this town there is no such thing as Methodist mumps, Baptist domestic troubles, Presbyterian poverty, or Catholic broken legs," he said.[30] Similarly, he condemned people who "designate Italians, Negroes, Mexicans, Hungarians, and Chinamen as 'wops,' 'niggers,' 'greasers,' 'bohunks,' and 'chinks.'"[31] He treated everyone as a member of his flock and built a following one at a time.

His first conquest was Mollie Levy—one of the young women who had giggled at his nervous stutter. Mollie was a native Texan with a dry wit to combat the rabbi's constant teasing. She was also a frugal financial manager, a practical woman one year older and a few inches taller than the five-foot one-inch rabbi. Their differences proved compatible, and the couple married within nine months of his Texas arrival. On the Fourth of July in 1890, they celebrated the birth of their daughter, Ruth. A son, Harry, followed in 1893. The Cohens were proud that both of their children were B.O.I.—born on the island, a boastful acronym that sets apart Galveston natives.

The family of four moved into the corner house at 1920 Broadway and Avenue I, a three-story, wood-frame Victorian that became a magnet for people in need. Temple benefactor Eliza Kempner paid the mortgage on the dwelling, a hospitable landmark that townsfolk called the "rabbinage." Here, more so than at the temple, Henry Cohen held court and gave counsel. Word of the rabbi's tutelage brought a student in need of a loan, an ex-convict optimistic that the rabbi would find him a job, and a Hollywood crew that screened a reform-school movie, *Prison Without Bars,* in the rabbi's study.[32] Outdoors, Cohen's front porch served as a reception area for the multitudes who talked, sipped lemonade, and munched Mollie Cohen's home-baked cookies while waiting to confer with the rabbi.

Cohen was always on call; if not at home, then throughout the city and beyond. The death of an elderly man in Victoria, Texas, put Cohen on a midnight train to officiate at his morning funeral. An anti-Semitic vaudeville act touring the state prompted letters of protest from the rabbi and cancellation of the offending scenes that showed Jews kissing money.[33] Was an Episcopal youth unable to afford the courses for seminary admission? Cohen tutored him in Christology.[34] Was a musically gifted medical student without a piano? The next day a red spinet was delivered to the youth's fraternity house, courtesy of the rabbi's connections to the Balinese Room, a gambling den and dining room on a Galveston pier.[35]

For a cosmopolitan port of call, Galveston's educational resources were slim, so Cohen built a personal library that grew to twelve thousand volumes. The rabbi's quest for knowledge led him to the medical school. Accepted as an honorary faculty member, he scrubbed down with physicians and stood alongside them during surgery. Everyone on campus called Cohen "Doctor," a title gratuitously granted pastors of the era. Cohen found the title fitting and demonstrated the connection by writing a paper on medical advice in the Talmud, the compendium of ancient rabbinical discussions and commentaries. The rabbi understood that healing was part medicinal, part psychological, and delighted in the dual role. One summer while Cohen was en route to Boulder, Colorado, a weary traveler asked whether there was a doctor on the train. The rabbi answered in the affirmative and relieved the voyager's sickness with aspirin and a show of concern.[36]

The rabbi's search for intellectual peers led him to Galveston's Catholic clergy. The rapport was immediate. At a banquet in 1896 for Cardinal Francesco Satolli from Rome, Cohen was the only non-Catholic guest.[37] Such ecumenical bonds, rare anywhere in the nineteenth century, helped Cohen persuade Galveston's bishop, Nicholas A. Gallagher, to sign an 1898 petition protesting the French government's handling of the Dreyfus Affair, in which a Jewish military officer was falsely convicted of treason and later exonerated. The bishop signed a second petition in 1903 protesting the Kishinev pogroms that left two thousand Jewish families homeless, and he later donated money for victims of Russian persecution.[38] Cohen's warm ties with the bishop were all the more remarkable because parishioners perceived the prelate as distant and authoritarian.[39]

The appointment in August, 1896, of a young priest to Galveston's St. Mary's Cathedral was welcomed by the city's three thousand Catholics, as well as by the rabbi.[40] Father James Martin Kirwin, twenty-four, an Ohio native and a graduate of Washington, D.C.'s Catholic University, arrived in

*Msgr. James Martin Kirwin, ca. 1895, Rabbi Henry Cohen's best friend
and coworker for civic causes and social justice in Galveston.*
Courtesy Catholic Archives of Texas, Austin.

Galveston like a Gulf Stream breeze. The personable priest compensated
for the bishop's aloofness. Cohen and Kirwin became instant cronies. Although they were a decade apart in age and at least a foot apart in height,
their interests and backgrounds meshed. They became a familiar pair,
"Little Henry" and "Big Jim," dashing around town to hospitals and public meetings. One was small and energetic with a British accent; the other,
tall, muscular, and handsome with an Irish American brogue. Like Cohen,
Kirwin was conversant in several languages and read liturgical Latin, Hebrew, and Greek. Like Cohen, Kirwin came from a large family with no extra money for frills. Both enjoyed a jigger of whiskey and a ribald tale. Co-

hen researched the history of Jews in Texas, and Kirwin studied the state's Catholic past. Both lobbied the legislature—Cohen for a pure milk law in 1893; Kirwin for restrictive saloon legislation in 1909. Cohen returned to the legislature time and again pressing for prison reform. Kirwin was back and forth to Austin to keep public money flowing to Catholic schools and to block the state from inspecting convents. The rabbi and the "padre," as Cohen called his friend, were strangers to none.[41]

ILL WINDS

Catastrophe catapulted both clerical activists to national attention. On Saturday, September 8, 1900, a cataclysmic hurricane swept a tidal wave over Galveston Island, making rubble of thirty-six hundred homes and killing more than sixty-five hundred inhabitants—one-sixth the city's population. The death toll stands as the nation's worst in a natural disaster. Looting became rampant, even ghoulish as thieves cut fingers off corpses to plunder rings. Kirwin, a Spanish-American War chaplain and the ranking soldier on the island, met with the mayor, the chief of police, and other civic leaders to write the proclamation placing the city under martial law.[42] He and Cohen served on the Central Relief Committee. The priest patrolled on a black steed, rounding up the able-bodied to clear debris and remove corpses from the rubble. When bodies buried at sea washed ashore, Kirwin ordered the corpses cremated—a practice contrary to Catholic law and a decision destined to stall Kirwin's advancement within the Church hierarchy.[43] At the time, Kirwin's concern was public health. Cohen had no superiors second-guessing his decisions. The rabbi patrolled on foot, a shotgun under the crook of his arm as he attended to the suffering of all faiths. Clara Barton, famous organizer of the Red Cross, reached Galveston nine days after the storm and triggered an international relief effort that funneled money, clothing, and food to an island falling prey to dysentery, yellow fever, and despair.[44]

The storm demolished all but five of the island's twenty-eight churches, with the temple among the institutions spared. The Sunday morning after the storm, the rabbi opened the doors of B'nai Israel to Christians, whose churches were a shambles. The temple sustained "comparatively little damage," the rabbi told reporters. "Twenty-five hundred dollars will cover this."[45] The Jewish community suffered forty-one casualties and immeasurable property damage. "The great majority of our people lost their domiciles entirely; no house in the city was left undamaged," Cohen wrote New York's *American Hebrew*. His own home, the rabbinage, was "seriously wrecked" but repairable. Although human needs came first, weighing on the rabbi's heart was damage to the Jewish cemetery. "Water to the depth of eight or ten feet swept through our cemeteries, the wind blew down nearly all the tombstones, and the combined elements tore away the iron railings—200 by 260 feet ... thus making our '*botai hajim*' [cemetery] grazing grounds for stray cattle," he reported.[46]

Hundreds of survivors fled Galveston. The killer storm, and subsequent hurricanes in 1910 and 1915, drove multitudes of merchants and residents inland to Houston. The rival city, which christened completion of its deep-water port in 1914, was better sheltered from the elements and eager to overtake Galveston's commercial lead. Gradually, Houston surpassed Galveston in population and trade.[47]

Yet Houston's Jews still looked to Galveston for leadership. Houston's spiritual leader was also a Briton, Rabbi Henry Barnston, a pastor five years younger than Cohen and only nine months in America when the Galveston hurricane pummeled the coast. Barnston was courtly, literary, humane, and ecumenical, a man who dashed off polished sermons from the pulpit but not slapstick jokes like Cohen. If only Barnston could be more like Cohen, a colorful people's pastor. Although Barnston served Houston energetically from 1900 to 1943 and became an insider among his city's sophisticates, he served in Cohen's shadow. His Jewish star would have shone brighter had he not been so close to Cohen's orbit.

Cohen's stock as a leader continued to grow. He remained in Galveston to help rebuild and fortify the island from future storms. Before the 1900 hurricane, Rabbi Cohen hinted at the possibility of leaving Texas for pulpits elsewhere. After the storm, moving was out of the question: "I have enjoyed the prosperity of my people; I cannot now forsake them in their poverty."[48] Cohen's congregants were fewer and his city of declining importance, but his fame and influence mounted.

THE GALVESTON MOVEMENT

The Galveston rabbi solidified his humanitarian reputation between 1907 and 1914, when a stream of immigrants elected to bypass New York harbor for Texas' Gulf Coast port. Cohen helped implement the Galveston movement, a plan to divert European Jews to the American Southwest and Midwest. The ambitious effort was fueled by a growing tide of anti-immigrant sentiment in the Northeast and Jewish self-consciousness over the squalor their brethren brought to New York. More than two million Jewish refugees had entered the United States between 1880 and 1907, with more than 75 percent of them settling in the Northeast. They crowded into tenements, drove up crime, provoked anti-Semitism, embarrassed old stock Jews, and taxed city services. New York banker Jacob Schiff, a godfather of American Jewish philanthropy, gambled that with a $500,000 subsidy and a convincing public-relations campaign, hordes of immigrants would choose the West over the congested Northeast.[49]

Schiff was not the only Jew of influence contemplating the future of the more than one million Eastern European Jews clamoring to escape stepped-up persecution. Other visionaries dreamed of Zion, restoring the land of Israel to its descendants in exile. A variant of the Zionist dream was proposed by Israel Zangwill, Rabbi Cohen's old schoolmate and head of the Jewish Territorial Organization. Zangwill believed Jews should claim some uninhabited territory as their own. For a time he proposed Jewish resettlement in Uganda. When the African alternative failed to catch on, he teamed up with Schiff and switched his attention to the American West.

Galveston was selected over other southern ports because it connected with a German passenger shipping line. Moreover, Galveston Island was a railroad terminus to the country's midsection and a city too small to tempt immigrants to remain. The goal was dispersal. Henry Cohen's presence in Galveston made the choice fortuitous. He was an old friend of the temperamental Zangwill. He was a committed anti-Zionist. As Texas' foremost rabbi, he could tap into a network of rabbis, lay leaders, and merchants to help resettle the refugees.

The going was rough. During the seven-year experiment, one hundred ships carried Jewish refugees from Germany's North Sea to Galveston Bay. Some years, as few as 126 immigrants chose the Galveston route. In peak years, one to three thousand were transported. On board, they complained that the food was rancid and meager and that the crews were surly toward lower-berth passengers. The journey lasted more than three weeks, rather than the usual two-and-a-half, prolonged by captains who slowed the engines to save costly fuel. Immigration authorities in Galveston were exceptionally strict. In 1913 they deported more than two hundred refugees a month after supposedly detecting hernias. Orthodox Jewish groups denounced the Galveston plan because applicants were forewarned that settlement beyond the Mississippi might entail working on Saturdays. Furthermore, the American West had few kosher butchers, making the Galveston route seem a mockery of traditional Judaism. The Yiddish press, which opposed the movement, magnified all complaints.[50]

Rabbi Cohen worked doggedly, despite the difficult odds. When the first eighty-seven immigrants disembarked in Galveston in July, 1907, he welcomed them with a brass band. Local lads, like the eager Sam Perl, were deployed as "runners" to escort immigrants to public baths, barbers, and post offices to mail letters back home. Cohen often intervened on behalf of refugees whom U.S. authorities were ready to deport. Alexander Ziskind Gurwitz, a Polish rabbi detained by immigration officials the day his ship arrived in 1910, attested to the weight of Cohen's personal touch: "When it came to me, the immigration officials cast a jaundiced eye. They regarded my silver-grey hair and began to mutter among themselves. I was frightened. . . . But Rabbi Cohen asked after my precise age and my profession. I showed him my passport, which showed my birth date as being fifty-one. I also informed him that I was a certified *shochet*. I added documented proof that 2,000 rubles had been transferred from my bank in Russia to an American bank. There was no danger of my becoming a public charge. I was permitted to pass."[51]

The immigrant recalled how Cohen congratulated him and offered him a kosher meal: "I thanked him warmly for his noble heart, and I saw that he was equally considerate of all the immigrants. With gently reassuring words, he did whatever he could do to make the adjustment for the immigrants easier. He sought out jobs for them, and until these materialized he saw to it that they had adequate food, drink, lodging. He was as a compassionate father to all of the poor, lonely immigrants. If all of the paid professionals . . . had fulfilled at least in part their responsibility, as did Rabbi Cohen, the immigrants would not have suffered even a fraction of what they had to bear."[52]

Statistically, the Galveston movement's grand design was deemed a failure. It altered no migration patterns. During the seven-year experiment, 10,000 refugees disembarked in Galveston—less than 4 percent of total Jewish immigration to the United States. Of those 10,000 arrivals, 3,000 stayed in Texas, including 300 in Galveston; 1,000 settled in the surrounding states of Arkansas, Louisiana, and Oklahoma; 6,000 elsewhere across the Midwest and Far West, including 375 in Colorado. In the meantime, another 100,000 Jews a year had entered the United States through New York.[53]

In personal and subjective terms, however, the Galveston movement was a success. As immigrants earned their livelihoods and sent for overseas relatives, small Jewish enclaves sprouted in places like Hamilton, Texas, where no Jew had lived before. Some faltering synagogues—in Sioux City, Iowa, for example—were spiritually strengthened by the infusion of newcomers more in touch with Jewish tradition. According to a historian who reviewed the movement in 1983, the Galveston plan led to "recognition of Judaism as one of the three great religious groups in the United States." It settled immigrants in twenty-five states and more than one hundred towns. Jewish people now permeated the nation. Small clusters of Jews, rather than a massive wave of refugees, succeeded in spreading awareness and respect for Judaism across America.[54]

Not every Texas rabbi was enamored of the refugee movement nor of Rabbi Cohen's role. Fort Worth's Rabbi G. George Fox resented the refuse—mainly prostitutes—that the Galveston plan unwittingly deposited in his city. The movement's guidelines barred single women from immigrating alone, because they were unlikely to find self-supporting jobs. Still, unaccompanied females routinely slipped through, posing as daughters of legitimate passengers. Another undesirable category of immigrant was the political malcontent who spouted Marxist, socialist, and anarchist ideologies. Finding work and lodging for political radicals was no easy task. Rabbi Fox fumed that Cohen got all the glory for the Galveston movement, while grunts like him hustled to find jobs and lodgings for less-than-welcome new arrivals.[55]

THE KU KLUX KLAN

The increased presence of immigrants bred fear and revulsion, particularly among status-conscious white Protestants ready to impose moral standards upon the nation. After World War I, these factors, compounded by unemployment, rising crime, and crowded urban settings, accelerated the revival of the Ku Klux Klan. In the Southwest, the Klan's push for law and order reinforced the region's vigilante streak. The masked fraternity traced its origins to post–Civil War Pulaski, Tennessee, and six Confederate veterans. Their secret society derived its alliterative name from *kuklos,* a Greek word for circle, and *klan* to reflect the founders' Scotch-Irish heritage. During its first heyday of violence from 1865 to 1871, the KKK evolved from a costumed group, terrorizing former slaves, into the military wing of the Democratic Party. White-robed night riders attacked blacks, scalawags, and carpetbaggers in the name of the Klan. In 1915, the lynching of factory manager Leo Frank, an Atlanta Jew falsely convicted of slaying a young girl, signaled a resurgence of mob-directed hate. The Frank case, coupled with the release that same year of D.W. Griffith's racist film *The Birth of a Nation,* led sixteen men on a pilgrimage to Stone Mountain, Georgia, a Confederate memorial site, where they founded the Knights of the Ku Klux Klan. The reincarnated Klan presented itself to prospective members as a positive force for Protestantism, chastity, and Prohibition.[56]

Cohen and Kirwin watched anxiously during the autumn of 1920 as the Klan organized across Texas. Much to their dismay, Galveston seemed as susceptible as other cities. The island had a Klavern—Galveston Klan No. 36, founded November 18 of that year.[57] William Moody III, offspring of one of the island's most powerful families, collected dues for the local Klavern.[58] *Colonel Mayfield's Weekly,* an eight-page Klan organ with hateful headlines about "Kikes and Katholics," was published in Houston and found a substantial Galveston readership.[59] Determined to stop the Galveston Klan from gaining momentum, Cohen and Kirwin conferred with city officials and secured a promise that no parade permit would be issued the KKK.[60] The Klan did manage to stage an initiation ceremony on the island on September 3, 1922, erecting two giant crosses, "blazing with red electric lights," on opposite ends of a fenced field. The Sunday morning before the rally, cloaked Klansmen interrupted at least one local church service to leave a monetary donation and an invitation to the rite.[61] Chartered trains filled with Klan members from Beaumont and Houston bypassed the Galveston depot and deposited the hooded hordes at the induction site. Although the Klan initiation ceremony caught the rabbi and his allies by surprise, the gathering was self-contained within the field's barbed-wire confines. Galveston witnessed no ghostly street parade of prejudice, as did other Texas cities. No tar-and-featherings or lynchings were reported on the island.

The rabbi and the padre publicly raged against the Klan. Cohen made certain that *The Birth of a Nation,* which portrays the Klan as savior of the South, was pulled from the schedule at Galveston's Queen Theatre. "The K.K.K. is arming its people with propaganda and the idea is that the 'Birth of a Nation' will give them just so much aid and comfort," Cohen wrote the movie house manager. "It would be better if the film were called off under the circumstances." It was.[62]

Kirwin angered the Klan by refusing to salute an American flag that the KKK erected on a Houston street corner to honor a fallen Catholic soldier. "That flag hid a dirty spot," the priest declared during the young Marine's funeral. The Klan responded with threats of violence against "Pappy Kirwin," whose defiance helped the public realize how the "super patriots" in the Klan were sullying the flag.[63]

Partly because of Cohen and Kirwin's moral authority and united front, the Klan never established as strong a presence in Galveston as it did in Austin, Houston, Dallas, Fort Worth, and Beaumont (which, like Galveston, had a sizable Catholic population). In those localities, Klan slates were swept into office in 1922. One difference between Galveston and those Klan-dominated cities was its relative stability. During the preceding decade, Galveston's population had grown by 8,600, compared with increases of more than 60,000 in both Houston and Dallas, where the Klan flourished.[64] Another factor keeping down Klan influence on the island was its advocacy of Prohibition—an issue winked at in Galveston, a port with a rum-running tradition. Also, Cohen and Kirwin, unlike some liberal religious leaders elsewhere, were never nonchalant or indifferent to the Klan but quick to perceive it as a threat. As one latter-day Galveston historian observed: "There was too much local resistance from people like Rabbi Cohen and Father Kirwin for the Klan to find growing room."[65]

GOOD-BYE TO A FRIEND

Sunday evening, January 24, 1926, Rabbi Cohen's dinner was interrupted and his composure shattered. A representative from the diocese came to his door with a message: Father Kirwin was dead. The fifty-three-year-old priest had died in his sleep, never rousing from a nap after mass and Sunday supper. The rabbi was shaken. "The shock of his sudden demise after three decades of close companionship has left me speechless," Cohen told a reporter.[66] "He was always to be found when wanted and always to be trusted when found."[67] Church bells tolled. Stores remained closed into the week as funeral masses were conducted over the next four days.

The only medical explanation for the priest's premature death was high blood pressure, weight gain, and long hours, combined with the stress of his multiple roles. Kirwin's responsibilities had grown to include president and professor at St. Mary's Seminary and vicar general of the Galveston diocese. The pope had finally elevated Kirwin to monsignor in 1922 after an apostolic delegate investigated the circumstances surrounding his long-ago order to cremate victims of the 1900 hurricane.[68] A celebrity in the Catholic world, Kirwin had received an honorary doctor of law degree in 1923 from Indiana's Notre Dame University and a medal from the French government. His death drew condolences from France, Ireland, and Italy, where he had traveled and conducted mass.

In Galveston, grieving contingents from the fire department, the police force, the Knights of Columbus, the American Legion, the Texas National Guard, and the Spanish War Veterans assembled to escort Kirwin's casket to the train depot for his final journey home to Circleville, Ohio. As Cohen's son, then editor of the *Galveston Tribune*, wrote: "Suffice it to say, that [was] the saddest day in the rabbi's life ... when bareheaded, with un-concealed tears flowing down his cheeks, he followed behind the bier of his dearest friend through the streets of a city they had loved and served so well."[69]

Intellectual peers, kindred spirits, and civic partners, Cohen and Kirwin had shared an irreplaceable camaraderie. "As a friend I know I shall not see his like again," the rabbi mourned.[70] For strength, he read from the Book of Job: "Though he slay me, yet will I trust in him." For solace, he repeated the Hebrew expression, *Zecher tzaddik livrachah*, "The remembrance of the righteous is for a blessing. God rest his soul."[71]

THE FINAL PHASE

Rabbi Cohen was by then sixty-three, a stage in life when he was more "father confessor" than friend to people he met. Particularly among Jews, he was mentor and role model. Because Cohen had been a circuit-riding rabbi when other Texas congregations were forming, he understood the politics inside most every temple and shul. If a rabbi in Waco or Austin was upset at the apathy or stinginess of his congregation, he confided in Cohen. If a pulpit became vacant in Fort Worth or San Antonio, applicants contacted Cohen instead of the search committee.

In 1922, Cohen had artfully pulled strings to bring his son-in-law, Rabbi Ephraim Frisch, from New York to San Antonio's Temple Beth-El. Cohen was delighted to have his daughter, Ruth, back in proximity. She was his kindred spirit, a soul of harmony and depth who could have been a rabbi had notions of equal suffrage triumphed sooner. Her son David visited Galveston every weekend and marveled at the shiny pennies—"Laffite's

Rabbi Henry Cohen, age sixty-eight, at the beach with his grandchildren, summer, 1931. Left: David Frisch, fourteen, son of Ruth and Ephraim Frisch, San Antonio's rabbi. Right: Henry Cohen II, age four, son of writers Ann Nathan and Harry Cohen. Young Cohen became a Philadelphia rabbi. Courtesy Henry Cohen II.

treasure!"—his grandfather discovered beneath the sand at the beach.[72] The Cohens and Frisches regaled one another with joke after joke. Rabbi Frisch, unfortunately, was not as relaxed and amusing among his own congregants. Unlike his father-in-law, he was no diplomat but an impatient idealist with a searing mind. Cohen did not mind intervening when San Antonio's temple elders complained about his son-in-law's obstinance. Frisch did so much good and let no injustice pass quietly.

Austin's Jewish community posed a different set of problems. The capital city could not keep a rabbi for long. David Rosenbaum, who served from 1911 to 1922, complained of a meddlesome president and miserly congregants. They resented the time he spent assisting university "shtoodents" who paid nothing to the temple trough.[73] The talented Rosenbaum, who hailed from Chicago, had accepted the Austin pulpit mainly to work within Henry Cohen's orb. He moved on to a West Virginia congregation, returning briefly to marry a Texas bride, with Cohen, of course, officiating at the ceremony.[74]

Waco had an altogether different congregational climate. Its rabbi, Wolfe Macht, confided to Cohen in 1922 that, after just three years in Texas, he was ready to quit. "I am embittered against Waco Jewry," he wrote the senior rabbi. "I must leave. . . . I get no encouragement whatever. Here you find the largest amount of prejudice, because here you also find [the] most indifferent coreligionists." To calm the rabbi, Cohen alerted Asher Sanger, an influential business figure, suggesting that a little appreciation toward the rabbi would go a long way. Cohen's ploy worked. Sanger and other business leaders began to consciously compliment their rabbi, and Macht remained at Waco's Rodef Sholom until his death in 1952.[75]

Cohen rightly perceived that personality, more so than ideology, orthodoxy, or scholarship, was what mattered in a Texas rabbi. In Brownsville, his former religious school student, Sam Perl, had evolved into an effective lay rabbi, mediating differences among Jews and representing his people to the community at large. Beaumont's rabbi, Sam Rosinger, had turned into a surprisingly good fit, despite his pro-Zionist columns in the *Texas Jewish Herald.* Rosinger was sincere, humble, and effective. Disagreements between the two rabbis were frequent, but intelligent and never personal. It was a pleasure to share the rabbinage with the Rosingers and their four children during their summer vacations. The rabbinage was also open to visits from the family of Isadore Garsek, the Orthodox rabbi from Fort Worth.

Texas rabbis institutionalized their camaraderie in 1927 with an annual *kallah,* or symposium, launched by Orthodox Rabbi Abraham Schechter of Houston. The kallah's purpose was solely Jewish scholarship. Cohen treasured the opportunity to retreat for a few days, mix with Jewish theologians of differing persuasions, and discourse over rabbinical law. He recognized that his Orthodox colleagues were deeper thinkers than he. They led philosophical seminars on mysticism and anti-asceticism, while he spoke about Texas Jewish history.[76]

Cohen was the first to admit his academic shortcomings. In fact, when Hebrew Union College asked him to apply for seminary president in 1921, he told the leadership, "I have not the adequate scholarship."[77] He chose not to share wife Mollie's reaction: she had no intention of becoming housemother to a bunch of rabbinical students.[78]

The young rabbis coming out of rabbinical school in the thirties and forties were more outspoken on racial issues than Cohen. To be sure, Cohen had helped people of color, but he never articulated his racial views as starkly as his younger colleagues. Perhaps his British colonial heritage held him back—all that time in Africa and the West Indies. His style was to work behind the scenes, helping one individual at a time. He had assisted black youths like Jack Johnson, a future heavyweight boxing champ. Jailed in the 1890s for pugilism, Johnson was furloughed, at Cohen's insistence, to work on the docks.[79] In 1907 Cohen backed a measure to integrate seating on Galveston's trolleys, but the proposal lost amid acrimony.[80] He had always spoken against bigotry, and Galveston's African American leaders knew that Cohen never turned down a request for a job, a loan, or a charitable deed. The new crop of Texas rabbis demonstrated brotherhood in ways Cohen had not. In the 1940s, Corpus Christi's Rabbi Sidney Wolf was taking teenagers on tours of African American churches. Houston's Rabbi Robert Kahn persuaded city police to put an African American on the force. Levi Olan, in Dallas since 1949, made race relations a routine part of his pulpit credo. Cohen approved. In order to lead, rabbis had to be ahead of their congregations and their communities.

Cohen had always been ahead of his flock, and he recognized the need for change. When he had first come to Texas in 1888, the state had only five other rabbis, some with questionable credentials. By 1950, there were thirty-six—most with seminary degrees. Many of these rabbis had been drawn to the Lone Star State simply to become acquainted with Cohen. His legend had spread with the hurricane, the Galveston plan, the prison-reform movement, and a clerical top-ten list that had ranked him among the nation's "Big Ten" ministers.[81] In his eighty-ninth year of life, well beyond the biblical threescore and ten, Rabbi Henry Cohen felt death approaching. As he neared the end of his rich lifetime and long career in June of 1952, he knew he was leaving the Texas rabbinate in good hands. As the dean of Lone Star rabbis, Cohen had fostered civic activism, moral leadership, warmth, humor, and a Jewish blueprint for Texas' future.

5

Cowtown's
Front-Page Rabbi

G. GEORGE FOX, FORT WORTH

THE RED-HEADED RABBI'S PULSE shot up—again. Try as he might to distance his flock from Hell's Half Acre, in the autumn of 1913 Rabbi G. George Fox overheard ranchers downtown muttering remarks about "Jew whores." What's more, the Sisterhood at his synagogue of seventy families was scandalized at the gossip. The women—chief among them his wife Hortense, a third-generation American—wanted those tramps gone.[1]

The Jewish prostitutes were Eastern European women who had ventured to Fort Worth's red-light district by way of Galveston, a port of entry for eight thousand fellow Jews since 1907.[2] Fox's colleague, the saintly Rabbi Henry Cohen of Galveston, was being lauded from Texas to New York for greeting each refugee at the dock. But as far as Fox was concerned, the refuse was riding the rails from the Gulf Coast to North Texas, bringing social disease and dishonor to Jews in Fort Worth. "As rabbi, I could not and would not escape the responsibility that was mine in this shameful business," the rabbi declared in his memoirs. "It was a drab affair."[3]

With the police commissioner and the mayor, Fox arranged a raid on brothels within "the Acre," a seedy neighborhood of saloons, dance halls, cathouses, and gambling dens in the blocks north of the Texas & Pacific depot.[4] Madams were advised to surrender their Jewish girls on charges of disorderly conduct, or face a shutdown. At the jail, Fox confronted twenty women.[5] Through a Yiddish interpreter, the American rabbi warned them to turn to legitimate pursuits—or else. In response, some tugged at the rabbi's heartstrings with sagas of children in foster homes. Others blamed hunger, violence, and deception for driving them into the "sordid" business. "One showed me a lavaliere bearing a picture of her father, so she said: an old, bearded, Eastern co-religionist," Fox recalled. "One asked me whether my rich, fat Jews would take her into their homes and give her a job. . . . A third challenged us, in Yiddish, to give her a job in some store. Of course we were stymied. . . . Two of the lot married the men who were their pimps and went into legitimate business. . . . The rest left town."[6]

When Christian clergymen asked the rabbi why his outrage extended only to Jewish prostitutes, he advised his brothers in the Tarrant County General Pastors Association to round up the gentile prostitutes themselves. Fox, however, had more legal ammunition at his disposal, mainly the White Slave Traffic Acts. The run-of-the-mill harlots were American-born. If arrested, they could be bailed out by pimps and madams, or fined and returned to the streets. The Jewish suspects, many masking their immigrant origins with American aliases, were subject to deportation as "alien prostitutes."[7] And so they were. Eighteen young Jewish women were deported to Europe, months before the outbreak of World War I.[8]

"The job made me unhappy, though I could see no other way," Fox wrote. Although the ambivalent rabbi was chairman of the Fort Worth Charity Commission and an organizer of a state welfare conference, he found it more prudent to remove than to try to reform the women. Truth be told, "Jew whore" remarks stirred anti-Semitism among the public and insecurity among Jews who prided themselves on being law-abiding Americans with a family-centered religion. Fox and his generation of upwardly mobile Jews wanted to retain their religious identity. Yet they were eager to be seen as part of the American mainstream, not a remnant of the Old World like their unwashed cousins pouring in from the *shtetls* of Eastern Europe.

Prostitution among Jews—documented in muckraking magazines and a federal immigration investigation—had prompted Jewish communities nationwide to police their own. B'nai B'rith, the Jewish fraternal organization, had helped the Justice Department apprehend Jewish prostitutes who crossed state lines. Chicago rabbis had worked with the district attorney and vigilantes to round up Jewish madams in the Windy City. Prosti-

tution was such a blot on Jewish morality that little attention was given to
its causes, its social solutions, or the men involved in the business. When
whispers of Jewish prostitution surfaced in Fort Worth's downtown cafés,
Rabbi Fox had precedents to follow.[9]

Fox was not as bold, or grandstanding, as his ministerial colleague, the
Rev. J. Frank Norris at Fort Worth's First Baptist Church. The year before,
Norris had announced from the pulpit the names of leading citizens who
owned brothels. This led not to arrests but retaliation, as arsonists set fire
to the minister's church and parsonage.[10] In contrast, Rabbi Fox's action
in ridding the community of Jewish prostitutes was met with sighs of relief. He had distanced Fort Worth's Jewish residents from the taint of im-
morality. He had gingerly worked with the authorities, without upsetting
the status quo. He had correctly gauged how far to stretch his moral authority in a town closer to the frontier than the Bible Belt.

CATTLE COUNTRY

Fort Worth was where the West began. Named for a general who never
made it to North Texas, Fort Worth traced its origins to an 1849 army outpost, built to protect towns farther east from marauding Comanches.[11] As
the American West grew to symbolize the cowboy, Fort Worth was part of
that culture, a watering stop for longhorns and horseback riders traveling
the Chisholm Trail. Here, cowboys spent their wages on a bath, a haircut,
whiskey, women, and gambling. Trail bosses stocked up on flour at Jacob
Samuels' dry goods store and sampled tobacco at Eichenbaum's Cigars, es-
tablishments owned by Jewish entrepreneurs.

Despite Jewish names on a score of Main Street storefronts, organized
Judaism was slow to gain a toehold in Fort Worth, much slower than
elsewhere. In a cow town where drunken gamblers unloaded six-shooters
into the air, law and order was more a priority than prayer. Among Fort
Worth's Jewish pioneers, the suggestion of a *minyan*—the ten-man quo-
rum required for a worship service—was met with ridicule. "Fort Worth
Jews were beyond redemption," wrote the daughter of an early Jewish
settler.[12] The religious-minded moved forty miles east to Dallas, a commercial crossroads and more of a magnet for Jews. By the time Fort
Worth's "Israelites" dedicated their first landmark—a cemetery on land
donated by a non-Jew in 1879—Dallas boasted a handsome synagogue

with a choir, a Sabbath School, and a secular school. Fort Worth remained without a Jewish congregation until 1892 when twenty men, mostly Eastern European immigrants, spearheaded the formation of Ahavath Sholom, a traditional synagogue with a name that means love of peace. A decade later, forty-three well-assimilated Jews, many of them born in Texas, Louisiana, Mississippi, and Tennessee, organized Congregation Beth-El, a Reform synagogue with English services. Ties between the two congregations were cordial, with some Jews belonging to both. However, in a town that identified with the frontier, each congregation had a hard time attracting and keeping a rabbi.[13]

As Fort Worth grew, cattle remained the cornerstone of the economy and "Cowtown" became its nickname. The Chisholm Trail faded into history, supplanted by stockyards and slaughterhouses. Swift's and Armour's multistory packinghouses employed several thousand workers, including immigrants from Poland, Greece, and Mexico. A dozen rail lines linked Fort Worth to the small towns and vast ranches across West Texas. Families from Abilene and Wichita Falls rode those rails to Cowtown to shop, finding high-topped shoes for the children, broad-brimmed bonnets for the ladies, and detachable collars for the gents. The leading restaurant was Joseph's Café, where Russian immigrant Sam Joseph and his German-born wife, Minnie, feted vaudeville stars and politicians. Fort Worth's signature haberdasher was another Jewish merchant, Memphis-born Leon Gross, a temple founder and the proprietor of Washer Brothers Clothier. Greenwall's Opera, managed by a Jewish family, featured Sarah Bernhardt on its marquee. Fort Worth was feeling cosmopolitan by 1910, its downtown streets no longer dirt, but red brick. The city was home to sixty thousand whites, thirteen thousand African Americans, five hundred Jews, fifty-nine Chinese, and fourteen Native Americans.[14]

As far as Texans were concerned, Fort Worth was a big city—the state's fourth largest. To Rabbi Fox, however, it seemed small. When the rabbi first traveled to Fort Worth by rail from Chicago in February, 1910, he had left behind a metropolis of 1.5 million—including 111,000 Jews—for a dusty town one-twentieth its size. En route, he was disheartened by the color line crossed when the train pulled out of Cairo, Illinois, and across the Mississippi. African American passengers filed out of the front cars and seated themselves in the back of the train. In the North, Fox had attended the University of Chicago, a racially integrated campus. By the time Fox's train pulled into Fort Worth, the twenty-five-year-old rabbi had decided that his inaugural sermon would be a Lincoln's birthday address. Within days, the young rabbi sent his photo to the local papers with an announcement of his sermon topic.[15]

He was stunned at the reaction. All week, the rabbi's phone rang with people urging him not to laud Lincoln from the pulpit. "Lincoln was all right up North, but this was Texas," he wrote in his memoir. Temple president Sam Levy, a wealthy cigar and liquor dealer, warned the rabbi, "I will not be responsible for what happens to you."[16]

February was Secessionist Month in Texas, anniversary of the debate in the legislature preceding the Lone Star State's 1861 withdrawal from the Union.[17] Confederate veterans, a number of Jews among them, bristled at the newcomer's audacity. But to the rabbi, a former Illinois schoolboy who quoted from the Gettysburg Address, Abraham Lincoln was more than the Civil War president, more than the Great Emancipator, more than a martyred leader. Lincoln was a Bible-quoting lawyer, a non-churchgoing Christian who practiced a personal brand of religion that conveyed a touch of the cowboy. The rabbi drew religious inspiration from Honest Abe: "[Lincoln] turned to the Bible as his companion and guiding light. He knew the Bible well."[18] So did George Fox. Against the wishes of his congregation, on his first Sabbath in Fort Worth, the young rabbi preached a sermon titled "Lincoln's Contribution to the Nation."

"Nothing happened," the rabbi reported, except that he had asserted his independence and articulated his passion for American history and ideals. "The next year I did the same," the rabbi remarked. "A northern Presbyterian minister joined me."[19]

This colorful rabbi, a Lincoln Republican in the land of Southern Democrats, seemed determined to proceed with candor, break some taboos, and raise the profile of the local Jewish community. Already, during his first week in Texas, he had persuaded the local ministers' alliance to open its membership to rabbis.[20] Although there was another rabbi in town— Charles Blumenthal, the Lithuanian-trained religious teacher at Ahavath Sholom—Fox quickly became the high-profile rabbi, particularly among the non-Jewish community.[21] Debonair, with a rusty mane of hair, Fox cut a fashionable figure with his dark, tailored suits, starched shirts, and a gemstone tie tack that complemented the sparkle in his eyes. The young rabbi wore rimless spectacles, a thin mustache, and projected a strong jaw that relaxed into a winsome smile. He was also a paradox: a Jew who looked like an Irishman, a minister without a clerical collar, and a Northerner comfortable backslapping with Texans.

FAMILY TIES

Lively Hortense Janette Lewis took notice. She spotted the rabbi's picture in the paper the week he arrived and assured her cousins that she and that candid rabbi would march down the aisle. Previously courted by a wealthy oil-pipe producer's son, Hortense had more status than a number of other eligible young Jewish women. She had grown up in Galveston—Texas' Jewish capital. After the death of her father, wholesale grocer Mose Lewis, Hortense's family had moved to Fort Worth to be closer to relatives. Her mother, Nettie Lowenstein Lewis, a widow with four children, was elected president of the local section of the National Council of Jewish Women. She married her first husband's cousin, Ike Stiefel, whom Hortense disliked because he was rough on one of her brothers.[22]

Many established Jews spoke disparagingly of the immigrants trickling into Texas from Russia, Poland, the Ukraine, and Lithuania. The newcomers—some of them socialists characterized as "negative . . . down-with-the-monarchy" types—arrived in Fort Worth at the rate of eight per month, placed there by the Galveston Immigration and Information Bureau.[23] Fox, too, resented the refugees who added to his workload as he scrambled to find them jobs and lodgings. Still, when the rabbi heard a rumor that Hortense had called a first-generation immigrant a kike—a vulgar epithet for a Jew—he was appalled. When he confronted Hortense with the allegation, her older sister Lillian took the blame. Once that unpleasantry was smoothed over, G. George courted Hortense the next eight months.[24]

When the couple said their vows on November 20, 1910, he was twenty-six and she was two weeks past her twenty-first birthday. Three rabbis officiated at the ceremony—Blumenthal of Fort Worth; Cohen from Galveston; and Leonard Rothstein of Alexandria, Louisiana. The bride and groom were married at the temple—a wood-frame and stucco building six blocks from the courthouse. Absent from the ceremony was the *chuppa,* the Jewish wedding canopy that symbolizes a couple's new household. Fox believed that the roof provided canopy enough. The chuppa was one of many traditions, linked more to superstition than Judaism, that Fox's Reform theology discarded. Another was the practice of stomping on a glass at the close of the marriage ceremony, a reminder of life's sadness and the destruction of Jerusalem's ancient temple. Fox put no stock in such customs. Hortense was no slave to tradition, either. Her mother, rather than her stepfather, gave away the bride. The maid of honor was sister Lillian; the matron of honor, her grandmother, Carrie Lowenstein, of Waco; the best man and attendants were a lawyer, two cigar wholesalers, and a jeweler, all members of the temple board of directors. The bridal gown was Parisian chiffon over satin; the bouquet, cascading lilies of the valley; and the honeymoon? Where else? Chicago.[25]

Chicago was his reference point, and it quickly turned into hers. There, in a city with stockyards and packinghouses that dwarfed Fort Worth's, Hortense met her in-laws, a close-knit family far different from her own. George's mother was Isabella Kuklin Fox, named for Queen Isabella of Spain. Four centuries earlier, Spain had expelled its Jews, including Isabella Fox's ancestors, who gradually migrated to Russia. Isabella's husband was Moses Fox, a dirt farmer forced to flee Russia in 1885—when George was an infant—after speaking against the czar in a local tavern. In North America, Moses Fox worked his way up from Canadian peddler to storekeeper in small-town Greenview, Illinois. He eventually moved into real estate and appraisal work in Chicago. Besides G. George, the couple had four sons and three daughters. J. Logan Fox—the J. was for Jacob— became a lawyer; Noah was a physician; Matthew, a podiatrist and pharmacist; Herschell a U.S. Department of Agriculture employee. All three sisters—Clara, Ethel, and Bessie—were schoolteachers, with Bessie also heading the Jewish Welfare Board in France during World War I.[26]

G. George was the eldest, born July 28, 1884. His first initial stood for Gresham, the Anglicized version of Gershom, the name the biblical Moses gave his first-born son. Fox felt about his name the way he felt about his religion. Both could be abbreviated and Americanized. "I don't want Jewish differences so marked that we may be mistaken for foreigners," he wrote.[27]

The Fox family joined Temple Isaiah, one of Chicago's leading Reform synagogues, and its rabbi, Joseph Stolz, became Fox's earliest religious role model. Fox gained further inspiration as a teenager from Dr. Emil G. Hirsch, Chicago's most prominent Reform Jewish leader—a rabbi of the rich, ambassador to the community, and champion of the downtrodden. Rabbi Hirsch, a theologian of note, disseminated his views in the *Reform Advocate,* the respected weekly that he edited. Fox, too, had dabbled in journalism, writing for the *Iron Age,* a magazine of the steel industry. He admired the way Emil Hirsch merged an array of skills and concerns into the role of rabbi. The vocation seemed limitless. Fox felt the "call."[28]

After graduating from the University of Chicago in 1904, Fox enrolled in Cincinnati's Hebrew Union College. There he developed close bonds with fellow students Jacob Singer, Samuel Schwartz, and David Rosenbaum. All were immigrants raised in the Midwest who enjoyed taking time out for practical joking. Most memorable was the evening Fox telephoned Singer's brother, a violinist with the Cincinnati Symphony. Affecting a thick German accent, Fox convinced the musician he was speaking with "Frrrritz Krrrreisler," a prominent soloist and composer visiting the city. The family was giddy over the famous musician's attention, until Fox confessed to staging the call. Several years later, when another premier violinist, Mischa Elman, actually telephoned the Singer household, no one took the caller seriously. They suspected another prank, à la Fox.[29]

Fox was ordained in 1908, the valedictorian among a class of three. Choosing from several pulpit offers, he selected Moses Montefiore Congregation in Bloomington, Illinois, because it was closest to home—one hundred miles southwest of Chicago. Because his congregation was small, Fox found time to study for a doctorate in philosophy and to teach biblical history at Illinois Wesleyan University. He was proud to be among the few Jews appointed to teach at a secular Christian university and joked that he was the "first Methodist rabbi in captivity." However, his sense of humor belied the irritations of the job. The rabbi's courses sparked complaints from Protestant quarters: his biblical history lectures contained too little religious dogma and too much critical thinking. His landlady reproached him for smoking in his room—a vice "against Methodist discipline." Fox scoffed at such conflicts. Then he ran into intolerance at his own congregation. The temple president vetoed Fox's suggestion that a young Jewish haberdasher be encouraged to join. "We don't want any *kikes* in our congregation," the lay leader told the rabbi, whose world shattered at the sound of the slur. "I was astounded," Fox wrote in his memoir. "That this vicious prejudice would extend to heads of congregations had never entered my mind." He resolved to leave Bloomington at the first chance.[30]

Texas materialized as the next opportunity. Rabbi George Zepin, ordained in 1900, had been at Fort Worth's Temple Beth-El more than a year and was ready to leave for Cincinnati and an administrative post with the Union of American Hebrew Congregations. Zepin felt obliged to find his replacement. Fox jumped at the opening but soon realized that he had not left prejudice behind. Even in a young state like Texas, attitudes separating old stock from new immigrants were evident. Jim Crow laws separating the races stared him in the face. The idealistic rabbi hoped to change minds, hearts, and attitudes. He perceived all Fort Worth as his pulpit and much of Texas as "unploughed territory."[31]

Fox anointed himself missionary to Jews across West Texas and in Oklahoma, which gained statehood in 1907. As a circuit-riding rabbi he reveled in trips to Ardmore—where he turned a vacant Oklahoma church into a synagogue—and to Drumright, an oil town three hundred miles north of Fort Worth, where he persuaded Jews to organize High Holy Day services. South of the Texas-Oklahoma line in Gainesville, the rabbi started a congregation that lasted "until the Jewish population there melted away." He fared better in Wichita Falls, where a frustrated Orthodox lay leader agreed to try Fox's less observant style of Judaism. In Amarillo, Fox helped Panhandle Jews launch a congregation and Sunday School to which he journeyed once or twice a month "until they got someone on a regular basis."[32]

EXTRA! EXTRA!

To link these congregations and to connect himself with rabbinical colleagues elsewhere, in 1914 Fox launched a regional weekly newspaper— the *Jewish Monitor*. His board of directors at Beth-El backed the venture and helped find investment partners for Monitor Publishing Company, the printing shop that put out the paper. Temple secretary Louis Morris, an insurance broker, put up one third of the cash and served as business manager. The rabbi became president and editor of the sixteen-page tabloid that circulated in forty cities across Texas, Oklahoma, Arkansas, and Louisiana.

Printed on glossy paper and published on Fridays, the *Jewish Monitor* sold for a nickel an issue or a dollar a year. It was sprinkled with photos of Jewish leaders and profiles of communities from Muskogee to Monroe. Speeches of Jewish content were reprinted from across the nation. Perhaps the *Monitor's* best-read columns were the social notes, chatty items such as the engagement of Fort Worth's Fannie Joseph to M. Wolfe of Wichita Falls; the visit of the Bermans of Henryetta, Oklahoma, to their in-laws, the Melaskys, in Austin; and Miss Marjorie Belisch's departure for the University of Pennsylvania.[33] Throughout World War I, a page a week was filled with letters and photos from "Our Soldier Boys in Camp and Abroad."[34] Enlivening the paper were opinion pieces from the re-

The Jewish Monitor, *March 5, 1920, promotes Fort Worth's annual Fat Stock Show. The lively weekly, launched in 1914 by Rabbi G. George Fox, circulated from Oklahoma to Louisiana, mixing religious symbolism with national pride.* From Klau Library, Hebrew Union College, Cincinnati.

gion's rabbis, most notably Fox's seminary friend, David Rosenbaum, now an Austin rabbi who dubbed his column "Chips from a Rabbinical Workshop."[35]

On the secular side, the *Monitor* promoted the region's cattle industry with banner headlines that exhorted: "Don't Fail to Attend the Stock Show."[36] Most vivid were Fox's accounts of regional news events, among them a gas tank explosion in Ardmore that shattered two blocks of buildings, injured two hundred people, killed sixty (among them one Jew), and sent the rabbi to that Oklahoma city to render assistance. "It's nothing but ruin," the rabbi reported in the aftermath of the 1915 disaster.[37]

With readership high, Fox was not averse to using the *Monitor* for self-promotion. The rabbi pushed sales of his first book, *Judaism, Christianity, and the Modern Social Ideals.* The "limited" edition, printed by Monitor Publishing Company, was available for a special price of $2.50 that included a *Monitor* subscription.[38] Through the news columns, the rabbi also pried charitable dollars from co-religionists, publishing lists of

donors to Jewish causes: "If your name is not here—and it is your fault—
you are derelict in your . . . duty."[39] The weekly proved to be an effective
sales vehicle and fund-raiser.

Imagery reinforced the *Monitor's* mission as a journal of Jewish American acculturation. Its front-page nameplate incorporated a Torah, a
menorah, a Star of David, and the rabbi's name. Its editorial-page emblem
was the Stars and Stripes. In keeping with its Jewish American creed, the
Monitor's editorials denounced formation of Jewish veterans groups. The
American Legion was open to all, Fox reasoned, and separation of vets was
bound to provoke "prejudice and malice." During Prohibition, the rabbi
opposed exemptions for sacramental wine. "The temptation will be there
for one to abuse the privilege," he warned, referring to rabbis implicated
in bootlegging scandals. Fox saw no reason for Jews to seek privileges in a
country that guaranteed equality.[40]

Despite the *Jewish Monitor's* push against separation and ghettoization,
the newspaper was quick to spotlight anti-Semitism in Texas and abroad.
When a Dallas wholesale clerk denigrated a Fort Worth clothier as "the
Jew," Fox editorialized against the slight. Within a week, the business firm
sent the *Monitor* an apology.[41] Another time, the paper reported that
Christian children had taunted students at the Fort Worth Hebrew Institute with cries of "dirty Jews" and "Jew noses." The "nagging offenses" occurred during the summer of 1915.[42]

Many readers linked the schoolyard taunts to odious headlines ema-
nating from Georgia, where Jewish businessman Leo Frank had been sen-
tenced to death for the murder of a girl in his pencil factory. Frank's conviction, more the product of prejudice than evidence, led to nationwide
outrage among Jews and non-Jews. The *Monitor* printed a petition, with
spaces for thirty signatures, beseeching Georgia's governor to commute
Frank's death sentence to life. The cause stirred such urgency that the
newspaper reprinted the petition in subsequent issues. When the *Fort
Worth Star-Telegram*—"our generally friendly contemporary"—questioned the logic of sparing Frank from the "gallows," Fox snapped back
that the defendant had been tried amid hostile surroundings. Georgia's
governor agreed and commuted Frank's sentence, but the act of clemency
did no good. A mob invaded a prison hospital August 16, 1915, and lynched
Leo Frank. Jews across the South shuddered, traumatized with fear that
their social acceptance was but a veneer. In a full-page editorial headlined
"Jewish Martyrdom," Fox lamented: "It is a blow to those who thought

America was the land of the free. . . . This outlaw spirit of ancient days has found itself anew."[43]

Propelled by the rabbi's prolific writing and energy, the *Monitor*'s reputation grew, along with its advertising revenue. The weekly came chockfull of ads. Not just Joe Greenberg's Kosher Delicatessen and Sanger Brothers' pitch to "Hooverize Your Rugs," but also Old Ripy whiskey, Martha Washington Wine, *Correct English* magazine, and Mistletoe Butter from the local creamery. The gentile world advertised aplenty in this Jewish voice. Full-page ads lured investors to newly discovered oilfields ("Mighty Gushers Roar . . . $100 will buy 100 shares . . . $500 . . . may make you a fortune").[44] The most lucrative ads were legal notices of courthouse sales, foreclosures, divorces, and lawsuits. By law, these ads had to run in publications of record, often for consecutive issues. And the *Monitor* cashed in.

The *Monitor* was not the Lone Star State's only Jewish weekly, although it was the liveliest. Houston's *Texas Jewish Herald*, begun in 1908, competed for readers, writers, and endorsements. Both tabloids touted themselves as the Southwest's largest, oldest Jewish journal. When the *Herald* mailed every Texas rabbi a questionnaire asking for opinions about its columns, Fox was among the few who did not respond.[45] He preferred to tout the *Monitor*. "It was unexpectedly successful from the beginning and became a real force in the South," Fox wrote of his publication. It acquainted readers with Jewish institutions nationwide and civic institutions in their home towns. As for its person-to-person influence, Fox noted, "I spoke to one of the ladies who met and married her husband through an exchange column in the *Monitor!*"[46]

SETTLING DOWN

The rabbi's own domestic life was blissful. He adored his lively wife, who worked with the temple Sisterhood to raise funds for the Sabbath School. The rabbinical couple initially moved around: summers in Chicago, where she enrolled in classes at the University of Chicago; a six-month leave of absence in New York during World War I for the rabbi to launch a Soldiers and Sailors Welfare League for B'nai B'rith. In Fort Worth, George and Hortense resided in a succession of rented, semi-detached houses as well as the Metropolitan Hotel, a downtown hostelry with a cigar stand in the lobby. By 1916, their household had enlarged by two children—

*Fox family portrait, 1912. Hortense Lewis Fox, Rabbi G. George Fox, and baby,
Samson George, who died in 1918.* Courtesy G. George Fox.

Samson George, born in 1912, and Ruth Elaine, born in 1915. The family of
four took out a mortgage on a home in Fairmount, a new middle-class
neighborhood with dirt streets serviced by three downtown trolley lines.[47]

The town and the temple were growing, and Fox was at the forefront.
Comfortable in any crowd, the rabbi joined civic groups from the Elks and
the Masons to the Shriners and the Kiwanis Club. He served as chaplain of
the Ad Club and a director of the Junior Chamber of Commerce. "George
Fox . . . has become widely known outside of the religious sphere on account of his whole-souled and energetic . . . participation in affairs of a
broad civic and benevolent nature," noted a local Who's Who that profiled
Fort Worth's most prominent civic figures. "He has taken an active part in
every drive both for war and peace."[48] Patriotism was foremost to this
first-generation American. During World War I, he was volunteer chap-

lain at Camp Bowie, the training base across the river where thirty-five thousand soldiers were stationed.

The rabbi emerged as a top fund-raiser for the Liberty Bond drive. So did a number of African Americans. At a Liberty Bond luncheon at which volunteers presented financial reports, the rabbi was disturbed to see the "Negroes" shuttled to a side waiting room: "When I asked why they were not with us, I was told that whites and Negroes did not eat together publicly. I arose and asked . . . would there be any distinction in the money raised, based on color or race? . . . I told the group that as far as I was concerned, I would not participate in the meeting if other Americans . . . were barred. There was a hush, some subdued excitement—then the Negroes were called in and a real Liberty Bond celebration was held."[49]

Postwar, General John J. Pershing, commander of the American Expeditionary Forces in France, visited Fort Worth for a parade and luncheon. The rabbi coordinated the publicity and the music and rode in the general's car. Working with the rabbi to organize the celebratory affair were newspaper publisher Amon G. Carter, former mayor B. B. Paddock, and department store owner William Monnig—public figures whose names survive on city landmarks. Serenading the luncheon crowd that day was Congregation Beth-El's "Temple Quartette."[50]

Participation in civic affairs came naturally, but interfaith endeavors were unexplored territory for Jews. When ministers in the Tarrant County Pastors Association outlined plans for a citywide religious-revival week, Fox was reluctant to explain that Jews do not stage salvation rallies. In Judaism, study, rather than proselytization or emotional appeals, is the traditional path to enlightenment. Nonetheless, when a minister turned to the rabbi and asked, "How about your congregation, Fox?" the rabbi decided on the spot that Beth-El, too, would host a revival. Its purpose: to "re-Judaize" Jews. Understanding Fox's predicament and his need to join in, fellow rabbis from Waco, Tyler, El Paso, San Antonio, Austin, and Dallas trekked to Fort Worth to assist. Fort Worth's recently arrived Orthodox rabbi, Abraham E. Abramowitz, also participated. Nightly, the rabbis alternated at the pulpit, sermonizing, praying, and encouraging Jews to join synagogues and participate in Jewish communal life.

"The pews were packed," recalled Frances Rosenthal Kallison, who was then eleven. "This was good entertainment, a nice diversion, a regular service with some organ music, no Bible-thumping. I went with my parents, my grandmother, her two aunts, and my grandmother's bachelor uncle, Isadore. Everybody kept asking for Dr. Cohen."[51]

By popular demand, Fox wired Galveston's Rabbi Henry Cohen, imploring him to join in: "The revival has been successful beyond all expectation. . . . Have had dozens of requests for you. Please arrange to come Sunday night, Monday night, or Tuesday night or as many nights as you can. Am earnestly hoping you will be here."[52] Cohen made an appearance.

Another interfaith opportunity arose when J. Frank Norris, the controversial Baptist minister, returned from Jerusalem preaching fervent Zionism. The Zionist District of Fort Worth invited the pastor to speak, with Fox on the program delivering general announcements. Fox was not a Zionist, but he held his tongue, choosing to applaud rather than challenge the minister's endorsement of a Jewish national homeland. When Fox wrote up the gathering for the *Monitor,* he noted that the Hebrew Institute band played *Ha-Tikvah,* the Zionist anthem, as well as *Dixie* and *The Star Spangled Banner,* lest anyone doubt the crowd's patriotism.[53]

DISAPPOINTMENTS

On the surface, Rabbi Fox was upbeat. Beneath his convivial countenance, he was in mourning. His six-year-old son, Samson, had died from meningitis in 1918.[54] The death of his son increased the rabbi's homesickness for the North. During periodic leaves of absence and summer vacations, he interviewed with Midwest congregations and searched for a pulpit closer to Chicago, the center of his universe. Aware of these feelers, the Beth-El board of directors gradually raised Fox's salary from $275 to $400 a month in hopes of retaining him.[55]

By Fox's ninth year in Fort Worth, the town had grown to 100,000 and Beth-El had more than doubled to 150 families. Fox had been hammering the congregation for years about the need for a larger, grander edifice. By 1919, the membership finally agreed. The land selected for a new temple was at Galveston and Broadway, a tree-shaded boulevard home to leading Methodist and Baptist congregations. The price of the lot was within reach: $10,000. Fox co-chaired the fund-raising drive with restaurateur Sam Joseph, who lived across the street from the site in a mansion with an upstairs ballroom.[56]

The $139,000 red-brick and white-limestone synagogue was not quite finished in time for the High Holy Days in September of 1920, so members worshiped in the basement.[57] Completion of the building was not without headaches. Temple elders passed out cigars to roofers and carpenters to keep them on the job.[58] Youngsters climbed inside the empty ark, which they called a "Torah box." Marion Weil, a fourteen-year-old who lived a block away, recalled stealing past the scaffolding with his buddies and roaming throughout the unfinished sanctuary. The pews were lined up but not yet nailed to the floor. "We got in behind the pews and pushed them, and they went down like dominoes," he chuckled. "The rabbi was furious."[59]

Further fraying nerves was a downturn in the economy. Capital dried up as oil investment schemes led to fraud indictments. Prohibition forced a number of Jews out of business. Beth-El's building deficit totaled $80,000, forcing the congregation to sell second-mortgage bonds. Half of Beth-El's congregants failed to donate money or follow through on building fund pledges, and temple membership dropped by one fifth. Fox was reduced to the role of bill collector and beggar, calling on lumberyards to ask donations of building material. "The rabbi had to borrow his monthly salary from the bank because the congregation was unable to pay it," recalled congregant I.E. Horwitz.[60] The new edifice was not half what Fox had envisioned. Still on the drawing board, and never constructed, were a gym, a billiards room, a rooftop garden, and two dance halls.[61] Frustrated, Fox resigned several times, then was coaxed back into service by congregational leaders.[62]

A dispute of a different sort led to Fox's resignation as editor of the *Jewish Monitor,* the paper that projected his personality. Many of the region's immigrants, unable to read English, were clamoring for a Yiddish newspaper that would keep them abreast of current events. Fox initially endorsed the creation of the *Yiddish Wochenblatt*—"so that émigrés can learn about America [through articles that] diffuse real Americanism and Jewish news." The *Monitor* printing company agreed to publish the foreign-language paper and appointed Rabbi Abramowitz of Ahavath Sholom as its editor. Although Fox knew no Yiddish save for a few words such as *chutzpah* (gall) and *meshugga* (crazy), he agreed to become the *Wochenblatt's* vice president and editorial consultant.[63]

After just two issues—and over Fox's objection—the editorial board voted to merge the *Monitor* and the *Wochenblatt* into a bilingual edition. The weekly's first sixteen pages would be in English; the next sixteen, in Yiddish. Because Yiddish is read from right to left, the *Monitor's* back page became the *Wochenblatt's* front page. The slick newspaper that Fox had nurtured since 1914 suddenly took on an alien appearance, half its pages filled with an alphabet indecipherable to most readers. Explaining that it "takes different training to supervise" an English/Yiddish newspaper, Fox wrote a farewell column on September 23, 1921, and removed his name from the *Monitor's* front page.

THE COWTOWN KLAVERN

Fox was restless and disappointed: The *Monitor* was half what it used to be; his congregation's edifice was but a fraction of what he had envisioned.

Politics in Fort Worth and the rest of the state had grown ominous. The Texas Ku Klux Klan was flourishing, with dens in one hundred towns by June, 1921. That month, Tarrant County's sheriff and county judge launched Klavern 101 with a gathering on the banks of the Trinity River. Even Fort Worth's mayor joined the vigilante society that excluded "colored races" and "non-Christians." Although the *Star-Telegram* refrained from editorializing for or against the Klan, it reported KKK activities. In July, and again in August, a Klan posse tarred, feathered, and whipped Benny Pinto, a purported bootlegger. Three other abductions and whippings made the local news that summer and fall.[64]

Fox was initially guarded in his response to the Klan—quite the opposite of rabbis in Galveston, Beaumont, and Tyler who publicly denounced the masked order. Fox knew who many of the Klansmen were. They were part of the local power structure, the same gentlemen who welcomed him at the Rotary and the benevolent Elks. "Among these false prophets are also some of my best friends," he conceded. "I shall not attack men—but movements."[65] Fox hoped that dialogue, rather than denunciations, could combat the local KKK's bigotry. The Klan was not all bad. Klavern 101 billed itself as a patriotic Protestant fraternity, and at times it seemed benign, even fielding a City League baseball team—the Ku Kluckers.

Following the Klan's initial episodes of vigilantism, Fox wrote, "We had hoped that the Ku Klux Klan would do some things that perhaps would add to the good and the glory of the nation. . . . We had hoped the Ku Klux Klan would do its duty as it saw fit without infringing on the rights of others."[66] His rhetoric got no bolder until February, 1922, when the Fort Worth Klan staged a massive nighttime parade down Main Street. That month Fox unleashed a full page of fury against "the men with masks." Noting that no law sanctioned "tarring and feathering [of] men and women," he deplored "the injection of religious fanaticism" into the body politic. "Our country has attained greatness because in it are mixed the best elements of a thousand peoples and multitudes of faiths. Let us continue to assimilate the best there is." He added that the Klan would have excluded Jesus Christ, a Jew who was not "100% American."[67]

Several months later, rumors circulated that the Klan planned to boycott Jewish businesses. Concerned, the rabbi contacted his friends among the KKK and received their "absolute word" that no boycott was in the offing. "[Don't take] these rumors too seriously," he wrote May 12, 1922, in a guest editorial. "The alleged prejudice against Jews in these organizations is exaggerated and . . . we can only make matters worse by consistently dwelling upon the unfortunate intrusion into the calmness of American life of racial and religious prejudice."[68]

While Fox scoffed at the Klan's economic muscle, others in the Jewish community felt its ill effects. Sol Rosenthal, who peddled meat to restaurants, found his beef supply reduced and his cold-storage unit mysteriously shut off at night. Rosenthal reacted by purchasing pastureland beyond the city limits and opening his own meat plant, which soared to prominence.[69] Attorney Theodore Mack, a Temple Beth-El founder, spotted Klansmen in the courtroom among the judges and jurors. Convinced there was no way to win a jury verdict, Mack switched his practice from trial work to appellate cases.[70] Haberdasher Leon Gross grew wary after Klansmen, unaware that he was Jewish, invited him to join the order. Fearing a boycott, Gross added to his letterhead stationery the name of an employee who did belong to Klavern 101.[71] Elsewhere in Texas, the KKK tried to cancel a performance by Fritz Kreisler, the violinist Fox had done such a rollicking impersonation of during rabbinical school.[72]

At home in Tarrant County, Fox continued dialoguing with his contacts inside the Klan. Meanwhile, a local anti-Klan movement, organized in the spring of 1922, did not include the rabbi in its ranks.[73] George Fox, the first clergyman in Tarrant County to champion Abraham Lincoln, remained cautious and ambivalent toward the Klan. As a newcomer in 1910, he had been confident of bucking the establishment. By 1922, Fox, the insider, was not so inclined.

HOMEWARD BOUND

During Fox's annual summer sojourn to Chicago in 1922, his brother J. Logan introduced him to a group of young professionals from Lake Michigan's suburban South Shore. Sociable, middle income, and integrated into

the American way of life, they wanted to start a "free will synagogue" without the fixed dues, assigned pews, or religious school tuition common in
other congregations. Moreover, each adult, whether male or female, was
to be a voting member—a departure from the practice of counting men
only.[74] The organizers invited Fox to become their spiritual leader. Although they could guarantee no salary, the experiment appealed to Fox,
who was eager to return to Chicago. As the rabbi conferred with the steer-
ing committee—which included his brother—Hortense met with a
group of women to organize a temple Sisterhood. The rabbinical couple
excitedly planned their future, agreeing to leave Fort Worth as soon as the
South Shore Congregation signed up 150 families.

The Foxes expected to move in a year, but within two months, the
idealistic congregation met its membership goal. Fox learned the news
from the *Sentinel,* a Chicago Jewish weekly that ran an item congratulat-
ing the new temple for hiring "Dr. George Fox . . . one of the strongest and ablest Jewish ministers in the entire South."[75] A shocked Fox
showed the clipping to Temple Beth-El President Max K. Mayer. Apolo-
getically, the rabbi promised not to leave without the congregation's
concurrence, and certainly not for another year. However, Fox recalled
in his memoir, the temple president exploded: "He took the paper, threw
it down on his desk and shouted: 'If you ever expect to leave, you might
just as well do it now.'. . . The next Friday I informed my congregation of
the state of affairs and told them that I had the president's permission to
leave now, and that I would avail myself of that permission. I was hit by a
storm of protest. Members stopped talking to us, and for a while things
were very unpleasant. Strangely enough, my non-Jewish friends came to
our rescue."[76]

The Chamber of Commerce arranged a farewell banquet at which
George and Hortense were presented with a sizable check—"a going away
present . . . to buy a new car when we got to Chicago."[77] Ironically, the man
presiding at Fox's departure luncheon was the head of the Ku Klux Klan—
presumably former state senator W. A. "Bill" Hanger, an attorney who
served as Klan kleagle, cyclops, and district titan.[78] Fox chuckled at the in-
congruity of the Klan befriending the rabbi who had integrated the Liberty
Bond luncheon. Fox never considered the Fort Worth Klan a serious
threat—perhaps because he knew its members and was hesitant to censure his friends, perhaps because his eyes were no longer on Texas, but out
of state.

WINDY CITY WELCOME

Home in Chicago, Fox was ebullient, building a congregation that within two months surged to three hundred families.[79] Although the rabbi went unpaid for months, his work and his surroundings invigorated him. Compared with Fort Worth's stable, low-key Jewish community, Chicago's was dynamic. In 1921 alone, Chicago had opened ten Jewish institutions, including four synagogues, a cemetery, and a country club.[80] The City of Big Shoulders had more than 225,000 Jews, 120 rabbis, and several Jewish newspapers.[81] Adding to the editorial mix, Fox wrote a weekly column, "The Watch Tower," for the *Sentinel*. He churned out the *South Shore Temple News*, a "breezy bulletin" full of retail ads and news about his temple's basketball team, sewing circle, debate club, and theater troupe. His background on the *Monitor* served him well.

When his congregation raised money for a building, Fox made certain that the gymnasium, club rooms, and auditorium (which doubled as a chapel) were constructed first. Much later, a spacious sanctuary was added, but not until the 1950s, when membership reached seven hundred families, who could afford a $400,000 addition. Fox had learned from his Texas experience that if he put communal needs first, the spiritual aspect would follow.[82]

The rabbi's brothers, sisters, and parents joined the South Shore Congregation. During services, Hortense sat up front and signaled her husband when his sermons droned on.[83] She widened her Jewish involvement, helping to organize the Illinois Federation of Temple Sisterhoods and serving as state president and a national Sisterhood director.[84] In 1925, G. George, Hortense, and ten-year-old Elaine toured the Mediterranean, taking in ancient sites from Athens to Jerusalem and Damascus. Serving as family scribe, Hortense sent letters to the *South Shore Temple News* signed, "Three Wandering Jews."[85] The family of three grew to four in 1926 when Hortense gave birth to another child, G. George Fox Jr.

The rabbi reconnected with his seminary friends—Singer and Schwartz—as well as David Rosenbaum, the Austin, Texas, rabbi who also worked his way back to a Chicago pulpit. After having served remote pulpits—the Singers in Nebraska, the Rosenbaums in West Virginia—these couples were happy to have left the back roads for the camaraderie available in a big city with a flourishing Jewish community.[86]

As in Fort Worth, Fox was an ambassador to the gentiles. He created a ministers' association and hosted Thanksgiving services and goodwill dinners. Ever the self-starter, he organized a Jewish chaplains' corps on call to state prisons and mental institutions. He launched the University of Chicago's Jewish students' group, served on city and state interracial commissions, and was president of the Chicago Rabbinical Association. He wrote five more books, most of them published by vanity presses, on subjects from biblical literature to Abraham Lincoln.

The Foxes kept up their Texas ties. They vacationed in Mineral Wells, north of Fort Worth, and often visited old friends with whom they corresponded the rest of their lives. The rabbi was keynote speaker at Beth-El's fiftieth anniversary celebration in 1952. Dan Levy, a groomsman at the Foxes' wedding, sent the couple a crate of Texas grapefruits every winter. When San Antonio rabbi Ephraim Frisch visited Chicago, he and Fox played a round of golf. A few years later, Texas rabbi David Jacobson and his wife, Helen, returned to San Antonio from a Chicago visit laughing at how Fox had talked a Windy City cop out of issuing a speeding ticket.[87]

Fox never slowed down. Into retirement, he penned his "Watch Tower" column and filled in at Southern congregations for the High Holy Days. When Hortense died in 1956, the rabbi reflected on forty-six years of matrimony and hung up a marriage counseling shingle. He drew a sizable clientele.[88] Fox was content with his career and the avenues the rabbinate had opened to him. Until his death at the age of seventy-six in 1960, he relished his role as rabbi.

Although his rabbinical work never ceased, Fox did not receive anywhere near the prominence in Chicago that was his in Fort Worth. Yes, his endeavors were innovative and valuable, but in Chicago he was one among dozens of rabbis, many with older, wealthier, more prestigious congregations. In the scope of Chicago Jewish history, Fox's congregation was of fleeting duration. Eleven years after the rabbi's death, the synagogue complex he built from scratch was sold to an African American congregation, The Old Landmark Church of God in Holiness in Christ. Chicago's South Shore, once a Jewish Gold Coast, had evolved into a black neighborhood, and Jews moved out in a flurry of white flight. A cluster of South Shore veterans reorganized as Congregation Kol Ami and relocated to a downtown high-rise. The names of G. George and Hortense Lewis Fox receded into the past, visible only as inscriptions on *yahrzeit* (memorial) plaques at Kol Ami. In *The Jews of Chicago,* a coffee-table book published in 1996, the South Shore Congregation receives scant attention. Rabbi Fox is not mentioned at all.[89]

In Fort Worth, Fox remains a standout—a pioneer, a publisher, and a Ph.D., one of two rabbis in the city of his time and one among fifteen in the state. He stayed longer and accomplished more than any previous Fort Worth rabbi. His civic involvement helped Jews feel part of the mainstream. His newspaper (published for another decade after his departure), put Fort Worth on the Jewish map and helped readers become more comfortable with their Jewish American identities. The synagogue Fox watched go up brick by brick became a city landmark, serving the congregation until the end of the century, the financial struggle long forgotten.

Fox's colorful memoir and positive contributions obscure the contradictions of his Texas tenure. Although an outspoken leader, he faced many cultural collisions that pitted pragmatism against idealism. The rabbi's roundup of Jewish prostitutes, his resentment toward the Galveston Immigration Plan, and his resignation from the bilingual *Monitor* indicate discomfort, if not embarrassment with Jews far less mainstream than he. His ambivalence toward the Ku Klux Klan is troubling, to say the least, at odds with his insistence on preaching about Lincoln and his ultimatum to integrate a public luncheon. Fox was bold and confident when preaching about American ideals, but allowed his friendships within Klavern 101 to curb his display of moral outrage. Nonetheless, congregants who recall G. George Fox lament his Texas departure because he had the personality and drive to accomplish a great deal in a developing state. His charisma carried him far.

Fox's career lends weight to the premise that Texas was often home to rabbis less likely to forge memorable careers elsewhere. Bright, urbane, and energetic, Fox was savvy and aggressive enough to land a Chicago pulpit but not a prestigious congregation. Although he was innovative and productive in Illinois, Fox, nonetheless, was just another rabbi at a second-tier temple. Had he stayed in Texas, he could have been a power broker.

6

The Mexican Connection

MARTIN ZIELONKA, EL PASO

THEIR PASSPORTS WERE FAKES—forged in Berlin. Their clothes were ragged. Their voices, hushed. But the four men who slipped into the study of Rabbi Martin Zielonka appeared robust and optimistic—"exceptionally splendid specimens with good educations," the rabbi recalled. Whispering in Yiddish, the language of Eastern Europe's Jews, they described their ocean voyage to Veracruz, their trek across Mexico, and the ruse they used—a U.S. address and auto tag numbers—to cross the international bridge into Texas.[1]

The month was January; the year, 1921. Congress was debating the nation's first immigration quotas and calling for a crackdown on illegal aliens.[2] The El Paso rabbi warned his visitors that, if apprehended, they faced imprisonment and swift deportation. The foursome said they would take their chances. So would many others. Lured by rumors of easy passage to the United States via Veracruz, thousands more wandering Jews were en route from Europe.

Within weeks, dozens of illegal Jewish refugees were arrested crossing from Mexico into Texas. Martin Zielonka, the only rabbi along the eight-hundred-mile Texas-Mexican border, scrambled to do what social work he could: food baskets from his congregation, clothing from local Jewish merchants, letters to the refugees' stateside relatives, pleas to immigration authorities. From their jail cells, the immigrants told the rabbi they were ex-soldiers, displaced by World War I and Europe's volatile borders. They had wandered across the Continent for several years, seeking visas and an escape route to America. If deported, they faced prosecution for desertion. "That meant torture or death," the alarmed rabbi telegrammed a friend.[3]

Woven together, the immigrants' tales of cunning and desperation touched Zielonka, an immigrant himself, but a rabbi better known for aloofness than warmth. The refugees' plight meshed with his theology and stirred his sense of mission as nothing had before. He believed that this unstoppable wave of illegal aliens could sow seeds of Jewish communal life in Mexico, a nation with a hidden Judaic heritage. Little did he realize the role he was to play in a seldom-told chapter of North American Jewish history.

As El Paso's county jail filled with Jews, Zielonka made an urgent trip to the Gulf Coast in March, 1921, to confer with several fellow rabbis. The region's rabbis had previously collaborated during the Galveston movement, which resettled ten thousand Eastern European Jews across the western half of the country prior to World War I. Now, Zielonka's colleagues in Galveston, Houston, and New Orleans informed him that illegal Jewish refugees were turning up in their port cities, landing in prison, and facing deportation. Zielonka believed that the only humanitarian alternative was to persuade the U.S. government to send these itinerants not to Europe but back to Mexico, which was willing to keep them. He envisioned relief committees in Mexico helping Jewish refugees find work, learn Spanish, and apply for Mexican citizenship. Fulfilling that vision would require diplomatic moxie and money. Zielonka's Texas colleagues backed his ideas and pressed him to proceed to New York and alert international Jewish relief officials to the impending human flood.[4]

In New York, however, the social workers and philanthropists Zielonka consulted were not enthused, but rather unmoved. Felix Warburg, the banker who headed the American Jewish Joint Distribution Committee, met with Zielonka but showed scant interest in the Texas trespassers. He explained that more than two million *law-abiding* European Jews were clamoring to enter the United States. The illegal Mexican migration could jeopardize their chances, especially with congress on the verge of passing restrictive immigration quotas. "Stop this movement . . . lest we be accused of conniving to help in the evasion of the law," a Warburg confidant advised the Texas rabbi, adding that he "would not sit *shivah* [in mourning] for any boy that found his way [illegally] into the U.S."[5] Instead, the New Yorkers suggested stemming the refugee tide by cabling the Yiddish press abroad with word that the Mexican route to the United States was a hoax.

By and large they had no zest for Zielonka's south-of-the border dream. Years before, in 1891, the American Jewish leadership had investigated Mexico's potential as a Jewish haven and vetoed the idea because Mexico's politics were unstable, its wages low, unemployment high, and prejudice against Jews historic. A Catholic country twice the combined size of Texas, New York, and New England, Mexico had no synagogues, no Jewish cemeteries, and no emotional ties to American Jewry.[6] For Zielonka, though, Mexico was the land next door, an exotic landscape visible from his front yard. He had stood on the hills of El Paso and watched rebel leader Pancho Villa march into Juarez. He had negotiated the release of a Jewish prisoner—a tense exchange that ended when Villa shot the lock off a jail-cell door.[7] Beyond the Rio Grande, the rabbi had wandered throughout Mexico's plateaus and Pacific shores. A nation of five million people with perhaps two thousand scattered Jews, Mexico seemed ripe with opportunity. And Mexico offered the only hope.[8]

Already, the rabbi's desk overflowed with telegrams and special-delivery letters from American Jews begging help for relatives stranded in Texas jails and Mexican provinces. "How much money is required . . . when the person lands in Mexico?" asked a grocer from Goose Creek, Texas, who scribbled a letter in pencil on lined paper. "One of my sisters . . . is an elderly young lady . . . in love with a young man . . . in Soviet Russia, . . . and he decided to go to Mexico."[9] Should she follow? Zielonka answered each correspondent. With or without official sanction, the rabbi had become a one-man immigration bureau.

Four months into the crisis, Zielonka and other Texas rabbis appealed to B'nai B'rith, the nation's oldest Jewish secular organization, founded in 1843.[10] The service fraternity's southern leadership, meeting in Dallas, endorsed Zielonka's Mexican scheme. Within weeks, the group's national executive board concurred and went to work. Among other tactics, B'nai B'rith's top echelon lobbied U.S. Secretary of Labor James J. Davis—directly by letter and indirectly through contacts at his Moose Lodge.[11] The lobbying campaign soon altered American foreign policy toward the apprehended Jews, permitting their return to Mexico.

Meanwhile, Zielonka teamed up with B'nai B'rith's second-vice president, Archibald Marx, a New Orleans contractor who became his close friend and correspondent for life.[12] The duo was dispatched on a fact-finding trip to Mexico, where they witnessed the squalor of the Jewish refugees. More than two hundred immigrants a month were landing at the port of Veracruz. Some hiked north toward the Rio Grande. Others hitched rides on carts to Mexico City, where they pawned their possessions and subsisted on a few centavos from Monte Sinai, Mexico's only Jewish relief society.[13] In Mexico's capital, Zielonka and Marx called a public meeting during which they unequivocally told some two hundred refugees that Veracruz was not a way station to the United States. "Seek a home in Mexico," the rabbi urged. He promised business loans, medical care, and Spanish-language classes—if they remained. The response was so positive that Zielonka wrote, "We started what so many said was impossible: to organize the Jews of Mexico."[14]

MEXICO'S HIDDEN HERITAGE

Until then, Mexico's Jews had been splintered by geography, ethnicity, and history. Zielonka knew firsthand. Thirteen years before, in the summer of 1908, the Central Conference of American Rabbis had sent him on a six-week mission to Mexico to gauge how hospitable the country might be toward Jewish settlers. In six dispatches to the *American Israelite,* he painted Mexico as an alluring land with prehistoric ruins, exotic flowers, and a leisurely pace.[15] Contrary to reports from the 1890s, the rabbi found the nation free of overt anti-Semitism. Yet the few Jews he tracked down were fearful of disclosing their identity. Indeed, the Spanish word *judio* was a pejorative, an idiom meaning "unbaptized," and an epithet for a "bad merchant."[16] The stigma was reinforced during Easter week, when cries of "Death to Judas" were often rephrased as "Death to Jews."[17]

In Chihuahua, a railroad, mining, and manufacturing center of thirty-five thousand, Zielonka located eight Jewish families and six bachelors. They told the rabbi they socialized at a club for foreigners where they identified themselves as Germans, Alsatians, Spaniards, and Americans—not Jews. In Guadalajara, a garden city of 125,000 in the central Mexican plateaus, the governor helped Zielonka contact six or seven Jewish families. "Many more . . . some . . . very prominent . . . do not wish to be known as Jews," the rabbi wrote. Some had married Mexican Catholics and said Judaism was a fading memory. Still others with Jewish surnames denied their Hebrew origins. In the river town of Torreón, the rabbi tracked down a dozen Syrian Jews who had settled in Mexico two years before, choosing a Latin American country because they were conversant in Ladino—an ancient Judeo-Hispanic dialect that the rabbi called "a Spanish jargon." These Syrian émigrés had conducted Torreón's first Rosh Hashanah and

Yom Kippur services, yet they made no effort to meet the city's three well-established European-Jewish families. The latter were Ashkenazim—Jews with customs rooted in medieval Europe. The Syrians were Sephardim—descendants of Spanish Jewry whose customs and Hebrew pronunciation differed from those of their European co-religionists. The Sephardim considered themselves more cultured than the Ashkenazim.[18]

In Mexico City, Zielonka encountered the same divisions on a larger scale. The teeming capital was home to five hundred Jews. A couple of dozen from Syria and Turkey conducted a daily worship service in a back room of an adobe house, where a cupboard pushed against an eastern wall housed a Torah scroll. Twenty-two men, their shoulders wrapped in prayer shawls, worshiped the Saturday morning in 1908 when Zielonka's mission landed in Mexico City.[19]

What kept Mexico's Jews apart was history. In this land spiked with cathedral spires, the Spanish Inquisition had flourished for almost three centuries, from 1528 until 1820. Jewish merchants and families had been tortured and burned at the stake in Mexico, as they had been in Spain. Many persecuted Jews converted to Catholicism yet came under suspicion, particularly as their businesses prospered. Officially, these converts were termed *conversos,* but Spaniards contemptuously called them *Marranos*—swine—suspecting that they practiced Judaism undercover. Zielonka, one of the first Americans to research the phenomenon of Mexico's crypto-Jews, developed a friendship with Francisco Rivas, a professor of classical languages who claimed to be a descendant of King David. Although fluent in Hebrew, Rivas knew little about Jewish beliefs or rituals. For several years, he had tried, unsuccessfully, to recruit Mediterranean Jews to Mexico.[20]

"With such a history, one need not wonder that the Jews did not flock to Mexico," Zielonka wrote. "The hand of the Inquisition still hangs heavy over Mexico and the word Jew is only whispered here and there and the Jews have not known each other as Jews."[21]

Determined to leave some imprint of his 1908 sojourn into Mexico, Zielonka called a meeting at Mexico City's Masonic Temple on a national holiday, when shops were closed and Jews most likely to attend. The twenty Jews who met with him that day in the summer of 1908 coalesced into the Jewish Relief Society of Mexico. Reorganized four years later, the group renamed itself Sociedad de Beneficiencia Aliance Monte Sinai, the last two words a gesture of gratitude to Zielonka, whose El Paso synagogue was Temple Mount Sinai. This was the same relief society that distributed a few centavos to the refugees crowding into Mexico City when Zielonka returned in 1921.[22]

ZIELONKA REVISITS MEXICO

With the lessons of his earlier mission to Mexico still fresh, Zielonka realized there was little chance of finding local people to supervise B'nai B'rith's relief effort. Mexico's Jews were too splintered and self-conscious for such an undertaking. Yet the rabbi considered it possible and imperative to overcome the nation's past. Returning to Mexico for the entire summer of 1921, he located several well-established American and European Jews and persuaded them to take major roles in B'nai B'rith's immigrant outreach.

Joseph Weinberger, an American movie distributor and B'nai B'rith member living in Veracruz, agreed to greet immigrants at the dock. "A boat never lands that some passenger hasn't been robbed [en route]," he reported. Weinberger delivered the grim news that entrance to the United States was not possible. He steered the new arrivals toward Mexican villages, loaning refugees up to $100 to put them on the road as peddlers, not beggars.[23]

Among the earliest arrivals was Isaac Serviansky, twenty-eight, a native of Filipova, Poland, who adapted to the Mexican economic and social milieu by peddling knives and love powders that came with promises of virility. Serviansky gamely sampled the foods of the region, biting into a jalapeño pepper that his poker-faced compadres convinced him was a "Mexican cucumber." Within a year, Serviansky was doing well enough to send for his wife, Tzipa—Cecilia in Spanish—and three children, who settled in Cordoba, where he opened a store. When a son was born in 1927, they named him Bernardo, for he was a child of Mexico, not Poland. Although Isaac Serviansky, a bearded man with an ever-present hat, put on his *tefillin* to pray each morning, he dropped the kosher dietary laws. To his children he spoke Spanish, not Yiddish. When his sons turned thirteen, there was no bar mitzvah ceremony, rather a photograph to mark the pivotal date and their passage to manhood.[24]

Not every family adjusted as well. Clara Aranowitz, a widow with six children ages six to eighteen, disembarked in Veracruz in 1921, wandered across Mexico, and reached Juarez sixteen months later, ragged and starved. Zielonka found work for Clara and two of the children in a secondhand shop. The youngest offspring went to school; the eldest son smuggled his way across the border and, reportedly, into Oklahoma City.[25]

Mania Kalinski, another refugee, alarmed her Stateside relatives with a plea for $300 to free herself from "white slavery." A skeptical Zielonka wrote his colleagues that Kalinski's story had "a *traefe* (unkosher) smell." Sure enough, the woman had fallen in love with a Mexican Catholic, married the young man, and spent her relatives' cash on furniture.[26]

Another questionable cry for assistance arrived in a letter from a Kansas City B'nai B'rith supporter. She told Zielonka that her seventeen-year-old cousin, Hessel Levy, had been spurned by B'nai B'rith's Mexican relief officials and was "in desperate straits and starving."[27] Investigators learned that the youth was simply not shrewd enough to peddle in the competitive Mexico City market. He owed money to fellow immigrants, who pestered him to repay. Jailed for selling food in an off-limits area, Hessel Levy had despondently watched the police eat his wares. "We gave him $33 to get his clothes out of pawn," reported Weinberger, who also arranged free lodging for Levy and a $115 loan to make a fresh start.[28]

By then, B'nai B'rith was operating a Mexico City settlement house— a twenty-room building at 5-A Calle de Mina. "Every spare room was crowded with beds and cots," according to the rabbi. The lower floor housed offices, a medical clinic, classrooms, bedrooms, a kitchen, and showers. Upstairs were a dental clinic, a sick ward, staff quarters, and a dining room where one hundred immigrants a day ate a hot meal. In a courtyard the size of a hotel lobby, the refugees gathered to socialize, "gesticulating wildly," Zielonka wrote, and speaking an array of Yiddish dialects.[29]

Between 1921 and 1930—the year Mexico put a lid on immigration because of rising anti-Semitism and the coming portents of the Great Depression[30]—8,164 Jews settled in Mexico. Some 5,000 remained in the capital.[31] Most were from Poland, with the next-largest group from Russia. With minimal start-up capital, they were making a major contribution to the Mexican economy. Small loans of $100 or less had put peddlers on the road to remote mountain villages. Larger loans of up to $400 had financed candy stands, carpentry stalls, and tailor shops. Because Mexico imported everyday items such as umbrellas, paper boxes, suspenders, belts, and furniture, the immigrants built small factories that produced such goods from native materials. Jewish vendors also introduced installment-plan purchases to Mexico, enabling the peon and servant classes to buy shoes, thread, and other items. The credit system created a consumer market that helped raise the standard of living among the poor. As Jews became self-sufficient, they repaid B'nai B'rith more than $230,000. They formed their own loan societies, as well as Jewish clubs, Yiddish schools, and kosher delicatessens. They spawned a flourishing Jewish community and a network of twentieth-century synagogues.[32]

"Jewish history is repeating itself in Mexico City!" an ecstatic Martin Zielonka declared in sermons and speeches to the Central Conference of American Rabbis and the National Council of Jewish Women. He envisioned the day when generations of Mexican Jews would recite the Kaddish, the Jewish memorial prayer, for the martyrs of the Inquisition. History was coming full circle. The success stories unfolding across Mexico fit into the rabbi's theology, ideology, and his own life experiences.[33]

THE RABBI'S PAST

Born in Berlin on February 15, 1877, Martin Zielonka was the oldest child of Bertha Sanger Zielonka and David Zielonka, a Prussian cabinetmaker. The family surname was a common one, similar to the Polish word *zielonkawy,* a shade of green that describes a field or a frog. In 1880, the Zielonkas boarded the first-class deck of a steamship bound for New York, then continued by train to Cincinnati, the Queen City on the Ohio River. Five more Zielonka children were born, four surviving into adulthood. Sam became a neurosurgeon; Erwin, a dry cleaner; Saul, an attorney who served as city solicitor and owned a chain of movie theaters. Regina, the only daughter, was a Pittsburgh secretary who married an immigrant in the movie business.[34]

From the time of his bar mitzvah in 1890, Martin told his mother he wanted to become a rabbi.[35] Although the Zielonkas attended a traditional synagogue, Martin was attracted to the preaching of Isaac Mayer Wise, rabbi at Congregation Bene Yeshurun (sons of God) and the foremost exponent of American Reform Judaism. Zielonka had followed the movement since 1885, when the denomination's nineteen leading rabbis convened in Pittsburgh and hammered out a set of religious tenets. Their Pittsburgh Platform defined classical Reform Judaism as a modern, adaptable religion that favored social activism and rejected Zionism. The Reformers disdained the skullcap and prayer shawl, as well as the kosher dietary laws prohibiting pork and shellfish. They believed that the mission of

the Jews was to disperse throughout the world and become a beacon of
justice, peace, and prophetic values.[36] Zielonka, the product of a successful immigrant family, was in accord.

With idealistic zeal, Zielonka enrolled in 1891 at Hebrew Union College
and was ordained in 1899 among a class of six.[37] (When his mentor, college founder Isaac Mayer Wise, died the following year, Zielonka proudly
noted that he was the last student the famous rabbi had ordained—due to
his place at the end of the alphabetical class roster.) Eager to spread Reform Judaism, Zielonka accepted a call in 1899 from Waco, Texas—a
stagecoach stop and Baptist stronghold geographically near the very heart
of Texas.[38]

Texas was a challenge and a change—a frontier state with fifteen thousand Jews, compared with Ohio's fifty thousand. Zielonka's closest rabbinical colleagues were at least half a day's travel away in San Antonio, Dallas, Houston, Tyler, and Galveston. In Waco, he was the hometown rabbi
for forty-eight families at Temple Rodef Sholom (pursuer of peace) as well
as a circuit-riding rabbi who routinely traveled ninety miles to Fort Worth
to perform a wedding or funeral.[39] "At a dance to which young Jewish
ladies came from great distances," his son later wrote, Martin met and fell
in love with a San Antonio girl, Dora Schatzky.[40] Shy and introspective,
Dora was rooted in the Old South. Her mother, Rebecca Schlenker, was
descended from antebellum Louisiana merchants, and her father, Louis
Schatzky, was a traveling salesman.[41] In February, 1900, six months after
the San Antonio girl met the Cincinnati-trained rabbi, the couple married
and set up house in Waco, but not for long. A pulpit in El Paso became vacant that summer, and the Zielonkas decided to build their future in
Texas' westernmost city.

WELCOME TO EL PASO

Ringed in high desert, cut off from the rest of Texas by hundreds of barren
miles, El Paso possessed a flavor all its own. A cultural crossroads, the city
was named for the pass at the southernmost point of the Rockies. The
town had begun as a trading station on the trail linking Mexico's Chihuahua Desert with Santa Fe. Surrounded by mountains and bisected by
the shallow Rio Grande, the region's topography reminded the rabbi of
Cincinnati—except here the hills were dotted with sagebrush, not trees.
Here the river was a boundary between nations, not states. Here lay a bor-

der town with 15,906 inhabitants, twenty-five saloons, and no paved streets. Mules pulled trolleys along tracks that led to hotels, shops, and a plaza where alligators, imported as a novelty, lazed in the public fountain. Both crude and cosmopolitan, El Paso was also the midpoint on the east-west rail line between St. Louis and San Francisco. Juarez, the border city across the Rio Grande, had become a free port in 1885, attracting traders who bartered with beaver pelts, blankets, piñon nuts, silver coins, and turquoise. Some Jewish merchants, tailors, and dry cleaners settled in El Paso to do business with the army's Fort Bliss. Others arrived with visions of branch stores across the Southwest managed by a network of sons, nephews, and uncles. "Border Spanish" came easily to these Jewish settlers, already conversant in European languages. Zielonka, however, never picked up more than a few Spanish phrases.[42]

Jewish women played a role in this frontier. During epidemics, they went door to door with buckets of chicken soup, dispensing broth with ladles.[43] Many a wife worked in the family retail store or turned her home into a boarding house. One retail family, the Krupps, provided lodging above their store for Mexican bandit and rebel leader Pancho Villa, who ordered troop supplies and uniforms from a host of Jewish merchants.[44]

Jews were always an integral part of El Paso commerce and politics. When a city government was organized in 1880, voters elected two Jews—Mayor Solomon Schutz and Alderman Adolph Krakauer. In 1887, a death in the Jewish community led thirty-two Israelites to pitch in $1.25 per quarter to maintain a Jewish cemetery, assist needy co-religionists, and create the Mount Sinai Association. Three years later, the El Paso Hebrew Sunday School started, with classes held at the county courthouse. Regular religious worship did not take root until 1898 when an Alabama rabbi, Oscar J. Cohn, moved to El Paso to recuperate from failing health. His presence invigorated Jewish communal life. The Mount Sinai Association transformed itself into a congregation that constructed a synagogue with an onion-domed, Byzantine-style tower. When Rabbi Cohn left El Paso for a pulpit in Dallas (where he died a year later), Mount Sinai recruited Zielonka at a salary of $150 a month.[45]

A PRODUCT OF HIS TIMES

On September 7, 1900, the day after Martin and Dora Zielonka arrived by train, the rabbi stood in a gas-lit sanctuary with 128 seats and led services

for a congregation of forty-five families. A well-groomed figure of medium height and stiff decorum, the rabbi made his debut wearing a pinstriped suit with a cutaway jacket accessorized with a pocket watch and
gold chain. With his pursed lips, waxed mustache, and hair meticulously
parted down the middle, Zielonka conveyed an imperious air as he peered
at worshipers through gold-rimmed spectacles that slipped down the
bridge of his nose. By his demeanor and his sermons, the rabbi quickly
gained a reputation as a moralizing preacher outraged by gambling, risqué
movies, and truancy from school or synagogue. He assailed parents who
took their children "automobiling" rather than to religious functions.[46]
He denounced newspapers that printed "lurid" headlines about murders
and divorces. To help civilize the town, he fell in step with the Citizens
League, a reform group that fought to regulate saloon hours, restrict gambling to basements and back rooms, and enforce an ordinance that required people to leave pistols at home.[47]

"Shootings were commonplace and fights were the order of the day,"
Zielonka's son, David, recalled. Seared into his memory was the Sunday in
June of 1910 when his father took him along for a convivial morning gathering of Jewish men at Ernst Kohlberg's Cigar Store. A drunken gambler,
evicted by Kohlberg from a downtown hotel, barged in, "whipped out his
gun and shot Mr. Kohlberg to his death, to the horror of all of us."[48] Such
violence was not an isolated incident in a city where Pat Garrett, the law-
man who killed Billy the Kid, served as customs collector. The rabbi was
once roused in the middle of the night to officiate at a real shotgun wedding. "It was a pioneer community in a pioneer city, where everything was
free and easy and where life was not taken very seriously," Zielonka recalled years later.[49]

The rabbi teamed with civic leaders to launch the city's first charities
and raise money for YMCA and Salvation Army facilities. He planted
seeds for the creation of a city university, served on the municipal planning commission, and was a charter member of El Paso's Rotary Club.
Dubbed the "Reform rabbi of the West," Zielonka had a circuit-riding territory that stretched eight hundred miles. Beyond El Paso, he helped
launch congregations in Albuquerque, Alamogordo, Santa Fe, Tucson,
Tucumcari, Phoenix, and Los Angeles.[50] He also spoke up for the Latino
population and accused the school board of "ignoring the obvious needs
of Mexican children."[51]

Despite the rabbi's defense of children, Jewish youth hardly perceived

Zielonka as an advocate or friend, but rather as a disciplinarian. At Sunday School, he ordered one student to sit in the corner with a wad of chewing gum on her nose. He expelled his next-door-neighbor's son from the confirmation class for giggling. The youth, Leonard Goodman, Sr., recalled: "The Hebrew words were strange for us and sounded funny, so we started laughing. He blamed me. I took it on the chin." Another student, Beulah Halpern Schnadig, had mixed emotions toward the rabbi: "There were times when I loved him and times when I hated him. He was very human, and he was a big influence on my life."[52] Few people drew close to this rabbi, who evaded congregants by dropping an unbaited fishing line into the Rio Grande and pretending to catnap.[53]

Dora Zielonka, quiet and in poor health, never felt at home with her El Paso neighbors. "She wasn't, let's say, popular socially," Goodman recalled.[54] Her closest companion was her widowed sister, Hattie Schatzky Harris, a hospital dietitian who moved to El Paso with her daughter, Rosalie, a child whom Dora doted upon.[55] Dora's health was precarious. The region's windstorms aggravated her allergies; a thyroid condition that dated from childhood flared up periodically. Her first child, David Leopold Zielonka, born October 21, 1904, was a fragile infant who weighed less than three pounds at birth but developed into a healthy child. Fourteen years later, on April 11, 1918, Dora gave birth to a long-awaited second child, Arthur Kline Zielonka. That autumn, the six-month-old was suddenly stricken with cholera, and he died the same day. Overnight, Dora Zielonka's hair turned white. "The scars of this loss were carried by Dad and Mother for the remainder of their lives," wrote their surviving son. A year later, fifteen-year-old David, the focus of Dora's life, left home for college and rabbinical school.[56]

Dora Zielonka, withdrawn to begin with, became more so. Congregants recall her as a stout, silent woman, with strands of white hair limply tucked into a bun. She wore loose-fitting, scoop-necked dresses when she posed for group pictures with the temple Sisterhood and the El Paso section of the National Council of Jewish Women. In both organizations, she participated as a fund-raiser and convention delegate at the state and national level.[57] When the Zielonkas moved to a new parsonage at a prestigious Sunset Heights address, each had a separate bedroom equipped with a pull chain that summoned their caretaker and cook, Robert Brown, from a basement apartment.[58] Dora needed the assistance. She was often unsteady on her feet and suffered from "nervousness." Twice, she and the

Dora Schatzky Zielonka and Rabbi Martin Zielonka, with a cigar in hand,
late 1930s. Courtesy Carl L. Zielonka, D.D.S.

rabbi journeyed to Minnesota's Mayo Clinic where part of her thyroid
gland was removed to treat a goiter condition.[59]

Dora found relief during trips to Mexico. While her husband worked in
the capital at B'nai B'rith's Mexican Bureau, Dora relaxed in the mountain
resort of Cuernavaca. She became a close friend and travel companion of
Bea Marx, wife of Archie Marx, the rabbi's B'nai B'rith partner.[60] Both
couples shared an appreciation for German poetry and music, and the
Mexican connection nurtured their friendship. Like his wife, the rabbi
seemed more relaxed in Mexico, more compassionate, too, as he worked
among the immigrants. At home in El Paso, he seemed the opposite—

El Paso rabbi Martin Zielonka, at right in coat and tie, with Temple Mount Sinai's
Y-Church League basketball team, 1917. Standing: Henry Blume, Ralph Aronson,
Max Katz, Herman Silberberg, Robert Marcus, Rabbi Zielonka. Seated: Harold
Potash, team captain Errold Lapowski, Isidore Grossblatt.
Courtesy Temple Mount Sinai, El Paso, Tex.

puritanical and disapproving, a minister of stern demeanor trying to civilize an untamed Western town. Early congregants seemed pleased with
his rectitude, his visibility, and his image in the community.

RELIGIOUS RIVALRIES

Temple Mount Sinai's impressive $50,000 synagogue, dedicated in
1916 at the corner of Oregon and Montana streets, was a soaring red-
brick edifice adorned with stained glass. Its basement gymnasium was the
home court for the temple's championship Church League basketball
team, whose athletes wore uniforms emblazoned with Jewish stars.[61] The

Mount Sinai gym, with its swimming pool, billiard tables, and large, wall-mounted American flag, was theoretically open to all Jewish youngsters. However, Zielonka expelled those who belonged to rival Congregation B'nai Zion, a Conservative synagogue. "On more than one occasion when we were there in the gym enjoying ourselves, Rabbi Zielonka would ask us the same question: 'What are you doing here? You belong at the shul,'" recalled an El Paso native affiliated with B'nai Zion.[62]

The rift between the temple and the shul, as the traditional synagogue was called, was mainly of Zielonka's making, born of jealousy and ideological differences. A number of El Paso's wealthier Jews paid dues to both congregations as a show of support for Jewish institutions. Zielonka had been receptive in 1912 when the city's traditional Jews—who came to El Paso through the Galveston immigration movement—started daily prayer services in the rear of stores and in private homes. The arrival in 1923 of Dr. Joseph Roth, a rabbi raised in New Jersey and ordained at New York's Jewish Theological Seminary, marked a strain in relations. Hungarian-born Roth was seventeen years younger than Zielonka and more educated, with a Ph.D. in philosophy from New York University. Roth donned clerical robes when he preached and therefore looked warmer and more spiritual than Zielonka did in his three-piece pinstriped suits. Yet Roth, much like his Reform counterpart, berated congregants who played poker and mah-jongg on the Sabbath. At Hebrew school he was impatient with inattentive youngsters. "He klopfed us on the knuckles," recalled Isadore Kahn. Critics called his air of decorum an "ice curtain." Yet Rabbi Roth could warm up to an audience in a way that Zielonka could not. "I do not drink, smoke, or chew, but I cuss," he wryly warned.[63]

The major bone of contention separating the rabbis was their outlook on Zionism, a political issue creating a chasm in El Paso and a rift among Jews around the globe. Zionism was then a burgeoning movement to resettle Jews in Palestine and turn the Promised Land into a modern Jewish nation. America's immigrant quotas and Europe's escalating anti-Semitism persuaded multitudes of rabbis and laity to lobby for a return to Zion. Not Zielonka. He was an advocate of Diaspora—the dispersal of Jews around the world. His humanitarian work in Mexico was infused with a prophetic component: a belief that Jews are international citizens with a mission to spread the ethics of the Ten Commandments. "We have been scattered more than twenty-five centuries in all lands," Zielonka wrote. "I believe that in God's economy, we have not been spared through centuries of acute suffering simply to be another nation." He cautioned that "Palestine is not an uninhabited region. . . . We occupied it for a comparatively short time. . . . We are creating anti-Semitism between Jews and Mohammedans."[64]

A growing number of El Paso women agitated to form a chapter of Hadassah—the international women's Zionist organization founded in Philadelphia in 1912. Hadassah supported public health and modern medical facilities in the Promised Land as well as Youth Aliyah, which resettled Jewish youth from war-torn Europe in Palestine.[65] Zielonka was opposed. He attacked the rapidly growing Hadassah network as a "nationalist" scheme full of "propaganda."[66] His mentor, Rabbi Isaac Mayer Wise, had condemned Zionism in his time as a "madman's dance" and a "prostitution of Israel's holy cause."[67] But the world stage was producing new role models, among them Hadassah's founder, Henrietta Szold. She visited Texas in 1912, 1914, and 1919 to organize chapters, but she received no invitation from El Paso.[68] El Paso women made three futile attempts—in 1928, 1936, and 1937—to organize a Hadassah chapter, but Zielonka had the clout to block them.[69] During the last attempt, Tamar de Sola Pool, a national Hadassah leader married to a prominent New York rabbi, visited El Paso to spur a grassroots movement. Zielonka was not swayed by her presence or her arguments. In his journal, he denigrated the effort, writing, "I told Mrs. Pool I felt we had enough women's organizations."[70]

El Paso's mainline Jewish families of German descent concurred with the rabbi. America had proven to be their promised land. They believed there were plenty of public health and community service measures to address close to home. Zielonka's work across the border demonstrated a better way to handle Jewish resettlement, via immigration to nations outside Palestine.

Rabbi Roth, although a Zionist, lacked the clout or the time to turn Hadassah into a cause célèbre. As a traditional rabbi, he had more rituals to observe and more services to conduct. Twice a day, in the morning and early evening, he rounded up a minyan, the ten men necessary to convene a service. One fourth of his congregants were too strapped to pay dues. When the Depression hit El Paso, the shul fell behind on its mortgage. Roth continued officiating without pay and went to work as chairman of the philosophy and psychology department at El Paso College of Mines. The position in academia gave him a high profile, with prestige rivaling Zielonka. At ecumenical events, Roth or Zielonka was usually seated on the podium between a priest and a minister. El Paso's citizenry had learned from Zielonka's example to respect the "office of rabbi." Few outside the

Jewish community knew that professional jealousy and political differences kept the rabbis from sharing more than a glance.[71]

LOOKING BACK

Martin Zielonka died unexpectedly January 1, 1938, after hospitalization for coronary sclerosis. He was sixty years old. By then, the younger, more traditional Rabbi Joseph Roth had eclipsed the senior rabbi in the hearts of El Paso Jewry. Congregants at Mount Sinai and B'nai Zion gradually forgot the bulk of Zielonka's work with the planning commission, the college, the Citizens League, the Rotary, and the resettlement of Jews in Mexico. What they recalled most vividly and vehemently was his crusade against Hadassah—which El Paso women finally joined in 1943. Among succeeding generations of local Jewry, few were aware that an El Paso rabbi had influenced Mexican history. Rabbi Floyd Fierman, a history buff who served at Temple Mount Sinai from 1949 to 1979, virtually ignored Zielonka when he researched the region's Jewish past. Perhaps influenced by people's disdainful reminiscences, Fierman, in his many books and articles, makes scant mention of Zielonka's thirty-seven-year presence.[72]

"A rabbi never expects gratitude," Zielonka had told the Temple Mount Sinai Brotherhood several months before his death.

Yet Zielonka's work had important and lasting effects. Stirred by the plight of homeless refugees and convinced of Mexico's potential, Zielonka became the catalyst for altering American foreign policy and an untold number of lives. From Texas to New York, he pleaded the cause of the illegal refugees. Rebuffed by philanthropists and social workers in New York, he refused to give up and wring his hands while Jews were being deported. He became their lone champion until B'nai B'rith endorsed his efforts and bankrolled his vision. The passion and zeal that Zielonka brought to the Mexican immigrant situation were rooted in his opposition to Zionism. So was his obstinacy toward Hadassah. He believed that Jews are not a nation but the Chosen People, selected to retain the core of their identity as they disperse across the world.

The migration of eight thousand Jews to Mexico in the 1920s constituted that nation's largest wave of Hebrew immigration in the twentieth century. Mexico's Jewish refugees did not remain peddlers for long. They thrived and multiplied. During the 1970s, these immigrants and their descendants donated more money per capita to Jewish philanthropy than

Jews of other nations.[73] In 1993, they commemorated B'nai B'rith's 150th anniversary with a book about the Jewish migration to Mexico—a volume dedicated to Rabbi Martin Zielonka.[74]

Did the times shape the man or the man shape the times? The answer is both. Reexamining Zielonka's Mexican endeavors, it becomes clear he had a Texas blueprint to follow. The Galveston immigration plan, from 1907 to 1914, had directed ten thousand Eastern European Jews to the western half of the United States. Zielonka watched participants in that migration wave succeed by virtue of their industriousness and the welcoming hand extended by Galveston's Rabbi Henry Cohen. Zielonka understood that new arrivals need language skills, monetary loans, and a warm reception to adjust smoothly. Although he lacked the warmth and social charm of Henry Cohen, he made certain that Mexico's B'nai B'rith Bureau hired workers who had these qualities. Zielonka's achievement is all the more remarkable because he lived far from centers of Jewish life, in a place remote even by Texas standards. Because of his isolation, the rabbi realized that there was no one else to resolve the crisis at his doorstep.

"The men who stand forth as leaders are not necessarily the men who occupy the biggest pulpits," Zielonka said in a baccalaureate address to his son's 1929 graduating class at Hebrew Union College. "The men who are influencing Jewish thought and adjusting the ancient heritages to modern needs are not those who shout the loudest or are most often in the public press."[75] And a rabbi, like Zielonka, who is not altogether applauded in his time or in his remote surroundings, may, nonetheless, exert a major influence on the course of the Chosen People.

7

Pearl of the Rio Grande

The Making of a Lay Rabbi

SAM PERL, BROWNSVILLE

SAM PERL WORE DOZENS OF HATS, and one of them was a *yarmulke.* For half a century this haberdasher, civic booster, radio host, and Shriner presided as lay rabbi of the lower Rio Grande, self-appointed to a pulpit that stretched from the toe of Texas into Mexico's Sierra Madre. A cigar-smoking immigrant with a Yiddish rhythm to his Texas drawl, Sam Perl orchestrated so many religious events—weddings included—that a county judge vested him with the authority to perform civil marriages for all.[1] Bearing the mantle of minister, this men's clothing merchant delivered invocations for the Kiwanis, the Chamber of Commerce, and the federal court, sometimes sharing the podium with a Catholic bishop. Publicly, he frowned on Jews eating pork, but if served a slice of ham at a Kiwanis Club luncheon, he winked, dug in his fork, and dubbed his serving "rare roast beef."[2]

Motivated less by piety than by conviviality, showmanship, and a deep attachment to his religious heritage, from 1926 to 1977 Perl forged a flexible set of rules to maintain peace among a splintered Jewish community. At Brownsville's tiny Temple Beth-El, three hundred miles from the nearest kosher butcher, members prayed in Spanish, English, Yiddish, and Hebrew. Some insisted on skull caps and prayer shawls, others resisted. If a worshiper sneezed, Mexican congregants reflexively shouted "Jesús!"[3] Too

Brownsville's lay rabbi Sam Perl, ca. 1965, takes aim with a pool cue.
Courtesy Frances Perl Goodman, San Antonio.

diverse, too few, and too remote to attract an ordained rabbi, local Jews recognized Sam Perl as their religious spokesman, even as their congregation multiplied from sixteen families to more than a hundred. The husky six-footer, with his high-pitched laugh and contagious grin, became an ecumenical figure and the Rio Grande Valley's most visible Jew.

Despite his lofty religious status, Sam Perl was no theologian. His familiarity with biblical and Hebrew texts went scarcely beyond recitation of Sabbath prayers. His Galveston high school diploma was the extent of his scholarship. Yet as the heart and soul of Brownsville's Temple Beth-El, Sam Perl gave direction and cohesion to a Jewish community that traced its his-

tory to before the Civil War but had floundered for years without leadership or edifice.

"My grandfather's temple was 'reconformadox,'" observed one of the
lay rabbi's grandsons, using a term that comically blends Judaism's denominations of Reform, Conservative, and Orthodox.[4] At the very least,
Brownsville's Temple Beth-El was unorthodox. A pianist softly played the
French composition "Clair de Lune" as a prelude to the mourners' *Kaddish*.[5] At Passover seders in Perl's home, the silver cup symbolically filled
with wine for the prophet Elijah was inscribed, *Perfect Attendance, Kiwanis, 1938*. Poker winnings retired the temple mortgage. Non-Jewish
spouses were allowed interment in the temple cemetery, a practice forbid-
den in Judaism's traditional realm. In another break with time-honored
rules, Perl deemed shrimp permissible fare for Gulf Coast Jews and was
chaplain to the Shrimp Producers Association.[6] Shrimping was a local industry, and Perl, who was referred to as both "rabbi" and "Mr. Brownsville," believed that what was good for the local economy was good for the
Jewish community.

DISCOVERING THE MAGIC VALLEY

Sam Perl first ventured to the border region during the summer of 1926, a
traveling salesman lured by advertisements trumpeting the Magic Valley.
His destination was Olmito, a lake front promoted as the future site of "the
most beautiful city in South Texas."[7] When Sam and his older brother
Leon reached Olmito, they shook their heads at a quagmire buzzing with
mosquitoes, stepped back on the train, and continued to the end of the
line—nine miles south, to Brownsville.

Here, they discovered the Magic Valley they had envisioned—a county
seat of sixteen thousand residents on the edge of Texas and the verge of
growth. They marveled at the high-rise El Jardin Hotel, under construction and already dazzling pilots with its height and glare. On palm-lined
Levee Street, which stretched into town from the Rio Grande, a Missouri-
Pacific depot was in the works. An international bridge, to supplant the
ferry crossing, was scheduled for completion within two years. Nearby, a
dilapidated warehouse dating from the Civil War was to be razed "to give
way to the advance of progress," according to the *Brownsville Herald*. In its
place would rise yet another hotel replete with baths, steam heating, ven-
tilated doors, and roof garden. Brownsville, touted as a crossroads "where

Mexico meets Uncle Sam," was emerging from rural isolation into a vacation land, and the brothers were impressed.[8]

The tip of Texas was a bicultural locale, more Latin than American, with store signs in Spanish and street signs in English. The region was predominantly Catholic as well, with church bells at the Immaculate Conception Cathedral tolling the time. Brownsville's commercial core, unlike those of most Texas county seats, did not radiate from the courthouse—a stolid, four-story building with a stained-glass rotunda. Instead, Brownsville's retail stores stretched along Elizabeth and Washington Streets, which began at a bend of the Rio Grande and funneled ferry traffic from Matamoros, the Mexican city four times its size across the river.

Sam and Leon noted the flowering bougainvillea, the parakeets in the trees, and the flourishing commercial climate. They also saw promise in two familiar commercial names: Dorfman's Jewelers and Edelstein's Furniture. Both of those families had ties to Galveston, where the Perl brothers had grown up. (Sam remembered seeing Morris Edelstein and his bride-to-be, Yetta Weisenthal, kissing behind the bushes as teens.) Both of those mercantile families had roots in Podhajce, a Polish town in the Austro-Hungarian Empire where the Perl brothers were born.[9]

Sam and Leon concurred that fate must have guided them to the lower Rio Grande Valley, a fifty-mile-wide region that is not really a valley but a delta where the sluggish river that forms Texas' southern border drains into the Gulf of Mexico. Over time, the meandering ribbon of river had changed course and left strands of narrow, bending, lagoons called *resacas*, which served as nesting grounds for wintering birds, breeding grounds for malaria, and condominium sites for future developers. A visionary, Sam Perl saw the region's interior as the Venice of Texas, and after taking a rowboat excursion to Padre Island, he forecast even more potential. The barrier isle, the nation's longest sand spit, with 113 miles of dunes, had no roads or bridges, but Sam predicted development of its white-sand beaches. He was prepared to remain in the region and fulfill his dreams.[10]

A men's shop called the Fashion was for sale on Elizabeth Street, the main thoroughfare. Fine haberdashery was new for Sam, a twenty-nine-year-old traveling salesman who sold butcher paper and men's underwear. Brother Leon, a thirty-eight-year-old veteran of World War I, had been working at their uncle Louie Perl's Beaumont hardware store. The brothers, both bachelors, agreed to invest their futures in fine men's clothing and the border town store.

FROM WHENCE THEY CAME

The Perl brothers had journeyed to Texas from Eastern Europe at the turn of the century. Sam, born June 24, 1897, loved to recount the tale of their difficult voyage. Their ship had been scheduled to dock in Galveston on September 8, 1900, but a catastrophic hurricane shattered the Island and forced the vessel—carrying Sam, Leon, sister Belle, and their mother, Rivka—to dock in New Orleans. The foursome later moved to Galveston to join father Wolf Perl, who had migrated in 1899. Another sibling, Joe, a promising student, had preceded the family to America and was in school in New York.

Wolf Perl, bearded and "wrapped in his religion," set a pious example. He earned a living selling produce and clothing, and always attended daily worship services and rested from work on the Sabbath. At home, he recited a blessing as he washed his hands before meals and chanted a prayer before and after he ate. The Perl patriarch was a kosher cook of note, a "grand master" of gefilte fish—a pâté of ground pike, carp, and whitefish, seasoned with grated onion, boiled, and served on a platter with horseradish. Deftly, Papa Perl formed gefilte fish balls between two spoons, shaping perfect spheres without soiling his fingers.[11]

As the youngest son, Sam was entrusted with carrying the family's *cholent*—a stew prepared in a cast iron pot—to a community oven on Friday afternoons. "The aromas were tantalizing and overwhelming," he later recalled.[12] The cholents simmered until midday Saturday when, after Sabbath morning services, Sam and other neighborhood youths ran home with their stew pots, being careful not to stumble and spill the family supper.

Young Sam was exposed to religious experiences of a different sort from Rabbi Henry Cohen, Galveston's humanitarian rabbi, who bicycled all over town and pastored to the community at large. The leader of Temple B'nai Israel, Cohen headed the Jewish Immigrants Information Bureau in Galveston, which relocated ten thousand Eastern European Jewish refugees to the Midwest and Southwest between 1907 and 1914. Sam Perl volunteered as one of Rabbi Cohen's "runners," an errand boy who escorted men from the boat to the public baths and the barber. Streetwise Sam Perl, with his fluency in Yiddish and English, was a natural for the task, which had its lighter moments. He regaled friends with descriptions of the immigrants' shock at how they looked after the first clean shaves in their lives.

In Europe, most had observed the biblical prohibition against putting a razor to the face. But in America, younger immigrants in particular were ready to venture into this new land bearing a new image. Young Sam approved of that flexibility.[13]

Galveston, an island city, was an international port where vice thrived and gambling was commonplace. Sam Perl learned at an early age how to deal a deck of cards and bluff a poker hand. After graduating from Ball High School in 1914, he headed to Austin and the University of Texas campus, but not for long. Academics was not a strong suit, and his extracurricular activity was cards. Running low on money, Sam sold his books before the end of the first semester to buy bus fare home. Back in Galveston, he attended a business school and went to work as bookkeeper at Texas Star Flour Mill.

In 1918, with the United States involved in World War I, Sam received a draft notice. The night before his induction, he partied with friends at Houston's Rice Hotel, a final fling before reporting for duty. Stumbling into the lobby in the wee hours, he found himself in the midst of an even larger party, a spontaneous celebration of the armistice ending the war.

Sam returned to Galveston, where he worked at the flour mill and spent his evenings at old haunts, often surrendering his wages at the gambling tables. To solve his financial problems, Perl changed jobs, going on the road in Texas and Louisiana as a salesman for Kraft Paper Company and BVD. He often joked that in his new position, he "slept between Edna and Inez"—two South Texas towns.[14]

When Leon suggested that the brothers look at the Magic Valley in the summer of 1926, Sam was ready to take a chance. Once settled in Brownsville, he became a joiner. Over the next several decades he was active in the Elks Lodge, the Propeller Club, and the Alzafar Temple Shrine—which custom-made a rhinestone-encrusted fez to fit Sam's extra-large, size 7¾ head. Also on his civic agenda were the Valley B'nai B'rith Lodge, the Brownsville High School Band Boosters, the Scottish Rite Consistory-Shrine, the Mexico Goodwill Trip Committee, and the International Good Neighbor Council.[15] With business on his mind, Perl passed out his professional card to each new face and rose to the presidency, chaplaincy, or exalted ruler status in each organization. Daily, he scanned the *Brownsville Herald*'s list of hospital admissions, visiting any friend, acquaintance, customer, or fellow Jew in ill health. A natural politician and pastor, Perl built a flock of friendships as he drummed up business.[16]

COFFEE AND CONVIVIALITY

Sam Perl began his workday dropping in on neighboring merchants. Promptly at 10:40 A.M., he entered Fisher's Café for a coffee break with his pals from the Kiwanis and the courthouse, a ritual so regular that each man had his own mug hanging on a restaurant hook. The morning rite began with a contest, a guess-the-number game with the winner a loser, surrendering coins to pay for the coffee. The men gathered for a second coffee break in midafternoon. They joshed and joked, cementing a congenial oligarchy that served mainly to boost Brownsville. During these casual tête-à-têtes, the men puffed cigars and tossed out ideas about civic projects that often gained fruition through the Chamber of Commerce, the Downtown Merchants Association, or the Brownsville Merchants Association. Sam, and most of his cohorts, served on the executive boards of them all.

Inside his own store, which was called the Fashion—Perl Brothers, Sam was master of sales and charm. He greeted each female customer with a kiss and counseled women about gifts for boyfriends or husbands. He remembered exactly what they had previously purchased and for whom. To each child, he gave a penny to dial a sweet from the gum-ball machine. Male customers on both sides of the border were initially drawn by ads in 1926 that highlighted the Fashion's high-class labels: Florsheim Shoes ($10 a pair), Hart Shaffner and Marx suits ($35–$65), Dobb's hats ($8–$10), linen handkerchiefs, and smoking jackets.[17] The Fashion became the town's top quality haberdashery, the Valley's Neiman-Marcus for men.

Sam's wide range of contacts led to contracts to outfit the police, the firefighters, and U.S. Customs agents. When cadets from the Border Patrol Academy arrived by the busload for uniforms, longtime employee Eli Konigsberg measured them from bottom to top for boots, trousers, holsters, shirts, and caps.[18] Commerce showed promise, but the religious side of Sam's life was lacking.

BROWNSVILLE'S JEWISH ROOTS

Yes, there were Jews in Brownsville. There always had been. The Perl brothers were actually latecomers to the region's Jewish family. One of the area's earliest Jewish settlers was a steamboat captain, Benjamin Moses, who carried freight in 1846 for General Zachary Taylor's army in what became a war against Mexico. The general had been dispatched to the Valley to resolve whether Texas' southern border ended at the Rio Grande or the Nueces River, 113 miles to the north.[19] During the ensuing hostilities, the general moved his headquarters into the empty home of John Melvin Hirsch, a Jew who had fled with his family to Matamoros.[20] That Mexican port city was already home to a handful of Jewish merchants and foreign trade brokers who imported European goods and exported cotton.[21]

After the United States won the war in 1848, Simon Mussina, a Philadelphia native and son of a Dutch Jew, moved to the region. From Matamoros he published a popular English-language newspaper, the *American Flag*. Mussina helped surveyors lay out the new Texas town, then moved his presses across the river to the American side. The city was named Brownsville after Major Jacob Brown, who died while his regiment defended the fortress at the bend in the river facing Matamoros.[22] Besides Mussina, other Jews migrated across the narrow strip of water, leaving Mexico for the political stability of the United States. More Jewish merchants from New York and Europe soon joined them, sensing opportunity. During the American Civil War of the 1860s, the twin ports at Brownsville and Matamoros functioned as back doors to the Confederacy.

By 1868, half a dozen Jewish families on both sides of the river had formed a Hebrew Benevolent Society that purchased a half acre in Brownsville for a Jewish cemetery. They enclosed the grounds with a five-foot, triple-brick wall and landscaped the premises with native palms. During the cemetery's first decade, most of those buried were "murdered in Mexico or on the frontier," according to a notary public of the time.[23] So remote was the region that for eighty-two years, that hallowed plot remained the only Jewish cemetery within a one-hundred-mile radius.[24]

Confederate soldier Adolph Bollack of New Orleans had carried home a favorable impression of Brownsville, site of the 1865 Battle of Palmito Ranch, and he returned with his family four years later. Most sacred among his family's possessions was a Torah, the handwritten Hebrew scroll containing the Five Books of Moses. It had been brought to America from France by Bollack's ancestors.[25]

Despite the sacred scroll and the well-tended cemetery, Brownsville's Jewish families had little in the way of organized religious worship when Sam Perl arrived in 1926. However, they mingled so easily with the rest of the populace that one of their own, Benjamin Kowalski, had been elected mayor in 1912. For lack of a Hebrew worship service, Jews sometimes attended the Episcopal or Catholic church.[26]

The autumn that Sam and Leon arrived, a rabbinical student from Cincinnati's Hebrew Union College conducted Rosh Hashanah and Yom Kippur services at the Masonic Temple. The High Holy Day worship gave impetus to weekly Friday night services at the smaller American Legion Post. Jewish mothers started a Sunday School for their children. But the religious school teacher, Mrs. Henry Grunewald, an elderly woman of Orthodox upbringing, felt unappreciated and quit. Further friction among Jews surfaced over whether or not to wear yarmulkes—"the matter of the hat," as one observer put it. Little had been resolved by the next High Holy Day season when Dr. Hyman Ettlinger, a math professor at the University of Texas, officiated as lay rabbi. Then in the fall of 1929, Milton Grafman, another student rabbi, spent three weeks in South Texas visiting small towns to assess the likelihood of forming congregations near the border. He found the Orthodox Jews "antagonistic," the Reform Jews, "indifferent," and many Jews suspicious of one another because of competing businesses. During a two-day stop in Brownsville, Grafman drummed up enough enthusiasm to supervise the election of officers and creation of a congregation. Although the rabbinical student's letters back to Hebrew Union College mention no names—save for Mrs. Grunewald "who finally consented to cooperate . . . [after] I did everything but get down on my knees"—the Jews he conferred with very likely included Sam Perl.[27]

Perl began leading Brownsville's Friday evening minyan, reviewing in advance the weekly Torah portion and preparing an explanatory sermon. He arranged for Berrera's Bakery, a Mexican sweet shop, to bake a traditional braided egg bread, or challah, each Friday. He ordered pickled herring by the barrel and *knishes* by the dozens during his buying trips to New York. Gradually, he brought a taste of Judaism and a degree of regularity to religious observance in Brownsville.

Sam realized that he, too, had let Judaism slide. His shop was open Saturdays, and his store sold tickets to Friday-night high school football games—the weekly fall social event. Unlike his father, who packed his own kosher chicken and pot when he traveled out of town, Sam had expanded his palate. He savored tamales, a Mexican treat wrapped in corn husks, with concentric layers of *masa* meal and a core of ground pork. He relished chile and enchiladas. Sam accommodated to his surroundings, but he had absorbed enough Judaism and ethnic flavor from his father and Rabbi Cohen to bring others into the fold.

To Sam's delight, the Jewish mothers involved in the budding Sunday School launched a building drive. They received a charter for the Temple Beth-El Sisterhood in 1931, then purchased a corner of land in a residential neighborhood at West Eighth and Saint Francis Streets. For $4,265 they hired a contractor to construct a white-stucco sanctuary and, as an afterthought, negotiated inclusion of kitchen and bathroom facilities for a mere $40 extra. Their little house of worship, completed in 1932, doubled as a religious school. On Sunday mornings, students and teachers gathered among the pews for classes, with the youngest children meeting in the back rows and the teenagers sitting up front. By the spring of 1933, the religious school had graduated its first students—a confirmation class of four adolescents.[28]

Sam spread knowledge of Judaism into the larger community, arranging for the Kiwanis Club to present informative programs prior to Jewish holidays. He persuaded newspaper publisher Mo Stein, another Jew, to explain the holidays in print. Jews and non-Jews began coming to Sam with requests for benedictions, liturgical advice, and invitations to serve on interfaith councils. One civic leader, in the depths of a painful divorce, turned to Sam for consolation when his church and pastor shunned him. "Sam sat down and gave me what he called a sound piece of Jewish advice: 'Don't look back.'" The man felt uplifted. Consulted and respected, Sam cherished his role as he became the ethnic broker and spokesman for the Jewish community.

Perl's rabbinical role and civic involvement were not without precedent in the American West—although his lengthy tenure elevates him to a select group of lay rabbis.[29] Where there was no rabbi, the Jewish community had a tendency to anoint a representative. A number of "Marryin' Sams" circulated in the Gold Rush days of California, performing weddings in the absence of credentialed rabbis.[30] They had just enough Judaic knowledge and civic stature to do so.[31] In Arizona, merchant Sam Drachman followed miners into the desert and served as lay rabbi of Tucson Jewry from 1867 until his death in 1911. "No wedding was official without Uncle Sam."[32] In Deadwood, South Dakota, tobacco store owner Nathan Colman was both justice of the peace and lay rabbi from 1877 until his death in 1906.[33] Another self-styled rabbi, Lewis Abraham Franklin, gave the first documented Jewish sermon in the West. His Yom Kippur address in 1850 was delivered from a pulpit inside a tent store on a San Francisco street.[34] Like the frontier West, Judaism is democratically based with little hierarchy. Biblically rooted, its rituals and daily practices evolved from commentaries and codes reinterpreted by succeeding generations. The core of the tradition is the ten-man prayer service, which any participant may lead. Sam Perl, like lay leaders in the past, did just that.

In Brownsville, his task was difficult considering the polyglot of Jews and the harsh economic times. The Great Depression severely affected the Valley, where wages were low to begin with because of the steady influx of workers from Mexico. The Brownsville school district, short on funds during the depression, paid teachers in scrip, rather than cash, redeemable for barter in the few stores willing to accept it. Perl Brothers did, and in exchange for the scrip, Sam and Leon received customer loyalty and used the paper credit to pay up to 57 percent of their property taxes.[35] Sam focused on better economic times to come. When a five-story post office and federal courthouse opened downtown in 1933, optimistic Sam was first in line to apply for a mailbox. The reason was evident in his store's new address: P.O. Box 1, Brownsville, Texas.[36]

ALL IN THE FAMILY

Sam and Leon shared a strong brotherly love. With a quick peck on the lips, they kissed each other in the morning and at the close of business, and they never quarreled publicly. Smartly dressed in brand name suits and ties, the brothers were nonetheless a study in contrast, and so were their brides. Leon was reserved, quiet, formal, and immaculate. His lithe frame helped his golf game. A former infantry soldier, he belonged to the American Legion, the Rotary, the Elks, and, of course, the temple, but did not aspire to leadership roles. His life centered around his wife, Corinne Pupkin Shapere, a Tennessee native sixteen years his junior and a divorcée from nearby San Benito. Pert and petite with emerald eyes, Corinne read the Sunday New York Times, ordered blouses and suits from New York and Houston, and was mother to one son, Dudley, from her first marriage. She and Leon dated for several years before marrying in the late 1930s.[37]

Corinne's bookkeeping expertise landed her a permanent spot behind the cash register at the Perl Brothers' store. Like a fixture, she sat at her cashier's stool throughout the business day, munching for lunch a grapefruit or salad that Leon delivered from the drugstore. When customers entered, Leon talked quality, price, fabric, and design. When customers departed, he returned to his wife's side, leaning against a counter, looking over her shoulder, chatting softly, closing his eyes, and catching a catnap.

Leon assumed that stance so often that the weight of his body wore a circular depression in the red-and-white checkered linoleum floor.[38]

Corinne ran the store and grew to function as Leon's eyes, for his vision, never perfect, dimmed each year. On the golf course, his caddie had to point him toward the greens. Yet Leon never delegated the task of carrying the day's receipts to the bank. He counted his paces down the street. Leon also never forgot the way to the store's water cooler. Inside the tank's refrigerated compartment, he stashed a bottle of whiskey and a dish of kosher pickles, the latter to hide the alcohol on his breath.

"He was the sweetest alcoholic," recalled his niece.[39]

Sam, on the other hand, was a Scotch-on-the-rocks man, an incurable storyteller who relished a drink and a joke among friends. He was forever tugging open gents' jackets, good-naturedly inspecting garment labels to make sure their clothing was from his store. One day an irritated acquaintance sewed an Edelstein's Mattress label in the lining of his sport jacket, and Sam was stunned. "Since when has Edelstein started making men's clothes?" he muttered.[40]

When business was slow, Perl Brothers lured customers with the promise that buyers could set their own easy-payment terms. Ben Freudenstein, a coffee-break crony, got the best of Sam. He paid a nickel a week for a new suit and insisted that he be mailed a receipt. As the months went by, the deal cost Sam so much postage and aggravation, he settled for less than full payment just to be rid of the bookkeeping and the ribbing.[41]

Sam Perl's busy routine took him home at lunchtime for a hearty meal, a thirty-minute nap, and in later years, episodes of *As the World Turns*. If a Kiwanis luncheon altered his routine, Sam reminded his wife to take notes on the soap opera. Sam also interrupted his afternoons with a quick drive to radio station KBOR–1600 AM. Beginning in the late 1940s, listeners heard Sam Perl's *Views on the News*, a daily five-minute monologue sponsored by the Fashion and packed with folksy hometown happenings. On the air, Sam's favorite word was "copacetic," a southern term possibly derived from the Hebrew phrase *kol b'seder*—everything is in order. His signature expression was, "At Poil Brudders we do lo-o-o-ve eva'body."[42]

Sam was beloved in return. Cohorts suggested that he run for mayor. Sam declined, convinced that politicians made enemies. "I want to have friends, friends, friends," he told his protégé, Emilio "Capi" Vasques, the Mexican immigrant who rose from stock boy to eventual owner of the Fashion.[43] Sam preferred to be Mr. Friendship, a title he was awarded in 1969 at a six-hundred-seat banquet attended by Texas senator John

Tower—a Republican he never voted for—as well as compadres from both sides of the border.[44] Guest speakers recalled the rowdy Chamber of Commerce junkets Sam led into the Mexican interior, trips during which a busload of Brownsville boosters toasted informal trade agreements with south-of-the-border towns. Sam's devotees also recalled how he shrewdly stockpiled Arrow shirts before the war. "Ahhrrr-row," his Mexican customers called the popular label. When white shirts were scarce, Sam doled them out to regular customers. He also set aside one Arrow for each hometown soldier returning from the war.

A DIFFERENT WOMAN

Sam's wife, Stella, unlike Leon's spouse, was private and introspective, a homebody who "took a lot of tending," her children recall. Some termed her emotionally fragile and distant. Prone to depression, she played a less active role in her children's upbringing than Sam—who kissed the youngsters good-bye every morning when he drove them to school. Daughter Frances was born in 1929. Her younger brother, Seinwil, born in 1934, derived his nickname—"Ito," which he legally added to his name—from the Mexican maids who endearingly called him "Samuelito." Many among Brownsville's middle class employed Mexican American workers as full-time household help. At the Perls' residence, housekeepers Felicitas, Toni, and later Morena were part of the family, a team that kept the two-story house immaculate and the kitchen humming. They adored Sam but confided that Stella was not an easy boss. At mealtime, she rang a handheld bell to summon the help to serve the next course. A number of family friends privately said that Sam's involvement in the synagogue and the community gave him the appreciation and reinforcement he did not get enough of at home.

Stella had endured a troubled childhood. Born in Indianapolis, she was the daughter of Isaac "Ike" Cohn, a Russian coat tailor who gambled away his wages and walked out on his wife and three children. Deserted, Stella's mother, Czech-born Hannah Lorber Cohn, moved her household to Houston and the embrace of a large extended family.

As a young woman, Stella worked as a milliner at Levy Brothers dry goods store. She and Sam had met during the High Holy Days in 1921, outside Houston's Congregation Beth Israel, introduced by another girl Sam had dated. Sam liked Stella's style and sensed her need of a caretaker. She

Stella and Sam Perl partying in Brownsville during the early 1960s.
Courtesy Frances Perl Goodman, San Antonio.

appreciated his attentions—constant compliments plus cards and flowers on Valentine's Day. The couple became engaged, but he broke it off. In early 1928, when he went back to Galveston for a hernia operation, Rabbi Henry Cohen's daughter, Ruth, suggested that Stella visit the hospitalized Sam. Their romance was quickly rekindled, and the couple planned a wedding for September 9, 1928. In the months preceding the ceremony, they corresponded daily between Houston and Brownsville: "I don't want you to worry a minute about your financial abilities in doing for me," Stella wrote on July 27, 1928. "You know, darling, that I am so happy with your love and whether we will be rich or poor will not matter so long as we always love each other. . . . I hope you are not worrying about the burden of taking unto yourself a wife. For you know, honey, I am not accustomed to riches. My demands will be very small."[45]

Two weeks before the wedding, Stella was stricken with appendicitis, and the doctor prescribed bed rest and an ice pack. Surgery was postponed until after the wedding, but Sam would later joke about his bride being packed in ice. The couple canceled their New York honeymoon plans: Broadway tickets, restaurant reservations, and a visit to his brother Joe, now a professor of classical languages. The newlyweds instead took the train to San Antonio for an overnight stay before Stella returned to Houston for surgery. Sam made the three-hundred-mile train ride home to Brownsville alone, bringing the couple's wedding gifts. The Jewish women of Brownsville unwrapped the presents and set up the Perls' new apartment with such efficiency that Stella never tracked down who gave her each gift.

Stella never stepped into the public role of *rebbitsin*, a term for rabbi's wife that implies maven, mixer, and ministering arm to the community. Although she was a charter member of the Brownsville Junior League Service and the Mercy Hospital Ladies Auxiliary, she was not one for the limelight. A regular synagogue-goer, she preferred the pews to the podium, but inevitably drew attention to herself because her armful of charm bracelets jangled as she fanned herself during the service. Hurricanes terrified Stella. During one Gulf Coast storm, she persuaded her husband to check the family into the Fort Brown Hotel, where Sam held court for out-of-town journalists covering the hurricane. The Perls's house weathered the storm, but the Brown Hotel lost its roof, drenching Sam and Stella.

Stella resented Corinne, her sister-in-law. Corrine directed style-show benefits on both sides of the border; she stored her furs in the refrigerated compartment at the Laundromat; she supervised the religious school and played piano at the temple. Stella almost never stepped inside the family store. The Fashion was Corinne's domain. For years, the sisters-in-law did not speak. Stella kept her distance from Corinne until Leon's death in 1969. As the sisters-in-law shared their grief, they finally grew close.[46]

THE TEMPLE NETWORK

Because Stella was no rebbitsin in the larger sense of the term, Sam found a substitute in Betty Rubinsky, a Lithuanian immigrant who came to Brownsville, like many congregants, by way of Mexico. A pious mother of four, Betty was not only versed in religious traditions, she observed them to the letter. Her journey to Brownsville began at the same time as Sam's, only hers was an odyssey, a pilgrimage that took years. Betty's fiancée, Josef Rubinsky, had fled Lithuania in 1926 to escape a twenty-year term in the army. Because America's immigrant quotas were full, he settled in Mexico and wrote for Betty to join him. She followed a year later, with the ship's captain marrying the pair on board the vessel before she stepped ashore.[47]

The newlyweds kept a kosher home, slaughtering chickens with a sharp knife to the jugular vein as prescribed in Jewish tradition. Beef did not present a problem, because they could not afford it. Josef worked as a peddler, traveling into the mountains to trade with Indians, then marketing his wares on Mexico City's streets, using a blanket as his display case. A son, Simon, was born in 1928. The next year the family moved north to the mountain city of Monterrey, then in 1933 to Matamoros. Their desire was proximity to Texas and ultimately American citizenship. After five years of Mexican residency, they were eligible for entry to the United States. Ironically, Mexico's immigrant quotas to the United States were full, but Lithuania's quotas were not. In the mid-1930s, Betty and Josef Rubinsky and their Spanish-speaking children moved across the bridge to Brownsville with the designation "Lithuanian" stamped on their visas. Spurned as "Juden" in Lithuania, labeled "Europeans" in Mexico, the Rubinskys entered America and found themselves called "Hispanics."[48]

At the little synagogue on West Eighth Street, the Rubinskys were among a cluster of Eastern European Jews who disapproved of Sam Perl's Americanized style of worship, and withdrew to another room to stage an alternative service. In an alcove without chairs, they stood at prayer, cloaked in fringed prayer shawls, moving forward and back, mumbling Hebrew verse by rote. Josef chanted the weekly Torah portion in a rich, soothing voice that filtered into the main chapel, filling Sam with nostalgia.

The Rubinskys were not only fellow Jews, but also Sam's neighbors. Rapprochement was in order. Betty and Sam casually conducted a series of neighborhood summit meetings. Sam wanted to recruit Joe Rubinsky as *hazzan*—Torah reader. However, the Rubinskys refused to enter the sanctuary unless, out of respect for tradition, the entire congregation donned yarmulkes and *talaysim*—skull caps and prayer shawls. A compromise was struck. Religious garb became required attire for participants in the worship service but optional for congregants seated in the pews.

Once Betty Rubinsky became part of Beth-El's inner circle, the temple gained a mistress of traditions. She taught Hebrew to youngsters, tutored bar mitzvah candidates, and reminded Sam about rituals for minor holidays such as *Succoth,* the fall harvest festival, and *Tu'Bshvat,* a Jewish arbor day. Her son, Simon, recalled, "They had a common interest: giving a Jewish education to the children."

MEET RUBEN EDELSTEIN

If Sam was the rabbi and Betty the unofficial rebbitsin, Ruben Edelstein stepped in to act as *shammes*—the caretaker or synagogue supervisor. Born in Brownsville in 1918, Edelstein got drawn into the workings of the temple when it was deeply in debt. A social hall had been added in 1951 with a partial donation from descendants of the Bollack family, but completion had saddled Beth-El with a $34,494 mortgage. With only thirty-five Jewish families and little formal organization, the temple had difficulty enough meeting its operating budget.

Edelstein went to work with a committee that turned the synagogue into a nonprofit religious corporation, exempt from property taxes. Bylaws were written and a board of directors, of which Perl was a perpetual member, oversaw administrative affairs. A dues structure was initiated and a committee appointed to maintain the historic cemetery. The number one goal was to straighten out the temple finances.

Edelstein made sure the mortgage payments were met. Edelstein supervised the cemetery. Edelstein served as temple president. Edelstein organized Israeli bond drives and United Jewish Appeal dinners, although Sam, the convivial master of ceremonies, generally got the credit. "I didn't need it," Edelstein said. "Sam was a good spokesman. He was a lot of show and no go as far as getting the nails and bolts together. He let someone else do that."[49]

Leave it to Sam to dream up the most imaginative money-raising scheme of all—poker games following Sabbath worship services. "That was the only way we could get a minyan to services and to pay off the social hall," Edelstein conceded. The Friday-night poker tradition lasted more than a decade, then evolved into a weekly social event at couples' homes. The husbands played poker while the wives played mah-jongg. Home-cooked food and homegrown stories rounded out those evenings.

THE FINAL JUDGMENT

Another sure money raiser for the congregation was the raffle. The person entrusted with pulling the winning ticket from the bowl was the Jewish community's Catholic friend, U.S. District Judge Reynaldo Garza. "Everybody would trust the federal judge," Garza explained.

Born in Brownsville in 1915, Garza had mingled with Jews as far back as his memory stretched. His aunt Victoria was a buyer for Bollack's Department Store. His father, Ygnacio Garza, a Mexican immigrant and a Brownsville bank accountant, served as pallbearer at many a Jewish funeral. During the 1950s, the Perls and Garzas lived catty-corner from one another on Hibiscus Circle and double-dated to community functions. "I knew Sam long before I finished law school," Garza recalled. "Sam was a good friend of my brother, Ygnacio, auditor of the housing authority. My brother bought clothes there [at Sam's store]. I did too." Reynaldo Garza's first suit was a Perl Brothers' purchase—ten installments at five dollars a week. The occasion was his 1939 graduation from the University of Texas Law School.[50]

Garza also occupied a seat at the table when the downtown boosters met for morning and afternoon coffee. When President John F. Kennedy appointed Garza the nation's first Hispanic federal judge in 1961, the kaffeeklatsches moved to the federal courthouse, where they were timed to coincide with the judge's morning and afternoon recesses. Elevated to the Fifth U.S. Circuit Court of Appeals in 1979, Garza chose his friend Sam Perl to deliver the benediction at the induction ceremony.[51] Garza had also appointed Perl "unofficial federal court chaplain." His chief duty: delivering a nonsectarian prayer at naturalization ceremonies, a cherished proceeding for both men.

"'Lay Rabbi Sam Perl' was the way I'd introduce him," Garza said. "He gave the same prayer so many times, I used to tell him I knew what was coming next. I told him if he ever forgot a word, if he ever hesitated, I'd be able to finish off for him. . . . It was a good invocation, too. He was a good preacher."

The courthouse connection brought business to the Fashion. Garza required that male jurors wear jackets and ties, although some had never owned formal attire. Jurors who looked as if they could afford new apparel were steered to Sam's clothing store three doors up the street. The others had their choice of three coats and ties, supplied from Sam's sale rack. "One tie was a bright yellow," the judge recalled. "One poor guy, the coat was four inches too long, and he got picked to serve on a jury." The juror, obviously uncomfortable, returned the next day in a suit from his own closet. Another juror, a large man with a belly hanging over his belt, wore a Perl Brothers' jacket that was so tight it strained at the seams. With it he wore the bold yellow tie, day after day during a tax evasion case that went on so long, the judge began to see the yellow tie in his dreams. "I told Sam, 'Come and see what you did to this poor guy.'"

Like Sam Perl, Reynaldo Garza was observant of his religion, attending morning mass and becoming active in the Knights of Columbus. Both men were multilingual and proud of their ethnicity. Garza knew a few Yiddish phrases, and Sam spoke passable Spanish—enough to make a sale, a deal, or marry couples in Mexico. The two friends were active in politics, Sam calling himself a "one-lever Democrat" and Garza leading a Valley group in the 1950s named Democrats for Eisenhower.[52] Tall and imposing like Sam, the judge rivaled his friend as kibitzer and storyteller. Both could put a comical ending on the most serious tale.

"EXTRA! EXTRA!"

"Sam Perl, Missing." *"El Millonario Sam Perl Perdido."*[53] The media in Mexico and Texas broadcast an alert on March 15, 1977, that men's clothing merchant Sam Perl, a personification of the border's multicultural mix, had vanished. Had he been spirited away? Crashed into a ditch? Kidnapped by bandits who had just robbed a Matamoros bank?

The Civil Air Patrol pressed a Cessna into service. Ham radio operators activated the airwaves. Customs and Border Patrol officers joined the alert as law enforcement agents on both sides of the river combed the countryside. Brownsville's chief of police set up a command post inside Sam's two-story house alongside Judge Garza, who maintained telephone contact with federal authorities.[54]

The seventy-nine-year-old haberdasher was still a fixture in the life of the lower Rio Grande. He was last seen driving from his house at 2 P.M., en route to a Chamber of Commerce meeting to deliver the invocation. Sam had stopped home at noon for his usual hot meal, half-hour nap, and the day's episode of *As the World Turns.* After adjusting his tie and pocket handkerchief, he had kissed Stella good-bye.

Thirty minutes later, sister-in-law Corinne Perl, at her perch behind the cash register at the Fashion, received a phone call from the chamber. They were delaying the meeting for Sam. Was he at the store? At 6 P.M., when KBOR radio did not broadcast Sam Perl's *Views on the News,* concern spread among the town of forty thousand that something was amiss.

Mayor Ruben Edelstein hurried to Perl's house to assess the situation. He found Morena, the housekeeper, hysterically wailing, "He's dead. He's dead." [55] Stella was calm, perhaps tranquilized. Sam's dog, fattened on kosher salami, caught no scent of his master. Dropping by to offer support and elicit information were Sam's flock from Temple Beth-El, including Harry Lawrence, a rabbi hired four years earlier as director of education to work in tandem with Sam, who was slowing with age.

Afternoon wore into evening and then a starry night. Perl's grown son, Ito, an engineer, was en route from Dallas. Grandson Herbie had dropped in unexpectedly after his bride-to-be got sick from an overdose of sun at Padre Island. Daughter Frances, in New York for installation on the board of the National Council of Jewish Women, boarded a series of flights to rush back to her hometown.

At ten o'clock the next morning, Sam was discovered, dazed but unhurt. Disoriented, soaked in sweat, with the car doors flung open, Sam Perl had spent the night parked on the shoulder of a highway in Olmito—the still-undeveloped town site that lured him to the Magic Valley half a century before. The diagnosis was never clear (a stroke? high fever? dehydration?). But the result was. During Sam's six-week hospitalization, the rest of the family decided that he and Stella would move to San Antonio and live near daughter Frances for the rest of their lives. [56]

Once Sam recuperated, he became his old self, mingling with new friends in San Antonio and being elected president of a Jewish senior citizens club. He corresponded with his Brownsville friends. The temple raised money to purchase for Sam a Torah rescued from the Holocaust. At an emotional ceremony in 1978, he donated the scroll to the synagogue.

From San Antonio, Sam telephoned Garza with a special request. He wanted copies of those Mexican newspapers that had headlined Sam Perl as a missing *millonario.* "If you can get ahold of any of those newspapers, I want as many as I can," he told the judge. "I want to show people that in Mexico, they think I'm a millionaire." [57]

Sam Perl never accumulated a million dollars, but he may have made a million friends. When he died August 5, 1980, his flock along the border did not forget him. The city of Brownsville renamed a street in his honor. A broad, four-lane highway leading to a border crossing, Sam Perl Boulevard is a path between cultures, a bustling monument to the legacy of the lay rabbi.

8

A Reverence for Art

ALEX AND ELEANORE KLINE, LUBBOCK

A LECTURE IN LONGHAND celebrating some ancient pharaoh's tomb fills one page of paper. The reverse side contains a different view of old age—a typewritten note to Rabbi Alex Kline warning that his pension plan premium is past due. Another sheet of paper outlines the Chinese dynasties from Shang to T'ang. The flip side bears the orange-and-blue logo of the Howard Johnson Motel where the rabbi lodged when he penned those thoughts. A third set of notes explains Buddhist art—on the back of a Girl Scout Council budget. And a fourth—scribbled on the blank side of discarded circulars—follows Cleopatra's legend from hieroglyphics to Hollywood.[1]

Aesthetic on one side, humdrum on the other, the art-history files of Rabbi Alexander Stanley Kline fill sixty-eight dusty boxes stacked against a wall at the Museum of Texas Tech University. Categorized by era and artist, these archives preserve the junk mail, the faraway thoughts, and the scholarly research of a small-town rabbi who recycled paper before the term was coined and interpreted the art of the ages to a country-western town. Before he died in 1982, Rabbi Alex Kline had spent the last two decades of his life lecturing at the regional museum in Lubbock. There, in a room now named after him, he enthralled West Texans with his humble, cut-and-pasted art collection: a lifetime of illustrations clipped from books and magazines, each glued to cardboard or brown paper and arranged in sequence to illustrate art from the pyramids to Picasso.

That Kline's title was rabbi—not curator or Ph.D. in art history—concerned no one. "This is West Texas. Nobody cares about your credentials if you can produce," said Winifred Vigness, former director of the West Texas Museum Association, which sponsored Kline's lecture series. "If you can build a better mousetrap, who cares if you went to Mousetrap University?"[2]

Moreover, the rabbi's expertise extended to music, literature, and philosophy. Eager to share his insights, the rabbi broadened the avenue—from commerce to culture—that linked Lubbock's seventy-six Jewish families to the rest of the populace. With Rabbi Kline at the lectern, fine arts became the region's universal religion.

BIRTH AND BACKGROUND

If Kline was not a professional authority, his reverence for art seemed intuitive. Religion and art were entwined in his Hungarian upbringing. His mother, Regina Katz Klein, was a seamstress who specialized in fine needlework and passed on her fascination for color, design, painting, and architecture. She traced her family tree to the Katzenellenbogens, a rabbinical dynasty that dated from the sixteenth century. Her husband, Joseph, the grandson of a Hungarian rabbi, was injured during the Austro-Hungarian War and returned home in 1912 partially paralyzed. He worked as a tinsmith, fashioning objects from metal. The family lived in Budapest where Alex, born June 18, 1902, was the oldest of four brothers, two of whom died in early childhood. Because of his father's disability, Alex was a breadwinner from an early age, learning to scrimp and save for things he valued. The lad's intellectual curiosity went hand in hand with his religion. His family adhered to Hungary's Reform Jewish movement, called Neology, a school of thought that stressed intellectual rather than spiritual and mystical elements of Judaism.[3]

To escape the poverty and political instability of Europe, Alex emigrated to the United States in 1921. His first step toward Americanization was changing the spelling of his surname from Klein to Kline—a modification more consistent with the rules of English usage. For an immigrant like Alex, fluent in six European languages, employment was not hard to find. He worked as a translator at a Pittsburgh bank that specialized in foreign currency. At night, he studied English and earned a high school equivalency certificate. A lucrative career in international finance was assured, but money was not what motivated him. The tug of his past persisted.

Kline attended services at Pittsburgh's Temple Rodeph Shalom and was captivated by the rabbi, Samuel Goldenson, a noted orator and advocate of social justice who wore a handsome silk top hat. Goldenson, who became a mentor to Kline, was a 1904 graduate of Hebrew Union College. Kline followed his path, moving west to the Cincinnati seminary campus in 1926.

Older than most students by four or five years, Kline found himself out of step with his classmates. Ideologically, he was a Zionist who believed that a Jewish nation would and should materialize in the Middle East. He was among the few students who sat at Professor Abraham Idelsohn's Hebrew-speaking table in the campus dining room, for he considered Hebrew a living language—a minority view twenty years before the creation of Israel. Also setting Kline apart was his Hungarian accent. Tirelessly, he worked with elocution instructor Cora Kahn to eliminate all traces of Europe from his diction. He nearly succeeded, for his speech retained only a faint Hungarian rhythm and a trill when he said words such as "thrrree."[4]

Art remained Kline's favorite pastime. In his dormitory room, he religiously cut out pictures of paintings and pottery, pasted them onto brown wrapping paper, then sorted them by subject into bundles he tied with string. When he accumulated one hundred pictures by a single artist, he turned the pile into a subject file of its own. "He was an amateur critic of art with a capital A," Professor Jacob Rader Marcus recalled.[5]

For Kline's rabbinical thesis, he examined the historical tension between Judaism and art. Because the Second Commandment forbids graven images and because the biblical prophets rage against "elaborate personal adornments," Jews were historically slow to produce the tapestries and tableaux that nourish artists' souls. Yet, Kline reasoned in his thesis, houses of worship are "sermons in stone, color, and stained glass. . . . Art is the eternal articulator of the soul of humanity, . . . the permanent expression and record of his best experiences." Art and religion share a "profound kinship" touching the spiritual realm.[6] He could not get enough.

PERIPATETIC RABBI

Upon Kline's ordination in 1933, the seminary placed him at a pulpit in Jackson, Tennessee (pop. 22,000), the remote hometown of legendary railroad engineer Casey Jones. Kline's congregation was small, his twenty-five-dollar-a-week salary meager, and his art history talks unappreciated.

Rabbinical student Alex Kline, senior picture from Hebrew Union College Monthly, *June, 1933.* Print from Jacob Rader Marcus Center of the American Jewish Archives, Cincinnati, Ohio.

Disappointed and disillusioned, the novice thirty-one-year-old rabbi could not help but believe that had he been younger and American-bred, a more sophisticated, urban congregation might have hired him. After a year in rural Tennessee, Kline negotiated a move to a slightly larger congregation in Asheville, North Carolina, a picturesque Blue Ridge Mountain town of fifty thousand.

Between jobs, Kline attended a summer rabbinical conference in Philadelphia, where an acquaintance arranged a blind date with twenty-four-year-old Eleanore Florence Spitz. Eleanore was a third-generation American, a Philadelphian pursuing a Ph.D. at the University of Pennsylvania in paleography—the study of ancient languages and inscriptions. On their first date, Eleanore knew she had met her match when Alex corrected her

Latin as they discussed the syntax of "hocus pocus." Like magic, the pair were engaged three days later and married within ten weeks on August 28, 1934. Her widowed father, a physician, was dismayed at the marriage because he lost his caretaker. Her mother, who had died three years before, would probably have been pleased. She had wanted Eleanore's brother, Armand, to become a rabbi, but he had dropped out of the seminary and ultimately soared to prominence in the field of astronomy.[7] Eleanore, too, left college behind. She was prepared to share the rest of her life with Alex in the combined roles of *rebbitsin*, intellectual partner, travel companion, financial manager, housekeeper, and chauffeur—because he never learned to drive.

The newlyweds moved to Congregation Beth Ha-Tephila (house of prayer) in Asheville, where their son, David, was born in 1935 and their daughter, Susanna Rose, early in 1938. The family's next move, in the fall of 1938, was to the Gulf Coast oil town of Port Arthur, Texas, near the Louisiana line. The Klines enjoyed Texas and the camaraderie of rabbinical couples serving in nearby Beaumont and Galveston. They vacationed at the Galveston shore, always dropping in at the home of Rabbi Henry Cohen, whose two-volume, unabridged dictionary on a tall wooden stand impressed young David Kline. Alex and Eleanore especially enjoyed the annual *Kallah* of Texas Rabbis, the scholarly symposium attended by rabbinical couples from the Lone Star State's Orthodox, Conservative, and Reform synagogues.

The Klines remained at Port Arthur's Temple Rodeph Shalom until 1943 when they realized that a dip in the local economy and a drop in the Jewish population were probably long term. The rabbi opted for an interim position at El Paso's Temple Mount Sinai while that city's Reform rabbi served as a World War II chaplain. Kline's three-year stint in El Paso, a border city with two synagogues and twenty-three hundred Jews, was a happy interval, passing all too quickly. The parsonage—a two-story brick-and-stucco home on a hillside—was walking distance from the synagogue, which had a busy gymnasium and a membership of several hundred families. The family dog, Kelly, followed the rabbi on his morning walk to work. All four of the Klines learned Spanish, mingling comfortably in the bilingual region. One summer, they took a two-day train ride to Mexico City and spent a month in the Latin American capital, with the children attending a Mexican school while their parents researched pre-Columbian and Aztec art. Back home in El Paso, the rabbi's art history lectures were popular at civic group meetings. He could have contentedly spent the rest of his career in El Paso, but the close of the war found him searching for a vacant pulpit.

Skeptically, Rabbi Kline accepted a position in Jamaica, New York, a suburban Queens congregation uncomfortable from the outset with his political and religious views. "They insisted he not speak about Zionism, the A-bomb, or Yiddish—all topics close to his heart," the rabbi's son recalled. Yiddish, the mother tongue of Eastern Europe's Jews, is a poetic language that the rabbi loved to quote and joke in. The atomic bomb, although it had brought World War II to an end, troubled the rabbi, who questioned what it might lead to. Zionism, the other taboo, was a pressing concern. Europe's homeless Jews had nowhere to go except to displaced persons camps. The Promised Land of old seemed the most humane destination, for the Holocaust had exposed the extent and depravity of anti-Semitism across Europe. Kline's own father had perished in 1943, when Nazi soldiers invading Budapest ordered elderly and disabled Jews lined up against a wall and machine-gunned to death. The personal tragedy, which Kline painfully pieced together from news accounts and never discussed with his children, intensified his commitment to his heritage.

At Jamaica's Temple Israel, tension grew and tempers flared. ("Rabbi, you always talk about the suffering Jews abroad. We are Americans.". . . "Rabbi, you sound like a communist!" . . . "Rabbi, we are sick of all this Zionist propaganda."[8]) Fed up, the rabbi resigned before his first year was up. During the summer of 1947, the family moved in with Eleanore's brother in Lansdowne, Pennsylvania, and Alex scrambled to find a job— his sixth pulpit in fourteen years.

The only position Kline could land was in Clarksdale, Mississippi, a Delta town of sixteen thousand residents, seventy miles south of Memphis. Resigned by then to spending his career in rural America, Kline promised his children stability, pledging to stay put until both youngsters were grown, so they would have a place to call home.

But adjusting to the Deep South was not without difficulty. David, age twelve, entered school after the term had begun, wearing a suit more appropriate to P.S. 163 in New York than the more casual E. Dorr Junior High in Clarksdale. "They called me a 'damn Yankee,'" bristled David, who had spent all but one year of his childhood below the Mason-Dixon line. His sister Susan formed a circle of friends yet found the town cliquish, with a pecking order dating back generations. "I was never an insider," she recalled. "I was not asked to be in a high school sorority, although some Jewish girls were. They were born there, and their heritage was there."

Clarksdale's Temple Beth Israel offered the rabbi a modest salary, supplemented with a house and later a new car from the local Chevrolet dealer. Grateful to have a rabbi, townspeople showered the family with professional courtesies. For the High Holy Days, the rabbi was presented a custom-fitted suit from Shankerman's. Eleanore enjoyed discounts from Sebulsky's Style Shop and other retail stores. The rabbi's favorite small-town perks were the movie passes that the Tyson Theatre extended to all clergy.

The Klines lived in Mississippi during its last years of segregation, before the arrival of the Freedom Riders demonstrating for change. White residents scarcely mixed with black residents, except those hired as domestics. Although this county seat was more than 50 percent African American, few white people were familiar with the Delta blues music that made Clarksdale a popular stop for blacks traveling from Arkansas to Memphis.[9] After the U.S. Supreme Court's 1954 ruling to integrate public schools, Clarksdale and the rest of Mississippi defied the mandate, with White Citizens Councils flourishing throughout the state. Although Kline was not an activist preacher and disagreed with rabbis who marched for civil rights, residents knew where he stood. He preached "in code," said son David. He discussed race relations on an abstract level, talking about ideals of equality and the belief that all people are created in the image of God. He urged congregants not to "conform" like their neighbors— meaning not to be racist. Kline did not betray his conscience, but he walked a tightrope. He needed to keep his job.

Clarksdale's Jews had their own peculiar problems. They were blackballed from the country club on the hill and knew good and well which gentiles would not patronize Jewish stores.[10] Kline perceived one aspect of his role to be the Jewish representative to the community at large. He became president of the Clarksdale Ministers Association and adviser to the Hillel Jewish students foundation at Ole Miss—the University of Mississippi at Oxford, a two-hour drive to the east. His passion for art made him a favorite with the local chapter of the American Association of University Women, which sponsored his weekly art lectures at the Carnegie Public Library. The rabbi was again disappointed that his lectures drew few Jews.

Conversely, the Jews were perturbed by Kline's preoccupation with art. Temple Beth Israel's membership covered a large swath of rural Mississippi, and there were plenty of pastoral duties. Some of the congregation's 110 families journeyed fifty miles to attend Friday night worship services, a social event for Delta Jews. "We never missed a Friday night," recalled

Shirley Levine Weinberg, who served as president of the Hadassah chapter launched by Eleanore. "Our social life was the temple." The Sunday School faculty consisted entirely of parents, all dedicated volunteers teaching Judaism to the next generation. They worked under Eleanore, who supervised the religious school. She also taught Hebrew to bar mitzvah students, for the rabbi was short on patience with preteens who would have preferred a less intellectual rabbi, someone more approachable and sociable with kids.

On the rabbi's part, he introduced more music into the worship service, most notably organ accompaniment that more traditional congregants were averse to. He obliged Orthodox members by hiring a *Ba'al Tefillah*— literally a master of prayer—for the High Holy Days so that those preferring traditional worship could *daven* separately. The Orthodox often convened for an early morning service; Reform congregants prayed from midmorning until noon, when the Orthodox reconvened. Although the sanctuary was small, Kline kept different strands of Judaism functioning under the same roof.[11]

The rabbi also kept his promise to his children, remaining in Mississippi for thirteen years until both offspring graduated from Bobo High School and completed college. David went to Brandeis University in 1953, then followed in his father's footsteps at Hebrew Union College. Susan went to the University of Illinois, graduated from Sophie Newcomb College in New Orleans, then married a Houston boy, Raymond Brochstein, at a Clarksdale wedding in November, 1959.

By then, the rabbi and Eleanore were ready and eager to depart Mississippi. Long uneasy with the state's racial and political climate, the Klines were among the few whites in town who supported the presidential candidacy of John F. Kennedy.[12] Alex Kline, already fifty-eight years old, was beginning to think about retirement but unable to afford it. He looked around for one last pulpit to sustain him into his final years and was intrigued by an opening in Lubbock, a West Texas county seat of 128,000 people. The city had one synagogue with two hundred Jews from seventy-six families. The salary in Lubbock was low—$5,800 after ministerial deductions—but included a six-room parsonage. The location was remote —327 miles northwest of Dallas—but Alex and Eleanore had grown accustomed to out-of-the-way places, and Texas had proven hospitable in the past. Culturally, the region was best known for the rock 'n' roll beat of Buddy Holly, but it was home to Texas Technological College, a respected state school moving toward university status. The surrounding landscape was nothing much to look at—a flat, parched, and treeless terrain on the edge of the Great Plains—but sunsets turned the evening sky into a palette of colors.

LUBBOCK'S PAST AS PROLOGUE

Organized Judaism began relatively late in Lubbock, the hub city of an arid farming region blessed with underground water. Lubbock's first Jewish family arrived in 1916, opening Grollman's clothing store. A second couple, the Kessels came in 1920, and a third couple, Jenny and Louis Feldman, became the proud parents in 1927 of Lubbock's first native-born Jew—a boy named Marvin. Not until 1929, when men's clothing merchant Morris Levine arrived, were there enough Jews for communal observance of Rosh Hashanah and Yom Kippur. That year, fifteen families—some driving ninety miles from Hobbs and Clovis, New Mexico—borrowed a Torah and rented a room at the Lubbock Hotel for High Holy Day services. Most of the participants were first- and second-generation Americans, traditional Jews with Eastern European roots, worshipers accustomed to praying in Hebrew. Although few kept kosher kitchens, they observed some of Judaism's dietary laws by refraining from shellfish and pork.[13]

The Great Depression drew additional Jewish retailers to Lubbock, an oasis of economic well-being thanks to bumper crops of cotton. "It was called the 'white spot' on the map," Norma Glassman Skibell recalled. Her family had moved there in 1932 after the banks closed in Electra, two hundred miles farther east. Another newcomer in the early thirties was Charles Laskey, a Kansan who persuaded his Orthodox friend—salesman Moshe Forbstein of Kansas City—to lead Lubbock's annual High Holy Day observance. From these beginnings evolved Congregation Shaareth Israel— Hebrew for remnant of Israel—chartered in 1934. Still, Lubbock's Jewish population was sparse. When Chicago architect Sam Kelisky and his Russian-born wife, Sadie, arrived with their two sons in 1937, they were the city's fifteenth Jewish family. Of those families, most were retailers advertising their names on downtown storefronts: Grollman's Fashion, Jaretts' Cinderella Shop, Levine's Department Store, Kligman's Pawn Shop, Kay's Mercantile, Houstman Dry Goods, Freed's Ready-to-Wear, and Leva's Hungarian Café.[14]

Outside of their busy shops, most Jews remained clannish, with low visibility in the general community.[15] Although the men joined the Masons, the Lions, the Elks, the American Legion, and the Veterans of Foreign Wars, and the women volunteered for Red Cross charity work, Jews mostly socialized among themselves. They were so few. Friday evenings were special with the lighting of the Sabbath candles at home and traditional foods on the table. There were often dinner guests—one or more Jewish traveling salesmen who made sure their routes put them in Lubbock for the weekend. Saturday and Sunday nights, Jewish couples gathered in homes to play cards while their teenagers turned on the radio and danced to pop tunes. Once a year, the Jewish community rented the ballroom at the Lubbock Hotel, set up card tables, charged fifty cents for cakes and sandwiches, and played pinochle, gin rummy, casino, and poker until the wee hours.[16]

As the only Jewish youngster in her public school class, Norma Glassman Skibell recalled how self-conscious she felt at Rosh Hashanah and Yom Kippur, when she missed school because of the religious holidays. Her absence underscored the fact that she was different from her classmates. Passover, the eight-day holiday when Jews eat no bread, was also difficult. She took a sack lunch to school and ate matzo instead of joining her friends for fifteen-cent burgers across the street at Logan's.[17]

Of course, being part of a close-knit Jewish community had its rewards. Everyone took pride in Shaareth Israel's first synagogue, a converted dwelling at Sixteenth Street and Avenue X remodeled into a "treasured house of worship." Every congregant was invited to Lubbock's first Jewish wedding in 1940—the marriage of Sarah Favorman to Ben Beaird. For the nuptials, the congregation invested in a *chuppa,* the canopy under which a Jewish bride and groom take their vows. Some doubted that the chuppa would ever be used again, but in January, 1941, Norma Glassman and Albert Skibell became the Jewish community's second pair of newlyweds.[18]

Officiating at both weddings was the community's first rabbi, Isadore Garsek, whose initial visit to Lubbock in 1938 was as a "supply rabbi," sent from Chicago's Hebrew Theological College to conduct High Holy Day services. The Jewish community invited the "yeshiva boy" to stay on as full-time rabbi. Garsek accepted, returning after his 1939 ordination, despite warnings from teachers who feared he was going to *ek-velt*—the end of the world. Garsek wanted a secular education and realized that he could enroll at Texas Tech and earn the bachelor's and master's degrees his yeshiva had not offered. That September, he matriculated at Tech. In November, he attended a Hadassah convention in Fort Worth, where he met Sadye Maye Carshon, a native Texan whom he married in June, 1940. The couple lived in Lubbock until 1944, when Garsek reported for active duty as an army chaplain. Immediately postwar, he was hired by Ahavath Shalom, his wife's synagogue in Fort Worth, where he spent the rest of his career.[19]

Lubbock had trouble replacing him. Over the next sixteen years, five rabbis came and went. "They didn't like us or we didn't like them," explained Skibell. One purported rabbi had bogus credentials and a mail-order ordination. "We were stunned when we found out," Skibell said.[20] Another rabbi unilaterally introduced the *Union Prayer Book,* a Reform Jewish prayer book with next to no Hebrew. "The congregation came into the temple to pray and found their books mysteriously gone," relates an account of Shaareth Israel's history. "Overnight, the congregation went from Orthodox to Reform."[21] The new books remained, but not the rabbi. Lubbock's next rabbi could not adjust to the Texas heat and wore shorts beneath his pulpit robes. His wife went bare-legged, refusing to wear nylons, a fashion faux pas regardless of the temperature. In a breach of faith, the same rebbitsin submitted a pork chop recipe to the Sisterhood cookbook.[22] When the congregation began searching for yet another rabbi during the summer of 1960, worshipers prayed for a rabbinical couple who would be as contented with Lubbock as they. They got their wish.

ART MEETS RELIGION

As Alex and Eleanore Kline packed up their household for a move from Mississippi to Texas, the Women's Council of the West Texas Museum Association was planning Lubbock's first extensive art exhibit. Museum Director W. Curry Holden had arranged to borrow a cache of original art from a Dallas couple that was redecorating their penthouse, leaving for Europe, and in need of a place to store fifty oils. The museum had no money for professional movers, much less insurance, so Holden's wife, Fran, and her friend, Pauline Bean, drove to Dallas to pick up the paintings. Loading the canvases in the back of a van, they trucked the multi-million-dollar art collection to Lubbock. Once the paintings were hung, the organizers realized they were at a loss to interpret the priceless Renoirs and Raoults for the public. "We had no idea what we were doing," Bean recalled. In what seemed a miracle of good timing, the *Lubbock Avalanche Journal* reported on August 5, 1960, the arrival of Rabbi Kline, a connoisseur of art whose private collection included "80,000 reproductions, . . . one of the largest in the nation."[23]

"It was just an act of God," Pauline declared. "We knocked on his door." Intrigued, the rabbi accompanied the women to preview the exhibit. Midway through the galleries, he paused by French artist François Raoult's cubist portrait of a colorful clown. "I'll never forget the rabbi's words," Pauline recalled. "He said, 'The artist's palette was like ground-up jewels.' After that, we were in the palm of his hand. We were insatiable for him—and for Eleanore."

Before long, the rabbi was delivering a series of well-attended lectures at the museum—with Eleanore his stage manager and partner. While the rabbi spoke of mummies and mosaics, Eleanore stationed herself in the back of the room operating the opaque projector. If the rabbi confused Rococo with Baroque, Eleanore corrected him. If he stumbled over a date, she piped up with the year. "There was a lot of banter back and forth," recalled a regular lecture-goer. The sixty to one hundred people who enrolled each semester in the ten-week seminar series felt well acquainted with the couple by the end of the course.

Among the lecture-goers were the region's elite: university faculty members, bankers, women's club presidents, officers' wives from Lubbock's Reese Air Force Base, and executives from surrounding towns. To the rabbi's delight, the audience was sprinkled with Jews from Shaareth Israel. The prestige of a museum setting had raised the rabbi's reputation from amateur to aficionado. He lived up to his billing, proving to be an artist with words. The Italian painters, he told his classes, thought of art as theater, with every "room and ceiling a stage and every scene a lively tableau."[24] The rabbi's favorite building the world over was the Parthenon, which displayed a "harmony of proportions like a piece of music . . . its seeming simplicity deceptive."[25]

Every October, the fine arts critic at the *Avalanche Journal* publicized the upcoming lectures, describing Kline as a "virtual volcano of knowledge, spewing up facts in unexpected emotional eruptions."[26] Everyone talked about how the rabbi made sense of contemporary art. Cubism came together like a jigsaw puzzle when the rabbi discussed Picasso. Impressionist paintings were no longer a blur of images, but "canvases with color and the brilliance of the sun." Pop artists, like the outrageous Andy Warhol, were serious thinkers who took a "confection of vulgarities" from honky-tonks and grocery shelves and transformed them into something permanent and arresting.[27] The rabbi did not overlook religious art, recounting biblical stories, like the temptation of Eve and the beheading of John the Baptist, that inspired famous canvases. The Bible, he noted, is also art: a literary anthology packed with drama, mythology, and verse.

The rabbi's lecture series led to guest appearances at campus philosophy classes and guest sermons from church pulpits. Lubbock's Methodists still remember the Sunday morning that Rabbi Kline conducted the eleven o'clock worship service at the First Methodist Church. "He didn't stand back in a corner," said Pauline Bean. "Everything was so easy with Rabbi and Eleanore."

Eleanore, too, guest-lectured at the university. Her topic was Roman family life. She spoke to Protestant Sunday School classes about Judaic customs and lectured around town about Jewish food, although she wasn't much of a cook. One season her culinary talks emphasized the Passover seder, the ritual meal that was also Jesus' last supper. From that season on, local churches started hosting Passover seders at Easter time.

"Before, there had been little interaction with the Jews, other than businesswise," observed Pauline Bean, whose family rented retail space to Levine's Department Store. "The town had been very clannish. There was no animosity. There was no crossing over. The Jews kept themselves secluded. The Klines bridged the gap between the Jewish community and the gentile community. It traveled on the back of art. . . . They opened the door."

Eleanore was best known for her monthly Conversations in Literature series at the public library. Her focus was bestsellers. Although her favorite author was Nobel laureate Saul Bellow and her favorite discovery was William Least Heat Moon, she was comfortable reviewing pulp fiction from Danielle Steel to Sidney Sheldon. No literary snob, she believed that popular books "reflected the age in which we live." However, if a novel was poorly written, she advised readers to use "the good old Jewish custom" and start the book from the back.[28]

Short, trim, and energetic, Eleanore generally dressed in tailored suits accented with artistic jewelry fashioned from polished stones and purchased in museums on trips abroad. Cats-eye glasses framed her eyes, and her salt-and-pepper hair was softly brushed back into a bun. In high heels, she stood five-feet five-inches, half a head shorter than the rabbi. Every photo of the pair in the *Avalanche Journal* shows her gazing up into his smiling face. The rabbi, too, was neat, trim, and formal, with a halo of

Rabbi Alex and Eleanore Kline brought their devotion to Judaism and reverence for art to Lubbock in the 1960s and 1970s. Frank Pontari, © *Fort Worth Star-Telegram.*

white hair on his balding pate, deep blue eyes, glasses, and always a suit and tie in public. "He was a rabbi you were proud to be seen with," Norma Skibell said.

If members at Shaareth Israel had a problem, however, they were apt to approach Eleanore, not the rabbi, for she was more flexible. "She kept an edge on his temper," congregant Bobbie Freid recalled. "He had a short fuse. . . . She'd say, 'Now, Daddy.'" That would help calm him down. Eleanore had a knack for smoothing over differences, whether they involved liturgy, ritual, or parents upset at the rabbi's frustration over bar mitzvah students. Rabbi Kline was driven to exasperation by his Texas students' enunciation and tried in vain to remove the drawl from their Hebrew.[29]

Just as Eleanore had taken charge in Clarksdale, she took command at Shaareth Israel, which by the 1960s was housed in a red-brick, L-shaped building at Twenty-third and Avenue Q. The sanctuary had seating for sixty worshipers, with double the capacity when bridge chairs were set up in an adjacent social hall. Eleanore ran the religious school, was active in the temple Sisterhood, and served two years as its president. Because Eleanore looked after day-to-day temple activities, the rabbi had the time to focus on arts and antiquities. "I would be completely helpless without her for even one day," the rabbi told the *Avalanche Journal* in 1973.[30]

Well into his seventies, the rabbi continued lecturing on the pulpit about Judaism and off the pulpit about art. Buoyed by appreciation and adulation, he worked well beyond retirement age, becoming rabbi emeritus in 1980. When he died March 29, 1982, after a heart attack at the age of seventy-nine, two lectures remained on his spring seminar series.

Jews as well as Christians gathered at the rabbi's house to mourn. In accordance with Jewish law, a minyan convened in the Klines' living room to participate in evening prayer services throughout the next week. Pauline Bean, a Methodist, was surprised at the open grieving she witnessed in the Kline household. As the days passed, the tears abated. People reminisced. By the end of the week, the atmosphere was more upbeat. The week of "sitting *shivah*," as the Jews refer to it, proved therapeutic for non-Jews as well.

Alexander Kline's lecture series did not end with his passing. Seven weeks after the rabbi's heart attack, Eleanore delivered the last two seminars in his Chinese art series. The next season, and into the next century, the lectures continued with scholars from Texas Tech University behind the podium.[31] Eleanore remained in Lubbock for four years after the rabbi's death, then moved to be closer to her children and grandchildren. She stayed in touch with her Lubbock friends until her death in Houston in 1993.

The cultural climate the Klines nurtured in Lubbock did not wane. Alex and Eleanore Kline helped set creative forces in motion: The museum expanded its offerings; an increasing number of classical music groups performed in the city; and the public library received Jewish books donated in the rabbi's memory. The *Lubbock Avalanche Journal* automatically wrote up Jewish holidays. Jewish parents routinely visited public school classrooms to explain the significance of menorahs and matzos. The Klines had sparked a great deal. They fostered relations not only between the Jewish and gentile worlds, but between a remote Texas region and the realm of fine arts.

Alex Kline, a Hungarian immigrant seeking to wed religion and art, had reached his zenith in Lubbock during the last two decades of his forty-nine-year career. At previous pulpits in Tennessee, North Carolina, New York, and Mississippi, he had tried to broaden his congregational flock through art history talks. Instead, he encountered indifference. Ironically, a West Texas region best known for its heritage of two-stepping music and rock 'n' roll was ripe for his message.

Reflecting on the contradictions of his ministry, Kline wrote an essay in midcareer about "The Rabbi in the Small Town." Outlining his professional journey, he observed that a rabbinical student often graduates from the "stimulating atmosphere" of the seminary into the "arid environment" of a backwater town where he is "compelled" to live with the "Philistine" products of "provincial" America. "Can this richness of mind and spirit continue to grow in the shallow soil of the average small town?" he asked. "Shall these dry bones live?" Cynicism takes over unless the rabbi, who is paid a paltry wage, learns to appreciate the challenges the "provinces" afford. Because small-town Jews see their Christian neighbors going to church, they too want spiritual inspiration, comfort, pageantry, and ceremonial beauty. "They want to be preached to and exhorted." They want biblical knowledge, albeit simplified and popularized. They want a rabbi who will visit their homes and become their friend. They want a "goodwill ambassador" to the community. A small-town rabbi's personal influence goes much deeper than an urban rabbi's.[32] Concluded Kline: "Rather to be a big frog in a little pond, they say, than a little frog in a big pond. . . . Where there are a thousand rabbis, what authority rests with one? Where there is only one, everything depends upon him. . . . The rabbi serving in a small town need not become a small town person."[33]

9

Evolution and Dissolution
of a Pulpit

EPHRAIM AND RUTH COHEN FRISCH,
SAN ANTONIO

THE IMAGE OF THE SHABBY BRIEFCASE haunted Lewis Lee. Clutching that battered leather attaché case was Rabbi Ephraim Frisch, the religious leader who had been an inspiration to Lee and other young adults coming of age in San Antonio between the world wars. Now Ephraim Frisch, sixty-four, was rabbi emeritus of Temple Beth-El, a title that belied his forced retirement and self-imposed exile to New York on a pension of $333.35 a month. Lee had encountered the rabbi in 1944 on a train bound for St. Louis. Upon his return to San Antonio, the Texan contacted several Frisch disciples, who chipped in to send their mentor a new briefcase.[1]

Frugality of pocket and fragility of spirit had led the usually well-attired rabbi to neglect his accoutrements. Depression, widowerhood, and a nervous breakdown had contributed to his debacle two years before at San Antonio's Temple Beth-El. Bitterness had followed. A volunteer stint with a rabbinical Social Justice Commission had fizzled in anger. In the New York apartment the rabbi shared with his sister, he toiled over a book he would never complete. He spent a year revising a philosophical article for Phi Beta Kappa's quarterly journal. He took predawn baths to ease his arthritis. Occasionally, he performed marriage ceremonies for interfaith couples grateful to find a tolerant rabbi who would unite them. Annually, the rabbi emeritus sent his Texas congregation a note with Jewish New Year greetings and a donation for prayer books. Simultaneously, he wrote New York's Congregation Emanu-El requesting a complimentary High Holy Day seat for himself, a courtesy extended to retired rabbis.[2]

This was what had become of Ephraim Frisch, the courageous rabbi who from 1923 to 1942 had stirred San Antonio's younger generation to strive for a better world. To them he was a rabbi who preached ethics rather than piety, a progressive who backed unions over industry, and a visionary who foresaw the rise of fascism in Europe. Their memories enshrined him as a "giant of justice," a man of erect posture, just under five-feet eleven-inches tall, with a serious gaze behind wire-rimmed bifocals, a broad forehead, and a fringe of chalky hair crowning his pate. Formally attired, he dressed for success with pointed starched collars, bow ties, pinstripes in winter, and dapper white jacket and light trousers in summer. He was an intellectual who read hieroglyphics for "personal satisfaction," a teacher who allowed teens to question the existence of God, and a highbrow who scorned *Time* magazine as a "smart alecky sheet." He angered hawks with his opposition to ROTC, and he caused a stir in Jewish circles when he blessed the hogs at the stock show.[3]

In his lonely retirement, Frisch sifted through news clippings, letters, and sermons accumulated during four decades in the rabbinate. He savored his triumphs. He drafted a magazine article, then a longer memo touting the times he had stood up for social justice.[4] He wanted the victories, not his defeats, to be his legacy. An embarrassing episode involving President Woodrow Wilson was among the papers he discarded. Letters tracking his flirtation with the incendiary anti-Zionist American Council for Judaism were removed from his files destined for the American Jewish Archives. His affiliation had been a mistake, which he renounced in 1943 as soon as he saw the movement turning away from religion and toward slick public relations. Such episodes would not go on Frisch's list of battles for social justice, the legacy he thirsted for.

One of Frisch's favorite skirmishes involved a bill that sought to outlaw the teaching of evolution in Texas' schools. Frisch wrote a column for the *San Antonio Express* in 1929 ridiculing the measure and received a letter of support from an angora goat rancher, a stranger spurred to action by the rabbi's words. The rancher, a Protestant, planned to reprint Frisch's column, distribute a copy to every Texas legislator, and undermine the measure.[5] The rabbi's pro-Darwin column also elicited a letter of censure from a dean at the University of Texas Medical school. Intellectually, the dean endorsed the rabbi's views. But he berated the rabbi for taking a swipe at academicians too "timorous" to challenge the legislature. The dean reminded Frisch that most Texas lawmakers were "country people" who firmly believed "that God created the world . . . in 6 days of 24 hrs. each." Provoking the politicians could lead to a curriculum that declared "the earth is flat."[6] Rabbi Frisch had more faith in Lone Star legislators than that. He believed evolution to be in step with God, Judaism, and Texas. He warned that Texas would become "the laughing-stock of the nation" if lawmakers banned discussion of Darwin's seventy-year-old theory of the origin of the species. "Evolution reveals God as the great designer," he wrote.[7]

The rabbi and the goat rancher never met, yet they were the victors in this fracas. In March of 1929, the anti-evolution bill died in the Texas House of Representatives.[8] Ephraim Frisch—a prophet to some, an irritant to others—had broadcast his unpopular views and triumphed again.

THE ALAMO CITY

Outspoken Ephraim Frisch was a rare clergyman in San Antonio, the Lone Star State's largest city throughout the 1920s, with a population that climbed to 231,000. A historic frontier town, San Antonio had grown up around the Alamo, a Catholic mission turned fortress, which had become a crumbling landmark with a gas pump at the curb. Historically a magnet for the military and a mecca for tourists, San Antonio was a segmented metropolis. Thousands of soldiers assigned to Fort Sam Houston mingled with the general populace in the shops and the rooftop honky-tonks, yet cultivated a military milieu that set them apart from the city. The eighty-two thousand Mexican Americans—half of them Tejanos or Tex-Mexicans whose family trees predated Anglo settlement—added an international accent to the landscape in their service role as gardeners, maids, and custodians. They too retired to their own world, a four-square-mile slum with no running water, several families per wooden shed, and high tuberculosis and infant mortality rates. San Antonio business leaders touted their town's abundance of cheap, unskilled labor available for a dollar-fifty to seven dollars a week. The Chamber of Commerce boasted of the town's healthy sunshine that drew tourists and asthmatics to the tile-roofed hotels. Absent from San Antonio was the civic boosterism that elsewhere in Texas fostered public works and public charities. Parochialism prevailed. Too much of the population was rooted elsewhere to care. An Irish-Catholic political machine ran city hall. Most of San Antonio's clergy exhibited what a national magazine condemned as "ministerial mildness," crusading against pinball machines and pornography rather than poverty and disease. The clergy tended to ally with business interests and console the masses with platitudes.[9]

Jews were 2 to 3 percent of the populace, three thousand people in 1920 and six thousand by 1930. Many of these Jews were retailers, a number of them factory owners grown wealthy off the low wages paid the Mexicans. The old-guard Jewish families were largely American-born descendants of nineteenth-century German immigrants. These proud German Jews tended to be high-end merchants, bankers, pecan distributors, and members of Frisch's Temple Beth-El, the city's oldest Jewish congregation. Less well-to-do clusters of Eastern European Jewish immigrant families operated retail stores and pawn shops concentrated in "Little Jerusalem," the three-block area stretching from city hall, across San Pedro Creek to Santa Rosa Street and the Mexican slums. These small storefronts—with names like *La Feria, La Estrella,* and *El Nuevo Mundo*—catered to the Latinos with such items as first-communion apparel and low-priced wedding dresses. Soldiers swarmed the area on payday, ordering chevrons, ribbons, and hand-sewn military insignia for their uniforms.[10]

Besides Frisch's Reform congregation, founded in 1874, the city had two, more traditional, synagogues: Agudas Achim (union of brothers) and Rodfei Sholom (pursuers of peace). The two shuls offered a mix of Hebrew worship and Old World nostalgia that appealed to more recent immigrants. Another segment of the Jewish population was unaffiliated with any synagogue, yet these people were culturally and intellectually Jewish just the same. These were the secular Jews, the "socialist Yiddishists," refugees radicalized by the currents of change and hope in Eastern Europe.[11] Some were members of the Arbeiter Ring, Yiddish for the Workmen's Circle, a fraternal order and mutual benefit society with long-term socialist goals. These talkers and theorists found San Antonio a lively ideological environment. In their midst were political exiles from Mexico—south-of-the-border socialists who had fled revolutionary turmoil. The Mexican expatriates and Jewish theorists were drawn to San Antonio politician Maury Maverick, Sr., who served as New Deal congressman, then mayor. They were all drawn to Ephraim Frisch's liberal agenda. Maverick used to drive to the rabbi's house—in his Model A Ford with his son, Maury, Jr., in tow—and join old-timers of different ethnic backgrounds as they thrashed out the ideas stirring across the world.[12]

ASCENT TO THE PULPIT

Frisch's predecessor at Temple Beth-El was Rabbi Sidney Tedesche [Tedésk-ee], a specialist in Greek languages who sermonized in generalities. Well liked for his comforting pulpit presence, Tedesche participated in ecumenical meetings across the city, then complained privately about anti-Semitic slurs—for example, an archbishop who "flashed the dollar" when he discussed Jews, and a Protestant colleague who "Jesus-Christed" everyone in his secular remarks.[13] Tedesche did not challenge such affronts. When other Texas rabbis acted in concert to censor the performance of a touring vaudeville act that featured Jews kissing dollar bills, Tedesche did nothing "except express regret that it was found impossible" to stop the show in San Antonio.[14]

In June of 1923, Tedesche resigned the San Antonio pulpit after two years in Texas to accept a call to New Haven, Connecticut. A behind-the-scenes campaign ensued to fill the vacant Texas pulpit. Leaders of B'nai B'rith's Anti-Defamation League lobbied for "a good, conscientious worker in San Antonio," a rabbi who would speak out on social issues previously ignored.[15] Rabbi Henry Cohen, Texas' rabbinical patriarch, had just the candidate: his son-in-law, Ephraim Frisch.

Frisch, a forty-three-year-old New York rabbi, had been searching for a position during the previous year. He had applied to a Tennessee synagogue, but Nashville's Congregation Ohabai Sholom rejected him in November, 1922, because his sample sermon was delivered in too strident a style.[16] New Haven also turned Frisch down in the summer of 1923, preferring the smoother Tedesche. That left a vacancy in San Antonio. An eager Ephraim Frisch wanted to apply immediately and wired his father-in-law in Galveston for advice. Cohen, Texas' senior rabbi, had already been speaking confidentially with San Antonio's temple president. The savvy elder rabbi wired his New York son-in-law: "Do not apply for the position. You must be called."[17]

San Antonio Jews were accustomed to auditioning applicants for the pulpit via trial sermons—a test Frisch might fail. Rabbi Cohen convinced temple president Morris Stern, a former Galveston resident, that rabbini-

cal auditions were becoming passé. He suggested a casual summer meeting between the temple president and the prospective rabbi, perhaps in
Williamstown, Massachusetts, where the Cohens and the Frisches planned
to vacation before the summer meeting of the Central Conference of
American Rabbis. The elder rabbi noted that many San Antonians were already acquainted, personally or by reputation, with Ephraim Frisch and
his wife, Ruth Cohen Frisch. The description of the couple's wedding
seven years before in the Texas Jewish press had gushed with superlatives.[18]

Over the summer, excitement built in both the Reform and Orthodox
communities around the possibility of luring Rabbi Cohen's relations to
South Texas. The maneuvering worked. On December 3, 1923, without a
tryout, Frisch was called to San Antonio's Temple Beth-El. Six hundred
people heard Frisch's first sermon, a message about spiritual goals and
righteousness that was written up in the morning paper.[19] San Antonio's
entire Jewish community seemed pleased to have landed a rabbi with
such a pedigree. Reform Jews basked in their pulpit's link to Galveston's
celebrated Rabbi Cohen—diplomat, humanitarian, and statesman active
in Texas since 1888. The more traditional Jews at Congregation Rodfei
Sholom and Agudas Achim extolled Frisch as well. "Temple Beth-El has a
renowned leader . . . son of pious Orthodox Jews, grandson of a rabbi,"
wrote Alexander Gurwitz, an Old World rabbi working as a kosher
butcher and Hebrew teacher. "He joins with the Orthodox rabbis, and
with the entire Jewish community in community endeavor."[20]

Frisch's first challenge to community standards came four months later,
when the local school board endorsed compulsory Bible reading in the
classroom. The new rabbi mailed an eleven-page, typewritten letter to the
editor: "I love the Bible, but I believe the places where it is best taught are
the church, the religious school, and the home," he wrote. "I myself would
not foist the Jewish Bible on any Christian or anyone else."[21] The Bible-
reading policy remained, but Frisch's entry into the debate kept the controversy alive. Later, when Protestant clergy asked the school board to
award scholastic credit for religious classes taken at church, Frisch defeated the measure.

Inside the Jewish community, the new rabbi participated in the San An-
tonio Jewish Social Service Federation, a charity network founded in 1922.
"Since we organized the Federation, there seem to be ten or fifteen San
Antonians in trouble every day," Frisch wrote his father-in-law in March,
1923, "and we are attracting the *tsoros* [misery] of the whole county."[22]
That same month, congregant Hannah Hirschberg alerted Frisch that the

Texas Federation of Women's Clubs was barraging Capitol Hill with telegrams in support of tighter immigration restrictions—measures Jews opposed. Frisch encouraged her to "get on the job" and ask other women's clubs—Jewish and non-Jewish—"to challenge that action." He asked his father-in-law to "muster forces in Galveston."[23] Frisch was responding exactly as Rabbi Cohen and the Anti-Defamation League had wished. He seemed part of a team poised to handle controversy.

During his second year in Texas, Frisch sparked tempers and admiration with a Sabbath sermon urging Filipino independence. At the close of the service, a congregant who had recently returned from an around-the-world trip rushed the pulpit and challenged the rabbi with a pointed finger: "That man is using the pulpit for political propaganda. What does the Rabbi know about the Philippines?" The rabbi quizzed the man, then pounded a fist on the podium and declared: "This pulpit must be free, or else I will not serve as your rabbi. If the congregation by a vote should declare that it is not free, I'll resign immediately." The congregation broke into applause.[24]

The rabbi kept speaking out, prepared to make any issue his Alamo—a defeat that would call others to action. He proposed an American boycott of the Berlin Olympics because of Adolf Hitler's ban against Jewish athletes.[25] He preached an end to the poll tax that blocked poverty-stricken Mexican Americans from voting. He argued for elimination of Jesus' name from public ceremonies. (His preferred appellation for Christ was "Rabbi of Nazareth."[26]) He urged charitable donations to the Pro-Falasha Committee, a group he had cofounded in New York to aid black African Jews in Abyssinia.[27] During the Roosevelt years, Frisch once stepped in front of his pulpit and exhorted congregants to vote for FDR and the New Deal—a plea that led a number of business leaders to walk out.[28]

HIS BETTER HALF

Ephraim Frisch's career mate and soul mate was his spouse, Ruth Cohen Frisch. The pair met at the University of Chicago's International House while enrolled in summer classes. He was thirty-five and she was twenty-five when they became engaged in July of 1915. He was a lively intellectual, conversant in world literature and abreast of articles in *Harpers,* the *Nation,* and the *New York Times.* Her intellectual expertise extended to music. She had studied piano at New York's Damrosch Conservatory and given piano lessons in Galveston on her family's baby grand. She also drew sketches to illustrate her recitals, published articles on music and Judaism, and wrote poetry lamenting war:

> *Loath to her labor repairs the Muse*
> *Over the page she bends*
> *Dips the pen in the scarlet ink*
> *Pauses and thinks—for the task offends.*
> *Slowly she writes: "On an August day*
> *In 1914 the world arose*
> *And went to battle." She cries aloud:*
> *"God that I might this chapter close."* [29]

Born in Galveston in 1890, Ruth was the first of two children of Rabbi Henry and Mollie Levy Cohen. She was B.O.I.—"born on the Island," a Galvestonian boast. The Cohens' parlor was a crossroads for all creeds and castes—from visiting dignitaries to paroled ex-convicts. Laughter was a key ingredient of the Cohen household, from naughty limericks to Jewish jokes. Ruth's public school education was classic Texan, and her elementary school papers record the catechism of dates she mastered: "Washington's Birthday is on Feb. 22; San Jacinto Day is on April 21; Texas Independence Day is on March 2." [30] An energetic child with brown pigtails, she produced plays in the attic—"admission, one pin"—romped at Galveston's seashore, and played outdoors with neighborhood children after school. [31] After dinner, she copied her schoolwork into lined-paper notebooks while her parents worked on their own civic projects. [32] She graduated from Ball Senior High in 1907 with high honors and kudos for her success on the literary magazine and the tennis team. As a young adult, Ruth hosted a musical group of six high school seniors—a "combination of talk, performance, cookies and lemonade." [33] Later in life, she invited whole classes of teenage Sunday School students into her parlor.

Ruth's radiant smile reflected her upbringing. Her face projected inner calm and warmth. A large woman unadorned by jewelry or makeup, she had plain features—bushy eyebrows, a straight nose, and a square jaw. Her hair was dark and straight, parted at the side and blunt cut above the earlobes. Her brown eyes were steady and strong, and her gaze, kind and matriarchal. Like Eleanor Roosevelt, she had an aura that lit up a room. [34] "She was outgoing and talented," recalled Helen Gugenheim Jacobson. "She could have been a concert pianist. She could have been a rabbi." [35]

Ruth Cohen Frisch in 1931, three years before her death from Hodgkin's disease. An educator, writer, and musician, she was the daughter of Galveston's Rabbi Henry Cohen and the wife of San Antonio's Rabbi Ephraim Frisch. Photo taken by Cones Studio, San Antonio. Courtesy Rose E. Frisch, Cambridge, Mass.

Engaged for a year, Ruth Cohen and Ephraim Frisch married in New York on August 17, 1916. The maid of honor was his sister, Janet. The best man was Ruth's brother, Harry, then working in the advertising department of the *New York Times*. The officiating rabbi, of course, was her father. Two hundred close friends, relatives, and congregants celebrated with a reception at the Gotham Hotel. Afterward, the couple honeymooned in Maine.[36] The newlyweds meshed like fine-tuned machinery. "She was the governor on his motor, a steadying influence," recalled Lewis Lee. She smoothed his harsh edges. The couple's liberal political views coincided, but Ephraim was the brusque, uncompromising Yankee, Ruth the soft-spoken southerner. A political argument from her lips seemed more palatable, less antagonistic. She was perceived as the ideal *rebbitsin:* "a strong right arm to the rabbi, and a ministering angel to the community."[37] During the wedding weekend, Ruth's mother proudly informed the Frisch clan of her German-Jewish roots and antebellum American lineage. The Frisches made no pretense of their origins. They joked that if they designed a family coat of arms, the insignia would picture a Baltic Sea herring wrapped in newspaper.[38]

FRISCH'S PAST

Descended from seventeen generations of rabbis, Ephraim Frisch traced his roots to the environs of Vilna (Vilnius), Lithuania, a center of Jewish learning under czarist domination. His maternal great-grandfather was Alexander Sender, a brilliant rabbi referred to as a *gaon,* or genius. This ancestral rabbi had written a nineteenth-century volume analyzing contracts and vows in the Talmud, the compendium of Jewish law annotated with centuries of rabbinical interpretations.[39]

Ephraim Frisch, born October 1, 1880, in Shubocz, Lithuania, immigrated to America in 1888, entering the United States through Duluth, Minnesota, on Lake Superior. Eight-year-old Eph [Ee-ff], as he was nicknamed, had journeyed with his older brother Sol to join their father, Rabbi David Frisch. Many Frisch relatives had preceded them to the region. Ephraim's father initially found work as a Hebrew teacher and *shochet* in Duluth. His wife, Hannah Baskowitz, and two-year-old daughter, Frieda, soon joined the rest of the family. During the next twelve years in Minneapolis, the family increased with the birth of five girls—Sarah, Janet, Ruby, Florence, and Helen. The Frisch youngsters grew up with a backdrop of labor conflict—epic battles that pitted landowners against lumber barons, farmers against grain-mill merchants, miners against steel manufacturers, and everyone against the railroads, which levied exorbitant shipping tariffs. Frisch kept abreast of current events, for he was a newspaper boy hawking extras on street corners, and apparently doing quite well because a customer bought him a navy blue sailor-boy suit to wear on the job.

Frisch's extended family remained enmeshed in crosscurrents influencing turn-of-the-century Judaism. One cousin, Leo Frisch, became director of Minneapolis's Galveston Immigration Bureau as well as editor of *American Jewish World.* An uncle, Rabbi Joseph Frisch, championed the

Haskalah, the Jewish enlightenment movement that encouraged study of secular texts. Eph's father, a six-footer with flowing beard and high fluted hat, followed the tenets of Orthodox Judaism. Still, he was pleased when Eph received a scholarship in 1896 for the eight-year course of study at Cincinnati's Hebrew Union College. Eph planned to carry on the rabbinical tradition, albeit in a modern branch of Judaism. Four years later, Eph's father was called to a pulpit in Union City, New Jersey. A short time after the move, tragedy struck. The Frisch patriarch died at age forty-three when a sore on his neck festered and proved fatal. In lieu of a widow's pension, his wife received a cart, a horse, and a kosher-meat delivery route.[40]

In his period of mourning, son Ephraim focused more energy on his studies. He won gold medals in Latin and oratory. He wrote for the *Hebrew Union College Monthly*, most noteworthy a witty essay about the Jewish predilection for secondhand merchandise. ("Jacob got his birth-right secondhand from Esau, and ever since the Jews have been dealers in old clothes.")[41] Frisch impressed classmates and future generations with his initiative by editing the seminary's first college annual in 1904. The 640-page volume featured scholarly pieces from faculty members and European Jewish thinkers, photos of graduates, and ads from Cincinnati matzo makers and multilingual print shops.[42]

Frisch's first pulpit was a world away in Pine Bluff, Arkansas, a forested, antebellum river town, home to the state's oldest Hebrew congregation— Anshe Emeth (people of truth), chartered in 1867.[43] Despite its isolation, this town with dirt-packed streets and twelve thousand residents had a sizable Jewish community—133 families with sixty students in the Sabbath School. Pine Bluff's Jewish residents had achieved local prominence: the city's oldest bakery was Jewish-owned, and a number of the town's Civil War veterans were Jewish. Scars from the war pocked the county courthouse, a limestone landmark occupied in 1863 by Union soldiers who barricaded themselves in with bales of cotton. Cotton bales were still essential to Pine Bluff, now for economic security. In a sarcastic newspaper column, Rabbi Frisch scolded the populace for paying closer attention to cotton bales than to social ills such as tuberculosis ("white plague"), school dropout rates ("people do not value a High School education sufficiently"), and juvenile crime.[44]

During Frisch's Arkansas tenure, from 1904 to 1912, he turned public attention from cotton bales to social action. He was founding president of the state's first county tuberculosis association. He spearheaded construction of the state's first public playground. He fostered creation of the Musical Coterie, a nondenominational troupe of singers accompanied by the temple organ and piano. The energetic rabbi was founding president of the Arkansas Jewish Sabbath School Teachers Association. When Russian Jewish refugees trickled into Pine Bluff, he launched Willing Workers, a Jewish charity with ninety-one volunteers. And when the refugee community totaled twenty-eight families, he welcomed the establishment in 1907 of a second congregation, B'nai Israel (sons of Israel), which conducted Orthodox services in the back room of a tailor shop.[45]

"The work of Rabbi Ephraim Frisch, who occupied the pulpit for nine years, has been of such far-reaching effect, and is so well appreciated that it is superfluous to elaborate upon it," commented his successor, who penned a fiftieth anniversary history of the temple in 1917.[46] Omitted from the temple's glowing retrospective is Frisch's testy debate with a minister who roused the rabbi's ire by calling the United States a "Christian nation." Frisch challenged the preacher to respond to three sermons debating the issue, but the minister desisted after two rounds.[47] Frisch was similarly peeved when a local paper, the *Daily Commercial,* drew snide comparisons between two famous American Jews: Judah P. Benjamin, a discredited member of the Confederate cabinet, and Oscar Straus, secretary of commerce and labor and the first Jew to serve in the U.S. cabinet. Frisch's reaction, printed beneath a four-column headline, pointed out factual errors and anti-Semitic innuendo.[48] Sensitive to slights, the rabbi in 1908 criticized Arkansas's interim governor, X. O. Pindall, for infusing his Thanksgiving Day proclamation with references to Jesus.[49] Omission of these verbal jousts from the temple history is an indication that the rabbi's sensitivity was not wholly shared by his congregation. Jews and non-Jews alike were especially uncomfortable with Frisch's support of the African American Rev. Isaac Fisher, a student of educator Booker T. Washington and the principal of Pine Bluff's Branch Normal College for Negroes. Under fire from whites and blacks for trying to host biracial gatherings of educated people, the Baptist minister resigned in 1911. Frisch wrote the local paper in support of his colleague's visionary efforts.[50]

By the time his African American colleague departed, Frisch had soured on southern morés. He looked north for a change. His sisters were in New York City, married, working, or raising children. He wanted to be near family and a university. He notified Hebrew Union College and was called to Temple Israel in Far Rockaway, a beach community in Queens. For his inaugural sermon in March, 1912, Frisch impressed the congregation of 160 families as he spoke without notes and quoted the Talmud, Ralph

Waldo Emerson, and Henry James.[51] Frisch's communal involvement continued. His congregation doubled in membership as he established a
temple social service department. That led, in 1914, to the creation of Children's Haven of Far Rockaway, an institution for temporary care of youngsters whose parents were hospitalized or poor.

Frisch's ministry and message appealed to a nucleus of artists and professionals. With encouragement and connections from his fiancée, Ruth,
in the spring of 1915 Frisch became founding rabbi of the New Synagogue,
an idealistic congregation that converted an existing building on Manhattan's West Eighty-sixth Street into a house of worship. The credo of this
congregation, which quickly grew from ten to seventy members, was humanitarian deeds, social action, flexible rituals, and liturgy augmented
with secular readings. Some Temple Israel members followed Frisch from
Far Rockaway. Many others were Manhattanites who had become enamored of Frisch while vacationing at the shore. Notables on the temple roster were sculptor Victor Brenner, the medal designer who crafted Lincoln's
head for the copper penny; Gotham Press editor Menko Wolfe; and social
worker David Bressler, who worked with Ruth's father to settle thousands
of Jewish immigrants across the Southwest. Ruth's music teacher, pianist
Clarence Adler, became a charter member and the New Synagogue's organist. Excitement over the New Synagogue was evident from a feature in
the *New York Evening Post*. The article described Frisch's approach as
"post/Darwin," waxed poetic about his Minnesota "boyhood," and detected in his demeanor "some of the spirit of the West."[52]

Frisch's religious circle included a coalition of Reform rabbis who
opposed Zionism and the 1917 British-issued Balfour Declaration that
promised a Jewish nation in Palestine. Frisch's thinking was typical of
nineteenth-century immigrants who believed that America was their
Zion. In the fall of 1918, President Woodrow Wilson endorsed the Balfour
Declaration in a Jewish New Year note to New York rabbi Stephen Wise.
When Frisch learned of this through an item in the *New York Times*, he
responded instinctively. Consulting no one, he wired the president that
"thousands" of Jews considered Zionism a "menace" and the creation of
a Jewish nation a mistake that would undermine Judaism and the patriotism of American Jews. To ensure that his telegram did not escape notice,
Frisch gave the text to the *New York Times*, which the next day identified
Frisch as acting chairman of a "Rabbis' National Committee" that opposed Zionism. Such a committee, tentatively named the League of Ameri-

can Jews, was in the embryonic stage. Its creation had been rumored but not announced.[53]

The following day, the *Times* reported that three pro-Zionist rabbis had ridiculed the telegram sent "in the name of a nonexistent organization." Publicly, these rabbis questioned Frisch's integrity—an insult that he never forgave or forgot. One of the trio contacted the New Synagogue's board of directors—"with the view of ruining me with my congregation," Frisch wrote his father-in-law, adding, "I went through a terrible ordeal." Even Frisch's colleagues in the anti-Zionist camp privately castigated him for writing the president and running to the press. Frisch's premature posturing aborted the committee's creation. Potential members and donors, including philanthropist Jacob Schiff, distanced themselves from Frisch. The *American Hebrew,* a New York weekly with a national circulation, hurled the final insult: an editorial recapping Frisch's folly identified him as "an obscure rabbi." Ephraim Frisch, the post-Darwin darling with the spirit of the West, now seemed naïve. The luster had rubbed off his rabbinate.[54]

Ephraim turned inward toward his family. Ruth was nursing their six-month-old son, their first and only child, David Henry. Ruth frequently journeyed back to Galveston, staying for weeks as their son grew into a toddler. With motherhood and travel, Ephraim noticed Ruth slowing down. She grew listless and anemic. Still, the doctor's diagnosis was a shock—Hodgkin's disease, a cancer that enlarges the lymph glands, spleen, and liver. With hospitalization, radiation, tender loving care, and Ruth's positive outlook, the disease went into remission.

TEXAS BOUND

The family of three was delighted at the chance to move to San Antonio in December, 1923. Ruth would be closer to home. David would be near his grandparents. Ephraim could start afresh. In San Antonio, the Frisches attracted an immediate following among Jewish teens and young adults. Ruth taught the high-schoolers as well as a college discussion group. Both classes were considered innovations in Texas where a Jewish education generally ended with a thirteen-year-old's bar mitzvah ceremony or confirmation exercises for fourteen-year-olds. The rabbi worked closely with the confirmation class, assuring questioning teens that no philosophical point of view was taboo. Frisch told students it was not unusual to ponder the existence of God or grow skeptical of religious liturgy. He left them guilt free to contemplate. "For him to point out that we had that option was incredible," recalled Bernice "Cris" Cristol Selman, who was confirmed in the 1930s. "Rabbi Frisch didn't criticize or ridicule. He wanted students to work it out for themselves."[55]

Lewis Lee, raised at the Orthodox congregation, Agudas Achim, enrolled in Beth-El's high school classes because his Jewish education at the shul had not gone much beyond the liturgy. "I was looking for more," Lee said. With Ruth Frisch as his teacher, he explored the ethics, history, and philosophy of Judaism. "I started finding answers to religious questions I was thinking about. It was filling my needs. You got a sense of ethics as well as religion."[56]

When the rabbi and his wife organized the Temple League for young adults, Lewis Lee and his wife-to-be, Charlotte Lippman, joined the circle. The league showcased local talent through amateur plays, vaudeville productions—among them a memorable spoof of *I Pagliacci*—instrumental music recitals, debates, and book reviews.[57] The league hosted socials at the Frisches' home and dances at the temple, where Ruth taught Charlotte Lippman the Texas two-step. Ruth steered the most talented young adults to the San Antonio Little Theatre, for which she was a board member. The prestigious playhouse, chartered in 1927, presented the city's first productions of controversial works such as Henrik Ibsen's *The Doll's House* and Clifford Odets' *Waiting for Lefty*, a drama sympathetic to the labor movement. The cross-pollination of talent between the Little Theatre and the Temple League led to collaboration with the San Antonio Civic Opera, whose director produced a Temple League performance of the Broadway hit *Awake and Sing*.[58]

On the civic front, the rabbi worked with educators to create the San Antonio Open Forum, an adult education effort backed by the U.S. Office of Education in cities across America. For San Antonio, this was a rare endeavor, because the open forum sought to include every resident. It staged free public lectures in dozens of venues, drawing participation from every race and domain. Local attorneys, clergy, physicians, educators, and politicians were among the speakers, along with a dozen national lecturers on cross-country tours. At its height in 1938, the San Antonio Open Forum staged 561 meetings, with total attendance of sixty-four thousand. More than one third of the meetings were in "Latin-American" neighborhoods and 10 percent at "Hebrew-American" institutions. The subjects ranged from health and citizenship to entertainment, with musical performances by local Mexican American and African American bands. The Open Forum helped a splintered town come together.[59]

The Frisches' first decade in San Antonio was a happy interlude. Several of the rabbi's sermons were published in pamphlet form—courtesy of congregants dazzled by his intellect. He completed his dissertation—*Historical Survey of Jewish Philanthropy,* published in hardback by Macmillan—and was conferred a Ph.D. in 1924 from New York's Columbia University. Son David, a tall, athletic young man with a knack for sports and physics, celebrated his bar mitzvah on March 14, 1931, with accolades from his father, who noted that his son "wrote his own speech."[60] The rabbi taught part-time at San Antonio College, joined the Rotary, the Boy Scout Council, and the Red Cross and headed the county Tuberculosis Association—as he had in Pine Bluff. His father-in-law got him appointed to the Texas Committee on Prisons and Prison Labor. Frisch's dissenting voice in school board controversies earned him an appointment to a University of Texas child welfare and parent education committee. When famed attorney Clarence Darrow took to the lecture circuit in 1931 to defend agnosticism, Frisch was part of a panel that debated the celebrity lawyer in San Antonio.[61] The rabbi also served on the San Antonio Chamber of Commerce Health Committee, where he attempted to draw attention to the squalor in the Mexican slum.

Frisch loved the podium. His oratory drew positive notice, despite his long-winded nature. (The rabbi joked that his son, David, "razzes me about my sermons, particularly their length."[62]) One Friday night message revolved around the "Revolt of Modern Youth" and was keyed to best-selling books on "marriage, mating, [and] genuine unrest among youth."[63] Other sermons warned of ill winds across Europe, where Benito Mussolini, "that little imitation of Julius Caesar," was guiding Italy toward "colossal" disaster. Only in Russia did Frisch see reason for optimism, because of the "sacrificial spirit of workers."[64]

The rabbi traveled to Mexico, the Middle East, Europe, and England, where he contacted leading thinkers, such as British historian Cecil Roth, who invited Frisch to join a gathering of friends in his living room.[65] Frisch brought home handsome souvenirs to decorate the custom-built stone house the family of three moved into in February, 1929—shortly after Ruth recovered from the mumps. Their Tudor house—north of the city

Rabbi Ephraim Frisch, second from left, before a debate featuring attorney
Clarence Darrow, far right. Panelists at the March 17, 1931, forum, from left
to right: Presbyterian minister Ilion T. Jones; Frisch; Henry B. Dielman, attorney,
moderator, and Open Forum chairman; Quin O'Brien, Catholic layman from
Chicago; and Darrow, who defended agnosticism. Print from the Institute
of Texan Cultures, the *San Antonio Light* Collection.

limits at 130 Luther Drive in Olmos Park Estates—was in a restricted
neighborhood with a property covenant limiting home ownership to
"persons of the Caucasian race and their bona fide servants."[66] The rabbi
was agog at his new home: "Everybody admires the little mansion. Being
now an English squire, you will always see me in knickers," he wrote his father-in-law.[67] A Mexican rug was artistically draped over a sofa. On one
wall hung the rabbi's "best beloved Mexican-wood . . . pictures," one of
them an oxcart scene. Another wall was the backdrop for an Egyptian
frieze of a camel caravan from the time of King Tut—a ruler whom Frisch
always referred to by his full name, Tutankhamen. From Frisch's trip to
Italy was a dark statuette of a lad with a thorn in his foot. The centerpiece
of the living room was Ruth Frisch's grand piano.[68] The kitchen, built with

two pantries, was stocked with Gulf Coast seasonings to spice Ruth's shrimp cocktail and seafood gumbo.

During Frisch's first four years in San Antonio, Beth-El's membership grew from 250 to 390 families. In 1927 the congregation moved into a new synagogue, a $230,000 domed sanctuary at the hilltop crossroads of Belknap and Ashby Places. Two hundred children attended the religious school, which had an impressive High School Division grooming thirty post-confirmands, ages fifteen to eighteen, for "future leadership."[69] In Jewish matters, Frisch was cordial with the city's other rabbis, co-officiating at weddings and funerals.

However, the rabbi spewed criticism at his alma mater, Hebrew Union College, dubbing its administrators "Bourbons" because of ties to affluent benefactors from the business sector.[70] He pushed to reinvigorate the Social Justice Commission within the Central Conference of American Rabbis and served as social justice chairman from 1925 to 1926. The commission's platforms ruffled feathers, in San Antonio and elsewhere, particularly the push for dissemination of birth control information. In that era, such information was judged "obscene" and banned from the U.S. mail. Frisch argued that social workers should hand out contraceptive literature, at government expense, to reach "those who are breeding who oughtn't to breed."[71] The Social Justice Commission also preached pacifism, endorsing war only after a national referendum. It condemned industrialists who refused to mediate with unions, advocated a five-day work week, and urged a "living wage," with salaries sufficient to cover sickness and old age.[72]

IN SICKNESS AND HEALTH

The summer of 1934, Ruth grew weak. A visit to her physician confirmed the couple's fears. Hodgkin's disease, which Ruth had battled fifteen years before, had returned.[73] Radiation therapy had little effect. Ruth returned to her childhood home and the care of her parents. Perhaps the Galveston seashore would invigorate her. Instead, one trip to the beach drained her so much, she entered John Sealy Hospital. Sensing that her illness was terminal, she implored Eph and David not to visit too often, for the sight of them turned her tearful. She reminisced with her mother about childhood ribbons and party dresses. She asked her brother to read aloud the latest issue of *Scribners,* particularly a serialized novel, and to buy the August issue so she could hear the next installment. As she weakened, Ruth called

for Ephraim to sit by her bed and read aloud the Book of Job, the biblical tale of woe about a righteous man who keeps faith in God despite
tragedy.[74]

Ruth slipped into a coma and died August 6, 1934. Her death stunned
Jewish circles across the nation. Just three years before, she had been honored as one of the first women to address the Union of American Hebrew
Congregations. Her subject: "The Ideal Synagogue." She had died in her
prime, at age forty-four. When Dallas's Rabbi David Lefkowitz learned of
her passing, he cut short his family's vacation in Yellowstone National Park
and returned to Texas to mourn: "Ruth's passing . . . took all the joy out of
our vacation." Houston's Rabbi Henry Barnston, in a memorial address,
observed that Ruth means *friendship;* Cohen is the designation for a *priest*
who ministers the Jewish people; Frisch is German for *fresh.* Ruth Cohen
Frisch was the sum of her names, and more. "Her passing away was a
tragedy, but her life was a benediction."[75]

Mourners came by train and caravans of cars. Rabbi Cohen, age seventy, conducted his daughter's funeral in his home. Over her grave, he in-
toned passages from Job: "The Lord hath given, He hath taken away,
blessed be His name."[76] The hard lessons of Job sustained Rabbi Cohen. At
a subsequent funeral for a man close in age to Ruth, Cohen consoled the
parents with assurances that their son and his daughter had traveled into
"the Beyond, which we call Heaven." In his eulogy, the rabbi said, "I cannot but think that I had a forty-four-year-old daughter taken suddenly,
while she was of use to her husband and to the community. I believe that
nothing is haphazard; there must be a plan, which we cannot understand
when we see young people leave us."[77]

The philosophy of Job and the belief in an omnipotent God with a divine plan sustained Rabbi Cohen as he mourned Ruth, who had been a
special angel on earth. His personal theology helped him cope with personal misfortune. Ephraim Frisch's more rational theology offered little
consolation for Ruth's death and the end of their eighteen-year marriage.
His deity was not personal or supernatural. He viewed God as a concept
embodying justice and love, a power moving humankind toward righteousness, not an anthropomorphic being overseeing each human endeavor. Frisch was critical of prayer books that spoke "*to* God instead of
about Him."[78] He interpreted the deity's role in biblical tales as "primitive
conceptions of God long abandoned."[79] If the Book of Job had helped
Ruth and her father face tragedy, it gave no comfort to Eph. In the note-

book where he recorded births, marriages, and deaths of congregants, the rabbi could not bring himself to chronicle his wife's passing.

People close to Eph discerned a change that did not wane. The strain of Ruth's death gave way to impatience and petulance. Confrontation had always been part of his persona, but Ruth had kept his temper in check, along with his public candor. Now the rabbi's combativeness was more apparent. Ephraim's sister, Janet Frisch Klein, moved down from New York for several months at a time to serve as hostess to the congregation and a crutch for Eph, who was losing self-confidence and privately falling to pieces. Criticisms the rabbi had nonchalantly withstood in the past left him shaken. In letters to friends, he later referred to himself as "depressed" and "under the weather."[80] At fifty-four, he felt advancing age. Arthritis afflicted his joints, waking him at dawn, prompting him to take early-morning walks and drop in for breakfast with his neighbors Frances and Perry Kallison. On the pulpit, he hammered away at his core issues—support for Roosevelt, disdain for big business, sympathy for the city's twelve thousand pecan shellers, who cracked and cleaned nuts for six cents a pound. Some of his sermons, particularly one backing the socialist Arbeiter Ring, "brought coals of wrath against him," recalled Frances Kallison. "The people exploiting the workers were very resentful about his sermon."[81]

Beth-El's board of directors objected to stands taken by the Central Conference of American Rabbis—controversial positions for recognition of conscientious objectors in wartime. Frisch's views were no different than his father-in-law's in Galveston, or his classmates' at pulpits in Pittsburgh and Cincinnati. Yet only Frisch was perceived as a radical. The reason may have been that rabbis who shared his views generally spoke out selectively on some issues and worked in coalitions to highlight other ills. Frisch's strident voice, on the pulpit and in the press, raged at almost every cause.

San Antonio, like other large, depression-era American cities, became a cauldron of labor conflict. The philosophical promises of communism and socialism inflamed the underclasses with hope, the upper classes with fear. Nationwide, a visible number of Jews were drawn toward these ideological movements. Many more Jews, particularly the German Jews in conservative places like San Antonio, were wary that radical politics would fan anti-immigrant fervor and strain business relationships with gentiles. A growing faction at Temple Beth-El questioned the rabbi's priorities.

During the summer of 1935, the rabbi's sixteen-year-old son, David, wrote that the temple was run by a clique of "scheming, uncharitable men who hate the poor and make their money from the presence of the Army in our city. . . . I'm boiling over with disgust at them now as I write because of their dislike of Dad from such base motivation."[82]

One reason for their discomfort was that Ephraim Frisch's sermons hit close to home. Labor unions were picketing Jewish-owned businesses, demanding living wages and shorter hours. San Antonio was not like New York or Boston, where activist rabbis had claimed a direct interest in mediating labor disputes that pitted Jewish strikers against Jewish manufacturers. In San Antonio the strikers were the invisible Latinos, the dominant minority with little class, clout, or education. Few local pastors shared the rabbi's righteous indignation for the poor. Jesuit father Carmelo Tranchese, who battled for federal money to clean up the Mexican slums, set up bread lines for strikers and worked with Frisch and the Tuberculosis Association to open health clinics. These efforts were at odds with the work of conservative archbishop Arthur Drossaerts, who built churches with non-union labor and criticized Rabbi Frisch for championing the poor at home and rebels abroad in the Spanish Civil War.[83]

Frisch believed he was following in the steps of the biblical prophets. He felt an "ethical compunction" to fight on the "battlefield of ideas." In a letter to a friendly congregant, he explained, "I would consider it a real honor . . . to be counted among the battlers for human rights."[84]

To Frisch, the most glaring violation of civil liberties in San Antonio occurred on June 29, 1937. Labor union leaders Emma Tenayuca and Robert Williams, accompanied by two hundred laid-off workers, crammed into the corridor outside the Works Progress Administration office in the Gunter Hotel—the downtown headquarters for cattle ranchers. When the shouting, chanting workers turned their assemblage into a sit-down strike, police ejected them. Some were jailed. Later that day, without a search warrant, police invaded the strikers' Workers Alliance headquarters, housed in a former funeral parlor. Armed with axes, police ransacked the premises and smashed typewriters, dishes, furniture, even the piano.[85]

Outraged, and out of the country in Mexico, Frisch penned a defense of the workers' rights, and three weeks later mailed his treatise to the press. By then his conclusions were moot. The Texas governor and the American Civil Liberties Union had decried the police brutality. The defendants had been acquitted and set free. The incidents had receded from the headlines, replaced by a cabdriver strike, arrests of pickets at an infant-clothing factory, and a 100-degree heat wave. Belatedly, on June 23, 1937, the *San Antonio Light* printed some of the rabbi's remarks under the headline, "Rabbi Frisch Hits S.A. Police in Labor Raid." The board at Temple Beth-El was irate and embarrassed. So was Frisch, but for different reasons. The newspaper had condensed his prose to four hundred words from twenty-five hundred. Frisch chafed at being censored. He arranged for his full remarks to be printed in pamphlet form and mailed to eight hundred congregants and colleagues in San Antonio and across the country. Some pamphlets were sent special delivery, eliciting a good-natured admonishment from a Cincinnati rabbi who responded: "Your special delivery air mail letter and its remarkable enclosure woke us out of bed the other night."[86]

Less supportive was Rabbi Julian Morgenstern, president of Frisch's alma mater, Hebrew Union College. The academician found the pamphlet's principles sound but the language "unnecessarily tactless" and bound to stir "some unnecessary opposition."[87] In the pamphlet, Frisch not only railed against the police. He also wagged a finger at "fashionably dressed, impeccably manicured and well-fed ladies" oblivious to the poverty surrounding their "swanky luncheons." He slammed San Antonio for donating the paltry sum of $30,000 to the Associated Charities. He warned that a community that tolerated substandard wages and living conditions was doomed to reap a "harvest of industrial strife."[88] Frisch was exhilarated by the ferment his mailing elicited, including criticism from temple board members. Among their objections: reinforcement of the "rampant" impression "that Jews are communists," the "untimely" appearance of his words, his interference in a non-Jewish sphere, and the inference that the rabbi spoke on behalf of Temple Beth-El.[89]

Frisch answered with a fourteen-page letter, copies of which he circulated among allies in San Antonio and beyond. He seemed in a frenzy over his right to expound his views. He was playing out a melodrama of his own, a showdown between himself and his "smug" detractors. He assured the congregation that he was not communist, not red, "not even egg-shell pink."[90] Calling himself an "unregimentable rabbi," he wrote a New York colleague that he felt emancipated as he fought his way out of his current "jam." Prophetically, he added, "I understand fully that my career here is at stake. . . . I take this risk . . . in order to remain a free man."[91]

He felt free but sapped. Early in 1938, the exhausted rabbi retreated to New York to seek medical care for a nervous breakdown and to recuperate with relatives. The temple politely termed his sojourn a leave of absence. While Frisch was convalescing, San Antonio's pecan shellers waged a bitter three-month strike. There was no voice at Beth-El to speak out. That summer, the temple hired an associate rabbi, David Jacobson, who was told that the senior rabbi was ill and might not return.[92]

In the fall, Frisch did return. His son, David, took time off from Princeton University to look after his father. Frisch supporters planned a gala to mark their senior rabbi's fifteenth anniversary in Texas. "Dad's getting better," David Frisch wrote his grandparents on December 10, 1938. "He grows daily more lively. This celebration will help him restore confidence in himself."[93]

But the cordial reception accorded the young associate rabbi evoked jealousy in Frisch, undermining his confidence. Associate Rabbi David Jacobson, while politically liberal like Frisch, was low-key, diplomatic, and conciliatory. His credentials were impressive—a Ph.D. from Cambridge University capped his rabbinical degree from HUC. He dazzled with his athletic frame and toothy smile. Two months after his arrival he married Helen Gugenheim, daughter of a wealthy congregant. The bride, who had a journalism job with NBC in New York, had met the rabbi during a trip home and been lured back to Texas by love. Frisch was suspicious of Jacobson's every move, from his marriage to a new practice of mailing congregants *yahrzeit* cards to remind them of the anniversary of a death in the family. On the civic front, Jacobson quickly allied with Frisch's friend, activist mayor Maury Maverick. In 1940, Jacobson headed a Citizens Welfare Survey Committee that delivered a harsh assessment of the city's social needs. When liberal archbishop Robert Lucey was assigned to San Antonio in 1941, Jacobson became his partner in social welfare causes. The young rabbi stepped into the role carved by Frisch, then moved forward amiably rather than abrasively.

Jacobson's chief diplomatic hurdle was the senior rabbi. "He was choleric," Jacobson recalled. "There was a lot of resentment toward me." Frisch complained to the Kallisons that the junior rabbi had turned the confirmation ceremony into a "pageant." He flew into a fit when a news article referred to Jacobson as "the rabbi" rather than "the *associate* rabbi." More than once, Jacobson consulted Frisch's father-in-law for advice on pacifying Frisch. Jacobson could reach no rapprochement with his senior rabbi. "I don't think I ever called him by his first name."[94] When the twosome co-officiated at Sabbath worship services, Frisch sometimes nodded off to sleep while Jacobson was at the pulpit. The cause was not boredom but weariness and nighttime insomnia.

Frisch's convalescent trips to New York increased. Relatives sympathized as he spoke of growing rebellion at the temple. Even Frisch's allies were concerned that, physically and mentally, he was not up to running a congregation. Frisch felt pressured into retirement. In June, 1942, despite two years remaining on the senior rabbi's contract, a congregational meeting was called. Allen Goldsmith, then twelve years old and present at the gathering because his parents lacked a baby-sitter, remembered the hostile setting. "It was a very divided house. . . . The group that backed David Jacobson wanted Frisch out." They had the votes. The issue in doubt was Frisch's pension. One congregant recommended $100 a week—$5,000 annually for life. The majority settled on $4,000.[95]

"He was not fired. He was retired," said Frances Kallison, a Frisch ally. "It had to be."[96]

Frisch had a graceful out. The Social Justice Commission of the Central Conference of American Rabbis was merging with its Peace Commission and needed an executive director. Frisch offered his services, gratis. But the imperious attitude that marked his final years in San Antonio eroded his service with the new commission. He felt demeaned to "a status of subservience" because his post involved clerical duties. He had to ask approval to accept speaking invitations or to expend sums as small as $25. "I am loath to believe that my colleagues . . . have such a low esteem of my abilities, judgment and experience," he wrote in a letter of resignation. "I can take it as I have taken many a thing before in my various skirmishes and battles for the right and the truth."[97]

Illness, irritability, arrogance, and professional jealousy were leading Frisch into isolation. Had he displayed more diplomacy, political acumen, or humility, he might have spent his final years as rabbi emeritus among his congregants or as a volunteer interacting with his colleagues. Instead, he went into bitter retreat, spending the last fifteen years of his life in relative solitude.

THE MAN AND THE MYTH

After Frisch's exile from San Antonio, many followers elevated him to near sainthood. "Rabbi Frisch was the physical embodiment of the Prophets to me, and I think to other kids," recalled Bill Rips, who was eighteen when his boyhood rabbi was "unceremoniously" ousted. "We felt alienated

from the temple." After Frisch's death on December 24, 1957, scores of ad-
mirers and detractors mistakenly linked the rabbi with Emma Tenayuca,
the charismatic union organizer and communist who led San Antonio's
striking pecan shellers. But the pair were barely acquainted: Frisch was out
of town when she waged her stormiest protests. Between the rabbi and the
labor organizer there is evidence of but one piece of correspondence—a
short thank-you note from Tenayuca regarding Frisch's police raid pamphlet.[98] Frisch devotees also recall him as a longtime ally of liberal archbishop Lucey, but the archbishop arrived only one year before Frisch's
forced resignation. The prelate did develop a long-term alliance with
Frisch's successor, David Jacobson. Lewis Lee insisted that an anthology,
Giants of Justice, had a chapter on Frisch, but it was actually an essay on
Frisch's father-in-law, Henry Cohen.[99] The power of Frisch's presence was
such that memory linked him to every progressive or radical issue of his
times. He inspired support for humanitarian causes, and, even if recollections are faulty, that is an honorable legacy.

The truth, however, is that the death of Ephraim Frisch's wife in 1934
dealt an irreparable blow to his psyche and his career. Beginning with their
courtship, his career moves had been aided by her congeniality and connections. His New Synagogue in Manhattan drew from her circle of
friends in the arts and social work. His call to San Antonio was accomplished through her father's maneuvering. Frisch's strident rhetoric and
modus operandi were ill suited to Texas, where successful clergy knew to
pick their battles, work in coalitions, and carry out unpopular acts with
bravado. To Frisch's credit, his uncompromising oratory and his focus on
injustice stirred and inspired congregants, especially young adults raised
with southern gentility and conservatism. He prodded congregants to
think about God and righteousness. His disciples recall him as a figure
ahead of his time.

Early in Frisch's career, his lengthy sermons and argumentative letters
to the editor seemed erudite. In retrospect, they sound redundant and
shrill, for he repeated himself time and again as he voiced moral outrage
and trumpeted his own work for social justice. When his columns and letters to the editor appeared in print, he mailed duplicates to newspapers,
journals, and colleagues—with postscripts about his latest altercations.
He basked in recognition, often generated through his own publicity.

At the start of Frisch's San Antonio tenure, he had pounded his fist on
the pulpit when a well-to-do congregant challenged his message. The incident resonated among future generations, mainly because Frisch himself

wrote it up seventeen years later for the *Hebrew Union College Monthly*. Frisch's version of the verbal clash was subsequently excerpted in two books that elevated the rabbi to martyr status. The first, *Justice and Judaism*, written in 1956 by two Jewish scholars, ranks Frisch with seven courageous American rabbis, including a Civil War rabbi run out of Baltimore for attacking slavery. The second book, *Jews, Justice and Judaism*, written in 1969 by a Christian scholar, recounts the pulpit-pounding incident and cites Frisch as a rabbi who advanced his prophetic heritage. Frisch would have been pleased at the description. The once "obscure" rabbi had secured himself recognition beyond the grave.[100]

10

The Celebrity Rabbi,
or Splintering over Zionism

HYMAN JUDAH SCHACHTEL, HOUSTON

A PRINCE OF ENGLAND was en route to Houston for a Friday night gala at the Rice Hotel. Rabbi Hyman Schachtel longed to attend but had a standing engagement, preaching from the pulpit at Congregation Beth Israel. This rabbi was drawn to celebrities and royalty. So was Houston. The synagogue's understanding directors gave the rabbi the night off. During the fete for royalty, Schachtel awaited his turn to meet the prince. When the pair were introduced, a startled Prince Philip inquired, "Rabbi, where is your hat?" To which the rabbi retorted, "Prince, where is your crown?" Hyman Judah Schachtel, a modern rabbi and a master of repartee, savored the moment.[1]

Houston was the only southern city to snare the prince for a social gala during his 1966 tour of the United States. Houston, after all, was on the move and on the make, an oil capital in the throes of a fifty-year boom ignited by the energy needs of World War II. Rabbi Schachtel, a London-born New Yorker with a British cadence to his voca*h*bulary, had been recruited to Houston in 1943. In that helter-skelter era, the lay leaders at Congregation Beth Israel—old guard Texans and nouveau riche entrepreneurs—had searched for a rabbi with energy that reflected their town, sophistication in tune with Houston's future, and a patriotic theology that rejected notions of a faraway Promised Land.

Rabbi Hyman Judah Schachtel in 1950 seated in his study at Congregation Beth Israel. © Houston Chronicle.

Past his prime was the congregation's longtime rabbi, Henry Barnston, at seventy-four the dean of Houston's clergy. The courtly Barnston had married and buried three generations of Jews since the turn of the century, when Houston was swampland and Beth Israel a synagogue with eighty-three families. By 1943, wartime Houston was concrete and skyscrapers, a wheeler-dealer, millionaires' capital. Temple Beth Israel was renowned as Texas' oldest (founded in 1854), largest (830 families), and wealthiest Jewish congregation. Its members were leaders of Jewish and secular institutions—from the B'nai B'rith fraternal order to the River Oaks Country Club. Their Jewish identities were strong, if invisible. No yarmulkes, *tefillin,* or kosher beef for them. Assimilated Texas Jews, Beth Israel's members were more likely to light up Christmas trees than kindle Sabbath candles. They were proud of their brand of religion and considered their temple a "citadel" of classical Reform Judaism.[2]

During the first two months of 1943, the oligarchy running the temple began pressuring the senior rabbi to retire. Barnston, a sixth-generation rabbi, had expected to retain the pulpit until his son Alfred, a rabbinical student, was called to follow. The board, however, wanted neither the father nor the son. In March of that year, a delegation officially asked Rabbi Barnston to change his status to emeritus. He refused. Two months later, board members approached him again, insinuating that they would go public with his shortcomings—mainly shaky delivery of sermons, poor health, and inability to draw a crowd. They showed him a photograph surreptitiously snapped at a recent Sabbath service. The sanctuary had scores of empty pews. Bitterly, the rabbi stepped down, claiming illness as the cause.[3]

The heir apparent to the pulpit was Associate Rabbi Robert I. Kahn. But the junior rabbi was absent, on duty as an army chaplain headed for the South Pacific. The temple's ruling clique prized patriotism, but the younger rabbi had caused discomfort in recent years. Kahn had urged the Red Cross to stop separating blood by the race of the donor.[4] He had hosted a Brotherhood Week meeting of the Houston Commission on Inter-racial Cooperation, a gathering that drew nine hundred African Americans to Beth Israel. Kahn's work with the interracial fellowship led the Houston Police Department to hire its first African American officer.[5] His involvement also sparked headlines when he decried as a "defense handicap" the lack of job training for blacks, nationwide.[6] The temple elders squirmed, preferring that the rabbi remain mum on such issues in their segregated city. Another complaint against the junior rabbi was his embrace of Zionism, the call for a Jewish homeland that many at Beth Israel perceived as a movement toward ghettoization. It was just as well that Kahn had departed Houston to serve his country. The junior rabbi's absence and the senior rabbi's forced resignation gave Beth Israel's leaders a window of opportunity to recruit an image maker in their own mold, a lieutenant who would follow their lead. The stage was set for Hy Schachtel.

THE NEW RECRUIT

Hyman Judah Schachtel was a Manhattan rabbi of note, a friend to celebrities, socialites, and politicians. Broadway songwriter Richard Rodgers called this rabbi "Reb" and supplied him with theater tickets.[7] New York governor Herbert Lehman appointed him to a state committee on marriage and family.[8] The *New York Times* routinely ran snippets from his sermons in its weekly roundup of rabbinical news and views.[9] No one had to coax the rabbi to the piano during penthouse parties, where he serenaded guests with a medley of pop tunes and a classical finale. The public took to this rabbi who had graduated from Hebrew Union College in 1931 directly to the position of assistant rabbi at Manhattan's Temple Shaaray Tefila, familiarly called the West End Synagogue, where diplomat Bernard Baruch was a member.

Born in London on May 24, 1907, and raised in Buffalo, New York, Schachtel had a religious upbringing rooted in the traditions of Eastern Europe—traditions that were anathema to the Houston Jews he would later represent. His mother, Janie Spector Schachtel, was the great-granddaughter of Lithuanian rabbi Isaac Elchanan Spektor, for whom a theological seminary at Yeshiva University is named.[10] Her husband, Bernard Schachtel, was born in the Polish border town of Kalicz and reared in London, where he became a Covent Garden opera singer. At his wife's insistence, Bernard Schachtel gave up the stage and its flirtatious sopranos for the more stable profession of cantor. Dreams of a position in the United States brought him to New York City in 1914, and soon after to a cantor's job at Buffalo's Temple Beth El—a Conservative congregation that also welcomed his services as a *mohel* for the ritual of circumcision. (He joked that he became a "Yankee clipper.")[11] Janie and the rest of the family soon followed him to New York, traveling aboard the British liner *Lusitania.* A nanny, nicknamed "Silly Lulu," accompanied them, but in a wrenching scene was turned back at Ellis Island because she could not read. "I can still see her screaming and my brothers and I crying because we wanted Silly Lulu to stay with us," the rabbi recalled years later.[12]

A talented family, the Schachtels shared a propensity for music and center stage. Hy, the eldest of four brothers and three sisters, played piano and accompanied his father at concerts; Irving mastered the violin; John, cello and saxophone; and Maury gravitated to jazz and saxophone and played at paid jobs with his brothers. Their father's instrument was his voice. Chaplain of the Cantors Association of Buffalo, Bernard Schachtel was a high baritone with a host of cantorial friends. Visiting Jewish singers, such as the celebrated Yussele Rosenblatt, spent Sunday afternoons in the Schachtel living room singing Hebrew classics and engaging in convivial a cappella competition. First a tenor might attempt a baritone melody; then the baritones reached for tenor notes.[13]

Hy's voice shone best at oratory. He won school and citywide competitions delivering famous speeches of Daniel Webster and John Adams, and finished second in a national oratory contest. At Hebrew Union College, which he entered at age seventeen, he composed the school's alma mater song and was a natural for entertainment chairman. When composer George Gershwin visited the Cincinnati campus, Schachtel showed him around. Polished and self-assured, Schachtel easily made the transition from the seminary into the spiritual and social life of his Manhattan congregation.

His glamorous public life gave little hint of personal loss. Schachtel's father, who suffered hypertension, died of a stroke at age forty-five, two months before his son's 1931 ordination. Hy also suffered from hypertension, a condition that kept him out of the armed forces. Two years after his father's death, in June, 1933, Hy married Henriette Strauss, a congregant and a Vassar College graduate studying at the National Academy of Design.[14] The marriage ended before the couple's sixth anniversary. Henriette suffered from a mental illness and had been periodically institutionalized, the rabbi told family and friends, explaining that her physicians had recommended the divorce.[15] The painful union and parting added a dimension of pathos and a degree of reflection and psychology to Schachtel's sermons. Life experience gave resonance to his words, already enhanced by the baritone timbre of his voice.

The voice. "That's what attracted me to him in the first place," recalled Barbara Levin Schachtel. Fourteen years his junior, Barbara was a high school senior when she first heard the rabbi's mellifluous voice at a Lake Placid resort. She was there studying piano. He had come to meet another rabbi. She overheard him talking about a book and joined the conversation. The year was 1938. "I knew he was married," she said. A year later, she heard about his divorce. Then a student at Wellesley College, Barbara mentioned the rabbi's single status to her campus friends, who urged her to phone him next time she planned a trip to New York City. She did, and romance blossomed, with Barbara opting for marriage rather than completing college. The couple wed October 15, 1941, in her hometown, Rochester, New York.[16]

INFIGHTING AND FLUX AMONG JEWS

During the early years of the Schachtels' marriage, the Jewish universe was in turmoil. World Jewry was splintered over solutions to the exodus of persecuted Jews fleeing Europe. Eyewitness accounts filtering into the West related grisly details about the slaughter of tens of thousands of Jews in Romania, Poland, Latvia, and Lithuania. Great Britain, the colonial overlord of Palestine, had placed a five-year, 75,000-person limit on the entry of Jewish refugees to its Middle East territory. The gates would shut in 1944, and Europe's Jewish refugees would no longer have a haven from certain annihilation. Prominent American Jews lobbied the U.S. State Department and the British government to relax immigration barriers at home and in Palestine. Emotionally, they pleaded that a sovereign Jewish nation be carved out of the Middle East. Within the Zionist Organization of America, egos clashed over tactical issues of leadership and diplomacy.

American Reform rabbis split over basic ideological issues. Their movement had been grounded since 1885 on the Pittsburgh Platform that defined Judaism as a universal religion, not an ethnic group or a nation in exile. However, Adolf Hitler's rise to power and the vulnerable state of European Jewry had begun to change many a theologian's view. A gradual "Zionization" of Reform Judaism had been occurring. The Central Conference of American Rabbis—the Reform rabbinate assembly—revised its position on Zionism in 1937 during a meeting in Columbus, Ohio. The majority adopted what became known as the Columbus Platform, a document sympathetic toward a Jewish national homeland. Dissenting rabbis refused to concede defeat. The debate raged white hot in 1942, when a push to create a Jewish army in Palestine, under its own flag within the Allied command, gained momentum and endorsement from two thirds of the rabbinical conference.[17] Schachtel was among the dissenters.

He was among the coordinators in June, 1942, when the holdouts convened a counterconference of rabbis in Atlantic City. The articulate New Yorker was also one of the youngest diehards at the gathering, leading the eldest to eye him for a larger role in their crusade. These rabbis made a distinction between *national* Zionism—a separate Jewish country, which they opposed—and *cultural* Zionism—a Hebraic renaissance in the desert, which they endorsed. Such distinctions, however, soon became lost in hostile debate.

By year's end, the legacy of the Atlantic City conference was the creation of the militant American Council for Judaism, an organization so named to stress its pro-American rather than its negative anti-Zionist mission. Although founded by rabbis, the American Council for Judaism enlisted the laity in its offense against Zionism. Another byproduct of the Atlantic City conference was a petition printed in the *New York Times* and signed by ninety cultural-Zionist rabbis, a group derided in the Jewish press as the "*goy* nineties."[18] Schachtel did more than sign his name to the petition stating the group's opposition views. He rounded up signatories; he helped draft the council's platform;[19] he filed the new group's incorporation papers with the state of New York. ("I received the certificate yesterday," he wrote the council's executive director, Rabbi Elmer Berger, on March 29, 1943. "We shall have it suitably framed and hung in your office.")[20] Later, Schachtel helped write a "Response to Zionism" for *Life* magazine. The essay ran under the byline of council president Lessing J. Rosenwald—former chairman of Sears Roebuck and President Franklin Roosevelt's choice for director of the World War II Bureau of Industrial Conservation.[21] Schachtel and the American Council for Judaism were allied across the country with Jews of prominence. Many were well-established Jews of German descent convinced that Zionism would lead outsiders to question their patriotism, just as accusations of dual loyalty dogged American Catholics. Philadelphia rabbi Louis Wolsey, Schachtel's mentor and a former president of the Central Conference of American Rabbis, assured the young rabbi that his role among the founders was a wise career move: "You have the opportunity of a lifetime in the American Council for Judaism. You can make yourself one of the outstanding leaders of a permanent movement—permanent because it is based on history. . . . You can render service to Israel—and to your career."[22]

Schachtel's career seemed on the rise nationally and locally. Earlier that year the *New York Times* had noted his election as vice president of the New York Council of Rabbinical Ministers, a union of Orthodox, Conservative, and Reform rabbis celebrating its sixtieth year.[23] Schachtel, who coordinated the group's anniversary events, was scheduled to become council president at a meeting in January, 1943. Three weeks before the election, however, the International Jewish Press Agency broke a story about two closed-door sessions of the embryonic American Council for Judaism. Schachtel was portrayed in the news account as one of the group's hawks, an "impatient" advocate who favored hiring a slick public relations agent to ignite controversy over Zionism.[24] Schachtel's quotes and his role in the new organization inflamed most of New York City's rabbis. Many among them branded the emerging American Council for Judaism an American *Cancer* for Judaism and "a stab in the back" to Jewish survival.[25]

Previously, Schachtel had seemed just another name on the alphabetical "*goy* nineties" petition. Revelation of his central role in the anti-Zionist organization poisoned his chance to lead his colleagues. During a stormy meeting of the New York Board of Jewish Ministers, Rabbi Stephen S. Wise—a firebrand, Zionist, social activist, and one of the lead-

ing national Jewish figures of his time—engineered the election of Orthodox rabbi Joseph Lookstein as president. Lookstein's selection was a double
insult to Schachtel because the top office traditionally rotated among Reform, Conservative, and Orthodox denominations. Sixteen rabbis who
sided with Schachtel walked out of the meeting, complaining of a "dis-
graceful browbeating."[26] The controversy demonstrated the divisions over
Zionism. Schachtel's defeat, rather than a crushing blow, raised his profile
as a spokesman. He was suddenly on call to debate the cultural Zionist
position—and he did, nationally at the June, 1943, meeting of the Central
Conference of American Rabbis in New York.[27]

Schachtel's Manhattan congregation was not thrilled with his sudden
notoriety. Temple Shaaray Tefila had recently promoted Schachtel to senior rabbi following the retirement of longtime spiritual leader Nathan
Stern. The congregation prided itself on being a stable institution with
only three previous senior rabbis in its ninety-eight-year history. Members
were not ardently pro- or anti-Zionist. They were definitely unaccus-
tomed to controversy and embarrassed by the headlines (so much so that
in later years members wrote Schachtel out of their official history and
omitted his photograph from a wall of temple rabbinical portraits).[28]

By mid-1943, Schachtel's name and byline had appeared in Jewish papers around the nation and at least twice in the columns of Houston's *Jewish Herald-Voice*.[29] By then, Houston's Beth Israel Congregation was
searching for a rabbi whose views meshed with the board's. Schachtel's
New York friend, Rabbi Jonah Wise, recommended him to the Houston
search committee, and soon the Schachtels began fielding calls from
Texas. "This persistent man kept calling," Barbara remembered, referring
to George S. Cohen, a Houston department store mogul and czar of Beth
Israel's ritual and music committee. Again and again, the Texan was on
the phone, finally announcing that he had arrived in New York to meet
Schachtel. The rabbi was wined and dined—and intrigued. Politically,
these Texans were on his wavelength. Of the ninety rabbis who signed the
cultural Zionists' petition, six were from Texas, and twenty-nine from the
South and Southwest.[30] The American Council for Judaism received its
strongest support in the South, where Jews were better integrated into the
community and more likely to perceive their faith as a religion without an
ethnic or cultural component.[31] Texas would certainly provide a more
hospitable home base than New York for Schachtel's platform.

Schachtel accepted an invitation to visit Houston in July—not as a rabbinical candidate, he insisted, but as a speaker for the American Council

for Judaism. The search committee arranged a country club reception for seventy-eight Beth Israel members so that the rabbi and a cross section of congregants would have a look at one another.

Schachtel's first view of Houston was admittedly insulated. Whisked from air-conditioned sedans into chilly, air-conditioned hotels, homes, and reception rooms, he remained oblivious to the jungle heat and humidity. When he phoned his wife to relay a firsthand report from Texas, he remarked: "It's freezing."[32] The people were warm, and therefore Houston seemed a comfortable climate. The southern hospitality was endearing in contrast to name callers in New York, who had labeled people of his persuasion "traitors" and "Munichmen."[33] Presuming that a call to the pulpit was in the offing, Schachtel invited retiring Rabbi Henry Barnston to his hotel room to share the British pastime of tea. Schachtel got a taste of Texas instead. The pipe-smoking gentleman preferred something stronger, and the pair conversed over scotch.[34]

REFLECTIONS OF A SENIOR RABBI

During their first encounter, Rabbi Emeritus Henry Barnston gave no hint of his forced resignation from Congregation Beth Israel. Dignity would not permit him to speak disparagingly of congregants who had turned on him after he had spent his forty-three-year career nurturing Beth Israel into Texas' premier Jewish institution. In his younger days, Barnston had been just as vehemently anti-Zionist as Schachtel. Now he refrained from joining the American Council for Judaism, preferring compromise over confrontation. At his feisty height two decades before, Barnston had corresponded with some of the same rabbis who were mentoring Schachtel. Barnston had once joked to his northern allies, "The Zionists here . . . swear that they will never rest until I'm scalped."[35]

Born in England on August 23, 1868, Barnston never lost his clipped accent, his fine penmanship, or his zest for playing British marches on the piano.[36] His father, Israel Barnstein, had served as rabbi of Dover, England, the white-cliffed coastal town and military garrison. His grandfather, who spelled his surname Barnstijn, was rabbi of Hoorn, a north Holland resort. Successive generations altered the spelling of the family name to adapt to their host countries. Henry Barnston, who went by "Barnstein" during his first two decades in Texas, legally Americanized the spelling of his name in March, 1920, after New York customs agents

*Henry Barnston, foreground, in 1928, at the Second Annual Kallah Convention
of Texas Rabbis. Behind him, from left, sit Maurice Faber of Tyler, Samuel Rosinger
of Beaumont, and David Lefkowitz of Dallas. From Kallah,
Volume II, Year Book, 5689.*

rudely detained him because they suspected his surname was of German origin.[37]

As a rabbinical student, Barnston had chafed under the Orthodox rituals practiced in England, where there was no comparable Reform Jewish movement. After the seminary, he earned a doctorate of philosophy at the University of Heidelberg. Exposure to changing religious currents convinced him to go west, where he was likely to find freedom of the pulpit and a congregation amenable to change. "I knew with my radical views I could never hold a place in England."[38] He corresponded with two congregations advertising for a rabbi: Lincoln, Nebraska, and Houston. When he learned that a dozen Houston couples were awaiting the arrival of a rabbi to get married, he accepted the call to Texas.[39]

At the turn of the century, Houston Jewry had two synagogues. The smaller, more traditional Adath Yeshurun (congregation of God), had bitterly split off from Beth Israel during the 1880s.[40] Beth Israel's membership, which was wealthier and more acculturated, included prominent merchants with German-Jewish roots. Among them were Jules Hirsch, who raised a family in a grand Victorian home where his youngsters serenaded neighbors with front porch concerts; Michael Westheimer, a hay merchant whose country lane turned into a major thoroughfare bearing the family name; Henry J. Dannenbaum, a school board president and state district judge; and the Levy brothers, whose dry goods store employed four hundred workers and whose Main Street mansion became a landmark. Philanthropist Ben Taub was the son of a Hungarian immigrant who launched the family fortune from a pushcart full of tobacco wares. Banker Emmanuel Raphael, son of the city's Civil War–era rabbi, Samuel Raphael, counseled millionaire William Marsh Rice to leave his fortune to create an educational institution that grew into Rice University.[41]

Beth Israel gained a contingent of congregants from Galveston after devastating hurricanes in 1900 and 1915 convinced merchants that Houston, fifty miles inland, was a safer, more sheltered base for shipping operations. Among the Galveston migrants were Russian-born brothers Simon and Tobias Sakowitz, retailers whose name became synonymous with fine taste. Their sister, Rebecca, founded the Houston Humane Society, and her husband, Max Nathan, a menswear merchant, founded the local American Jewish Committee, which fights anti-Semitism behind the scenes. Native Texan George S. Cohen was another Galveston transplant. The Galveston contingent looked down on the less cosmopolitan Houstonians and never gave Rabbi Barnston his due, comparing him always with Galveston's more senior rabbi, Henry Cohen, also a Briton.

Many other Beth Israel families were grounded in Houston's past, from the earliest city councils to the creation of the Houston Ship Channel Company and the Board of Trade and Cotton Exchange.[42] Business was their pursuit, as well as Houston's ruthless forte. Wealth abounded and helped Barnston spearhead projects beyond his temple. The rabbi launched Family Services for the poor. He became a charter member and vice president of the Houston Public School Art League, a forerunner to the Museum of Fine Arts. When the league hung prints of famous works of art in the city's dozen public schools, Baptist parents took offense at the bare-breasted Venus de Milo.[43]

Barnston yearned for classical music performances and noted the array of pianists and fiddlers who played background music at restaurants, vaudeville houses, and silent-movie theaters. With socialite Ima Hogg, the daughter of a former Texas governor, the rabbi helped gather thirty-five part-time musicians into a chamber orchestra. At the ensemble's first performance on June 21, 1913, the rabbi urged audience support for the new Houston Symphony Society—which became the catalyst for the heralded Houston Symphony Orchestra.[44]

Not all was harmonious. Houston's wealth from cotton, lumber, and oil barely camouflaged its racial bigotry. Barnston lived through the race riot of 1917, when African American soldiers stationed at nearby Camp Logan mutinied against police brutality and Jim Crow laws, leaving twenty-one people dead.[45] The rabbi did not comment on the riot in his sermons. He also lived through the terror of the Ku Klux Klan, which marched into Houston during the 1920 Confederate Veterans Parade.[46] The Klan's grand dragon worshiped at the First Methodist Church, where Rev. A. Frank Smith defiantly invited Barnston to set up headquarters while the temple constructed a new facility. For eighteen months, Jews worshiped inside the Methodist church, an ecumenical example in a time of bigotry. Smith later recalled: "Some of the 'saints' in First Methodist and some in Beth Israel raised their hands in holy horror. . . . A Jewish congregation worshiping in a Christian church was utterly unheard of in this section, . . . but Henry Barnston did not hesitate. . . . Small wonder such a bold adventurer should be in the forefront . . . of Houston."[47]

Small wonder that, two decades later, the rabbi resented the pressure to retire. He was Houston's reigning pastor, the clergyman with the longest tenure, a public figure touted for his "star quality."[48] His contract had been extended in 1928 into a lifetime covenant. However, since the start of 1943, Beth Israel's headstrong board had been pushing him to become more active in the American Council for Judaism, a step he would not take. The American Council's lay members made brash, emotional public statements at odds with Barnston's quiet style of leadership. On this matter, he would not do the board's bidding. Schachtel was definitely their man.

FROM THE FRYING PAN INTO THE FIRE

Two weeks after Schachtel's visit to Houston, he telegrammed his acceptance of a preliminary offer to become Beth Israel's senior rabbi at an annual salary of $11,000.[49] Although the wage was $1,000 less than his New York salary, Texas' lower cost of living meant that the money would stretch further.

Beth Israel's membership still had to confirm his appointment. Endorsement came August 4, but at a boisterous meeting, marred with scuffles and name calling. One contingent shouted, "kikes," and another faction yelled, "Nazi board members."[50] Schachtel's appointment was approved by a vote of 346 ayes to 91 nays.[51] Many among the nay voters—including David White, editor of the *Jewish Herald-Voice*—were incensed that the board had recruited an anti-Zionist leader at a time when news of Nazi Germany's mass exterminations reinforced the need for Jewish unity and a Jewish haven. Many other disgruntled congregants agreed with Schachtel's politics, but their sense of fair play led them to champion Chaplain Bob Kahn, the associate rabbi serving in the army. They felt strongly that the pulpit should stay vacant until his return. Board members, however, indicated that thirty-two-year-old Kahn was "too young" for the senior position. Yet Schachtel was thirty-six.

Barnston's ouster evoked another blast of resentment from the crowd. His retirement had "all the earmarks of a 'blitz' clearly marked 'made in Germany,'" according to congregant Jacob L. Farb. When board members insisted that Barnston was too old and sickly to minister to the congregation, his defenders snapped back that other cities had called rabbis out of retirement for the war's duration. Galveston's rabbi, Henry Cohen, was eighty; Richmond's rabbi, Edward Calisch, was "eighty and deaf"; yet Barnston, who was five years younger and "more vigorous physically and mentally than they" had been "unceremoniously shelved during a time of war crisis."[52] Beth Israel had violated a gentlemen's agreement among rabbis and synagogues not to permanently fill a pulpit while a young chaplain was off at war.[53]

Temple president Leopold "Lep" Meyer grew alarmed at the acrimony, concerned lest the Zionist forces multiply and dominate the congregation. "It became not only apparent but obvious . . . that there were hopelessly irreconcilable factions within our congregation, and shockingly, that a small segment of our members was more devoted to National Zionism than to Judaism," Meyer wrote.[54] To clarify Beth Israel's guiding religious principles, he appointed an ad hoc committee of ten members. Israel Friedlander—a past president, native Texan, lawyer, banker, and fanatical anti-Zionist—headed the committee that resolved to spell out what Beth Israel stood for. Friedlander, Meyer, and other congregational leaders believed that too many temple members were offspring of twentieth-century immigrants who infused the Jewish faith with *Yiddishkeit*—the culture of Eastern Europe's long-insulated shtetl Jews. Since 1936, some 250 families had joined Beth Israel, most of them newcomers to Texas or America. They did not understand that classical Reform Judaism revolved around morality and prophetic teachings, not Zionism or ancient rituals. Nor did these new members contribute their fair share to running the temple. An informal audit found that 13 percent of Beth Israel's members paid 45 percent of the costs. The big donors felt entitled to their leadership roles.

The manifesto that emerged from the ad hoc committee was titled "Basic Principles of Congregation Beth Israel." The seven-point declaration rested upon the Reform movement's original 1885 platform and reflected this Texas group's belief that religion was separate from culture and nationality:

> We consider ourselves no longer a nation. We are a religious community, and neither pray for nor anticipate a return to Palestine nor a restoration of any of the laws concerning the Jewish state. . . . Our religion is Judaism. Our nation is the United States of America. Our nationality is American. Our flag is the "Stars and Stripes." Our race is Caucasian. . . . While respecting the convictions of our Orthodox and Conservative brethren concerning the rabbinical and Mosaic laws which regulate diet, priestly purity, dress, and similar laws, we, however, as an American Reform Congregation, reject the religious obligatory nature of the same as having originated in ages and under influences of ideas and conditions which today are entirely unsuited, unnecessary and foreign to the beliefs and observances of progressive Judaism in modern America.[55]

The principles also discounted the Hebrew language as irrelevant and "unintelligible to the vast majority of our co-religionists."

Most inflammatory were the temple membership forms—pledges that paraphrased the Basic Principles and required the signature of congregants who wished to retain voting privileges or serve as officers. Beth Israel would have two tiers of members: those who subscribed to the principles and those who did not. A vote to accept or reject the Basic Principles was set for November 23, 1943. The "Beth Israel revolt" was under way.[56]

TEXAS BOUND

That autumn, Hy, Barbara, and their six-month-old son, Bernard—named for his grandfather and nicknamed "Bard"—boarded a train for the two-day trip to Houston. The three arrived November 3, unaware that they were stepping into a hornet's nest. Schachtel would have no honeymoon. Awaiting him was a stack of mail from rabbis who assaulted the Basic Principles and urged him to stall their adoption. "Democracy or Autocracy?" complained the *Beth Israel Sentinel,* a tabloid the local opposition cranked out. Also in the stack of mail was a letter from Chaplain Bob Kahn, welcoming Schachtel to Houston.[57] On duty in the South Pacific, Kahn knew nothing of the Basic Principles and said nothing about his resentment at having been passed over.

The Basic Principles were familiar to Schachtel, for he had proofread a draft several weeks before, making "minor revisions" by mail. The rabbi had suggested dropping the offensive reference to "Caucasians," but the committee stood firm. It meant to emphasize that Jews are not a race of people and that Beth Israel's members descended from the same racial stock as their Caucasian neighbors.[58]

What was clear to the committee proved outrageous to the Jewish press. Would Beth Israel reject an Ethiopian Jew or a Yemenite Jew? asked the *American Jewish World.* Were these "*Basic* or *Base* Principles?" inquired the *Jewish Review and Observer.* "Believers in Traditional Judaism Barred," headlined the *B'nai B'rith Messenger.* Rabbis of all persuasions, including three of Schachtel's American Council for Judaism allies, urged him to intervene, modify the language, and delay the vote on the Basic Principles. Schachtel refused. The Basic Principles were a product of the lay leadership. The new rabbi made a strategic decision to remain neutral for the time being.[59]

Once the Basic Principles passed—by a vote of 612 to 168—Rabbi Schachtel backed his congregation from the pulpit, the podium, and in the press. Mainstream media picked up on the furor. The *New York Times* reported that the "big money" groups at the South's largest congregation were behind a new credo that "hits observers of dietary laws." *Time* magazine illustrated its "Storm over Zion" piece with a photo of Schachtel captioned: "A set of Nürnberg laws?" Zionist leader Stephen S. Wise, Schachtel's nemesis at the New York Board of Jewish Ministers, published his monthly *Opinion* magazine with a headline that echoed for years: "The Shame of Houston."[60]

Schachtel went on the offensive. When *Reader's Digest* published an article attacking Zionism, he praised it.[61] When anti-Zionists in Lincoln, Nebraska, drafted their own set of Basic Principles in July, 1944, Schachtel visited as an emissary of the American Council for Judaism. In Dallas,

differences between Zionists and anti-Zionists also intensified, but conciliatory lay leaders prevented a schism by patiently reminding both camps
of their common interests.[62] In Little Rock, Arkansas, where more than
14 percent of the city's 1,140 Jews were members of the council, talk of creating an anti-Zionist congregation was scotched when the state's leading
rabbi, Ira Sanders, declared, "Over my dead body."[63]

Nowhere did controversy flare or polarization set in rivaling that in
Houston, a city of such rapid change that its old guard Jews fought to preserve what seemed sacred. These self-described champions of American
democracy held tightly to their nineteenth-century-based platform. Their
attitudes were a reflection of Houston. During the post-war Red Scare, this
metropolis galloping toward the future became the nation's most reactionary urban setting. Among Houston's Methodists, a lay revolt would lead to
creation of the Committee for the Preservation of Methodism, a right-
wing coalition that challenged the denomination's social gospel bent.[64]

Houston's Jewish community, which in 1943 included eight thousand
Jews and seven synagogues, was no stranger to patterns of conflict. Orthodox synagogue Adath Yeshurun was born of an acrimonious schism at
Beth Israel in the 1880s. As early as 1906, Houston had competing B'nai
B'rith lodges—one Orthodox, the other Reform—although the fraternal
order seeks to bridge such differences. Still later, disputes inside Adath
Yeshurun and the Conservative Adath Israel led disgruntled members at
both to bolt and form new congregations.[65] David White, longtime publisher of the *Jewish Herald-Voice*, observed that Houston's "migration in-
vasions" brought a continuous influx of new residents, who inevitably
upset the status quo. Not surprisingly, Beth Israel's November, 1943, showdown vote over the Basic Principles led to rumors of mass resignations. By
the end of January, however, only ten families had withdrawn.

THE OPPOSITION

When Chaplain Bob Kahn learned about the Basic Principles through letters from home, he began mulling over his future. "I was in an untenable
position," he recalled. "The temple decided that you couldn't be a good
Jew and a good Zionist. I thought I was a good Jew. I knew I was a good
Zionist."[66]

It had been a "bitter winter" for Kahn, disappointed at having been
passed over for senior rabbi. As assistant rabbi to Barnston since 1935, he

Lt. Robert I. Kahn, with a tallis *(prayer shawl) draped over his uniform, reads from the Torah at a Boston synagogue while attending training sessions in 1942 for Army Chaplains School at Harvard University. The carved poles or staves that hold the Torah scroll are barely visible at bottom right and left.*
Courtesy Congregation Emanu El, Houston.

had "expected" to succeed his mentor to the pulpit. "It seemed logical," he said years later in an oral history. The previous spring, while home on leave for Beth Israel's confirmation ceremony, Kahn had lobbied for the senior rabbi post, visiting friends and asking them to hire a temporary, interim rabbi until he returned from the war. He found few allies:

> Everyone of them had some reason for not pushing my candidacy. . . . The *good* of the congregation was regarded as more important than the welfare of an individual. That fall, of course things broke open, and Congregation Beth Israel passed the Basic Principles, which made it literally impossible for me to ever think about becoming rabbi of that congregation. . . . I'm not sure I wanted to go back to Houston with all these ghosts of friends who had deserted me. . . . If I were to die overseas without having made a definitive

statement in opposition to the Basic Principles, I would somehow have played false to my own ideals.[67]

On March 1, 1944, Kahn mailed his wife, Rozelle, a handwritten letter of resignation, which she edited, typed, and forwarded to the congregation March 27. The absent rabbi wrote that he could no longer "acquiesce by silence" to the Basic Principles, which he denounced as a "poorly written hodge-podge of theology, anti-defamation, anti-Zionism, and anti-Orthodoxy." He added, "I am a first class officer in the U.S. Army. But, by implication, I have been placed in a second class category in the congregation I have served for almost eight years."[68]

Two months later, scores of disaffected Beth Israel members met to discuss creation of a breakaway congregation. By the end of June, 125 families had signed a mass resignation petition. Their dramatic exit split many extended families affiliated with Beth Israel for generations. Beth Israel's losses from the schism soon totaled 142 families.[69] The secessionists—led by William Nathan, Mose Feld, and Nathan Klein—cabled Lt. Kahn on July 11. They invited him to become their rabbi at war's end, a bid he accepted.[70]

The new congregation, named Emanu El, gained more supporters ten months later when the *Houston Chronicle* gave front-page coverage to Rabbi Schachtel's Memorial Day address. In his holiday speech, Schachtel called Zionism a "hopeless" effort to "ghettoize" Jews and to "nullify their spiritual mission to mankind." Four Houston rabbis rebuked Schachtel for delivering such remarks "at a time when the broken remnant of the Jewish people in Europe needs the most sympathetic support."[71]

Soon after, in June, 1945, Kahn returned to Houston—and a hero's welcome—wearing three battle stars and a Philippine Liberation ribbon. His waiting congregants, under the leadership of interim rabbi Alan S. Green, had been crowding into Central Presbyterian Church for worship services. By 1947, Houston's second Reform Jewish congregation had grown to 750 families.

MAKING PEACE

Revelations of the Holocaust's full extent soon horrified the world. The United Nations voted November 29, 1947, to partition Palestine into a Jew-

ish state and an Arab state. Six months later, on May 14, 1948, Israel issued
its declaration of statehood. Schachtel, one of the last six rabbis to remain
involved in the American Council for Judaism, used his insider's position
to urge reconciliation. It was "futile to argue with history," he reasoned.[72]
The council's incendiary rhetoric would only fan violence between Arabs
and Jews. Another six months passed before Schachtel finally quit the anti-
Zionist council. "Anti-Semitism is being defeated by the courage of Israel,"
he stated in his letter of resignation dated November 29, 1948. "The name
Jew is now associated with courage, stamina, heroism, fighting power—
the anti-Semites have been confounded."[73]

Schachtel tried to begin mending fences by raising money for Israeli
bonds and Israeli causes, even soliciting dollars from gentiles. He and Barbara took a two-week trip to Israel in 1951 as guests of the Israeli government. In speeches, he praised the oratory skills of his former foes—Zionists such as Stephen F. Wise and Joshua Loth Liebman, a Boston rabbi who
had come to Houston in hopes of halting the vote over the Basic Principles. Schachtel wanted to put the past behind him, but in Jewish circles
it was not forgotten.

"There was so much hatred," Barbara Schachtel recalled. "He had to
rise above it."

LIFE GOES ON

Despite the rancor and factionalism among Houston's eight thousand
Jews, Schachtel found the door wide open for harmonizing with Houston's larger community of more than 400,000 residents. Beth Israel's longtime Methodist ally, A. Frank Smith, was now a bishop who welcomed
Schachtel into the Ministers Association of Greater Houston. Together,
the duo persuaded other clergy to say a simple "amen" at the close of public benedictions rather than "in Jesus' name."[74]

During his first months in Houston, Schachtel had launched a Sunday radio show, and he continued broadcasting weekly for more than
forty years.[75] He also penned a newspaper column in the *Houston Post*,
sharing a page with political insider Jack Valenti, who became a good
friend. Schachtel's local following grew, particularly among the non-Jewish community, and audiences topping one thousand bought tickets for
his book reviews. One admirer called Schachtel the Richard Burton of the
rabbinate.

His radio sermons were soothing, rather than controversial. His thespian voice was so polished that he spent one broadcast in 1952 reciting thirty minutes of Shakespeare: "'Now is the winter of our discontent.' ... 'Cowards die many times before their deaths.' ... 'Friends, Romans, countrymen.'"[76] His 1953 Washington's Birthday talk demonstrated his knack for moving from the folksy—"And they named him George"—to the universal, and infusing a half-hour broadcast with recommended reading (James Truslow Adams' *The Epic of America*) and a relevant Talmudic quote.[77]

A lifelong student of oratory, the rabbi made it a point to watch the televised sermons of his Christian colleagues, studying how they developed ideas, sustained thoughts, and held an audience through cadence, rhythm, and the rise and fall of emotion. "Preaching is essentially an art, and therefore must touch emotions," Schachtel said in a series of lectures to rabbinical students at Hebrew Union College. He recommended that a rabbi or minister exhibit "glibness" and "erudition" from the pulpit: "It is impressive to quote from other classical sources, to use a Latin or a French proverb, to throw in a Greek word from Plato and Aristotle or a quotation from Shakespeare." Schachtel further advised students that staging, lighting, and gestures were important. As an example he described how Cleveland rabbi Abba Hillel Silver, a major Zionist figure, "would close his eyes just before he poured forth a cascade of brilliance and poetry." Schachtel incorporated such mannerisms into his own style of preaching.[78]

"Schachtel was eloquent. He would certainly have been ranked among the leading pulpiteers of that era," said the Rev. Dr. John Eugene Fellers, director of the Institute of Religion at Texas Medical Center, an ecumenical organization that hosts a Hyman Schachtel lecture series in medical ethics. "Schachtel was Houston's most visible clergyman reaching across to men and women of all creeds. He was well-read, with a tremendous breadth of the liberal arts. ... We perceived him as a great spiritual presence, very urbane, sophisticated, impeccably groomed, charming, yet with genuine spiritual depth. Christians felt like, 'he's our rabbi, too.'"[79]

THE HOME FRONT

Rabbi Schachtel often remarked that his life revolved around "four Bs—Bach, Beethoven, Brahms, and Barbara." The woman who interrupted her Wellesley education to marry him and move to Texas subsequently earned a Ph.D. in epidemiology and behavioral sciences and a seat on the county hospital board—a position she retained for two decades. She spoke out for abortion, medical care for the poor, and the dire need for new charity hospitals. She fostered creation of a hospital endowment foundation that continues to raise millions. In 1982 a Houston foundation named Barbara Schachtel among the "Great Texans of the Year." In quintessential Lone Star style, the *Houston Chronicle* photographed her with the award's previous winners, a gossip columnist and a place-kicker.[80]

The daughter of a Rochester dentist, Barbara took to Houston more so than her husband. He was the cosmopolite, cut off from the cultural hub of New York City. He had walked into a thicket of controversy. He had to be diplomatic with temple elders who clocked his sermons to the minute and hosted ritual committee meetings at the River Oaks Country Club. He grimaced during compulsory Christmas morning visits to George S. Cohen's home, where each Schachtel child received a Yuletide gift. Barbara, however, had no regrets about exchanging a New York apartment for a two-story rental house with a garage and a lawn in Houston. Baby-sitters were available and affordable. At Beth Israel, she saw her place as member, not leader. As soon as her youngsters were in kindergarten, Barbara enrolled at the University of Houston.

Whenever Hy, in exasperation, contemplated leaving Houston, Barbara, son Bard, and daughter Ann Mollie, born in 1945, pleaded to remain. In the early 1960s, a pulpit in St. Louis seemed in the offing. A desperate Barbara telephoned Lep Meyer for an assist. Meyer, a masterful manager who had headed everything from the Houston Horse Show Association to the National Retail Credit Association, helped persuade Schachtel to stay. Then, too, the Schachtel's home, designed by the temple building committee in 1958, would have been difficult to leave. The custom-built house in the tree-shaded Old Braeswood neighborhood was constructed with natural wood and stone, with cathedral ceilings and an expansive living room suited for large or intimate entertaining. The couple's grand piano overlooked a picture window to the outdoors.

Beyond the walls of their abode, the Schachtels found Houston full of culture shocks from the day of their arrival. Texas' largest city was a clubby town, where liquor by the drink was available only in private homes and private clubs. Municipal decisions were made by a cluster of self-made men playing poker in Room 8-F at Jesse Jones' Lamar Hotel.[81] Deals made sub rosa led to relocation in 1943 of Baylor Medical School from Dallas to Houston. Rice University was white only (until 1964), a restriction written into its founding documents.[82] In comparison with New York, Houston was a cultural desert. The nation's twenty-first largest city had no professional acting troupe until 1947 (when the Alley Theatre opened in a back alley studio), no civic opera (that would come in 1955), and no ballet. The part-time symphony teamed up with pro wrestlers to sell war bonds at a function where the action was accompanied by the "William Tell Overture" and the final punch driven home with Chopin's "Funeral March."[83] As a welcome-to-Houston present, congregant Jake Sam gave symphony tickets to the Schachtels, who found the musicianship so abysmal that they walked out during intermission. "We'd leave at the half," Barbara recalled. Music buffs later appointed Rabbi Schachtel to the symphony board.

Houston's celebrities were of a different mold than New York's. The rabbi shared coffee with the colorful chief of police, "Pappy" Bond. At the Schachtels' first home on Rio Vista Street, the rabbi got acquainted with neighbor Leon Jaworski, chief prosecutor of the army's War Crimes Trials Section and one of the first witnesses to the Nazi death camps. On hospital rounds, Schachtel struck up a friendship with heart surgeon Denton Cooley, a third-generation Houstonian, and with Cooley's chief rival, Dr. Michael De Bakey. Maxine Mesinger, society writer for the *Chronicle,* name-dropped the rabbi in her columns. "I saw him at parties," she recalled. "He was always invited. Very big on the piano. He wasn't the entertainer per se. He would run over to the piano and play in friends' homes."[84]

It goes without saying that the rabbi made the guest list for Texas' party of the century: the opening, March 17, 1949, of millionaire Glenn Mc-Carthy's eighteen-story Shamrock Hotel. The oilman's rowdy reception, immortalized in novelist Edna Ferber's *Giant,* drew fifty thousand curiosity seekers who mobbed the grounds of the high rise. Some 175 Hollywood personalities arrived via chartered planes, trains, and limousines. The rabbi, who had previously taken a few spins in McCarthy's private plane, rated two reserved seats in the coffee shop. Of course, the coffee shop patrons coveted tables in the hotel's fancier restaurants, and the restaurant diners envied the guests in the Emerald Room. Those in the Emerald Room wished they had stayed home, especially when gate-crashers disrupted Dorothy Lamour's nightclub act with expletives and barnyard hoots picked up on the NBC microphone. The ensuing melee halted the network broadcast. Within two years, Glenn McCarthy's empire was $55 million in debt.[85]

POLITICAL VIBRATIONS

In Houston, the pursuit of money and the rewards of capitalism were celebrated with flash. In contrast, the pursuit of justice had to be low-key.
Houston's citizenry distrusted movements to eradicate poverty, unionize
labor, and subsidize school lunches with farm surpluses. That hinted of
socialism. Never mind that federal contracts had pumped millions into locally produced airplane fuel, synthetic rubber, chemical explosives, steel,
and aluminum. That fostered capitalism. In Houston, a major postwar
concern was creeping communism. Public officials and radio commenta-
tors—among them Schachtel—altered their rhetoric accordingly.

The Minute Women of the U.S.A., Houston's most militant Red Scare
group, in 1954 published a twenty-five-page list of "individuals . . . affiliated with . . . Communist-Front Organizations."[86] Schachtel's name appeared on the dossier. The rabbi scoffed at the absurdity, finding himself
in good company with three university presidents and Catholic archbishop Robert Lucey. Schachtel's appearance on the list was surprising,
because his radio broadcasts seemed tempered to give right-wing listeners what they wanted to hear—that communism was "godless," "atheistic," "evil," and "intolerant." His well-received George Washington's
Birthday sermon had contained a parallel between the fight against communism and the nobility of America's Revolutionary War. An Easter
Sunday sermon compared communism with the "bondage of Egypt."[87]
During one of the few radio sermons in which Schachtel criticized Mc-
Carthyism at length, he balanced his condemnation of blacklists and witch
hunts with an appeal to patriotism, asking listeners to "rise and with me"
recite the pledge of allegiance to the flag.[88] Most assuredly, thousands of
listeners did.

During the civil rights era, Schachtel kept his rhetoric low-key, convinced that his friendships with African American pastors and their congregations demonstrated far more than words. When students from Texas
Southern University, a black institution, staged sit-ins at Houston lunch
counters in the spring of 1960, Schachtel was appointed to a forty-one-
member Citizens' Relations Committee headed by friend Leon Jaworski.
The committee achieved little more than a two-week halt to the picketing.
In typical Houston style, lunch counters were integrated by fiat and without fanfare. Bob Dundas, "political fixer" and longtime public relations

manager at Foley's Department Store, brokered an agreement among seventy stores to integrate quietly at the end of the summer. Local news media consented to a ten-day press blackout on the issue. Without headlines, heroics, or police brutality, Houston dropped its most blatant Jim Crow practices.[89]

Among the relics of segregation was Houston's Jefferson Davis Hospital, a building named after the Confederate president and exposed in 1964 as a filthy, penurious, roach-invested facility.[90] A new public hospital, woefully understaffed, was headed in the same direction. During Barbara Schachtel's tenure on the hospital board, the situation was addressed and a state-of-the-art facility constructed. She suggested naming the institution Abraham Lincoln Hospital. But Quentin Mease, an African American on the board, knew the Daughters of the Confederacy would have a fit. He proposed a more politically astute namesake: Lyndon Baines Johnson.[91]

Johnson was another friend to the Schachtels. The rabbi had met LBJ through political adviser Jack Valenti, whose column in the *Houston Post* ran alongside Schachtel's. In no time at all, LBJ was referring to Schachtel as "my rabbi." When Johnson was inaugurated president of the United States on January 20, 1965, Schachtel delivered an inaugural prayer. Eyes heavenward, Schachtel prayed to the nation: "We ask for no miracles beyond the miracle which is always with us, if we will only use it, the power of love to transform foes into friends, slaves into free men, the curse of war and poverty into the benediction of concord and plenty."[92]

"It was the high point of his ministry," his wife recalled. During another visit to Washington, the Schachtels joined the Johnsons for a White House family dinner. Seated around the dining room table, they partook in a home-style meal of corned beef, cabbage, and vanilla-wafer flavored "cabinet pudding." When the Schachtels visited Europe and Israel in 1965, Valenti arranged for them to meet with Israeli prime minister Levi Eshkol as well as embassy officials, with the rabbi filing a report of his impressions. Johnson periodically telephoned the rabbi to ask how he thought his administration was faring. Schachtel disagreed with the president's buildup in Vietnam, and as the war dragged on he tried to protect LBJ from critics. Barbara Schachtel recalled: "On one of his radio talks, he spoke about how LBJ had to rely on reports from his generals in the field, etc. He sent a copy of the talk to LBJ. The result was a brief thank-you note. Their friendship had come to an abrupt ending. Later we learned that he allowed no criticism about 'his war.'"[93]

RELIGIOUS RIVALS

The person with whom Schachtel most sought rapprochement and colle-
giality was rival Rabbi Robert I. Kahn. That friendship eluded him. The
tension separating the two rabbis and their congregations took more than
forty years and two generations to dissipate—and still haunts those who
recall it firsthand. In 1949, a joint board meeting merely reinforced the
freeze. A decade after the split, Anne Nathan Cohen, who was partial toward Schachtel, wrote Congregation Beth Israel's centenary history, gingerly referring to the split as "a matter of principles." Fearful that her sub-
jectivity would show, Cohen delegated to her son the task of writing up
the schism.[94]

Splinter groups remained. Lep Meyer turned ardently pro-Zionist and
condemned Beth Israel for its initial reluctance to participate in Israeli
bond drives. Meanwhile, thirty-seven families, disturbed at the temple's
drift away from classical Reform Judaism, splintered off in 1957 to create
the Houston Congregation for Reform Judaism. Before breaking away, the
group members told Schachtel they felt no animosity toward him, but
they simply wanted their children to learn Judaism exactly the way their
grandparents had. The new congregation, which uses the out-of-print
Union Prayer Book, grew to around one hundred families and remains
viable.[95]

Beth Israel continued to grow and prosper, constructing an impressive,
multimillion-dollar building on a twenty-one-acre campus in the 1960s.
Because of the edifice's dozens of outside pillars, some congregants good-
naturedly called the temple the "Taj"—others called it "Taj Schachtel."
Visitors from less affluent congregations marveled at the podium, which
rose at the push of a button, and the telephone on the pulpit that led children to ask if their rabbi talked with God.

After Israel's victorious 1967 war, Texans and southerners in general became boosters of Israel. The following year, on December 8, 1968, Beth Israel finally and unanimously repealed the Basic Principles—the platform
"adopted midst such controversy twenty-five years ago," Schachtel stated
in a letter to Jacob Rader Marcus, founding director of the American Jewish Archives.[96] "While these principles have de facto been forgotten for
many years, last night they were officially eliminated." The Basic Principles
had hardly been forgotten as far as Rabbi Bob Kahn was concerned. He felt
a weight lifted at the news of their repeal. In his oral memoir, Kahn re-

*Rival rabbis Robert I. Kahn, left, and Hyman Judah Schachtel, together
for a joint ceremony in Houston, undated.* Courtesy Hyman Judah
Schachtel Library, Beth Israel of Houston, Texas.

called, "Finally, when . . . Beth Israel rescinded the Basic Principles, . . . I
felt fully vindicated in the stand I had taken."[97]

For decades, Kahn and Schachtel moved in overlapping circles, their
demeanor toward each other restrained. Both wrote several books. Both
wrote weekly columns for competing newspapers. Both served on boards
of social agencies and received awards indicative of meritorious service to
social causes, although Kahn was the more outspoken of the two. Both
taught locally on the campuses of the University of Houston, St. Mary's
Catholic Seminary, and the University of St. Thomas. Both served terms as
president of the Houston Rabbinical Association and the Kallah of Texas
Rabbis. Nationally, both participated in the Central Conference of American Rabbis. Schachtel served on the conference executive board in the

mid-1960s but was never tapped for the presidency—a slight linked to lingering scorn over the Beth Israel revolt.[98] "The other rabbis took Rabbi Kahn's side," said historian Abram Goodman, a New York rabbi who served in Austin from 1935 to 1941. "Rabbi Schachtel was sort of an outlaw."[99] In 1973, Rabbi Kahn was tapped for the prestigious post of rabbinical conference president.

Schachtel retired in 1975, adopting the title "rabbi at large" rather than emeritus. His affinity for celebrity never waned. In retirement, he led High Holiday worship at Martha's Vineyard, a vacation destination for the affluent and prominent. His participation in nonprofit causes multiplied, and so did the accolades and awards. Rabbi Kahn retired in 1978 with the traditional title of rabbi emeritus and continues in that capacity.

The two rabbis' names were joined in 1982 when philanthropic Houston Jews contributed to a Kahn-Schachtel Fellowship Fund to underwrite scholarships for Christian scholars studying at Hebrew Union College. Despite a joint testimonial dinner, the Schachtels still perceived Kahn as aloof. Finally, in 1986, when Schachtel was seventy-nine, Kahn made what Schachtel interpreted as a collegial gesture. He seconded Schachtel's nomination as vice president of the National Organization of Retired Reform Rabbis. Flattered, Schachtel served as the group's vice president and then its president, savoring the nod of the rabbi he had displaced.[100] Kahn, however, was unaware of any extraordinary gesture: "A motion was made to accept the slate, and I simply seconded the motion."[101]

LEGACIES

Hyman Judah Schachtel's legacy remains contradictory and controversial. To Houston's Christian community, he stands as a symbol of harmony, an ecumenical figure who ministered to Texans from high society to the city jail. President George Bush phoned his condolences upon Schachtel's death on January 11, 1990.

In the Jewish world, however, Schachtel's name evokes discord. The American Council for Judaism still rankles those who worked for the creation of Israel. In 1976, Schachtel angered members of the Texas Jewish Historical Society when he objected to the Jewish exhibit at the Institute of Texan Cultures, which showcases the state's ethnic groups. In a throwback to the rhetoric of the Basic Principles, Schachtel wrote the institute's director that "Jews are essentially a religious community." He was "surprised" to see them featured as a distinct cultural group.[102] Volunteers who had pushed for inclusion of the Jewish exhibit in the public hall heard echoes of the 1943 controversy.

The battle over the Basic Principles remains affixed to Schachtel's résumé. The fight also tempered his style. Rebuked because he would not or could not quell the Beth Israel revolt, after 1949 Schachtel rarely ventured back to the front lines of controversy. His initiation at Beth Israel had turned him cautious. During the Red Scare and the civil rights era, he muted his public remarks. At rabbinical conferences, he was reticent when controversy flared. "He turned more inward, more pastoral, more psychological. He eschewed the political arena," said Eugene Mihaly, the Hebrew Union College professor who eulogized Schachtel in the *Central Conference of American Rabbis' Yearbook.* The two became acquainted during visits to Martha's Vineyard and a rabbinical mission to the Soviet Union, but they never discussed the Basic Principles. "That whole point of view became discredited," Mihaly said. "It was a painful reminder for him. The whole profile of Judaism changed. The Holocaust came to haunt us."

In 1943 Schachtel was recruited to Texas to lead a divided Jewish congregation that eventually splintered into three. He rose above controversy by mixing with the larger Houston community. After the nation of Israel was born, he worked for Jewish unity and embraced a cause he had previously disavowed. The heated rhetoric of his early years in New York and Houston reflected the fervor of the times, confidence in his cause, and the ambitions of a younger rabbi. His later career is a testament to his skill at interfaith dialogue. Many gentiles funded memorials to Schachtel, including an ongoing lecture series and the Congregation Beth Israel library. Schachtel's positive high profile throughout Houston raised the status of all Jews, dispelled negative stereotypes, and opened doors for his co-religionists. Those who recruited him hoped to leave just such a legacy. Schachtel had come to Houston on the strength of his anti-Zionist credentials, a path to prestige that turned into notoriety and that his later accomplishments never quite eclipsed.

11

Conscience of a Community

LEVI OLAN, DALLAS

12:40 P.M. We interrupt this program to bring you a special bulletin from ABC radio. . . . Three shots were fired at President Kennedy's motorcade today in downtown Dallas, Texas."

—UPI RADIO BROADCAST, NOVEMBER 22, 1963

THE MURDER SUSPECT was Lee Harvey Oswald. Another culprit was the host city of Dallas, a place where hatred of federal authority reached such depths that schoolchildren cheered at news of the president's death. A full-page ad framed in black in the *Dallas Morning News* labeled the president a traitor and agent of the enemy.[1] One month earlier, United Nations Ambassador Adlai Stevenson was booed, picketed, and shaken by a crowd that rocked his limousine. Three years before, vice presidential nominee Lyndon Johnson and his wife had been spat upon by a society crowd.[2]

Cognizant of an "evil brooding for some time," Rabbi Levi Arthur Olan ascended the pulpit at Temple Emanu-El eight hours after President John F. Kennedy's assassination and preached about the "shame of a city." Dallas had permitted extremism to fester for years. "The guilt is all our guilt," he reasoned. Exposed to international glare, the luster of Big D was tarnished. Two days later, on his Sunday morning radio show, which reached more than 200,000 listeners, the rabbi blasted Dallasites and analyzed their "special" shame: "It happened here. He was our guest. . . . This was not the act of one misguided assassin. . . . Hate spewed out. This was the final act of all our hates in one insane moment. . . . We reap what we sow."[3]

The mayor disagreed. He told reporters that this chance tragedy could have happened in Podunk.[4] Dallas's black eye was undeserved. Some business leaders sought cosmetic solutions, perhaps a public relations firm to pretty up the municipal image. Most belittled the call from Olan and a handful of theologians for "communal psychoanalysis."[5] One of the rabbi's Methodist colleagues received death threats after CBS cameras filmed his sermon comparing the city with Pontius Pilate washing his hands of responsibility. Dallas, the Southwest's chic outpost of fashion and finance, was reluctant to acknowledge its intolerance or give evidence of atonement. Rather than eulogize the slain president or condemn the assassin, Dallas became engrossed in its self-image.[6] Recalled Stanley Marcus, a confidant of the rabbi's and president of the luxury Neiman-Marcus store, "There was a general question Dallas was struggling with: whether they wanted to accept any moral censure from the rest of the country and the world, or whether they wanted to fight it and tell the rest of the world to go to hell."[7]

Dallas's top political leaders heeded Olan's words. Nine days after the assassination, the rabbi and a handful of his close associates were among twenty people appointed by the mayor and county judge to serve on the Citizens Memorial to JFK Committee. Creation of the panel was a small turning point and a focal point for community soul-searching. Also serving on the panel were Dr. Willis M. Tate, president of Southern Methodist University, an educator who had stood up to Red-baiting just two years before; African American minister Caesar Clark, at whose church Olan had preached; and Marcus, the city's best-known ambassador. The committee included business titans and politicians. Together, they launched a drive to solicit money and ideas for a JFK memorial.[8]

Hundreds of ideas poured in, but few pledges. Olan, at times smug about his fund-raising clout, found the JFK memorial committee a hard sell. From a former temple president, he solicited but $250.[9] Another congregant wrote the rabbi that he had a different Dallas project in mind for his money. He would give the JFK memorial further thought after a trip to

Europe.[10] Dallas Jews also wanted assassination details to fade. Jack Ruby, the nightclub operator who killed Lee Harvey Oswald two days after the assassination, was Jewish and a member of local Congregation Sheareth Israel.[11] In the end, the committee raised $200,000. "It wasn't a large amount," recalled committee member James M. Stemmons, a millionaire developer.[12] Of the sum, $75,000 was donated to the John F. Kennedy Presidential Library in Massachusetts as an expression of sympathy from the people of Dallas. The rest was earmarked for a memorial.[13] Constructed seven years after the assassination, the monument is a cenotaph, or empty tomb, symbolic of the void left by JFK's death. The monument's starkness won few fans, but as Olan had told his radio audience in the days after the president's death, "Let us not turn our sorrow into a vain thing."[14]

TRUE TO FORM

That Rabbi Levi Olan was a voice pushing unpopular sentiments was par for his Texas tenure, which ran from 1949 to 1984, and typical of his career. The man whose message and presence reverberated across the airwaves of the nation's tenth-largest city was more than a moralizing preacher or gadfly. He was Dallas's civic conscience, a master rabbinical teacher who put issues into a moral framework and then helped search for philosophical and secular solutions.

All his life, Levi Olan had spoken to issues and ethics, sometimes in unorthodox fashion. In his youth, he had stood on a Rochester, New York, street corner spouting socialist maxims, until a police officer sent him scurrying off. In rabbinical school, he had heckled teachers from the back of the class and run with a clique of rebels who questioned the omnipotence of God and the scholarship of their professors.[15] At his first pulpit in Worcester, Massachusetts, the young rabbi upbraided the community because its Easter passion play dredged up centuries of prejudice: "Christianity persists in being Christless," he railed.[16] In Dallas, a city with a "most unhumble penchant for desiring to be first," he listened to a Baptist pastor boast that his congregation was the biggest in the nation and a Methodist minister brag that his church was the largest in his denomination. How did Olan's synagogue rank? He frankly told them, "We have the largest mortgage."[17]

A clergyman with mocking retorts and unsettling observations, Olan riveted a wide segment of the public through his half-hour Sunday morning radio sermons. On the air, he castigated those decadent Dallasites who plumbed their faucets with champagne but voted down federally subsidized school lunches for the poor. He sneered at glassy skyscrapers—modern-day "golden calves"[18]—that cast shadows across the unpaved roads of the city's Little Mexico. ("We glory in private initiative: we vote down public housing on high principles.")[19] He warned that America's racial tension could erupt into riots, for "prejudice is an evil which can explode an atomic or a hydrogen bomb."[20] More than negative harangues, Olan's radio addresses challenged listeners to draw contemporary meaning from religious subject matter. He infused each message with a hopeful, modern theology that urged a fusion of the Ten Commandments and technology, rather than an idealized return to the past. He translated the philosophy of Martin Buber into a twenty-five-minute radio sermon that contrasted the worship of God with the reverence of objects.[21] He called the Bible the "least-read bestseller" and startled listeners by branding the creation story a "beautiful myth," beautiful in that it ascribes no race or religion to Adam and Eve, only "a spark of the spiritual."[22] He embraced the theory of evolution as a "breakthrough" toward understanding the universe.[23]

Unlike other radio rabbis—David Lefkowitz before him in Dallas and Hyman Judah Schachtel, his contemporary in Houston—Olan rarely soothed and never appeased. Head on, he confronted troubling issues such as anti-Semitism, McCarthyism, and errors of the Vietnam War. Again and again, he returned to the arrogance of racism. ("The fact is, [the black man] is down in the pit because we put him there.")[24] As churchgoers across the region readied for Sunday School and Sunday worship, many who listened to Olan's provocative words incorporated his thoughts into their own sermons and lessons. In that manner, the rabbi's discomforting observations became part of the community dialogue.

Far from alienating his Bible Belt community, Olan gained stature. The mayor tapped him for participation in Goals for Dallas, a drive to make the city more democratic in the post-JFK era. The governor appointed him to the University of Texas Board of Regents. He headed the Dallas Housing Authority and served on a plethora of human relations councils and nonprofit agency boards. His colleagues elected him president of the Central Conference of American Rabbis. When *Fortune* magazine took a critical look at Dallas in the wake of the Kennedy assassination, it deemed Olan the area's "most powerful religious voice."[25] In a city where McCarthyism did not ebb until the death of JFK, the conservative *Dallas*

Morning News dubbed the rabbi a "Dallas Prophet" as well as a "born dis-turber of the peace."[26]

UNLIKELY PATH TO THE RABBINATE

A native of the Ukraine, Levi Arthur Olanovsky was born near the town of Cherkassy on March 22, 1903, the only child of immigrant parents who fled the pogroms of Russia when he was three. An Ellis Island clerk short-ened the family surname to Olan, and, in like style, Levi's father Ameri-canized his first name from Mordecai to Max. The family settled in Rochester's congested Jewish ghetto, where hundreds of refugees found jobs in the needle trades but placed their hopes in the socialist platform of the local Workman's Circle. Initially, Max Olan eked out a livelihood sell-ing odds and ends from a bicycle that he pedaled along the streets and al-leys of the Jewish enclave. Soon he opened a little store, then a little larger store where he sold groceries and dry goods.[27] New York's blue laws closed businesses on Sundays, a restriction that kept Max Olan's friends from shopping altogether, for they worked long hours during the week and re-frained from handling money on Saturday, the Jewish Sabbath. To assist a few co-religionist friends, Max Olan quietly opened his shop on Sundays and stationed young Levi outdoors as a lookout.[28]

The Olans lived above the family store at 253 Hudson Avenue in a household where Yiddish was spoken and Judaism was pervasive. In the kitchen was a *"pushke,* a little tin box" into which Levi and his younger sis-ter Bertha dropped coins to help buy acreage in the Promised Land. "It wasn't called the state of Israel then," Olan noted. "Ultimately, we would own the land that was promised to us." Levi's mother, Bessie Leshinsky Olan, kept a kosher household. His father was treasurer at the Hasidische Shul, a Lubavich synagogue without a rabbi, where men sat apart from women and chanted the liturgy by rote. Levi accompanied his father to services, but often ducked outdoors during the Torah reading and com-mentary. At home, Levi studied Hebrew with a bearded tutor who was paid "fifty cents, a glass of tea, and Mother's delicious cookies." The social center of the neighborhood was the Baden Street Settlement House estab-lished by uptown, assimilated German Jews. Olan joined the settlement house debate team, arguing the merits of the jury system and public own-ership of utilities.[29]

Levi's favorite settlement house memories were from the Boys Literary Club, of which he was a charter member. His best buddies in the BLC, as it was called, were future rabbis Milton Steinberg and Sidney Regner. Steinberg, who became an important thinker in the 1940s Reconstructionist movement, was already pondering why God permitted a world with poverty and war. He persuaded Levi to study with him after school at the neighborhood Talmud Torah school, where the principal, Mr. Rosenberg, doubled as Hebrew and philosophy teacher.[30] Levi's good friend Milton moved to New York when he was sixteen and ultimately enrolled in the Jewish Theological Seminary that ordains Conservative rabbis. Levi's other boyhood chum, Sidney Regner, graduated from high school in Rochester and enrolled in Cincinnati's Hebrew Union College, the institution that trains Reform rabbis.

Initially, Olan dismissed thoughts of a rabbinical career: "I was not one of those who was a gung ho religious person. I wasn't 'called.'"[31] Instead, the legal profession seemed to beckon this boy who warmed to a debate. He was also fascinated with history, philosophy, and the theory of evolution. A career in academia might have followed had Ivy League doors been wide open to Jews. The University of Rochester, a mile's walk from the Olan store, had the courses he sought. And it was affordable, thanks to financial aid available through George Eastman, founder of the local Eastman Kodak Company. After two years at his hometown university, Olan hankered for an out-of-town campus. Hebrew Union College, which his friend Regner urged him to attend, was tuition-free and offered a joint curriculum with the University of Cincinnati. Olan applied. "Why do you want to come to Hebrew Union College?" several rabbis inquired during his 1925 entrance interview. "Because I have a friend here," young Olan replied. "They laughed like the Devil."[32]

BECOMING A RABBI

Rabbinical school proved less than satisfying. "Theoretical absolutes were handed to us," Olan complained.[33] One history teacher lectured from note cards arranged out of chronological sequence. College president Julian Morgenstern—"Morgie" behind his back—threatened to expel Olan for his "attitude," but his scholastic performance kept him in. Although Levi tended to be a comic and a smart aleck in the classroom, professors could

*Levi Olan, front, joking around with six other rabbinical students at the Hebrew
Union College campus, ca. 1926. Behind Olan, from bottom to top, are Sidney
Regner, class of '27; Phineas Smoller, '30; Norman Goldburg, '29; Leon Feuer, '27;
B. Benedict "Babe" Glazer, '26; and Maurice Eisendrath, '26.* Photo from Jacob
Rader Marcus Center of the American Jewish Archives, Cincinnati.

tell from his cocked head and his sardonic comments that he absorbed
their lessons. The class that most impressed Levi was Dr. Moses "Butsy"
Buttenweiser's course on the prophets, which presented a biblical basis for
social activism. Although Olan mimicked "Butsy's" thick German accent,
he was moved by the professor's "passionate diatribes" on behalf of Nicola
Sacco and Bartolomeo Vanzetti—the Italian immigrants executed in 1927
after convictions based more on their anarchist views than the evidence.[34]

Upon his 1929 ordination, Olan moved to Worcester, Massachusetts,
and Temple Emanuel, which met in a converted private girls' school. To a
congregation reeling from the stock market crash, he naively preached
utopian ideals. Most congregants had strong traditional backgrounds and
disliked the English that Olan inserted into the service. They were of-
fended when the young rabbi insisted that a Jew could be an atheist. They
were attentive when a community forum, presided over by Olan, brought
to town Socialist Party president Norman Thomas, who became the rabbi's friend. They observed their rabbi becoming more empathetic after a
term as president of the United Jewish Charities brought him face to face

with the gap between charitable donations and earthly needs. They endorsed his interfaith forays and his practice of trading pulpits with Methodist, Baptist, Congregational, and Unitarian ministers.[35]

Despite a calendar full of clerical and civic activities, Olan sensed a void. He puzzled over the role of the rabbi, a word that literally means teacher. "I didn't feel that I was really getting anywhere. . . . I really wanted to put my teeth into something." For advice, he visited Harvard University professor Harry A. Wolfson, one of the foremost historians of Jewish Western philosophy, whom Olan knew by reputation only. Introducing himself, the junior rabbi candidly told the philosophical giant, one of the greatest Jewish scholars of his day, "Dr. Wolfson, I just became rabbi in Worcester, Massachusetts, and I don't know what to do." The philosopher "roared" at that. "He began to talk to me and outline a course of study. And that's how my career really was fashioned," Olan recalled years later. "I got into the discipline of spending mornings studying some of the things we talked about, particularly philosophy . . . then I'd go to the temple in the afternoons."[36]

Olan's self-guided curriculum began with the works of John Dewey (1859–1952), the American educator who applied the scientific method to social problems. "He influenced . . . my reasoning and thinking," Olan said. "It had nothing to do with theology." From Dewey, Olan moved to German philosopher Friedrich Hegel (1770–1831), who emphasized the progress of history and ideas, then to American psychologist/philosopher William James (1842–1910). Hegel and James influenced Dewey's thinking. "William James proposed the idea that progress makes life significant," Olan wrote.[37] Concurrently, the rabbi studied the Babylonian Talmud, meshing its ancient theological insights with modern philosophy. He delved into the ideas of contemporary Jewish philosophers such as Franz Rosenzweig (1886–1929), who worked with and influenced Martin Buber (1878–1965), and Henri-Louis Bergson (1859–1941), the French philosopher who tried to combine philosophy with action. Methodically, Olan pieced together the evolution of ideas and filtered the concepts into his sermons.

He gradually arrived at a basic definition of religion—"a conviction that there is God." He believed in a "limited" God who created a "moral universe"—not the omniscient God of Job or the omnipotent God of Exodus. Olan preached that perceptions of God change with human experience. The God concepts held by Moses or Job or Jesus, he said, were incongruent with contemporary times: "We have difficulty in accepting

literally the crossing of the Red Sea, the walking on the water, the miracu-
lous creation of the world in six days. . . . This whole pattern of ritual and
miracle just does not fit the modern mental and intellectual climate."[38] By
the mid-1940s, the horror of the Holocaust and the atom bomb had popularized Friedrich Nietzsche's dictum that "God is dead." Hebrew Union
College became home to a professor espousing a "death of God" theology.[39] Freudian psychiatry gave excuses for irrational behavior. Disturbed
that so many worshipers had replaced God with absolute faith in science,
technology, and psychology, the studious rabbi argued for religion's relevance: "Religion certainly does have something to say about war, about
strikes, about social discrimination, about poverty. It believes that there is
a moral law as absolute as the physical law. Just as the law of gravity operates all the time and we respect it, so the moral law operates all the time,
and when we fail to respect it we get violence, war, and disorder."[40]

The rabbi projected his weighty thoughts in an authoritative baritone,
a resonant rumble that jolted listeners to think in new ways. Those who
heard his sermons for the first time were surprised to shake his hand and
realize that the rabbi's voice belied his physical size. He was a bantam of a
man, five-feet five-inches tall, with athletic shoulders and a tendency to
cross his arms and engage in conversation with a fixed, unblinking eye. He
could be intimidating: berating a man who found a sermon "enjoyable"
rather than "challenging," or ordering a chattering congregation to "shut
up."[41] He could also be warm: exchanging affectionate notes with an elderly woman who showed him her Yiddish poetry.[42] Off the pulpit, Olan's
pipe added a professorial air to his appearance, while his idealism drew
college youth. Not overly concerned about his attire, he wore standard
business suits with white shirt and tie and rarely thought to buy new shoes
until his wife pointed out holes in the soles of the pair he was wearing.

Olan's wife, Sarita, was his opposite—a shy woman and a fashionable
dresser who wore tailored outfits with matching hats and gloves. The
daughter of a Cincinnati builder, Sarita Messer Olan was Levi's one and
only girl, his wife since 1931. Her given name was Sadie, which she changed
to Sarita, a name she took from a song.[43] Sarita had met Levi during a
dance at Hebrew Union College. Her parents invited the rabbinical student to their home for dinner, and, forever after, Olan liked to tease Sarita,
"I married you because I was hungry."[44] She taught school until their marriage and her move to Massachusetts, where she became a full-time home-
maker. Uncomfortable in the public eye, she left the theatrics to her hus-

band and her brother, Samuel G. Messer—a musician whose bass voice and hefty physique led to a Hollywood career under the stage name Robert Middleton. Many a night, Levi and Sarita stayed up past midnight to catch her brother's Westerns and classic films noir on late-night television.[45] When Olan's colleagues caught him yawning, he blamed his lack of sleep on his brother-in-law.[46]

CALL TO THE SOUTH

After nearly two decades in Worcester, the rabbi and the congregation had grown comfortable with one another—although it irked Olan that any temple member over age sixty still thought of him as "this young man just out of college." Olan's routine of morning study, afternoons at the temple, and year-round community involvement was set. His home was alive with the antics and growing pains of three children—Elizabeth, age twelve; Frances, better known as "Buzzy," age seven; and David, who was only a year old.

Then a call came from Texas during the spring of 1948. David Lefkowitz, former president of the Central Conference of American Rabbis and long-time spiritual leader at Dallas's largest congregation, was retiring. The Dallas search committee wanted a seasoned rabbi who could not only guide and inspire the congregation but step into the role of civic leader in their city of 400,000. The congregational elders wanted a progressive rabbi who would help counter Dallas's image as parochial and inbred. The committee consulted Boston's Rabbi Joshua Loth Liebman just weeks before his untimely death. Liebman, author of the 1946 bestseller *Peace of Mind,* endorsed Levi Olan.[47]

Olan agonized over the pulpit offer; Sarita was negative. She had no desire to uproot herself or the children, especially for a region so different and distant.[48] Dallas, twice as populous as Worcester, had about the same number of Jews—close to ten thousand. Texas Jews had absorbed the local culture so well that Dallas had nary a bagel shop. Olan's liberal cronies told him he was "off his rocker" to even consider preaching in Dallas, a reactionary region where Eleanor Roosevelt remained controversial and Harry Truman was regarded as a communist.[49] Quite the contrary, the southern political climate intrigued Olan, who was unperturbed by the naysayers. "My answer to them was, 'It's very easy to stand for [liberal] things in New England. . . . The real place to stand for them is where they are challenged, and if you're really going to do anything about them, that is the place to do it.' "[50]

Also pushing Olan toward Texas were two heavyweights in the Reform Jewish movement: Hebrew Union College president Nelson Glueck, a popular biblical archaeologist, and Jacob Rader Marcus, founder of the American Jewish Archives. They discerned a population trend of Jews moving to the Southwest and forecast the region's importance to organized Judaism. They viewed Dallas as an ideal pulpit for introducing changes in liturgy, ritual, and direction that the Reform movement had embraced but the South had largely ignored. Temple Emanu-El, the Lone Star State's second-largest Jewish congregation, could become a beacon to the region.[51] Olan, an innovator and activist, seemed well suited for the mission. Moreover, he had the personality and "pizzazz" that Marcus considered a necessary ingredient for success in Texas.[52] A harbinger of change, he would also usher in an era of Eastern European influence on Texas Reform Judaism.

Despite his mental preparation, the rabbi's introduction to Texas was an unexpected blast of hot air. As he stepped off the plane for his initial August interview, the rabbi remarked, "Who opened the furnace?" Summer heat aside, Olan found the environs agreeable. The Dallas skyline conveyed a playful optimism—from the neon-lit radio antenna atop the Mercantile Bank to the red-winged Pegasus soaring over the Magnolia Building and visible across the prairie. The city's top capitalists—an oligarchy of self-made men who set the city's agenda—impressed Olan.[53] A number of those business leaders served on the temple board: cotton broker Louis Tobian; Republic Bank president Fred Florence; advertising whiz Sam Bloom; philanthropist Julius Schepps; and national chain-store jeweler Morris Zale. The synagogue's president-elect, Alex Weisberg, was president of the Dallas Art Museum.

Dallas's fine arts were well endowed—if not well attended. The rabbi chuckled when he heard banker R. L. Thornton remark, "I'll give you all the money you want for a symphony on one condition: you'll never make me go."[54] Olan saw that there was a great deal to do in Dallas, as well as a great deal of raw material to work with. One more plus—life in Texas guaranteed year-round tennis, a bonus for Olan, who enjoyed the camaraderie of a doubles game.[55]

Olan and his family moved to Texas the last day of 1948, arriving in time for the New Year's Day Cotton Bowl. At the annual football classic, the rabbi sat in shirtsleeves among seventy-two thousand fans reveling in the balmy winter weather. He did not realize the import of his presence—or the scope of his mission—until another gridiron contest. When he tried to leave the stands for the restroom during a tight fourth-quarter situation, he was blocked by Texas governor Allan Shivers, who said, "Sit down. We can't spare you now."[56]

Of course, the transition from Worcester to Dallas entailed more than shirtsleeves, spectator sports, and gridiron blessings.[57] The blunt, forty-five-year-old rabbi and his reserved wife could not begin to fill the shoes of David and Sadie Lefkowitz, a seasoned rabbinical team. Lefkowitz—"the doctor" to some—was more pastor than preacher, a soothing rabbi with an affinity for hospital visits and empathy toward all creatures.[58] Sadie Lefkowitz—"Aunt Sadie" to the temple family—was a dynamo in the Visiting Nurses Association, the leading voice in the Sabbath morning choir, and a key member of the local Sisterhood and the National Association of Temple Sisterhoods.[59]

From the start, Olan made certain the search committee understood that it was hiring him, not his wife.[60] He let them know his strength was big ideas, not small talk. He was more prone to challenge than comfort. ("Rabbi Olan didn't suffer fools," remarked a congregant. "He had little use for mediocrity," concurred another.)

Fortunately, the new rabbi and the retiring rabbi achieved a comfortable rapport. Lefkowitz continued performing the hospital rounds, house calls, and hand-holding that were second nature to him. Olan took over Lefkowitz's Sunday morning radio show. Thanks to Lefkowitz, Olan received an automatic appointment to the Perkins School of Theology at Southern Methodist University, where he became a visiting professor of contemporary Judaism. "He had established the office of rabbi so that it was highly respected," Olan said in praise of Lefkowitz. "While our approaches were different, he had made a platform for acceptance that I could easily stand on."[61]

A DIFFERENT SORT OF RABBINATE

Olan knew his mission was to alter the direction of this synagogue, already a vigorous institution proud of its past. Founded in 1872 by prosperous German-Jewish merchants, Temple Emanu-El was launched the same year the railroad arrived in Dallas, and it grew in step with the city. The city became accustomed to finding strong civic figures on Emanu-El's board and pulpit. Under the temple's first rabbi, Aron Suhler (1875–78), Emanu-El operated the city's first nonsectarian school. Its early twentieth-century rabbi, William Greenburg (1901–19), sparked formation of the Humane Society, the Art League, and the Critic Club—an "intimate circle of influential leaders" and a think tank for civic improvements.[62]

The year Olan arrived, the temple had one thousand families on its roster, with five hundred children in its Sunday School. The operating budget approached $100,000. With Southern Methodist University, the temple's Community Course Committee cosponsored appearances by folksinger Burl Ives and U.S. Senator J. William Fulbright. The Temple Youth League sponsored canasta tournaments and a weekend at Wiley's Dude Ranch. The Brotherhood watched college football highlights.[63]

Olan wanted weightier programs, more participation from young adults, and greater emphasis on Jewish culture. Temple Emanu-El's worship service was in English, save one Hebrew prayer, the *Shema.* The temple quartet and organist, who led the congregation in American hymns, were not Jewish—"all goyim," Olan noted. The synagogue rarely celebrated a bar mitzvah, the coming-of-age ceremony for thirteen-year-olds that most Reform congregations abandoned in favor of confirmation, a graduation ceremony from religious school. The Sunday School curriculum taught no Hebrew and very little Jewish history. "In Dallas the job was to make Jews out of goyim," the rabbi quipped. He recruited a Jewish music director who built a volunteer choir with a professional sound and a repertoire of liturgical music sung in Hebrew. A second rabbi was hired as director of education.[64]

More than a few parents shuddered when they saw their children wrapping Hanukkah gifts in the same blue and white colors as the Israeli flag. Many congregants were still active in the American Council for Judaism, the rabid anti-Zionist group that had fought the creation of Israel. The suggestion that an Israeli flag be placed in the sanctuary was the last straw.[65] "We are being taken over by the third wave of immigration," a congregant of German descent complained, referring to Eastern Europeans like Olan.[66] When several hundred disenchanted temple members met with Olan and accused him of leading the congregation toward Orthodoxy and Zionism, the rabbi was bemused. Olan was never a flag-waving Zionist. He had been raised among Lubavitch Jews and socialists who quibbled with Zionists for reasons spiritual and theoretical. Yet he closely identified with Israel's role in Jewish history and culture. He spurned the American Council for Judaism, referring to its director, Rabbi Elmer Berger, as "that prick, Berger."[67] Confronted with rebellious Dallas congregants, Olan firmly told the crowd that his aim was to teach Judaism, not what "laymen told me to teach." The next day the leadership apologized.[68] The board that hired Olan believed in him, even when it disagreed with him.

Other adjustments were in order. Olan refused to raise money for day-to-day temple operations, although he had innovative ideas for spending whatever came in and more. "I'm a very expensive rabbi, and I don't mean my salary," he used to say.[69] "Indeed, when I accepted the pulpit, it was with the understanding that laymen raised the money, and I was the religious teacher."[70] He reserved his fund-raising clout for causes innovative or unheralded (such as the JFK memorial, a literacy program for Texas adults, and a book-signing party for a controversial colleague whose previous volume was titled *Christ Without Myth*). The temple officers accepted this stipulation from their rabbi, and board member Sam Bloom took charge of raising funds to finance Olan's innovations.

INTELLECTUAL HIRED HAND

The congregation had yet another adjustment to make: mornings found Rabbi Olan not at the temple but on the SMU campus. There, in the second-floor stacks of the theology school's Bridwell Library, the rabbi retreated to a study carrel, where he continued his philosophical journey. "Levi felt that he was the intellectual hired hand at the temple," explained Bridwell's chief librarian, Decherd Turner, who became Olan's closest friend.[71] To fulfill this role as "the learned man in the Torah," the rabbi spent thirty to forty hours a week absorbed in study.[72] Olan considered his SMU faculty appointment the most important honor conferred upon him in Dallas, for it allowed him to build a nest in academia.[73]

Olan arrived at the theology school library by nine o'clock, poking his head into Turner's office. He kibitzed with the staff a few moments and often passed along a joke—especially if he was just back from a rabbinical conference, a sure source of new quips. Then the rabbi disappeared into the stacks until noon. Calls from home or the temple rarely interrupted Olan. Assistant Rabbi Gerald Klein, hired in November, 1952, handled hospital rounds and routine congregational crises.

In his academic hideaway among the bookshelves, Olan became available to theology students like Zan T. Holmes, Perkins class of '59. "We would debate the critical issues going on," said Holmes, a leading Dallas civil rights figure in years to come. "He would challenge me, raise questions."[74] Paul Boller, popular assistant professor of American intellectual history, likewise looked forward to "bull sessions" with the rabbi alongside a study carrel piled high with books and papers.[75] "His counsel was sought regularly, and it counted," said theology professor Rev. Dr. Alfred Outler, who knew that Olan rarely attended department meetings but could be found on the library's second floor.[76]

Olan never missed lunch. He and Turner often ate at Mrs. Miller's, a restaurant where lentil soup was the specialty. With Schubert Ogden, a theologian who arrived at SMU in 1956, Olan usually lunched at Phil's Deli or Kuby's, a German sausage house a block from the campus. Stanley Marcus, whom *Fortune* magazine called the "conscience of the Dallas leadership," was another regular lunchtime companion.[77] Temple members Joseph Rosenstein and attorney Irving Goldberg, later appointed to the federal bench, shared noontime meals with the rabbi.

More important than the soup du jour was the conversation. "We left religion alone," said Stanley Marcus, a nonpracticing Jew. According to Ogden, "The agenda was culture, art, novels, events in Dallas, politics." Added Outler, "He was very good at repartee . . . and at gossip, for a little bit. He would talk a while and then fix you a question, and woe betide if you hadn't been listening. . . . He always saw local issues in their global perspective and always came at global issues with a sense of their relevance for here at home."[78]

Turner, Ogden, and Boller—all non-Jews—often attended Sabbath services at Temple Emanu-El. Their purpose: to enjoy the "divine" music and to catch Olan's sermons. "I could count on hearing a sermon that said something that made a difference," explained Ogden. "Levi did not, as a matter of conviction, talk down to his congregation."[79]

Books were an object of reverence to the rabbi. When the school of theology opened a new library on December 18, 1950, Olan was the first patron to check out a volume. Over the next thirty years, he was the library's most active user. The myriad of books and journals the rabbi requested ultimately shaped the library's collection.[80]

The rabbi also developed a warm friendship with Lon Tinkle, whose Sunday book column in the *Dallas Morning News* was one of the city's few windows to enlightenment. The rabbi and the reviewer, who was also an

SMU French teacher, commiserated over the condition of the Dallas Public Library, a neglected, turn-of-the-century Carnegie building. One million dollars in library bond money, approved in 1945, was still unspent in 1949. The rabbi and Tinkle, along with twenty-one other prolific readers, became charter members in March, 1950, of Friends of the Dallas Public Library, a group with the clout to move the library onto the city council agenda. At the Friends' initial meeting, disagreement erupted. Col. Alvin Owsley, a lawyer and former American Legion commander, objected to the group's name. It was too similar to the "Friends of Soviet Russia," and too "overworked as a name in communist-front organizations." Olan was appalled. "We liberals won," he joked, but the semantic skirmish was a harbinger of political collisions to come.[81]

The next clash over words was not resolved as quickly. In December, 1951, the head of SMU's English department, John O. Beaty, privately published one thousand copies of *The Iron Curtain Over America*. The book's theme was communist infiltration of America, and its thrust was that Jews are communists.[82] Olan was livid. In a February 17, 1952, radio sermon, "What Shall We Do with Our Prejudices?" the rabbi declared: "It is not uncommon for a college professor to be a man of extreme prejudice. The Nazi universities were full of professional bigots. . . . The fact is that the most educated people and the most widely read and traveled can be the most prejudiced."

Olan expected other voices to repudiate Beaty and his bogus scholarship. But in Dallas, the only public denunciation came from a student newspaper, the *SMU Campus*. Among both the Dallas Jewish community and the SMU faculty, the consensus was to ignore the menacing book rather than draw attention to it. (Besides, some SMU trustees were Beaty backers.) Nationally, the Anti-Defamation League of B'nai B'rith sounded an alarm—a four-page exposé in its monthly newsletter detailing Beaty's previous anti-Semitic speeches and warning of further excesses.[83] However, the American Jewish Committee, which fosters behind-the-scenes methods to overcome anti-Semitism, was closer to the controversy, with a Southwest regional office in Dallas. It counseled caution and quiet consultation with the media. It formed an ad hoc committee with the Dallas Jewish Federation and the National Council of Christians and Jews. When advertisements for *Iron Curtain* appeared in the *New York Times* and the *New York Herald Tribune,* the American Jewish Committee persuaded both papers to refuse future advertising. In Dallas, the *Times Herald* and the *Morning News* agreed not to review the book and to pay Beaty scant attention, perhaps a few sentences when he made a public appearance, but no headlines.[84]

SMU president Umphrey Lee, a man who dodged controversy, had ignored letters of complaint dating back to 1947 regarding Beaty's anti-Semitism. To gingerly demonstrate the university's pro-Jewish stance, Lee wrote a half-page preface to Rabbi David Lefkowitz's collection of essays, *Medicine for a Sick World,* and the SMU Press speeded up the book's publication date.[85] Such timid measures did nothing to dent the effect of *Iron Curtain,* which gained national notoriety with nine printings and sales of forty-five thousand copies. The *Houston Chronicle* raved about the book and quoted Beaty when he accused the Dallas press of censorship.[86]

Olan wanted Dallas Jewry to take a more aggressive stance. So did Stanley Marcus, who argued that the American Jewish Committee's quarantine approach was as futile as fencing in weeds.[87] In late 1953, Paul Boller, the assistant professor who specialized in the history of ideas, grew exasperated at the silence and wrote in the *SMU Campus* that Beaty's book was "a dreary performance, full of distortions, omissions, and half truths." Olan's friend Tinkle then published an end-of-the-year column in the *Dallas Morning News* placing *Iron Curtain* in a special category: books "that should never have been published." Beaty's response, in early 1954, was a mass mailing of an eight-page pamphlet, "How to Capture a University," which slammed B'nai B'rith as a "Jewish Gestapo," attacked the SMU/Temple Emanu-El speaker series, and insinuated that Stanley Marcus was a leftist.[88]

Time magazine assigned a correspondent to cover the controversy, and Boller felt it imperative that the university take a stand before the article got into print. "How would it look if there was no comment?" he asked years later. At Boller's instigation, the Beaty affair was placed on the agenda of a February meeting. The faculty condemned the anti-Semitic professor, 114 to 2. A few days after the vote, seven Dallas clergymen issued a statement denouncing Beaty. SMU's trustees followed with a mild chastisement.[89]

Beaty continued his anti-Semitic assaults in public speeches and unsolicited mailings to students and alumni. Not until Umphrey Lee retired as SMU president in May was the English department chairman rebuked by the administration. The school's next president, Willis M. Tate, confronted Beaty, and the professor's anti-Semitic behavior waned.

The episode had lasted two and a half years. The struggle cemented Olan's ties with kindred spirits on the faculty and identified liberal clergymen in the community. Activists like Boller felt a resurgence of hope. Triumph was possible. They felt invigorated for battles ahead. Observed Schubert Ogden, "Levi did not talk about the Dallas that *was*. He talked about the Dallas that could be. Levi belonged to the future."[90] The same month Beaty was silenced, the U.S. Supreme Court handed down the landmark *Brown v. Board of Education* decision ordering desegregation of public schools. The rabbi and Boller became involved with Dallas Citizens for Peaceful Integration and also signed on as charter members of the Dallas branch of the American Civil Liberties Union. Olan and others at SMU defended Boller's scholarship when the state textbook committee in 1961 impugned a high school history book he coauthored because it included discussions of slavery, Native Americans, and the Salem witch trials. "This was one of the most exciting periods of my career," Boller recalled. "Real issues came up: school integration, McCarthyism, anti-Semitism, charges of communism."[91]

CULTURE WARS

The Red Scare continued to plague Dallas. When a new public library building opened at long last in 1955, the city council denounced as "junk" an abstract metal sculpture in the library lobby, setting off a public outcry against tax dollars underwriting something both politically suspect and incomprehensible. The contractor removed the $8,500 piece. Olan and other "friends of the library" went to work raising private dollars to restore the sculpture to the public domain. During a subsequent art exhibit at the library, the staff capitulated to demands that it remove Pablo Picasso paintings from the walls.[92] Picasso's crime? He had championed the leftist side in the Spanish Civil War.

The Dallas Museum of Art also came under reactionary attack. The American Legion, the Veterans of Foreign Wars, the Dallas Patriotic Council, and the Public Affairs Luncheon Club denounced the museum for exhibiting works of "Red" artists. On their list were Diego Rivera, the Mexican muralist whose radical politics seeped into his work, and Ben Shahn, the Russian-born, American-Jewish painter whose work reflected sympathy toward leftist causes.[93] For an eight-month period in 1955, the

Dallas Museum of Art agreed not to exhibit works from a list of artists tinged by communist ideology.[94] Disgusted at the "emotional explosion," Olan repeatedly preached to the issue over the radio: "Anything we disagree with we call communism. . . . The angry passions can only weaken the nation."[95]

No issues were settled overnight, only over time. Olan derived pleasure from poetic justice. His final response to the art hysteria came a decade later. The temple Sisterhood had raised thousands of dollars from Olan's quarterly "Significant Book" lecture series. He proposed using the proceeds to commission a Ben Shahn tapestry. The rabbi spent a memorable afternoon in Shahn's New Jersey studio talking politics and swapping Yiddish stories. Ben Shahn's massive tapestry, which weaves the words of the 150th Psalm around six musical instruments, became a centerpiece of the temple's art collection. Olan later remarked to a *Dallas Times Herald* reporter, "This is the man [whose paintings the] Dallas Art Museum threw out . . . because he was a liberal."[96]

QUESTIONS OF RACE AND RIGHTS

Olan felt a historical kinship with African Americans: both blacks and Jews endured slavery; both had been dispersed from their native lands; both drew reassurance from the Hebrew Bible, particularly the prophets. Jim Crow laws kept blacks from intruding into white society. Gentlemen's agreements steered Dallas Jews to their own country club and their own law firms.

Dallas's black population realized from the start that it had a rare ally in Rabbi Levi Olan, a white clergyman willing to speak up for them. Olan's earliest radio broadcasts had conveyed his shock upon finding water fountains for "colored" and "white." Dallas was such a segregated town that jukeboxes placed black recording artists into a special category—"race." By 1950, the city had 21,500 black households, but just 14,800 rental units available to African Americans. Most of that housing consisted of shanties serviced by overworked sewage systems. Such apartheid pained the rabbi, who preached that racism is the antithesis of biblical teachings that "each person is a special creation and therefore is sacred." A push to accept federal public housing money became a cornerstone of Olan's preaching. He insisted that housing was a human right and denial of such a "blasphemy against God."[97]

When school integration became the law of the land, Dallas defied the court ruling for seven years—in court with legal challenges and in public with billboards that demanded, "Impeach Earl Warren," the Supreme Court chief justice. White supremacists linked civil rights efforts to communist agitation, but Olan turned their rhetoric inside out. On the radio he declared, "The discrimination against a man because of his color is basically Marxist, a doctrine in which men are like matter, not the creation of God."[98] When peaceful integration of Dallas's public schools finally occurred, Olan refused to join the chorus of praise. The motivation, he noted, was the dollars and cents of the convention trade, not conscience. The effort was token—18 first-graders in 1961, and 131 blacks integrated by 1964.[99]

Integration of schools led to the possibility of an integrated school board, but a schism developed among the African American leadership over which candidate to endorse. Apprised of the discord, Olan met with black ministers and convinced them that a divided minority would lose at the polls. By the close of the meeting, the ministers had agreed upon one candidate, a physician, Emmett J. Conrad, who served on the Dallas school board for the next decade.[100]

Olan's racial views were not without opposition. Hate mail arrived at his home and at the temple; threatening phone calls, too. Opponents tossed eggs at his door.[101] In 1958, days after a synagogue in Atlanta was bombed, police received word of a bomb threat in Dallas. Quietly, authorities stepped up patrols at local Jewish institutions. The threats did not materialize. Olan brushed off such intimidation. The positive response to his message was far more overwhelming than the negative reactions.[102]

Olan received warm support whenever he delivered a guest sermon at Good Street Baptist Church, an African American house of worship where the pastors, Rhett James and Caesar Clark, became his friends and allies. "The rabbi was an unusual man," Clark recalled. "Race or denomination did not pose a problem for him. That was unusual, thirty and forty years ago."[103]

These African American clergymen were always battling the poll tax—the $1.75 cent levy voters paid each election year to register to vote. A vestige of the post-Reconstruction era when white southerners rewrote state constitutions, the poll tax remained law in five states—Texas, Alabama, Arkansas, Mississippi, and Virginia. The levy effectively kept white political oligarchies in power and closed the voting booth to poor, less-educated adults who were most likely to feel a financial pinch or forget to reregister.

*Rabbi Levi Olan, center, and the Rev. Dr. Martin Luther King, Jr., far right,
at poll tax rally in Dallas Fair Park Auditorium, January, 1963. Far left, the
Rev. H. Rhett James. Between Olan and King stands the Rev. J. A. Stansfield.*
Photo by Marion Butts.

Black leaders tried to remind their people to register by hosting poll tax
rallies featuring speakers guaranteed to draw a crowd. On January 4, 1963,
an audience of more than two thousand filled the Fair Park Auditorium to
hear the Rev. Dr. Martin Luther King, Jr., the nation's leading civil rights
leader and advocate of civil disobedience. On stage sat the rabbi, one of
the few white members of the Dallas County United Poll Tax Committee.
A bomb threat an hour before the speech proved to be a hoax, although
the States Rights Party picketed outdoors. King's appearance was front
page news in the *Dallas Express,* the black community's weekly. It received
inside coverage in the *Dallas Times Herald,* which identified the famous
civil rights figure as a "prominent Negro rights leader. . . . [who] gained
national attention as leader of an integration movement in Montgomery,
Alabama." Dallas had a tendency to ignore the outside world as long as
possible.[104]

Yvonne Ewell, an African American educator in the Dallas public schools, sat in the audience the day Martin Luther King spoke and noted the rabbi's presence on stage. For years she had listened to Olan's radio sermons and been impressed with his grasp of institutional racism. He understood that Jim Crow laws and poll taxes were not the only barriers to equality. Solutions required deeper analysis. "Levi was one of the few people in Dallas who understood that racism is embedded in the system," she said. Within two years, Ewell was acquainted with the rabbi and involved in a Temple Emanu-El project that went to the heart of the issue.[105]

It was during the soul-searching aftermath of the Kennedy assassination that the temple's Community Affairs Committee developed a plan for an experimental preschool. For its pilot project, the committee selected Rhoads Terrace, a subsidized housing complex and home to 450 impoverished African American families. At that time, Dallas was the largest city in the nation without public kindergartens. By the time children of the poor enrolled in first grade, most lagged in such basic skills as identifying colors. Many youngsters' learning difficulties were rooted in medical problems easily corrected with eyeglasses, speech therapy, nutrition, or one-on-one attention. The temple committee teamed up with seven county agencies to help such youngsters and to demonstrate the worth of preschool education for the disadvantaged. Rhoads Terrace Pre-School opened in September, 1965, with twenty-nine children, ages four and five. It was to be a two-year, pilot program with a $25,000 budget. Hundreds of temple members pitched in. The rabbi signed his name to a congregational fund-raising letter—a rarity. Volunteers donated paint and built cubbies, cabinets, and play equipment. The temple youth refurbished toys. Women cooked hot lunches at the temple and transported meals to the preschool house. Volunteer drivers took Rhoads Terrace students on weekly field trips to the world beyond their ghetto. A Dialogue Dinner Series, initiated by the preschool parents, enabled Rhoads Terrace adults to meet with teachers and temple members and discuss racial issues. Volunteers, black and Jewish, addressed the school board about the need for public kindergartens.[106]

Rhoads Terrace Pre-School proved its worth, expanded, and became a catalyst for citywide change. Its graduates performed well academically in public school and presented fewer discipline problems than other youngsters. By the early 1970s, the preschool was receiving federal grants. In 1974 it became part of Rhoads Terrace Institute, a nonprofit entity with 70 percent of its funding from the Texas Department of Public Welfare and the rest from private donations. By then, public kindergarten was also a reality in Dallas, a development aided by the Rhoads Terrace example as well as the rabbi's work as a member of the Goals for Dallas Education Committee.[107]

A TIME FOR CHANGE

Dallas was clearly changing from a city too timid to fight anti-Semitism into a more democratic metropolis with grassroots political stirrings. Olan was changing, too. He was aging. He wanted to free himself of the weekly task of writing sermons and focus more time on his studies. He yearned to complete a book that synthesized his lifelong philosophical quest. He became rabbi emeritus in the fall of 1970 and was invited to London for a semester of teaching at the esteemed Leo Baeck College. Although Olan had never earned a Ph.D.—save for honorary doctoral degrees—his intellect and philosophical reach were a match for many of those among the faculty.

The rabbi's philosophical journey had led him into process thinking— a philosophical system in which change is seen as fundamental to reality. Its seminal philosophers are Charles Hartshorne and Alfred North Whitehead. Hartshorne, coincidentally, was appointed to a philosophy chair at the University of Texas in 1962, a semester before Olan began a six-year term on the university's Board of Regents. As was Olan's habit, he cultivated a scholarly friendship with the famous philosopher over lunch. In 1977, when Olan's friends published a book of philosophical essays in his honor, Hartshorne contributed a piece.[108] Olan completed three books during fourteen years of retirement. The first, *Judaism and Immortality,* explores the Jewish view of death and is geared to scholarly readership. The second, *Maturity in an Immature World,* is a compilation of radio sermons and illustrates the rabbi's gift for communicating complex thoughts to a general audience. His final book, *Prophetic Faith and the Secular Age,* coherently blends his philosophical research with the theological journey of the Jewish people. It is dedicated to Sarita, "who translated an illegible scribbling into the final manuscript."[109] The volume, and a series of monographs Olan wrote, led to his recognition as one of the earliest rabbis to combine Judaism and process philosophy. He is one of six Jewish theologians included in the 1996 anthology *Jewish Theology and Process Thought,* a book that contains an essay by Rabbi Harold S. Kushner, popular author of *When Bad Things Happen to Good People.* The anthology's introduction also pays tribute to Milton Steinberg, the boyhood friend who led Olan to his first philosophy teacher. Academicians classify the teachings of those theologians as "constructive postmodernism," a creative synthesis of science, ethics, aesthetics, and religion.[110]

A thinker, a preacher, a public personality, and a public servant, Olan reigns among the most influential of Texas rabbis. In theological circles, his prophetic hope argued against a sense of postwar disillusionment. In lay circles, his scholarship connected Judaism to the secular world. He was a mixer and ambassador to the gentiles, although never a glad-hander. His position as rabbi of Dallas's most prominent synagogue gave him entrée to the city's power centers where his views were listened to, if not immediately heeded. In a region that acquiesced to reactionaries and prided itself on conservatism, Olan made the liberal point of view respectable.

In November, 1975, Rabbi Olan's picture made the cover of upscale *D, The Magazine of Dallas.* In October, 1987, the *Dallas Observer,* the city's hip, alternative newspaper, extended its compliments. The irreverent tabloid listed the "best of everything" in Dallas and named Olan the city's most outstanding rabbi.[111] The selection came as a surprise for two reasons: Olan, who died in 1984, had retired seventeen years before.

Notes

PREFACE

1. David Ritz, "Inside the Jewish Establishment," *D, The Magazine of Dallas,* Nov., 1975.
2. T. R. Fehrenbach, *Lone Star: A History of Texas and the Texans,* p. 287; Simon Wolf, *The American Jew as Patriot, Soldier and Citizen,* pp. 72–75; Mordecai Podet, *Pioneer Jews of Waco,* p. 6.
3. Mark K. Bauman and Arnold Shankman, "The Rabbi as Ethnic Broker: The Case of David Marx," *Journal of American Ethnic History* 2 (spring, 1983): 51; Hollace Ava Weiner, "The Mixers: The Role of Rabbis Deep in the Heart of Texas," *American Jewish History* 3 (Sept., 1997): 289.
4. Jacob Rader Marcus, taped interview with author, Cincinnati, Dec. 13, 1992.

CHAPTER 1

1. Jacob Rader Marcus, founder of the American Jewish Archives, maintained that Schwarz was Texas' first rabbi and discounted as "free-lancers" rabbis who previously served in Houston and Galveston. Marcus interview; Descendants of Rev. Zacharias Emmich (1817–1901), Houston Jewry's first spiritual leader from 1860–62, have long claimed he was Texas' first ordained rabbi. However, the family lacks documentation. Emmich previously served, from 1856–57, in Lafayette, Indiana, where he signed a contract as *hazzan, shochet, mohel,* and teacher, according to "The First Century of Temple Israel," a congregational history of Lafayette Jewry. A favorable write-up of Emmich published in the *Occident,* Mar. 15, 1860, p. 306, makes no mention of ordination, referring to him as "Hazan," "Shochet," "Mohel," "minister," and "Mr. E."; see also Helena Frenkil Schlam, "The Early Jews of Houston," master's thesis, Ohio State University, 1971, p. 47; Weiner, "The Mixers," pp. 296–300.
2. "Rabbi H. Schwarz Dead," *Houston Post,* Oct. 19, 1900.
3. A. Suhler to Alex Sanger, Mar. 15, 1891, Dorothy M. and Henry S. Jacobus Temple Emanu-El Archives, Dallas.
4. *Houston Post,* Oct. 19, 1900.

5. Ibid., Sept. 6, 1915, Oct. 5, 1918; *Texas Jewish Herald,* July 6, 1916.

6. Charlotte Schwarz Friedman, telephone interview, Apr. 10, 1996; prayer book inscription, family papers, Hempstead; *American Jewish Year Book* (hereafter *AJYB*) 9 (1907–1908): 410–11; *AJYB* 21 (1919–20): 570; Malcolm Stern to Betty Friedman Kyle, Sept. 8, 1986; *Houston Post,* Sept. 6, 1915.

7. Edwin Gale, interview with author, Beaumont, Jan. 15, 1995; Bertram Schwarz, telephone interview, Apr. 29, 1996; Erwin Klinge, e-mail correspondence with author, July–Aug., 1997; "Marks Schwarz Funeral Rites," *Houston Chronicle,* Oct. 9, 1961.

8. *Jewish Encyclopedia* (New York, London: Funk and Wagnalls, 1901–1906), s.v. "Texas"; *AJYB* 16 (1914–15): 352.

9. Marcus interview.

10. Alan J. Lefever, *Fighting the Good Fight: The Life and Work of B. H. Carroll,* p. 60.

11. Rabbi Alexander Ziskind Gurwitz, "Memories of Two Generations," part 2, p. 6, box 3A187, Texas Jewish Historical Society Collection, Center for American History, University of Texas, Austin (hereafter TJHS).

12. Lefever, *Fighting the Good Fight,* pp. xii, 27, 48; Eugene W. Baker, *Nothing Better Than This: The Biography of James Huckins, First Baptist Missionary to Texas,* p. 12; Heinrich Schwarz, "Our Aims," Schwarz notebook, family papers.

13. Henry Barnston, "History of the Jews of Houston," ms.

14. Rev. Goldberg, son of a Polish rabbi, fell ill while peddling in Missouri and was nursed back to health in the home of a minister who converted him to Christianity in 1847. In Texarkana, this ecumenical minister tutored bar mitzvah students, led High Holy Day services attended by Jews and non-Jews, and never proselytized among Jews. *American Israelite,* Oct. 6, 1876; Louis Schmier, ed., *Reflections of Southern Jewry: The Letters of Charles Wessolowsky, 1878–1879,* p. 123; Carolyn Gray LeMaster, *A Corner of the Tapestry,* pp. 71–72; David Max Eichhorn, *Evangelizing the American Jew,* pp. 117–18.

15. William Kramer and Reva Clar, "Rabbi Abraham Blum: From Alsace to New York by Way of Texas and California," *Western States Jewish Historical Quarterly* (hereafter *WSJHQ*) 11 (Oct., 1979): 73–88.

16. Mention is made of Heinrich Schwarz's ordination by the Malbim in *American Israelite,* Nov. 1, 1900, and in Schwarz's notebook; *Encyclopaedia Judaica* (Jerusalem: Keter Pub., 1972), s.v. "Malbim, Meir Loeb ben Jehiel Michael," "Semikhah."

17. Rudolf Glanz, "Vanguard to the Russians: The Poseners in America," *Yivo Annual of Jewish Social Science* 18 (1983): 1–38; *Encyclopaedia Judaica,* s.v. "Prussia," "Poznan"; Gale interview.

18. "Baruch Schwarz, private teacher of Hebrew, died the 20th of December, 1848, after twelve hours in the sickbed of cholera that rages through the area here. Born 1798 in Widawa in Russian Poland, he was taught by his father, a famous

Talmudic scholar who sent Baruch to Hebrew school in Warsaw and elsewhere in Poland. . . . Baruch was very talented and came very early on to Kempen. . . . At a young age he knew Talmud and Hebrew very well. . . . In 1845 he passed a government exam in Posen to become a teacher of religion. . . . He had contact with Julius Fuerst [Jewish intellectual and editor of the *Orient*]. His son is an elementary school teacher in Rawicz. . . . In a brief time a sample of his writing will be published." Obituary from the *Orient*, Jan. 2, 1849, copied into Schwarz's notebook, translated from German by Tobias Brinkmann.

19. Reichenbach, located in Silesia, is Dzierzionow in Polish; Allenstein is Olsztyn.

20. Schwarz notebook, Hebrew translations by Alex Rofé.

21. "Schwartz [*sic*] Samuel, Co. A, 18 South Carolina Infantry. Confederate Statement of Service Reference Slip," military service records, Edwin Gale papers.

22. Ruthe Winegarten and Cathy Schechter, *Deep in the Heart: The Lives and Legends of Texas Jews, a Photographic History*, pp. 26, 65.

23. *Texas Jewish Herald*, Aug. 26, 1915; Gale interview; Adolph Harris became a Dallas department store magnate. Leon Harris, *Merchant Princes: An Intimate History of Jewish Families Who Built Great Department Stores*, pp. xxii, 28.

24. Minna Schwarz, eulogized as "the mother of Hempstead," died of fright Aug. 14, 1916, when she mistook a backfiring car for gunfire. Gale interview; *Texas Jewish Herald*, Aug. 24, 1916.

25. Waller County Historical Survey Committee 1973, *A History of Waller County, Texas*, pp. 124, 385.

26. *History of Waller County*, pp. 10–11, 36–40, 92, 123, 155.

27. Leo Schwarz, "Journal of Leo Schwarz of His Journey to America, November 24–December 18, 1872." Family papers.

28. *Encyclopaedia Judaica*, s.v. "Lyck."

29. Michael Meyer, *Response to Modernity*, pp. 75, 383; Louis Jacobs, *The Jewish Religion: A Companion*, 293–94.

30. *American Israelite*, Nov. 1, 1900; *Encyclopaedia Judaica*, s.v. "Ha-Magggid," "Der Israelit"; Schwarz notebook.

31. Heinrich Schwarz to editor of *Der Israelit*, Schwarz notebook.

32. T. R. Fehrenbach, *Lone Star*, p. 654.

33. "Our Aims," Schwarz notebook.

34. "Why sit here waiting for death?" refers to the siege of Samaria.

35. *Houston Telegram*, May 18, 1873, quoted by Frank MacD. Spindler in "Concerning Hempstead and Waller County," *Southwestern Historical Quarterly* 59 (Apr., 1956): 496.

36. *Brenham Weekly Banner*, May 31, 1873.

37. *American Israelite*, June 20, 1873.

38. Selma Schwarz, "Statement made to me in Fort Worth, Texas, April 10, 1939," Texas box, Jacob Rader Marcus papers, American Jewish Archives (hereafter AJA); *Dallas Daily Herald*, May 30, 1876.

39. *Dallas Weekly Herald,* Sept. 2, 1876; *Waco Daily Tribune,* Mar. 1, 1916; Bill Suhler, interview with author, Rockville, Md., July 20, 1995; *American Israelite,* June 20, 1873; "Brief History of Temple Emanu-El," Temple Emanu-El Archives, Dallas; Selma Schwarz statement; *Dallas Daily Herald,* May 30, 1876.

40. *Dallas Weekly Herald,* Sept. 2, 1876. Within two years, the Suhlers moved to a pulpit in Vicksburg, Mississippi. They were back in Texas by 1883, with Aron Suhler serving as rabbi at Waco's Temple Rodef Sholom. A father of nine, he resigned in 1885 because the congregation's fifty families paid him with chickens rather than cash. Suhler sold insurance, edited a German newspaper, and opened A. Suhler's Select English and German School in the synagogue basement. He filled in on the pulpit and served on the temple board. *Waco Daily Tribune,* Mar. 1, 1916; *Dallas Weekly Herald,* March 16, 1882; Podet, *Pioneer Jews of Waco,* pp. 24–26; B. Suhler interview.

41. [Koppel Von Bloomborg, pseud.] Jacob Voorsanger, "Lone Star Flashes," *American Israelite,* Oct. 19, 1880. Voorsanger, whose name means "singer" in Dutch, was a cantor in Washington, D.C., and Providence, R.I., and received two honorary degrees from Hebrew Union College (hereafter HUC). Kenneth Zwerin and Norton Stern, "Jacob Voorsanger: From Cantor to Rabbi," *WSJHQ* 15 (Apr., 1983): 195–202; Stanley Rabinowitz, *The Assembly: A Century in the Life of the Adas Israel Hebrew Congregation of Washington, D.C.* pp. 209–21.

42. Gale interview; *History of Waller County,* pp. 151, 155, 513–15.

43. Brenham Jews built B'nai Abraham, an Orthodox synagogue, in 1892. Robert P. Davis, "Virtual Restoration of Small-Town Synagogues in Texas," Internet Web site, www.neosoft.com/~tjhs/identity.html.

44. Schmier, *Reflections of Southern Jewry,* pp. 86–87.

45. "Passover in a Texas Town in 1891," *Jewish [St. Louis] Voice,* May 1, 1891, in *WSJHQ* 11 (July, 1979): 324.

46. Photo Archives, Texas Jewry Collections, the Texas Collection, Baylor University, Waco, Texas.

47. Gabriel and Jeanette Schwarz lived in Brenham in the early 1870s. He ran a dry-goods store and she, a hat boutique. *Brenham Weekly Banner,* July 26, 1873.

48. Bernice Davis, interview with author, Dallas, June 19, 1995.

49. Heinrich Schwarz's articles in *Die Deborah* include: "On the New Year Festival 5637," Sept. 15, 1872, p. 2; "On the Year 5639," Sept. 27, 1878, p. 1; "Poem: New Year's Eve 5653," Sept. 22, 1892, p. 1; "Moses Mendelssohn, Sketch Found by Local Pastor in Posthumous Papers of His," May 25, June 1, and June 8, 1893; "Translation: A Wonderful Deliverance from Shebet Yehudah of R. Solomon Aben [*Ibn*] Verga, 15th Century Spain," Aug. 16, 1898, p. 6; "Rashi," Sept. 15, 1898, p. 6; "At the Turn of the Year," Sept. 11, 1898, pp. 5–6; "Humoresque from Talmud and Midrash," Sept. 15, 1898, p. 3; "Strength of Character," Dec. 2, 1898, 5–6; "Memorable Days of Death from the Literary Remains of Dr. Leopold Zunz," Dec. 29, 1898; "The Holy Scripture," Jan. 19, 1899, p. 5; "Wine, a Rab-

binic Legend," May 18, 1877, p. 1; "The Oldest Source Known for the Three Rings in Jewish Literature," Sept. 1, 1898, pp. 5−6; "Elegy for the Day of Jerusalem, Tisha Beab Poem," Aug. 4, 1892, p. 1; "Elegy on the Day of Jerusalem," Sept. 9, 1897, p. 1; "Our Abodah," Sept. 29, 1898, p. 5; "General Charity Among our Ancestors," Dec. 1, 1898, p. 5; "The Dew-Drops," from Schwarz's notebook.

50. Felicia Joy Zeidenfeld, group discussion, Schwarz family reunion, Santa Fe, N.M., Oct. 25, 1997.

51. Robert Strauss, interview with author, Dallas, July 14, 1995.

52. Ellen Suhler, interview at Schwarz reunion.

53. UT's earliest Jewish fraternity chapters were Phi Sigma Delta, established in 1920; Sigma Alpha Mu, 1922; Tau Delta Phi, 1926; Alpha Epsilon Pi, 1941. The Jewish sororities were Alpha Epsilon Phi, 1925; Phi Sigma Sigma, 1929; Delta Phi Epsilon, 1934, and Sigma Delta Tau, 1939. The PhiSigs later merged nationally with Zeta Beta Tau. *Cactus,* yearbooks 1920−41; Edwin Gale pointed out that a number of Schwarzes graduated Texas A&M, but the campus, which was a male, military institute during this time frame, attracted a lower percentage of Jews and has had less impact on Jewish networks in Texas.

54. *Texas Jewish Herald,* July 6, 1916; *Houston Chronicle,* Apr. 19, no year, Edwin Gale papers.

55. Spindler, "Concerning Hempstead," p. 469.

56. Edis Schwarz to Gertrude and Don Teeter, May 27, 1991; Rabbi Robert Kahn and Rozelle Kahn, telephone interview, Oct. 7, 1997.

57. Congregation Emanu El, Houston, "If Our Ark Could Talk"; Rabbi Mathew Michaels, interview with author, Houston, Oct. 7, 1997.

CHAPTER 2

1. Samuel Rosinger, "Deep in the Heart of Texas," in *Lives and Voices: A Collection of American Jewish Memoirs,* ed. Stanley Chyet, p. 134; Gale interview; *Beaumont Daily Journal,* Aug. 25, 26, 29, 1910.

2. Rosinger, "Deep in the Heart," p. 134; Gale interview.

3. Frank W. Johnson, *A History of Texas and Texans,* vol. 2, pp. 696−99; Lorecia East, *History and Progress of Jefferson County,* p. 47; Florence Stratton, *The Story of Beaumont,* passim; Seymour Connor, *Texas: A History,* p. 318.

4. Eleanor Perlstein Weinbaum, *Shalom, America: The Perlstein Success Story,* pp. 61−62.

5. "$am $olinsky, Dec. 4, 1867−Sept. 29, 1934." Hebrew Rest Cemetery, Beaumont.

6. *Beaumont Daily Journal,* Aug. 24, 1910.

7. W. T. Block, "A Brief History of the Early Beaumont Jewish Community," *Texas Gulf Historical and Biographical Record* (hereafter *TGHBR*) 20 (Nov., 1984): 42;

W. T. Block, "From Cotton Bales to Black Gold: A History of the Pioneer Wiess Families of Southeast Texas," *TGHBR* 8 (Nov., 1972): 39–60.

8. Rosinger, "Deep in the Heart," pp. 114–33.

9. Ibid., p. 134.

10. *Beaumont Daily Journal,* Aug. 24, 1910.

11. Ibid., Aug. 26, 1910.

12. Rosinger, "Deep in the Heart," p. 135.

13. Ibid., p. 141.

14. Irving Goldberg, "Some Reflections About Reform Judaism—Yesterday and Today," speech, Dallas, 1988, Temple Emanu-El Archives, Dallas.

15. Rosinger, "Deep in the Heart," p. 137.

16. *Texas Jewish Herald,* Aug. 16, 1917.

17. Ibid., Aug. 10, 1916; Rosinger, *My Life,* p. 427–29.

18. *Texas Jewish Herald,* June 29, 1916.

19. Adele Feinberg Silverberg, interviews with author, Beaumont, July 7, 9, 11, 1997; Helen Goldstien Breen, interviews with author, Beaumont, July 7, 9, 1997; Lawrence Blum, interview with author, Beaumont, July 10, 1997.

20. In 1930 Rosinger joined the Reform movement's Central Conference of American Rabbis, and until 1947 he maintained membership in the Conservative movement's Rabbinical Assembly of America. He is one of the few rabbis to have concurrent membership in both groups. Chyet, *Lives and Voices,* p. 114.

21. Rosinger, *My Life,* p. 353; Rosinger, "Deep in the Heart," p. 135–36.

22. Bernard "Buster" Klein, Address at Golden Deeds Banquet, Apr. 5, 1960, Tyrrell Historical Library Archives, Beaumont.

23. *Beaumont Enterprise,* Feb. 13, 1933.

24. Wesley Norton, "Negro Trail-Driver, Jean Spence Perrault, and His Beaumont Descendants," *TGHBR* 19 (Nov., 1983): 35–50.

25. Judith Walker Linsley and Ellen Walker Rienstra, *Beaumont, a Chronicle of Promise: An Illustrated History,* pp. 69–71.

26. "Public School Troubles," *Texas Jewish Herald,* Dec. 31, 1914.

27. Rosinger, *My Life,* pp. 284–88.

28. *Texas Jewish Herald,* Dec. 31, 1914.

29. Rosinger, *My Life,* pp. 284–88, 446–47.

30. Charles C. Alexander, *Crusade for Conformity: The Ku Klux Klan in Texas, 1929–1930,* p. 5.

31. Ibid., p. 10; Thomas E. Kroutter Jr., "The Ku Klux Klan in Jefferson County Texas, 1921–1924," master's thesis, Lamar University, Beaumont, 1972, pp. 4–6, 55.

32. Ibid., p. 24.

33. Alexander, *Crusade for Conformity,* p. 11.

34. Kroutter, "Klan in Jefferson County," pp. 8, 35–36, 39, 41, 48, 55, 59, 71, 74, 84, 87, 95.

35. Ibid., pp. 39−41; Norman D. Brown, *Hood, Bonnet, Little Brown Jug: Texas Politics, 1921−1928*, p. 74.

36. Brown, *Hood, Bonnet, Little Brown Jug*, pp. 17, 42−43, 48, 51, 94.

37. Rosinger, *My Life*, pp. 255−58.

38. Kroutter, p. 65.

39. Herman Horwitz, interview with author, Beaumont, July 9, 1997.

40. Weinbaum, *Shalom, America*, p. 85.

41. Col. William Joseph Simmons' statement from *Beaumont Journal*, June 30, 1923, quoted in Kroutter, "Klan in Jefferson County," p. 115.

42. Artist Zeev Raban designed the windows. Helen Goldstien Breen, *History of Temple Emanuel: Its First Hundred Years*, pp. 12−19; For history of Bezalel School, see Nutrit Shilo-Cohen, ed., *Bezalel: 1906−1929*.

43. Breen, "History of Temple Emanuel," pp. 4−8; Rabbi Peter Hyman, interview with author, Beaumont, July 10, 1997.

44. The vote was 504 to 160 favoring the $50,000 hospital bond package. Jefferson County Commissioners Court Election Records, Oct. 10, 1922; *Beaumont Daily Journal*, Oct. 11, 1922.

45. David Grenader, telephone interview, Houston, Sept. 24, 1997.

46. *Beaumont Enterprise*, n.d., in Lena Milam papers, MS-18, scrapbook 34 (Nov.−Dec., 1935), Tyrrell Historical Library, Archives and Special Collections.

47. The Uhrys' grandson is Broadway playwright Alfred Uhry, author of *Driving Miss Daisy, Last Night of Ballyhoo*, and *Parade*, which dramatize tensions within Atlanta Jewry. Myrtle Uhry, telephone interview, LaGrange, Tex., Oct. 20, 1998.

48. Texas State Board of Health, Death Certificate no. 1897, Jefferson County.

49. Grenader interview.

50. Rosinger, "Deep in the Heart," pp. 139−40.

51. Ellen W. Schrecker, *No Ivory Tower: McCarthyism and the Universities*, pp. 165, 275−76, 280; Lawrence Kaelter Rosinger's books include *China's Wartime Politics: 1937−1944* (Princeton: Princeton University Press, 1944), *China's Crisis* (New York: Knopf, 1945), *Restless India* (New York: Holt Co., Foreign Policy Assn., 1947).

52. "Tribute Paid Child Victim of Car Crash: Eloquent Eulogy delivered by Rabbi Rosinger at Funeral Service," *Beaumont Enterprise*, Apr. 6, 1937.

53. Blum interview.

54. Ibid.; Shirley Alter, interview with author, Beaumont, July 11, 1997. Edgar Jones, 54, died April 8, 1934; Cipora Jones, 84, died Nov. 12, 1965.

55. Mendel Melasky, Goldberg's brother-in-law, telephone interview, July 7, 1997; Goldberg sat on the three-judge panel that decided *Roe v. Wade*, which upheld a woman's right to an abortion. Winegarten, *Deep in the Heart*, p. 184.

56. Lloyd Friedman, interview with author, Houston, Mar. 6, 1997.

57. *Beaumont Enterprise* clippings, in *Beaumont Exchange Club Book of Golden Deeds*, vol. 4 (1960) Tyrrell Historical Library, Beaumont, Texas.

CHAPTER 3

1. Maurice Faber to James E. Ferguson, Sept. 20, 1916, family papers of Eugene Lipstate (hereafter LP), Lafayette, La. Correspondence reprinted in *Alcalde* 5 (Aug., 1917): 699–702.

2. *Dallas Morning News* (hereafter *DMN*), Aug. 10, 1917; *Journal of the Senate, State of Texas, Second Called Session Thirty-fifth Legislature, Convened in the City of Austin, August 1, 1917 and Adjourned Without Day August 30, 1917* (hereafter *Impeachment Proceedings*), p. 634.

3. John A. Lomax and Alan Lomax, "Rye Whiskey," *Best Loved American Folksongs*, p. 199; *DMN*, Aug. 10, 1917.

4. *Facts on Ferguson*, July 10, 1918, pp. 70–71, William Clifford Hogg papers, Barker Texas History Center, Center for American History (hereafter CAH); "His Own Words to Discover His Motives," *Alcalde* 5 (Aug., 1917): 745.

5. Bruce Rutherford, *Impeachment of Jim Ferguson*, p. 8; Ex-Students Association of the University of Texas, *Ferguson's War on the University of Texas: A Chronological Outline January 12, 1915 to July 31, 1917, Inclusive*, p. 38; *San Antonio Express*, Dec. 17, 1916; *DMN*, June 15, 17, 1917.

6. "His Own Words," *Alcalde* 5 (Aug. 1917): 716.

7. Ferguson to Faber, Sept. 11, 1916; *Impeachment Proceedings*, pp. 163–65.

8. Faber to Ferguson, Sept. 13, 1916, LP.

9. R. L. Batts to J. P. Buchanan, Oct. 20, 1916, Robert L. Batts papers, CAH.

10. Doris Kivel, interview with author, Tyler, Nov. 23, 1996.

11. Harry A. Merfeld, contributor to *In Memoriam: Rabbi Maurice Faber, His Memory for Blessing*, 1935, unnumbered pages, LP.

12. Florence Wolf Leonard, interview with author, Tyler, Nov. 22, 1996.

13. *Tyler Courier-Times*, Sept. 16, 1934.

14. Ouida Ferguson Nalle, *The Fergusons of Texas or "Two Governors for the Price of One,"* p. 121; *DMN*, June 3, 1917.

15. Ex-Students Association of the University of Texas, "Governor Ferguson and Our University," Aug. 1, 1917, flier, Hogg papers; Robert E. Vinson, "The University Crosses the Bar," *Southwestern Historical Quarterly* 43 (Jan., 1940): 282.

16. Mann, "Temple Beth El, 1887–1987: Centennial Journal," p. 5; Maurice's parents were Fannie Better and Leon Faber. Biographical Sketch prepared for *DMN* in "Faber, Maurice," vertical file, CAH.

17. Circuit Court of Delaware, 11–184, New Castle County, Oct. 14, 1884.

18. U.S. Census, 1900, Soundex records, Keokuk, Iowa, vol. 44, ed. 65, sheet 6/15; Eugene Lipstate, telephone interview, July 20, 1996.

19. *AJYB* 2 (1900–1901): 452.

20. David Philipson in *In Memoriam*.

21. *Official Record of Rabbi M. Faber,* handwritten logbook, Collection Congregation Beth El, Tyler.

22. Simon Glazer, *Jews of Iowa: A Complete History and Accurate Account of Their Religious, Social, Economical and Educational Progress in This State,* pp. 303–307.

23. *Official Record of Rabbi M. Faber.*

24. *Congregation Beth El [Tyler] Minute Book 1895,* July 6, 1900 entry.

25. Jacobs, *Jewish Religion,* pp. 92–95.

26. Vicki Betts, *Smith County Texas in the Civil War,* pp. 2–31.

27. Winegarten, *Deep in the Heart,* p. 46; Mann, "Temple Beth El Centennial," p. 4.

28. Harvey Wessel, "A History of the Jews of Tyler and Smith County, Texas," in *Tyler and Smith County, Texas: An Historical Survey,* pp. 201–55.

29. Ibid., p. 204–205; Mann, "Temple Beth El Centennial," p. 5.

30. *Beth El Minute Book,* July 1, 1900 entry; "Seventy-fifth Anniversary of Ahavath Achim Congregation," TJHS; "Temple Beth El Centennial," p. 5; Wessel, "History of the Jews of Tyler," pp. 204–205.

31. "Seventy-fifth Anniversary"; *Fort Worth Star-Telegram* (hereafter *FWST*), Nov. 28, 1996.

32. Jewish Masons who bolted were from both Tyler synagogues and included Jacob Lipstate, Max Krumholtz, Leon Levinthal, Gus Taylor, Philip Golenternek, and Sam Cohen, according to Pete Martinez, lodge historian and author of "A History of Tyler Masonic Lodge No. 1233," *Chronicles of Smith County Texas* 35 (summer, 1996): 22–27; Lipstate interview.

33. Patricia Banister, "Regent Protest," ms., p. 4, Faber vertical file, CAH.

34. Marilyn McAdams Sibley, *George W. Brackenridge, Maverick Philanthropist,* p. 223.

35. James M. Smallwood, ed., *Will Rogers' Weekly Articles,* vol. 2, *The Coolidge Years: 1925–1927,* p. 124.

36. "Governor Ferguson and the 'Chicken Salad' Case," Hogg papers.

37. James L. Haley, *Texas: From Spindletop Through World War II,* pp. 99, 145; *Impeachment Proceedings,* p. 714.

38. *Impeachment Proceedings,* pp. 561–62; Nalle, *Two Governors for the Price of One,* pp. 13–15, 19; Sibley, *Brackenridge,* p. 224.

39. Sibley, *Brackenridge,* p. 224; Ferguson to V. H. Reed, Sept. 8, 1900, Thomas S. Henderson papers, CAH.

40. *DMN,* May 28, Aug. 10, 1917.

41. *Austin American,* Oct. 25, 1916.

42. Nalle, *Two Governors,* p. 105.

43. Statistics from Seymour V. Connor, *Texas: A History,* p. 321; Ferguson quote in *DMN,* Dec. 18, 1916.

44. Vinson quoted in *Austin American,* Oct. 18, 1916; Ex-Students Association, *Ferguson's War,* p. 26.

45. Ex-Students Association, *Ferguson's War,* p. 10.

46. "Durst, Lt. Col. Jno.," vertical files, CAH; "Ferguson 'Staff of Colonels,'" *Galveston Tribune,* n.d., Harry Cohen's scrapbook, Henry Cohen papers (hereafter HCP), CAH.

47. A biographical form Faber filled out in 1932 mentions no college degrees, honorary or otherwise. Nonetheless, the Keokuk, Iowa, newspaper put the letters "D.D., Ph.D." after the rabbi's name. *The Gate City,* Aug. 28, 1900.

48. James Ferguson, "The Cloven Foot of the Dallas Jews," *Ferguson Forum,* reprinted in *Colonel Mayfield's Weekly,* Mar. 24, 1923.

49. Board of Regents Certificate, LP.

50. Ex-Students Association, *Ferguson's War,* p. 27; Nalle, *Two Governors,* p. 117.

51. *DMN,* Dec. 17, 1916.

52. Ex-Students Association, *Ferguson's War,* p. 34.

53. Ibid., pp. 17, 34–35.

54. John A. Lomax, *Cowboy Songs and Other Frontier Ballads;* Nolan Porterfield, *The Last Cavalier: The Life and Times of John A. Lomax, 1867–1948,* pp. 195–204, 512.

55. *New Handbook of Texas,* s.v. "Ellis, A. Caswell"; "Mayes, William Harding"; "Potts, Charles S."; "Mather, William."

56. *Alcalde* 5 (Aug., 1917): 704.

57. Charles K. Lee to Batts, Oct. 7, Oct. 11, 1916, Batts papers.

58. Sibley, *Brackenridge,* p. 226.

59. Ex-Students Association, *Ferguson's War,* p. 7.

60. S. J. Jones to Ferguson, Oct. 2, 1916, copy sent to Faber, Oct. 15, 1916, LP.

61. Jones to Faber, Sept. 19, 1916, LP.

62. Alexander Sanger to David Harrell, Sept. 18, 1916, LP.

63. Harrell to Faber, Sept. 15, 1916, LP.

64. Faber to Ferguson, Sept. 20, 1916, LP.

65. Ibid.

66. Ibid.

67. Will Hogg's father, James Stephen Hogg, was the state's first Texas-born governor, serving from 1891–95.

68. Hogg to Faber, Sept. 26, 1916, LP.

69. *Austin American,* Oct. 17, 1916; *Alcalde* 5 (Mar., 1917): 239.

70. *Austin American,* Oct. 16, 24, 25, Nov. 18, 1916.

71. Ibid., Oct. 18, 1916.

72. *San Antonio Express,* Dec. 17, 1916.

73. Ibid.

74. Faber to Ferguson, Nov. 20, 1916.

75. Ex-Students Association, *Ferguson's War,* p. 9.

76. *DMN,* Nov. 25, 1916.

77. *San Antonio Express,* Dec. 17, 1916.

78. Tom E. Hogg to Faber, Dec. 17, 1916; Hal Lattimore to Faber, Dec., 19, 1916, LP. Hal Lattimore became a state district court judge and led the fight against the KKK in Tarrant County. His father, O. S. Lattimore, was elected to the court of criminal appeals in 1918.

79. John Duncan to Faber, Dec. 19, 1916; William Bell to Faber, Jan. 15, 1917; Frederick W. Cook to Faber, Nov. 22, 1916, LP.

80. Sibley, *Brackenridge,* p. 230.

81. Charles Lee to Batts, Dec. 7, 1916, Batts papers.

82. Ralph W. Steen, "The Ferguson War on the University of Texas," *Southwestern Social Science Quarterly* 35 (Mar., 1955): 356–62.

83. Ibid., p. 361; May Nelson Paulissen and Carl Randall McQueary, *Miriam: The Southern Belle Who Became the First Woman Governor of Texas,* p. 78.

84. *New Handbook of Texas,* s.v. "Ferguson, James Edward."

85. Fehrenbach, *Lone Star,* pp. 638–39.

86. *Impeachment Proceedings,* pp. 163–65.

87. Lomax later worked as secretary of the Ex-Students Association. Porterfield, *Last Cavalier,* pp. 211–16; Vinson left Austin in midsemester 1923 to become president of Western Reserve University in Cleveland, where he became friendly with prominent rabbi Abba Hillel Silver. Marc Lee Raphael, *Abba Hillel Silver: A Profile in American Judaism,* pp. 70–72.

88. Smallwood, *Will Rogers' Weekly Articles,* vol. 2, p. 123.

89. "The Cloven Foot," reprinted in *Colonel Mayfield's Weekly,* Mar. 24, 1923; The *Texas Jewish Herald* also ran the column and editorialized against Ferguson because of it. The column refers to Jews who refused to trade Ferguson linoleum products for advertisements. "Jim said that first the Jews crucified Christ, and now they were crucifying him," according to Paulissen in *Miriam: The Southern Belle,* p. 111.

90. Rutherford, *Impeachment of Jim Ferguson,* pp. 121–32.

91. Jacob Faber to M. Faber, 1924, translated from Yiddish by Batya Brand, Collection of Temple Beth El, Tyler; *In Memoriam,* p. 1.

92. Merfeld in *In Memoriam.*

93. H. W. Stillwell, contributor to *In Memoriam.*

CHAPTER 4

1. Cohen to Superintendent J. W. Hopkins, May 16, 1906, reprinted in *American Israelite,* Feb. 12, 1907; Cordell Hull to Cohen, Oct. 16, 1911, and M. Zielonka to Cohen, Jan. 8, 1923, HCP.

2. Raymond C. Mensing, Jr., "A Papal Delegate in Texas, the Visit of His Eminence

Cardinal Satolli," *East Texas Historical Journal* 20 (fall, 1982): 20; Webb Waldron, "Rabbi Cohen—First Citizen of Texas," *Reader's Digest*, Feb. 1939, pp. 97–100; "An American Ballad," NBC, July 4, 1948.

3. David Henry Frisch, "Some Memories of 1920 Broadway," in *Henry Cohen: Messenger of the Lord*, ed. A. Stanley Dreyfus, p. 44.

4. Henry Cohen II, "Portrait of a Rabbi," in *Messenger of the Lord*, p. 20.

5. Ibid., p. 30.

6. Gary Cartwright, *Galveston: A History of the Island*, p. 146.

7. Abraham Cronbach, "Henry Cohen, Humanitarian," in *Messenger of the Lord*, pp. 55–56.

8. David G. McComb, *Galveston: A History*, pp. 1–63; *AJYB* 16 (1914–15): 352.

9. *Jewish Encyclopedia*, s.v. "Texas"; James Lee Kessler, *B.O.I.: A History of Congregation B'nai Israel, Galveston, Texas*, Ph.D. diss., HUC, California, June 1988, pp. 14, 23.

10. *Galveston Daily News*, Nov., n.d., 1866, in Kessler, *B.O.I.*, p. 29.

11. *B.O.I.*, p. 32.

12. A cotton "factor" was a broker who not only bought and sold on behalf of farmers and planters but also advanced credit and supplies. Harold M. Hyman, *Oleander Odyssey*, p. 284.

13. Rabbi Joseph Silverman left for Congregation Emanu-El in New York. Kessler, *B.O.I.*, p. 66.

14. Jews College began ordaining rabbis in 1896. *Encyclopaedia Judaica*, s.v. "Jews College."

15. Henry Cohen, "Three Years in Africa," HCP, personal writings, box 3M325; Basutoland is now Lesotho.

16. Anne Nathan and Harry Cohen, *The Man Who Stayed in Texas: The Life of Rabbi Henry Cohen*, pp. 9–72; *Messenger of the Lord*, pp. 7–13.

17. Vorspan, *Giants of Justice*, p. 134.

18. Leo and Evelyn Turitz, *Jews in Early Mississippi*, p. 6.

19. *Woodville Republican*, Oct. 3, Nov. 14, 1885.

20. Turitz, *Jews in Early Mississippi*, p. 3; Isaac Hart to Leo N. Levi, Mar. 16, 1888, papers of Ellis Hart, Winona, Miss.

21. Turitz, *Jews in Early Mississippi*, pp. 6–7,

22. *Woodville Republican*, Oct. 17, 24, 1885. *Woodville Republican* also mentions Cohen and the local Jewish community Oct. 3, Nov. 7, 14, 1885; Sept. 12, 1886; Jan. 7, Feb. 18, Mar. 3, 17, 24, 31, and June 2, 1888.

23. Ibid., Oct. 31, 1885; Mar. 24, May 19, 1888.

24. Ibid., Dec. 12, 1885.

25. Nathan and Cohen, *The Man Who Stayed in Texas*, pp. 56–61.

26. Ibid. p. 13.

27. "Galveston, YMHA Congregation and Hebrew Institute," n.d., TJHS, box 3A189.

28. M. E. "Mefo" Forster, column, *Houston Chronicle,* June 26, 1924; Henry Cohen II, interview with author, Philadelphia, May 24, 1998.

29. *Messenger of the Lord,* p. 31; Banker Morris Lasker's son, Albert, was an advertising whiz whose fortune endowed the Lasker Awards for Scientific Achievement.

30. Waldron, "Cohen—First Citizen of Texas," p. 97.

31. *Galveston Daily News,* Nov. 11, 1936, in *Messenger of the Lord,* p. 30.

32. *Houston Press,* May 10, 1939.

33. Leo Greenwood to Cohen, Dec. 17, 1921; Cohen to Greenwood, Dec. 20, 1921, HCP.

34. Cartwright, *Galveston,* p. 146.

35. Louis Greene, M.D., interview with author, Houston, Mar. 7, 1997.

36. Cohen interview.

37. Mensing, "A Papal Delegate in Texas," p. 20; Nathan and Cohen, *The Man Who Stayed in Texas,* p. 104.

38. Cohen's eulogy to Gallagher, excerpted in *Diamond Jubilee: 1847–1922 of the Diocese of Galveston and St. Mary's Cathedral,* p. 116, Texas Catholic Archives.

39. James Talmadge Moore, *Through Fire and Flood: The Catholic Church in Frontier Texas, 1836–1900,* p. 220.

40. Population figures extrapolated from *Hoffman's Catholic Directory Almanac and Clergy List 1896,* pp. 310–13, which lists six churches and five Catholic schools enrolling 970 Galveston students.

41. Marguerite Meyer Marks, "Memories of Rabbi Henry Cohen As I Knew Him," *WSJHQ* 18 (Jan., 1986): 120–25; Stephen P. Brown, unnumbered pages in *Memoirs of Monsignor James M. Kirwin 1928;* James F. Vanderholt, "Gentle Giant from Ohio," *East Texas Catholic,* Apr. 23, 1982.

42. Cohen, "Father Kirwin as Patriot."

43. "Homily, Anniversary Death of Monsignor James M. Kirwin at Mass in Annunciation Church, Houston, Texas," Msgr. Kirwin Post Catholic War Veterans, Jan. 24, 1980, pp. 2–3, Catholic Archives of Texas; Cremation is a denial of Catholic teaching, especially the concept of resurrection of the dead. Religion News Service, "Cremated remains OK'd at Catholic funerals," *Anchorage Daily News,* Sept. 6, 1997.

44. Clarence Ousley, *Galveston in Nineteen Hundred,* pp. 120, 256–57. Ike Kempner, Ben Levy, and Morris Lasker were also on the relief committee. Paul Lester, *The Great Galveston Disaster,* pp. ii, vii, 99, 344; McComb, *Galveston,* p. 133; Frank W. Johnson, Eugene C. Barker, *A History of Texas and the Texans,* vol. 3, p. 1068.

45. Ousley, *Galveston in Nineteen Hundred,* p. 120.

46. *American Hebrew,* Oct. 12, 1900, p. 622.

47. McComb, *Galveston,* pp. 48, 150.

48. *FWST,* Dec. 17, 1937.

49. *AJYB* 16 (1914–15): 352.

50. Bernard Marinbach, *Galveston: Ellis Island of the West,* pp. 157–61, 181–95; Henry Cohen, "The Galveston Movement: Its First Year," *B'nai B'rith [Los Angeles] Messenger,* Apr. 16, 1909, in *WSJHQ* 18 (Jan. 1986): 114–19.

51. Gurwitz, *Memories of Two Generations,* pp. 205–208.

52. Ibid., p. 208.

53. "Rabbi Cohen on Immigration Work," *Texas Jewish Herald,* Apr. 22, 1915; Marinbach, *Galveston,* pp. 104, 114, 181–95.

54. Marinbach, *Galveston,* pp. 104, 114, 181–95.

55. Fox, "End of an Era," in *Lives and Voices,* pp. 279–90; G. George Fox Jr., series of telephone interviews with author, Chicago, 1995–98.

56. Charles C. Alexander, *The Ku Klux Klan in the Southwest,* pp. 1–82; Stanley F. Horn, *Invisible Empire: The Story of the Ku Klu Klan, 1877–1871,* pp. 1–291; David M. Chalmers, *Hooded Americanism: The History of the Ku Klux Klan,* pp. 8–38, 71; Wyn Craig Wade, *The Fiery Cross: The Ku Klux Klan in America,* pp. 143–45; Casey Edward Greene, "Apostles of Hate: The Ku Klux Klan in and Near Houston Texas, 1920–1982," master's thesis, University of Houston, Clear Lake, 1995, pp. iii, 1–2, 4, 7.

57. Alexander, *Crusade for Conformity,* p. 5.

58. Harry Hawley Sr. to W. L. Moody III, Mar. 16, 1923, Hawley papers, 96-0019, box 4/4, Rosenberg Library, Galveston.

59. *Col. Mayfield's Weekly,* June 17, 1922.

60. Although city commissioners minutes mention no accord barring Klan parades, the *Galveston Daily News,* Sept. 4, 1922, implies such an agreement in an article on a Klan initiation ceremony. An Associated Press dispatch of Aug. 6, 1926, reports that Klavern 36 sought an injunction from 56th District Court after the city commissioners declined on Aug. 5 to grant a permit for a KKK parade. Several secondary sources credit Kirwin and Cohen with securing a ban on KKK parades. These include McComb, *Galveston: A History,* pp. 170, 211, and Haley, *Texas: From Spindletop Through World War II,* p. 137. Casey Greene, archivist at Galveston's Rosenberg Library and scholar of the Texas Klan, concurs that an unwritten promise was likely secured.

61. *Galveston Daily News,* Sept. 4, 1922; *Col. Mayfield's Weekly,* Sept. 9, 1922.

62. Cohen to Charles E. Sasseen, Mar. 14, 1923, HCP; movie ads from Mar.–Sept., 1923, promote only one D. W. Griffith film, *One Exciting Night,* with an ad that states, "Why waste your time on old things? See the only new thing in films this year. . . . A different story told in a different way." *Galveston Daily News,* July 1, 1923.

63. *Galveston Tribune,* Sept. 6, 1921; *Col. Mayfield's Weekly,* June 17, 1922; Stephen P. Brown in *Memoirs of Kirwin;* Greene, "Apostles of Hate," p. 38;

64. Alexander, *Ku Klux Klan in the Southwest,* p. 28.

65. McComb, *Galveston: A History,* p. 211.

66. *Southern Messenger,* Jan. 28, 1926.

67. *Galveston Tribune,* Jan. 30, 1926.

68. The apostolic delegate was Pietro Cardinal Fumasoni Biondi, according to "Homily, Anniversary Death of Msgr. Kirwin," pp. 3–4.

69. Harry I. Cohen, "Father Kirwin," *America,* July 21, 1934, reprinted in *Galveston Tribune,* July 27, 1934.

70. Cohen, "Father Kirwin as Patriot."

71. Ibid.

72. *Messenger of the Lord,* p. 47.

73. David Rosenbaum to Cohen, June 26, July 7, 1922, HCP.

74. Rosenbaum to Cohen, Dec. 16, 1922, HCP.

75. Macht to Cohen, Sept. 28, Oct. 10, 1922, and Sanger to Cohen, Oct. 21, 1922, HCP.

76. Kallah, Third Annual Convention, program, 1929.

77. *Messenger of the Lord,* p. 16.

78. Cohen interview.

79. Arthur "Lil' Arthur" John Johnson (1878–1946) was World Heavyweight Boxing Champion, 1908–15. *Handbook of Texas,* s.v. "Johnson, Arthur John"; Cartwright, *Galveston,* pp. 157–59; Cronbach, "Henry Cohen, Humanitarian," in *Messenger of the Lord,* pp. 56–57.

80. Hyman, *Oleander Odyssey,* p. 192.

81. At the request of the Seven Arts Feature Syndicate, Rabbi Stephen Wise compiled a list of the nation's ten foremost clerical leaders, with Henry Cohen the only Jew among them. *Galveston Daily News,* Sept. 23, 1930, *New York Times* (hereafter *NYT*), Sept. 22, 1930; Rosella Horowitz, "A Church Leader: Rabbi Henry Cohen," *Unity,* Mar. 30, 1931, pp. 72–75.

CHAPTER 5

1. G. George Fox, "The End of an Era," in *Lives and Voices,* pp. 279–81; G. George Fox, "Why the State and the Church Should Require Health Certificates Before Marriage," in *The New Chivalry—Health,* pp. 159–64.

2. Marinbach, *Galveston,* pp. 42, 46, 55, 92, 112, 129, 149, 161.

3. Fox, "End of an Era," pp. 279–81; G. George Fox, Jr., telephone interviews with author, Chicago, 1995–98.

4. Richard F. Selcer, *Hell's Half Acre,* pp. 1–32.

5. *Fort Worth Record,* Nov. 11, 15, 1913.

6. Fox, "End of an Era," pp. 279–81.

7. The White Slave Traffic Act of 1910 rescinded a three-year residency limit, allowing deportation regardless of time in the U.S. Roy L. Garis, *Immigration Restriction: A Study of the Opposition to and Regulation of Immigration into the U.S.,* p. 114.

8. The deportees were Annie Appelbaum (a.k.a. Annie Wilson), Henne Becker (a.k.a. Lizzie Schiff), Regina Fisheimer (a.k.a. Regina Werner), Mary Fischer, Minnie Glasner (a.k.a. Minnie Baxter), Ida Guez (a.k.a. Annie Smith), Rachel Kappel (a.k.a. May Clark), Minnie Krauss, Yetta Madf (a.k.a. Yetta Rosen), Anna Marcovictz (a.k.a. Annie Schwartz), Sarah Muehler (a.k.a. Sarah Miller), Ida Novicki, Gussie Reichlin (a.k.a. Rosie Goldstein), Clara Rozenfeld (a.k.a. Jenny Goldberg), Byley Salesky (a.k.a. Betsy Brown), Rosa Schmidt, Etta Schwartz, and Bessie Weinstein. Supervising inspector, Immigration Service to the commissioner general, Oct. 14, 1913, 52809/73, National Archives.

9. Edward J. Bristow, *Prostitution and Prejudice: The Jewish Fight Against White Slavery 1870–1939*, p. 177; Howard Sachar, *A History of the Jew in America*, pp. 164–68.

10. Homer G. Ritchie, *Life and Legend of J. Frank Norris, the Fighting Parson*, pp. 80–84; Selcer, *Hell's Half Acre*, pp. 271–72.

11. Caleb Pirtle III, *Fort Worth: The Civilized West*, pp. 17–19.

12. Flora [Weltman] Schiff, "History of the Jews of Fort Worth," *Reform Advocate*, Jan. 24, 1914.

13. *Fort Worth Press*, Mar. 30, 1934; "History," ms., Jan. 13, 1949, Congregation Beth-El folder, *Fort Worth Star-Telegram* Archives, University of Texas at Arlington; *Beth-El Congregation 1902–1972, 5662–5732, 70th Anniversary Yearbook*, unnumbered pages.

14. Ellen Mack, "Jews in Fort Worth 1888 and Following," ms., Congregation Beth-El Archives, Fort Worth; Marion Weil, taped interview with author, Fort Worth, July 31, 1994; Federal Writers Project, Texas, *Research Data Fort Worth and Tarrant County, Texas: Consolidated Chronology*, vol. 2, 1889–1923, Fort Worth Public Library Unit, 1941, pp. 7778–79.

15. Fox, "End of an Era," p. 278.

16. Ibid.

17. *FWST*, Jan. 31, 1910.

18. Gresham George Fox, *Abraham Lincoln's Religion: Sources of the Great Emancipator's Religious Inspiration*, p. 116.

19. Fox, "End of an Era," p. 278.

20. *FWST*, Feb. 1, 1910.

21. Lithuanian-born Charles Blumenthal (1871–1957) came to the U.S. in 1890 and taught Hebrew school in Detroit, Toledo, and Buffalo before serving in Fort Worth from 1908 to 1913. He later worked in Savannah, El Paso, Shreveport, and Waco, and returned once to Buffalo and twice to Fort Worth. "Chronology of Charles Blumenthal," Texas Jewry Collections, the Texas Collection, Baylor University, Waco.

22. "Fox Family Overview," G. George Fox Jr. papers; Fox Jr. interviews.

23. Schiff, "History of the Jews of FW," p. 12.

24. Fox Jr. interviews.

25. Best man was lawyer/cotton broker Felix Bath; attendants, father and son Sam and Dan Levy, Ben Levy, no relation; ushers, Jake Gernsbacher, Nathan Gens, Louis Cohen, Meredith Carb, James Weltman, Will Friedman, Joe Colton, Marcus Alexander, Arthur Lewis, Simon Zeve. *FWST,* Nov. 27, 1910; "Fox Family Overview"; "End of an Era," pp. 302, 307; Rosten, *Joys of Yiddish,* pp. 91–92, 522.

26. Fox Family Overview; *Who's Who in American Jewry, 1938–1939,* s.v. "Fox, Gresham George," "Fox, Jacob Logan," "Fox, Noah," "Fox, Hortense Lewis"; *Who's Who in Chicago and Illinois, 1945,* s.v. "Fox, Gresham George," "Fox, Jacob Logan"; Winegarten, *Deep in the Heart,* p. 104.

27. Fox, "End of an Era," p. 305.

28. Emil Hirsch (1851–1923) merited a front-page article on his 70th birthday, *Monitor,* May 27, 1921; Fox, "End of an Era," p. 302.

29. The violinist was Julius Singer. Bernice Singer Baron, telephone interview, Aug. 31, 1995; Rachel Baron Heimovics, telephone interview, Aug. 31, 1995.

30. Fox, "End of an Era," pp. 275–76.

31. Ibid.

32. Ibid., p. 278–83; *Monitor,* Sept. 3, 1915.

33. *Monitor,* Oct. 7, 1921.

34. Ibid., Apr. 18, 1919.

35. David Rosenbaum papers, box 1, Chicago Jewish Archives, Spertus Institute of Jewish Studies; rabbis listed on the editorial page are, from Texas, Henry Cohen, A. Werne, Martin Zielonka, David Lefkowitz, David Rosenbaum, Wolfe Macht, R. Farber, Samuel Rosinger; from Oklahoma, Joseph Blatt, Merrie Teiler, Charles Latz; from Arkansas, Leonard Rothstein (then in Pine Bluff), Jerome H. Mark; from Louisiana, A. Brill and Harry A. Merfeld, who succeeded Fox at Beth-El. *Monitor,* Sept. 2, 1921.

36. *Monitor,* Mar. 5, 1920.

37. Ibid., Oct. 1, 1915.

38. Ibid., Mar. 28, 1919.

39. Ibid., Aug. 5, 1915.

40. Ibid., Dec. 24, 1920, May 27, 1921.

41. Ibid., Mar. 26, 1920.

42. Ibid., July 8, 1915.

43. The *Monitor* wrote up the Frank case May 14, 21, June 3, 10, 24, July 1, 8, 22, 29, Aug. 13, 20, 1915; *FWST,* Aug. 4, 17, 1915; Leonard Dinnerstein, *The Leo Frank Case,* pp. 118–47; Georgia's Board of Pardons and Parole gave Frank a posthumous pardon 71 years later, on March 12, 1986. Eli Evans, *The Provincials: A Personal History of Jews in the South,* pp. 308–15.

44. *Monitor,* June 6, 1919.

45. *Texas Jewish Herald,* Sept. 27, Oct. 19, 1916; the *Texas Israelite,* a monthly, was published in Fort Worth from April, 1908, until 1912. Houston's *Jewish Herald,* begun in 1908, became the *Texas Jewish Herald* Nov. 26, 1914. (In 1937 it com-

bined with another paper to become the *Jewish-Herald Voice*.) "List of Jewish Periodicals," *AJYB* editions 1908–15.

46. Fox, "End of an Era," p. 283.

47. The Foxes lived at 1329 Hurley Street, a corner house now vacant and dilapidated. *Fort Worth City Directory*, 1911, 1912–13, 1914, 1916, 1918, 1920.

48. B. B. Paddock, *History of Texas: Fort Worth and the Texas Northwest Edition*, vol. 4, pp. 573–74.

49. Fox, "End of an Era," p. 281–82.

50. Fort Worth Chamber of Commerce, "Luncheon Complimentary to General John J. Pershing," Feb. 7, 1920.

51. Frances Kallison, taped interview with author, San Antonio, Jan. 7, 1997; *Monitor*, April 6, 1922.

52. Fox telegram to Cohen, Apr. 7, 1922, HCP.

53. *Monitor*, Nov. 26, Dec. 10, 1920.

54. Fox Jr. interviews; no death certificate is on file for Samson Fox.

55. Temple Beth-El [Fort Worth] congregation minute book, Aug. 24, 1919, May 2, 1920.

56. Ibid., Feb. 25, 1919; *70th Anniversary*.

57. Itemized bill, Bryce Building Co. General Contractors, Dec. 16, 1920; *Temple Beth-El Bulletin*, Sept. 1920.

58. *70th Anniversary*.

59. Weil moved from Birmingham, Ala., to Fort Worth in 1920 and lived at 610 Broadway.

60. *70th Anniversary*.

61. *Monitor*, Aug. 22, 1919.

62. Beth-El minute book, Jan. 2, Mar. 3, Apr. 20, 1922; Sam Levy to Henry Cohen, Jan. 31, 1922, HCP.

63. *Monitor*, May 27, 1921.

64. *FWST*, July 3, 6, Aug. 7, 8, 10, Sept. 16, 18, Nov. 27, 1921; Hollace Weiner, "KKK Skeletons," *FWST*, Feb. 25, 1990; *FWST* of July 9, 1927, reported the flogging of a Jewish businessman, Morris Strauss; Alexander, *Crusade for Conformity*, p. 10.

65. *Monitor*, Feb. 3, 1922.

66. Ibid., Sept. 9, 1921.

67. *Monitor*, Feb. 3, 1922; *FWST*, Feb. 17, 1922; *Fort Worth Record*, Feb. 17, 1922; Federal Writers Project, *Research Data Fort Worth*, vol. 2, pp. 4203–4206.

68. *Monitor*, May 12, 1922.

69. "Jewish Businesses," box 7/4, Fort Worth Jewish Archives.

70. *FWST*, Feb. 25, 1990.

71. Weil interview.

72. Brown, *Hood, Bonnet, Little Brown Jug*, p. 60.

73. *FWST*, May 17, 1922.

74. *South Shore Temple News*, Sept. 19, 1924; Fox, "End of an Era," p. 288.

75. Fox, "End of an Era," pp. 288–89; *Sentinel* article reprinted in *Jewish Monitor,* Sept. 15, 1922.

76. Fox, "End of an Era," pp. 288–89.

77. Ibid.

78. Hanger's name is suggested by Tom Kellam in "The Mind of an Anti-Semite: George W. Armstrong and the Ku Klux Klan in Texas," *Chronicles: A Publication of the Texas Jewish Historical Society* 1 (1994): 28; "End of an Era," p. 289; *FWST,* Jan. 3, 1924.

79. Fox, "End of an Era," pp. 288–89.

80. "Supplemental Organizations," *AJYB* 23 (1921–22): 250.

81. *AJYB* 21 (1919–20): 360–67.

82. *South Shore Temple News,* South Shore Temple Collection, Chicago Jewish Archives.

83. Adelle Isaacson Bass and Lorraine Solomon Moss, taped interview with author, Chicago, Nov. 6, 1995.

84. *Chicago Daily News,* June 22, 1956.

85. *South Shore Temple News,* July 24, 31, 1925.

86. Peggy Singer Leibik, interview with author, Chicago, Nov. 5, 1995; Ruth Schwartz Panter, telephone interview, Nov. 6, 1995.

87. David and Helen Jacobson, interview with author, San Antonio, Apr. 6, 1997.

88. *Chicago Daily News,* Mar. 6, 1956.

89. Irving Cutler, *The Jews of Chicago: From Shtetl to Suburb,* pp. 206–207; Joe Mitchell of the Old Landmark Church of God in Holiness in Christ, interview with author, Chicago, Nov. 5, 1995.

CHAPTER 6

1. Martin Zielonka, "The Jew in Mexico," *Central Conference of American Rabbis Yearbook* (hereafter *CCAR Yearbook*) 33 (1923): 432.

2. Nativist sentiment led Congress to pass the "Quota Act" May 19, 1921, limiting immigration to 3 percent of U.S. residents of the same nationality counted in the 1910 Census. Garis, *Immigration Restriction,* pp. 142–43; Thomas J. Curran, *Xenophobia and Immigration, 1820–1930,* p. ix.

3. Zielonka, "Jew in Mexico," pp. 425–43; Zielonka telegram to Adolf Kraus, May 27, 1921, Mexico Bureau Collection, B'nai B'rith Archives, Washington, D.C. (hereafter, MBCBB).

4. The rabbis were Henry Cohen, Galveston; his house guest, David Lefkowitz of Dallas; Max Heller in New Orleans; and New York's Stephen Wise, who was lecturing in New Orleans. "Report of Rabbi Zielonka's Trip to N.Y.," Mar. 23, 1921, "Immigrants and Immigration [up to 1924]," Small Collections, AJA; Felix Warburg telegram to Zielonka, Mar. 8, 1921, Felix Warburg papers, box 195/15, AJA.

5. According to the "Report of Rabbi Zielonka's Trip," he met with top officials of the American Jewish Committee, Industrial Removal Office, and Hebrew Immigrant Aid Society. Among them were IRO director David Bressler, Jewish Theological Seminary president Cyrus Adler, and attorney Louis Marshall, leader of the AJC. Cyrus Sulzberger, a key worker during the Galveston movement, relayed Warburg's response and added his own comments about sitting shivah.

6. Martin Zielonka, "Romance of the Jew in Mexico," p. 2, MBCBB; Corinne A. Krause, "Mexico—Another Promised Land? A Review of Projects for Jewish Colonization in Mexico: 1881–1925," *American Jewish Historical Quarterly* 61 (June, 1972): 327–33; Corinne A. Krause, "Letters from Mexico in 1908 by Martin Zielonka: Background and Commentary," part 1, *WSJHQ* 12 (Apr., 1980): 220.

7. The late David Leopold Zielonka (rabbi at Congregation Shaarai Zedek in Tampa, Fla., 1930–77) typed these undated reminiscences about his father. Papers courtesy of Carl L. Zielonka, D.D.S., Tampa, Fla.; Haldeen Braddy, *Cock of the Walk: The Legend of Pancho Villa,* pp. 97, 99, 100, 103; Larry A. Harris, *Pancho Villa: Strong Man of the Revolution,* pp. 61–62.

8. Martin Zielonka, "Romance of the Jew in Mexico," MBCBB; "Correspondence and Reports of Rabbi Zielonka on Mexican Bureau of B'nai B'rith, 1921–33," micr. 600–600B, AJA.

9. Micr. 600–600B, AJA; Alexander Grenader of Goose Creek (now part of Baytown, Tex.) to Zielonka, Nov. 15, 1925, and Zielonka to Grenader, Nov. 19, 1925, MBCBB.

10. B'nai B'rith is Hebrew for sons of the covenant. Edward E. Grusd, *B'nai B'rith: The Story of a Covenant,* pp. 170–73.

11. "Confidential . . . 'Secretary Davis is at the head of the Loyal Order of the Moose. . . . I have a friend here, Sam Hart, who is a member of the executive committee from this section and he [and] Davis . . . are very intimate.'" Archibald Marx to Zielonka, May 28, 1921, MBCBB.

12. Marx's father was Salomon Marx, a German immigrant and New Orleans philanthropist who amassed a fortune in the cottonseed oil business. *Jewish Monitor,* Feb. 11, 1921.

13. Hannah Sinauer, "A Report of the History and Activities of the B'nai B'rith Mexican Bureau (1921–1931)," July, 1982, pp. 1–2, MBCBB; Zielonka, "Jew in Mexico," p. 433.

14. Zielonka, "Jew in Mexico," p. 433.

15. *American Israelite,* June 25, July 9, 16, 23, 30, Aug. 15, 1908.

16. "Material from Martin Zielonka Collection," micr. 46, AJA; Zielonka, "Jew in Mexico," p. 441.

17. Anita Brenner, "Making Mexico Jew Conscious," *Nation,* Sept. 9, 1931, pp. 252–55. *Encyclopaedia Judaica,* s.v. "Mexico."

18. *American Israelite,* June 25, July 9, 1908.

19. Ibid., July 16, 23, 1908.

20. Francisco Rivas (1850–1924). Martin Zielonka, "El Sabado: A Spanish American Jewish Periodical," *Publications of the American Jewish Historical Society* 23 (1915): 129–35; Martin Zielonka, "Francisco Rivas," *Publications of the American Jewish Historical Society* 35 (1939): 219–25; Zielonka, "Jew in Mexico," pp. 428–32; Krause, "Mexico—Another Promised Land?" p. 334; David M. Gitlitz, *Secrecy and Deceit: The Religion of the Crypto Jews,* pp. 55–58.

21. Zielonka, "Jew in Mexico," p. 427.

22. *American Israelite,* July 30, 1908.

23. Joseph Weinberger to Zielonka, micr. 600–600B, AJA.

24. Rosi Schwartz, interview with author, Eilat, Israel, May 17, 1994.

25. Immigrant roster, MBCBB.

26. Zielonka to Mexico City Bureau, May 26, 1922, MBCBB.

27. Jeanette Kram to Adolf Kraus, Dec. 28, 1924, MBCBB.

28. Weinberger to Zielonka, Jan. 20, 1925, MBCBB.

29. Zielonka, "Jew in Mexico"; micr. 600–600B, AJA; Sinauer, "Report of the History," p. 2; Boris D. Bogen, "B'nai B'rith Mexican Bureau," miscellaneous files, AJA.

30. Brenner, "Making Mexico Jew Conscious," pp. 252–55; Krause, "Mexico—Another Promised Land?" p. 340.

31. Sinauer, "Report of the History," p. 3.

32. Brenner, "Making Mexico Jew Conscious," pp. 252–53; *Encyclopaedia Judaica,* s.v. "Mexico"; *Texas Jewish Herald,* Sept. 17, 1925. Sinauer's "Report of the History," pp. 3–4, credits HIAS with donating $1,000 in 1923 and the Committee of Emergency Relief with donating $50,000 in 1926; Martin Zielonka, "My Impressions of Jewish Conditions in Mexico," Aug. 1, 1925, p. 4, MBCBB.

33. Zielonka, "My Impressions of Jewish Conditions in Mexico," Aug. 1, 1925, p. 4, MBCBB; *Texas Jewish Herald,* Nov. 4, 1926.

34. Family papers and telephone interviews with relatives: Carl Zielonka, Tampa, Aug. 30, 1994; David M. Zielonka, Gastonia, N.C., Oct. 17, 1993; Robert Zielonka, La Crescenta, Calif., Aug. 30, 1994.

35. *El Paso Times,* May 25, 1934.

36. Meyer, *Response to Modernity,* pp. 387–88.

37. Evelyn Rosing Rosen, "Martin Zielonka, Rabbi and Civic Leader in El Paso," *El Paso Jewish Historical Review* 1 (Sept., 1982): 5–12.

38. Podet, *Pioneer Jews of Waco,* p. 86.

39. Zielonka to Max Heller, May 26, 1900, Max Heller papers, AJA.

40. David L. Zielonka, reminiscences.

41. Carl and David M. Zielonka interviews; Hazel Friedlander Weisman, telephone interview, Shreveport, La., Aug. 30, 1994.

42. Frank Mangan, *El Paso in Pictures,* pp. 32, 40; El Paso Temple Mt. Sinai, *1898–*

1928 Temple Mt. Sinai Yearbook, pp. 10–12; Assorted El Paso family files, Fierman papers, Bloom Southwest Jewish Archives.

43. Galatzan file, Bloom Southwest Jewish Archives.

44. Floyd Fierman, "Haymon Krupp, Economic Adventurer in the Southwest," *Password* 26 (summer, 1981): 51–77.

45. El Paso Temple Mt. Sinai, *75th Anniversary Temple Mt. Sinai, 1898–1973,* pp. 4–5.

46. "Martin Zielonka, sermons, lectures, newspaper clippings dealing with his career, Mexico City Jewish community; necrologies, resolutions of sorrow. El Paso, Texas. 1900–38," micr. 484, AJA.

47. Photo collection, Temple Mount Sinai, El Paso; Mangan, *El Paso in Pictures,* p. 40.

48. David L. Zielonka, reminiscences; Ernst Kohlerg, cofounder of International Cigar Co., was killed June 17, 1910. *Letters of Ernst Kohlburg: 1875–1877,* p. 7; Fierman, "Insights and Hindsights," pp. 152–55.

49. Micr. 484, AJA.

50. Herman Lefkowitz to Harry Barnett, Nov. 18, 1935, and Joshua Bloch to Temple Mount Sinai, Nov. 21, 1935, Carl Zielonka papers; David L. Zielonka, reminiscences; Fanny Sattinger Goodman, "In the Beginning, the Jewish Community of El Paso, Texas," 1970, pp. 1–26, "El Paso, Texas," histories file, AJA.

51. Rosen, "Zielonka, Rabbi and Civic Leader," pp. 5–12; Francis Fugate and Linda Robinson, *Frontier College: Texas Western at El Paso, the First Fifty Years,* pp. 27–35.

52. Paso del Norte Jewish Historical Society Meeting, El Paso, group discussion with author, Oct. 29, 1995; Leonard Goodman Sr., taped interview with author, El Paso, April 9, 1994.

53. David M. Zielonka to author, Nov. 22, 1994.

54. Goodman Sr. interview.

55. Weisman interview; Paso del Norte discussion.

56. Texas Death Certificate No. 39384, El Paso County; David L. Zielonka, reminiscences; Dora Zielonka died Nov. 28, 1939.

57. Photo collection, Temple Mt. Sinai.

58. Tussell Acosta, current occupant of former parsonage at 837 W. Yandell, interview with author, El Paso, Apr. 9, 1994.

59. Zielonka/Marx correspondence, MBCBB.

60. Ibid.

61. *American Hebrew,* Dec. 8, 1916, p. 154.

62. Archie Goodman, during Paso del Norte meeting.

63. Hymer Elias Rosen, "I planted me Vineyards: The Story of Rabbi Joseph M. Roth," *El Paso Jewish Historical Review* 1 (Sept., 1982): 13–22.

64. Ibid; micr. 484, AJA.

65. Sally Rosen, interview with author, El Paso, Apr. 8, 1994; Rose Zeitlin, *Henrietta Szold: A Record of a Life,* passim; Gerald Sorin, *A Time for Building: The Third Migration, 1880–1920,* pp. 225–26.

66. Zielonka notebook, 1936–37, in micr. 484, AJA.

67. James G. Heller, *Isaac Mayer Wise, His Life, Work and Thought,* p. 604.

68. Rosinger, "Deep in the Heart of Texas," p. 126. One of the South's oldest Hadassah chapters was founded in San Antonio in 1912.

69. Fanny Sattinger Goodman, "Beginning of the El Paso Chapter of Hadassah," notes, Apr., 1974, speech, Barbara Goodman Ettinger papers, El Paso.

70. Micr. 484, AJA; Tamar de Sola Pool, three-time Hadassah president, was a Palestinian-born lecturer and language teacher. Her husband, David, was rabbi of New York's Spanish and Portuguese Synagogue Shearith Israel. *Who's Who in American Jewry 1938–1939,* s.v. "Pool, Tamar de Sola," "Pool, David de Sola."

71. Rosen, "I planted me Vineyards," pp. 13–22.

72. Fierman's papers at Bloom Southwest Jewish Archives record only the dates on Zielonka's tombstone, according to a search by this author and discussion with archives' founder, Abe Channin.

73. Krause, "Letters from Mexico," p. 220.

74. Alicia Gojman de Backal, *Memorias de un Desafío: Los Primeros Pasos de B'nai B'rith en Mexico,* pp. 108–109.

75. Louis Wolsey, "Memorial Addresses: Martin Zielonka," *CCAR Yearbook* 48 (1938): 214; David Lefkowitz, "Rabbi Martin Zielonka," *Publications of the American Jewish Historical Society* 35 (1939): 326–28.

CHAPTER 7

1. *New Handbook of Texas,* s.v. "Perl, Sam"; Ruben Edelstein petitioned County Judge Oscar Dancy and the Cameron County Commissioners Court in the early 1950s to empower Sam Perl to marry couples without a justice of the peace. Ruben Edelstein, interview with author, Brownsville, Feb. 11, 1997.

2. Walter Rathjen, interview with author, Brownsville, Feb. 10, 1997.

3. Simon Rubinsky, interview with author, Brownsville, Feb. 11, 1997.

4. Bill Goodman, telephone conversation with author, July 20, 1995.

5. Gay Greenspan, interview with author, Brownsville, Feb., 12, 1997.

6. The dietary laws stem from Leviticus 11 and Deuteronomy 14:3–21. Fish without fins and scales are unkosher. Jacobs, *Jewish Religion,* pp. 124–25.

7. *Brownsville Herald,* Aug. 1, 1926.

8. Texas Historical Society, *Historical Encyclopedia of Texas,* n.d., s.v. "Brownsville"; *Brownsville Herald,* Aug. 1, Dec. 5, 1926.

9. Frances Perl Goodman, taped interview with author, San Antonio, Aug. 9, 1996.

10. June Naylor Rodriguez, *Texas Off the Beaten Path: A Guide to Unique Places,* p. 95; Robert R. Rafferty, *Texas Coast,* pp. 255–59.

11. *Houston Chronicle,* Jan. 28, 1951; Molly O'Neill, *New York Cook Book,* pp. 40–41.

12. Frances Perl Goodman, "Cholent," in *The Melting Pot: Ethnic Cuisine in Texas,* Institute of Texan Cultures, p. 145.

13. Anecdotes, F. Goodman interview; Leviticus 19:27 is a source of the shaving restriction. Jacobs, *Jewish Religion,* pp. 47–48.

14. Reynaldo Garza to author, Apr. 24, 1998; sometimes Sam substituted Alice or Elsa. Ito and Marian Perl, interview with author, Dallas, Feb. 3, 1997.

15. Sam Perl Boulevard dedication ceremony program, Oct. 17, 1981.

16. Emilio "Capi" and Lily Vasques, interview with author, Brownsville, Feb. 10, 1997.

17. *Brownsville Herald,* Dec. 2, 5, 19, 1926.

18. Vasques interview.

19. Fehrenbach, *Lone Star,* pp. 270–73.

20. Winegarten, *Deep in the Heart,* p. 14

21. Ornish, *Pioneer Jewish Texans,* 263–64; "History of the Brownsville Hebrew Cemetery," p. 1, and "History of the Jewish Community of Brownsville," pp. 1–2, Ruben Edelstein papers.

22. Fehrenbach, *Lone Star,* p. 271.

23. B. B. Kowalski letter to *American Israelite,* July 28, 1876, in *WSJHQ* 10 (July, 1978): 306–307.

24. "History of Brownsville Hebrew Cemetery," pp. 1, 4.

25. Edelstein interview; Rabbi Edward Rosenthal, interview with author, Brownsville, Feb. 12, 1997.

26. Ito Perl interview; Harriet Denise Joseph and Sondra Shands, "Sam Perl: Mr. Friendship and Mr. Temple Beth-El of Brownsville, Texas," *Locus* 5 (spring, 1993): 153.

27. Milton Grafman letters to Rabbi Louis I. Egelson, HUC, Cincinnati, Oct. 3, 6, 11, 1929, Stephen Grafman papers, Potomac, Md.

28. Harriet Denise Joseph, "Temple Beth-El, 1931–1981," in *Studies in Brownsville History,* pp. 230–44.

29. William M. Kramer and Norton B. Stern, "The Layman as Rabbinic Officiant in the Nineteenth Century," *WSJHQ* 16 (Oct., 1983): 49–53; Rochlin, *Pioneer Jews,* pp. 202–206.

30. Sachar, *A History of the Jews in America,* p. 191.

31. Hasia Diner, *A Time for Gathering: The Second Migration, 1820–1880,* p. 125.

32. Rochlin, *Pioneer Jews,* p. 203.

33. Ibid.

34. Samson H. Levey, "The First Jewish Sermon in the West: Yom Kippur, 1850, San Francisco," *WSJHQ* 10 (Oct., 1977): 4–5.

35. Ledger books, the Fashion–Perl Bros., Sam Perl papers, CAH; Bruce Aiken, interview with author, Brownsville, Feb. 11, 1997.

36. Ledger books; Vasques interview.

37. F. Goodman interview.

38. Lily Vasques interview.

39. F. Goodman interview.

40. Rubinsky interview.

41. This is Reynaldo Garza's version of an oft-told Brownsville story.

42. "Views on the News," KBOR radio, Dec. 27, 1965, vinyl recording, Ito and Marian Perl collection.

43. Vasques interview.

44. *El Heraldo de Brownsville,* Nov. 24, 1969; *Brownsville Herald,* Nov. 23, 1969; Ito Perl interview; F. Goodman interview.

45. Stella Cohn to Sam Perl, July 27, 1928, Sam Perl papers.

46. Family interviews; Leon Perl died June 22, 1969, and received a front-page obituary. *Brownsville Herald,* June 23, 1969. Corinne Perl died in Brownsville March 29, 1994.

47. Rubinsky interview.

48. Ibid.

49. Edelstein interview; Joseph, "Temple Beth-El, 1931–1981," pp. 3–7.

50. Garza interview; Louise Ann Fisch, *All Rise: Reynaldo G. Garza, the First Mexican-American Federal Judge,* p. 34.

51. Ibid., p. 154.

52. Ibid., pp. 65, 80; F. Goodman interview.

53. Garza said he read the headline in *El Bravo.* A search of the Matamoros newspaper's bound editions by this author did not turn up the headline. Francis Goodman, Ito Perl, and Herb Goodman recollect the Spanish headline.

54. "Sam Perl Located," *Brownsville Herald,* Mar. 16, 1977.

55. Bernice Edelstein, conversation with author, Brownsville, Feb. 12, 1997.

56. Stella Cohn Perl died in San Antonio Aug. 18, 1987.

57. Garza interview.

CHAPTER 8

1. Alexander Kline papers, Egypt/box 3, Chinese Art III/box 65, India/box 62, Museum of Texas Tech University, Lubbock.

2. Winifred Vigness, interview with author, Lubbock, June 25, 1993.

3. Biographical details on Eleanore and Alex Kline, unless indicated, are drawn from interviews with Susan Kline Brochstein, Houston, Mar. 5, 1997; and David Kline, rabbi of Temple B'nai Israel, Monroe, La., March 18, 1998; *Encyclopaedia Judaica,* s.v. "Katzenellenbogen," "Neology."

4. Abraham Idelsohn held the chair of Jewish Music and Liturgy at HUC from 1924 to 1934. Cora Kahn, unofficial faculty member, taught elocution, stressing the importance of manners and appearance on the pulpit. Michael A. Meyer, "A Centennial History," in *Hebrew Union College–Jewish Institute of Religion at One Hundred Years,* ed. Samuel Karff, pp. 95, 105.

5. Jacob Rader Marcus interview.

6. Alexander S. Kline, "Social Functions of Art," rabbinical thesis, HUC, 1933, pp. 1–6.

7. Armand Spitz (1904–71), called the Henry Ford of astronomy, invented a low-cost projector used in planetariums. Brent Abbatantuono, "Armand Spitz: Seller of Stars," Internet Web site www.Griffithobs.org/IPSArmand.html.

8. Alexander S. Kline, "The Rabbi in the Small Town," *CCAR Journal,* 5 (Apr., 1954): 11.

9. Clarksdale's musical native sons include John Lee Hooker, Sam Cooke, Ike Turner, and Muddy Waters, who grew up about eight miles away. For African Americans, Clarksdale was a lively stop on a frequently traveled route between Arkansas and Memphis, according to Joel Pargot, Delta Blues Museum, telephone conversation with author, June 16, 1998.

10. Floyd Shankerman, telephone interview, Clarksdale, Miss., June 18, 1998.

11. Shirley Levine Weinberg, telephone interview, Northbrook, Ill., Mar. 17, 1998.

12. "I am amazed at the number of men and women who are against Jack Kennedy," visiting Rabbi G. George Fox wrote in Chicago's *Sentinel,* Oct. 13, 1960.

13. Lee Bradley Inselberg, "Changing Worlds: Jewish Women in Lubbock, Texas," master's thesis, Texas Tech University, Lubbock, 1982, p. 31; Richard Dasheiff, "Marvin Feldman Dinner," Internet Web site www.shamash.org/reform/uahc/congs/tx/tx002/feldman.html.

14. Norma Skibell, "History of Temple Shaareth Israel," Internet Web site www.shamash.org/reform/uahc/congs /tx/tx002/nskibell.html; Inselberg, "Changing Worlds," appendix C; scrapbooks compiled by Sadye Mae Garsek, Fort Worth.

15. Inselberg, "Changing Worlds," p. 64.

16. Norma Skibell and Bobbie Freid, interview with author, Lubbock, June 24, 1993; Skibell, telephone interview, Mar. 23, 1998.

17. Skibell interview, 1993.

18. Skibell, "History of Temple Shaareth Israel."

19. Isadore Garsek (1913–85) was born in Russia and raised in Des Moines, Iowa. *FWST,* Feb. 24, 1985; Sadye Maye Garsek, interview with author, Fort Worth, June 10, 1998.

20. Lubbock's short-term rabbis were Julius Kerman, Adolph Phillipsboerne, Stanley Yedwab, Israel Kaplan, and Frank Rosenthal. Skibell interview, 1993.

21. Dasheiff, "Marvin Feldman Dinner."

22. Trudi Post, telephone interview, Mar. 17, 1998; Skibell and Freid interview, 1993; Inselberg, "Changing Worlds," p. 33.

23. *Avalanche Journal,* Aug. 5, 1960.

24. Kline papers, Late Italians/box 16.

25. Ibid., Greek Art/box 4.

26. *Avalanche Journal,* Sept. 16, 1976.

27. Ibid., Oct., n.d., 1971.

28. Ibid., Oct. 19, 1983.

29. Skibell and Freid interview.

30. *Avalanche Journal,* May 20, 1973.

31. "Reports to the West Texas Museum Association," 1982, 1990.

32. Kline, "The Rabbi in the Small Town," p. 10.

33. Ibid., pp. 14, 25.

CHAPTER 9

1. Temple Beth-El, Resolution, June 1, 1942, Ephraim Frisch, Nearprint files, AJA; Lewis and Charlotte Lee, interview with author, San Antonio, July 20, 1996.

2. Ephraim Frisch, "The Book and the People of the Book," *American Scholar* 14 (autumn, 1945): 435–46; Temple Beth-El to Frisch, Nov. 26, 1956, Nearprint files, AJA.

3. Ephraim Frisch to David Frisch, Sept. 25, 1935, correspondence files, HCP; Kallison interview.

4. Ephraim Frisch, "The Work of Justice Is Peace," *HUC Monthly,* Nov., 1942, pp. 6, 19–20; "Letter by Dr. Ephraim Frisch on his contributions in the fields of Social Justice," spring, 1947, box 2/12, Ephraim Frisch papers (hereafter EFP), Collection 187, AJA.

5. W. J. Lockhart to Frisch, Feb. 27, 1929, box 1/ 4, EFP; Meyer, *Response to Modernity,* pp. 173–74.

6. William Keiller to Cohen, Feb. 28, 1929, box 1/ 1, EFP.

7. Ephraim Frisch, "Time to Wake Up," *San Antonio Express,* Feb. 22, 1929; Frisch, "No Chosen People," ms. May 7, 1924, box 3/5, EFP.

8. Sidney Wolf to Frisch, July 9, 1947, box 2/12; *San Antonio Express,* Mar., n.d., 1924, box 3/5, EFP; Meyer, *Response to Modernity,* p. 312

9. Derived from *U.S. Census Data on Race, Nativity, Country of Origin,* 1930; T. R. Fehrenbach, *San Antonio Story,* pp. 155–59, 169; *Will Rogers' Weekly Articles,* vol. 2, p. 267; Lewis F. Fisher, *Saving San Antonio,* p. ix; Ruben Munguia Sr., telephone interview, Apr. 30, 1997; Green Peyton, *San Antonio, City in the Sun,* passim; Ralph Maitland, "San Antonio: the Shame of Texas," *Forum,* Aug., 1939, pp. 51–55.

10. Population numbers from *AJYB* 24 (1922): 314 and 34 (1932): 249; Munguia interview; Peyton, *City in the Sun;* Fehrenbach, *San Antonio Story,* pp. 155–59.

11. Gurwitz, "Memories of Two Generations," pp. 277–78.

12. Maury Maverick Jr., taped interview with author, San Antonio, Apr. 4, 1997.

13. Sidney Tedesche to Cohen, Dec. 5, 1921, HCP.

14. Ibid.

15. Archibald Marx to Cohen, Aug. 2, 1923, HCP.

16. Nathan Cohn to Cohen, Nov. 16, 1922, HCP.

17. Frisch to Cohen, June 29, 1923; Morris Stern to Cohen, June 30, 1923; Cohen telegram to Frisch, June 30, 1923, HCP.

18. *Texas Jewish Herald,* July 8, 1915.

19. *San Antonio Express,* Dec. 8, 1923.

20. Gurwitz, "Memories of Two Generations," pp. 282–83.

21. Ephraim Frisch to *San Antonio Express,* Mar. 14, 1924, correspondence file, EFP.

22. Frisch to Cohen, Mar. 20, 1924, HCP.

23. Ibid.

24. Ephraim Frisch, "The Work of Justice Is Peace," *HUC Monthly,* Nov., 1942, pp. 6, 19–20; The congregant who challenged Frisch was apparently former temple president Nat Washer. In a letter to Rabbi Samuel Goldenson, Frisch writes, "I have exercised [freedom] whether my people liked it or not, ever since that Nat Washer incident in 1925 or 1926." Frisch to Goldenson, Sept. 7, 1937, EFP.

25. *Texas Jewish Press,* Jan. 3, 1936.

26. Ephraim Frisch, "Why I am a Jew," booklet, p. 10, Mar. 17, 1931.

27. *Universal Jewish Encyclopedia,* 1939, s.v. "American Pro-Falasha Committee."

28. Allen Goldsmith, interview with author, San Antonio, Mar. 4, 1997.

29. Ruth Cohen Frisch, "History," n.d., Ruth Cohen (Frisch), box 3M309, HCP.

30. "English papers, 1897, 1898," Ruth Cohen (Frisch), HCP.

31. Nathan and Cohen, *The Man Who Stayed in Texas,* pp. 130, 287–89.

32. Ibid.

33. Marks, "Memories of Rabbi Henry Cohen," p. 124.

34. Lee interview; Ruth Kempner, telephone conversation with author, June 25, 1996.

35. David and Helen Jacobson interview.

36. "Galveston Man's Daughter Weds," n.d., Ruth Cohen (Frisch), HCP.

37. Rosten, *Joys of Yiddish,* p. 303.

38. Ruth Littauer Herwitz, telephone interview, New York, June 26, 1996; Charles Frisch, telephone interview, Minneapolis, June 20, 1996.

39. Alexander Sender's Talmudic commentary, *Hatarat N'dorim [The Redemption of Vows],* was printed in Vilna and Jerusalem in 1880. Written in Aramaic with some Hebrew, it includes an endorsement by Rabbi Elchanan Spektor, ancestor

of Houston Rabbi Schachtel; Ruby Frisch to Florence Frisch, Aug. 2, 1975, Frisch family, biographical file, AJA.

40. Leo Frisch to Ruby Moses, n.d., Frisch family file; David Klein, telephone interview, New York, June 24, 1996; Charles Frisch interview; *NYT,* Dec. 26, 1957; *Who's Who in American Jewry,* 1938–39, s.v. "Frisch, Ephraim," "Frisch, Leonard Herman."

41. Ephraim Frisch, "*Babel und Bibel a la Delitzch,* an Imitation," *HUC Journal,* Apr., 1903, pp. 200–205.

42. Ephraim Frisch, editor, *Hebrew Union College Annual* (1904); The next HUC yearbook was published in 1919. A third attempt in 1924 took hold, and the yearbook has been an annual ever since. Meyer, "A Centennial History," p. 113.

43. LeMaster, *Corner of the Tapestry,* pp. 53–58.

44. *Daily [Pine Bluff] Graphic,* n.d., circa 1910, EFP.

45. *AJYB* 9 (1907–1908): 130; LeMaster, *Corner of the Tapestry,* pp. 78, 84.

46. Raphael Goldenstein, *History and Activities of Congregation Anshe-Emeth, Pine Bluff, Ark. 1867–1917,* p. 29.

47. Ephraim Frisch, "Contributions in Social Justice," p. 1.

48. *Daily Graphic,* Nov. 11, 1906.

49. LeMaster, *Corner of the Tapestry,* p. 56.

50. Ibid.; *St. Paul Dispatch,* Aug. 23, 1957; Constance C. Fisher to Ephraim Frisch, Sept. 21, 1957, box 1/1, EFP.

51. "Installation at Far Rockaway Temple Israel of Far Rockaway," n.d., box 3/5, EFP.

52. *American Hebrew,* July 30, p. 312; Sept. 24, pp. 582–83; Oct. 8, 1915, p. 642; *New York Evening Post,* Sept. 4, 1915; *Encyclopaedia Judaica,* s.v. "Brenner, Victor," "Bressler, David."

53. *NYT,* Sept. 5, 1918; *American Hebrew,* Sept. 13, 1918; Bobbie Malone, *Rabbi Max Heller: Reformer, Zionist, Southerner, 1860–1929,* p. 183.

54. *NYT,* Sept. 6, 7, 8, 15, 1918; Ephraim Frisch to David Philipson, Sept. 5, 10, 1918, box 1/5, David Philipson papers, AJA; David Feder, "The Zionist Controversy in the United States: September–December 1918," term paper, AJA; *American Hebrew,* Sept. 13, pp. 485, 492; Sept. 20, 1918, p. 514; Frisch describes the "Balfour Declaration controversy" to his father-in-law in order to explain why he snubbed Tamar de Sola Pool, whose husband was among rabbis who embarrassed him. Frisch to Cohen, Nov. 11, 1936, HCP.

55. Bernice Cristol Selman, telephone interview with author, Tyler, Mar. 24, 1997.

56. Lee interview.

57. *Jewish Record,* Oct. 28, 1927.

58. *San Antonio Express,* Feb. 22, 1929; Herschel Bernard interview with author, San Antonio, July 21, 1996.

59. "San Antonio Public Affairs Forum, Final Report, Second Season, July 1, 1938 – February 28, 1939," Texana/Genealogy Collection, San Antonio Public Library.
60. *Record book of Ministerial Functions,* 1923–38, EFP.
61. *San Antonio Evening News,* May 20, 1931.
62. Ephraim Frisch to Henry Cohen, Sept. 30, 1936, HCP.
63. *Jewish [San Antonio] Record,* Nov. 18, 1927.
64. *San Antonio Evening News,* Sept. 4, 1936.
65. Frisch to Cohen, Sept. 30, 1936, HCP.
66. Kenneth Farrimond, MD., current homeowner, e-mail to author, July 30, 1996.
67. Frisch to Cohen, Feb. 27, 1929, HCP.
68. Frisch to Cohen, Sept. 25, 30, 1935, HCP.
69. The new building was planned before Frisch arrived. Ephraim Frisch, "Temple Beth-El—A Retrospect and a Forecast," *San Antonio Jewish Weekly,* Apr. 29, 1927.
70. Frisch to Cohen, Mar. 20, 1924, HCP.
71. Meyer, *Response to Modernity,* pp. 312, 462.
72. Albert Vorspan and Eugene Lipman, *Justice and Judaism: The Work of Social Action,* pp. 255–60.
73. Kempner interview.
74. Nathan and Cohen, *The Man Who Stayed in Texas,* pp. 287–89; *San Antonio Light,* Aug. 6, 1934; *San Antonio Express,* Aug. 7, 1934.
75. David Lefkowitz to Cohen, Aug. 6, 1934; Henry Barnston to Cohen, Aug. 6, 1934, HCP.
76. Marks, "Memories of Rabbi Henry Cohen," p. 124.
77. Henry Cohen, "Eulogy for Marcus Meyer," Feb. 27, 1940, Henry Cohen II papers, Philadelphia.
78. Emphasis added by author to Frisch quote in Meyer's *Response to Modernity,* p. 320.
79. Ephraim Frisch, "Why I Am a Jew," Mar. 17, 1931, pp. 8–9.
80. Frisch to Samuel Goldenson, Sept. 7, 1937, box 2/12, EFP; Frisch to Charlotte Lippman, May 31, 1938, Lee family papers.
81. Kallison interview, Jan. 7, 1997.
82. David Frisch to Henry and Mollie Cohen, July 10, 1935, HCP.
83. Peyton, *City in the Sun,* 161–67; *New Handbook of Texas,* s.v. "Drossaerts, Arthur"; Frisch to Wolf, pp. 5–6.
84. Ephraim Frisch to Sidney (no last name), Aug. 13, 1937, box 2/12, EFP.
85. Karl Preuss, "Personality, Politics, and the Price of Justice: Ephraim Frisch, San Antonio's 'Radical' Rabbi," *American Jewish History* 85 (Sept., 1997): 263.
86. Victor Emanuel Reichert to Ephraim Frisch, Nov. 3, 1937, box 2/12, EFP.
87. Julian Morgenstern to Frisch, Nov. 3, 1937, box 2/12, EFP.
88. Ephraim Frisch, "The Police Raid: A Blow at Civil Liberties," pamphlet, July 24, 1937.

89. Unnamed board member to Ephraim Frisch, Aug. 8, 1937, box 2/12, EFP.

90. Kallison interviews.

91. Frisch to Samuel Goldenson, Sept. 7, 1937, box 2/12, EFP.

92. David Jacobson oral history interviews with Ruthe Winegarten, transcript, Nov., 1989, p. 44, box 3A174, TJHS.

93. David Frisch to Mollie and Henry Cohen, Dec. 10, 1938.

94. Jacobson interview with author.

95. Goldsmith interview.

96. Kallison, telephone interview with author, June 19, 1997.

97. Ephraim Frisch to Social Justice Commission, Jan. 24, 1943, EFP.

98. Emma Tenayuca to Frisch, Aug. 10, 1937, box 2/12, EFP; Sharyll Teneyuca, interview with author, San Antonio, July 20, 1996.

99. Albert Vorspan, *Giants of Justice,* pp. 132–44.

100. Ephraim Frisch, "The Work of Justice Is Peace," *HUC Monthly,* Nov. 1942, pp. 6, 19–20; Vorspan, *Justice and Judaism,* pp. 6–9, 17–18; Robert St. John, *Jews, Justice and Judaism,* p. 284.

CHAPTER 10

1. Barbara Schachtel, taped interviews with author, Houston, Mar. 3, 7, 1997; *Houston Chronicle,* Feb. 27, 1966.

2. Ann Nathan Cohen, *The Centenary History, Congregation Beth Israel of Houston, Texas: 1854–1954,* pp. 1, 33, 78–81.

3. Bobby Brownstein, "The Battle of the 'Basic Principles': Congregation Beth Israel and the Anti-Zionist Revolt in American Reform Judaism," master's thesis, University of Houston, 1991, pp. 37, 39, 42–44, 47; Jim Kessler, "A Study of the Split of Congregation Beth Israel, Houston, Texas, 1942–44," term paper, 1971, pp. 7–8, 12, Small Collections, AJA.

4. Israel Friedlander, "The History of the Official Adoption of 'The Basic Principles' by Congregation Beth Israel and Additional Correspondence, Articles and News clippings"; Exhibit F: articles from *Houston Post,* Feb. 9, 1942, and *Houston Press,* Aug. 24, Sept. 5, 1944, Beth Israel Collection 132, AJA.

5. Robert I. Kahn, letter to author, Aug. 11, 1997.

6. "History of the Basic Principles," Exhibit F, Beth Israel Collection, AJA.

7. Barbara Schachtel interviews.

8. Cohen, *Centenary History,* p. 61; Brownstein calls Governor Lehman one of Schachtel's mentors in "The Battle," p. 22.

9. *NYT,* Nov. 7, 1932, Oct. 16, 1941.

10. Rabbi Isaac Elchanan Theological Seminary (RIETS). *Encyclopaedia Judaica,* s.v. "Spektor, Isaac Elchanan."

11. Maurice Schachtel, telephone interview with author, July 2, 1997.

12. *NYT,* Apr. 21, 1931; *Houston Chronicle,* June 29, 1986; *New Handbook of Texas,* s.v. "Schachtel, Hyman Judah." Maurice. Schachtel interview; Barbara. Schachtel interviews.

13. Maurice Schachtel interview; *NYT,* Apr. 21, 1931.

14. *NYT,* Nov. 7, 1932; June 15, 1933; Alumnae Office at Vassar College, Poughkeepsie, N.Y.

15. Barbara. Schachtel interviews.

16. Ibid.; *NYT,* Oct. 16, 1941.

17. Howard R. Greenstein, *Turning Point: Zionism and Reform Judaism,* pp. 33–49; Henry L. Feingold, *A Time for Searching: Entering the Mainstream, 1920–1945,* pp. 100–103; Meyer, *Response to Modernity,* pp. 331, 388–89.

18. Petition in *NYT,* Aug. 30, 1942; phrase from Houston's *Jewish Herald-Voice,* July 22, 1943.

19. Brownstein, "The Battle," p. 22.

20. Schachtel to Elmer Berger, Mar. 29, 1943, Louis Wolsey papers (hereafter LWP), box 4/7, AJA; Brownstein, "The Battle," p. 23.

21. Schachtel to Wolsey, June 24, 1942; Schachtel to Morris Lazaron, July 13, 1942; Schachtel to Wolsey, Nov. 17, 1942, box 4/7, LWP; *Life,* June 28, 1943, p. 11; Brownstein, "The Battle," p. 23.

22. Wolsey to Schachtel, Jan. 22, 1943, box 4/7, LWP; Brownstein, "The Battle," p. 2.

23. *NYT,* Jan. 4, 1941.

24. *Congress Weekly,* Dec. 18, 1942.

25. Stanley Novicke, *Milton Steinberg: Portrait of a Rabbi,* p. 131.

26. *Congress Weekly,* Jan. 8, 1943; *Jewish Herald-Voice,* Jan. 14, 1943; Berger to Irving Reichert, Feb. 12, 1943, box 4/7, LWP.

27. "Are Zionism and Reform Judaism Incompatible? Affirmative: William H. Fineshriber, Hyman J. Schachtel. Negative: Felix A. Levy, David Polish," pamphlet, *CCAR Convention,* N.Y., June 24, 1943.

28. Rabbi Harvey Tattelbaum, Shaaray Tefila, telephone interview with author, May 16, 1998; "Temple Shaaray Tefila 1845–1995," booklet, p. 18.

29. *Jewish Herald-Voice,* Jan. 7, 14, 1943.

30. Texans include Barnston, Cohen, Frisch, Jacobson, Lefkowitz, and a chaplain at Camp Wolters in Mineral Wells. *NYT,* Aug. 30, 1942.

31. Thomas A. Kolsky, *Jews Against Zionism: The American Council for Judaism, 1942–1948,* p. 83.

32. Hyman Judah Schachtel, "A Book Review of *Texas,*" St. Luke's United Methodist Church, n.d., tape.

33. *Congress Weekly,* Mar. 27, 1942.

34. Barbara Schachtel interviews.

35. Henry Barnstein [Barnston] to David Philipson, Jan. 27, 1919, Henry Berkowitz papers, box 1/3, AJA.

36. Marguerite Barnes Johnston, *Houston, the Unknown City, 1836–1946,* p. 136.

37. *Texas Jewish Herald,* Mar. 25, 1920, quoted in 90th anniversary issue, *Jewish Herald-Voice,* Apr. 11, 1998, p. 10; "Barnston Family, Barnstein / Barnstijn, Barnston," genealogies file, AJA.

38. *Houston Post,* Jan. 21, 1949.

39. Jack Barnston, telephone interview with author, New Haven, Ct., Apr. 15, 1997.

40. Cohen, *Centenary History,* p. 30.

41. Johnston, *Houston, The Unknown City,* pp. 75, 96, 99, 111, 113, 130, 186, 221; Winegarten, *Deep in the Heart,* pp. 56, 96, 118.

42. Cohen, *Centenary History,* p. 13.

43. Johnston, *Houston, the Unknown City,* p. 161.

44. Ibid., pp. 184–85.

45. Death toll included four policemen. Robert V. Haynes, *A Night of Violence,* pp. 168–70, 204. 298.

46. *Galveston Daily News,* Oct. 9, 1920.

47. "Dr. Henry Barnston Memorial Issue," *Temple News,* Feb., 1950.

48. Johnston, *Houston, the Unknown City,* p. 136.

49. Annual Report, Congregation Beth Israel, May 30, 1944, p. 19.

50. Brownstein, "The Battle," p. 48.

51. Annual Report, 1944, p. 36.

52. Jacob L. Farb to Beth Israel Board, May 22, 1943, from "History of the Official Adoption of the Basic Principles"; J. L. Farb, "An Open Letter," *A Journal of Jewish Opinion,* Feb., 1944, pp. 12–13.

53. The Beth Israel controversy was among the factors leading the CCAR to pass a 1944 resolution requiring congregations to keep pulpits open until rabbis returned from active duty. "Principles on Replacement of Chaplains," *CCAR Yearbook* 54 (1944): 273; Beth Israel argued that Schachtel had not replaced Kahn, who was still associate rabbi, but Barnston, the retired senior rabbi.

54. Annual Report, 1944, p. 36; *The Days of My Years: Autobiographical Reflections of Leopold L. Meyer,* pp. 193–97; Brownstein, "The Battle," p. 31.

55. "Basic Principles of Congregation Beth Israel, Houston, Texas," Congregation Beth Israel Archives, Houston.

56. Meyer, *Response to Modernity,* note 111, p. 465.

57. Kahn to Schachtel, Oct. 29, 1943, Beth Israel Archives.

58. Brownstein, "The Battle," pp. 52, 108.

59. *American Jewish World,* Nov. 19, 1943; *Jewish Review and Observer,* Dec. 1943; *B'nai B'rith Messenger,* Nov. 12, 1943; *Beth Israel Sentinel,* Nov. 22, 1943, in William Nathan file of Beth Israel Collection, AJA.

60. *NYT,* Jan. 3, 1944; *Time,* Jan. 17, 1944, pp. 38–40; *Opinion,* Feb., 1944, p. 5.

61. *If God Were King: The Times and Words of Rabbi Alan S. Green,* pp. 33–42.

62. Ritz, "Inside the Jewish Establishment," p. 109.

63. Figures from Kolsky, *Jews Against Zionism,* p. 81; LeMaster, *A Corner of the Tapestry,* p. 64.

64. Don E. Carleton, *Red Scare! Right-Wing Hysteria, Fifties Fanaticism and Their Legacy in Texas,* pp. 103–11, 155–57, 174.

65. D. H. White, "A Hundred Years of Jewish Communal Life in Houston," *Jewish Herald-Voice,* Apr. 3, 1947.

66. Robert I. Kahn, interview with Louis Marchiafava, Houston, Aug. 6, 1975, transcript, TJHS, box 3A174.

67. Robert I. Kahn, "Oral Memoirs," Houston, May 30, 1977, cassette C-10, AJA.

68. Kahn to Beth Israel officers and board, Mar. 1, 1944, Congregation Beth Israel Archives, Houston.

69. Cohen, *Centenary History,* p. 58

70. Brownstein, "The Battle," pp. 86.

71. Ibid., p. 91; *Houston Chronicle,* n.d., William Nathan papers, Beth Israel Collection, AJA.

72. Kolsky, *Jews Against Zionism,* pp. 81.

73. "Rabbi H. Schachtel Quits Council," *National [Indianapolis] Jewish Post,* Apr. 15, 1949.

74. Barbara Schachtel interviews.

75. Brownstein, "The Battle," p. 81.

76. Humanitarian Hour, KXYZ Radio, transcript, H. J. Schachtel, "The Greatness of Shakespeare," Dec. 7, 1952.

77. Ibid., "George Washington: Man of Character," Feb. 22, 1953.

78. Hyman Judah Schachtel, "Varieties of Preachers and Preaching," in *Aspects of Jewish Homiletics,* vol. 7, Department of Midrash and Homiletics, HUC, Jan. 20–23, 1964, pp. 27, 32–33, 41.

79. John E. Fellers, telephone interview with author, Mar. 7, 1997.

80. Houston Oilers place-kicker Toni Fritsch and *Houston Chronicle* columnist Maxine Mesinger pictured with Barbara Schachtel in *Houston Chronicle,* May 23, 1982.

81. Carleton, *Red Scare!,* pp. 70, 74.

82. Ray Miller, *Ray Miller's Houston,* pp. 159, 164, 181, 187–88, 205; Marvin Hurley, *Decisive Years for Houston,* pp. 58–78.

83. Irving Wadler, essay in *Yesterday, Today and Tomorrow: Greater Houston Section of the National Council of Jewish Women,* pp. 41–44.

84. Maxine Mesinger, telephone conversation with author, Mar. 4, 1997.

85. Edna Ferber, *Giant,* pp. 47–63; David McComb, *Houston: A History,* pp. 135–36.

86. Carleton, *Red Scare!,* p. 129.

87. Humanitarian Hour, KXYZ Radio, "Easter Parade," April 13, 1952.

88. Ibid., "Our Growing Fear," March 16, 1952.

89. Thomas R. Cole, *No Color Is My Kind: The Life of Eldrewey Stearns and the Integration of Houston,* pp. 36–57.

90. Jan de Hartog, *The Hospital,* pp. 116, 119.

91. Quentin Mease, telephone interview with author, Mar. 7, 1997.

92. Three other clergymen, including San Antonio archbishop Robert Lucey, were on the inaugural program. Don R. Petit, *Threshold of Tomorrow: The Great Society: The Inauguration of Lyndon Baines Johnson, 36th President of the United States,* Jan. 20, 1965, p. 39.

93. Barbara Schachtel, letter to author, Oct. 14, 1997.

94. Anne Nathan Cohen Friedman, daughter-in-law of Galveston rabbi Henry Cohen, interview with author, Houston, Mar. 6, 1997.

95. Lois Edel Levy Grenader, charter member, telephone interview, Mar. 4, 1998; "Congregation for Reform Judaism, 1957–1989," subject files, AJA; Maas, *Jews of Houston,* p. 112.

96. Schachtel to Jacob Rader Marcus, Dec. 9, 1968, Beth Israel Collection, box 1/3, AJA.

97. Kahn, "Oral Memoirs."

98. Rabbi A. Stanley Dreyfus, former placement director for the Reform movement, explained the politics of the CCAR during an interview with the author, Brooklyn, May 26, 1997.

99. Abram Goodman, interview with author, Hot Springs, Ark., Nov. 15, 1997.

100. Barbara Schachtel interviews.

101. Kahn, letter to author, Aug. 11, 1997.

102. H. J. Schachtel to Jack Maguire, Dec. 14, 1976, Selma Weiner, personal papers, San Antonio.

CHAPTER 11

1. *DMN,* Nov. 22, 1963.

2. Darwin Payne, *Big D: Triumphs and Troubles of an American Supercity in the Twentieth Century,* pp. 305–20; Richard Austin Smith, "How Business Failed Dallas," *Fortune,* July, 1961, pp. 157–62, 211–18.

3. Levi Olan, "In Mourning," Nov. 22, 1963; "In Memoriam—John F. Kennedy, Radio-RLD," Nov. 24, 1963; "In Memoriam—President John F. Kennedy," sermon notes, Nov. 25, 1963, Levi Arthur Olan papers (hereafter LAO), box 26/3, AJA.

4. *NYT,* Nov. 24, 1963.

5. Smith, "How Business Failed Dallas," p. 159.

6. Rev. William A. Holmes, telephone interview, Washington, D.C., Aug. 2, 1997; Marie-Luise Keller, "A Report on the Political Developments and Theological Decisions in Dallas 1963," *Perkins Journal* 41 (Oct., 1988): 1–11.

7. Stanley Marcus, interview with author, Dallas, July 28, 1997.

8. "Joint Statement of County Judge Lew Sterrett, Mayor Earle Cabell," Dec. 2, 1963, box 13/15, LAO.

9. Irving L. Goldberg to Olan, June 2, 1964, box 13/15, LAO.

10. Leslie L. Jacobs to Olan, June 3, 1964, box 13/15, LAO.

11. Mark Briskman, director Dallas Anti-Defamation League, telephone interview, Nov. 7, 1997.

12. James Stemmons, telephone interview, Aug. 21, 1997.

13. Marcus adds that he arranged for architect Philip Johnson to donate his fee. "It was courageous of him. It was a good way to get blackballed in Dallas."

14. *Dallas Times Herald,* Apr. 29, 1968; Stemmons interview; "11/24/63 notes for KRLD," "11/25/63 notes for sermon," box 13/15, LAO.

15. Jacob Rader Marcus interview; Among Olan's "clique" of rebels were Sidney Regner and Leon I. Feuer, Class of '27; B. Benedict "Babe" Glazer, Class of '26, and Adolph H. "Rube" Fink, Class of '30. "Levi Olan: Oral History Interviews," conducted by Gerald Saxon, parts 1 and 2, 1983, tape and transcript, Texas/Dallas History and Archives Division, Dallas Public Library; Levi Olan, "Autobiography," box 30/8, LAO.

16. Levi Olan, "A Jew Views the Freiburg Passion Play," Apr., 1931, box 25/5, LAO.

17. Levi Olan, "Religion in Dallas," box 28/4, LAO.

18. Levi Olan, "Wanted: Moral Leadership," Apr. 3, 1960, WFAA Radio, transcript.

19. Ibid.

20. Levi Olan, "Religion and the Social Problem," April 10, 1949, WFAA Radio, transcript.

21. Levi Olan, *Maturity in an Immature World,* pp. 61–65.

22. Levi Olan, "My Christian Neighbor and I," WFAA Radio, transcript, Dec. 25, 1949.

23. Olan, *Maturity in an Immature World,* pp. 61–65.

24. Olan, "From Birmingham to Memphis," Apr. 28, 1968, KRLD/WFAA Radio, transcript.

25. Smith, "How Business Failed Dallas," p. 163; *Dallas Times Herald,* Oct. 20, 1984.

26. Paul F. Boller Jr., *Memoirs of an Obscure Professor,* pp. 1–33; *DMN,* Oct. 19, 1984.

27. "Olan Oral History," part 1, Dallas Library.

28. Decherd Turner, interview with author, Austin, Aug. 14, 1997; In a show of religious solidarity, many Jews, particularly the tailors, operated their shops on Sundays. Stuart E. Rosenberg, *The Jewish Community in Rochester, 1843–1925,* p. 183.

29. "Autobiography," p. 1; The shul was Agudas Achim Nusach Ari, later called the Morris Street Synagogue.

30. Steinberg (1903–50) became rabbi at New York's Park Avenue Synagogue and a popular, scholarly author whose books remain in print. Simon Noveck, *Milton Steinberg: Portrait of a Rabbi,* pp. 1–13.

31. Olan became a settlement house club leader during his two years at the University of Rochester. Rosenberg, *Jewish Community in Rochester,* p. 222; "Olan Oral

History," part 1, Dallas Library; Jack Cravetz, Olan's brother-in-law, telephone interview, Rochester, May 6, 1998.

32. Cravetz interview.

33. "Olan Oral History," part 2, Dallas Library.

34. Sidney Regner, "Levi Olan, Memorial Tributes," *CCAR Yearbook*, 95 (1985): 301–302; "Autobiography," p. 4.

35. Olan joked that a Worcester Baptist was the equivalent of a Dallas Unitarian. In Dallas, he traded pulpits only with Unitarian minister Bob Raible. "Autobiography," p. 7.

36. "Olan Oral History," part 1, Dallas Library.

37. Levi A. Olan, "A Preliminary Summing Up," in *A Rational Faith: Essays in Honor of Levi A. Olan,* ed. Jack Bemporad, p. 192.

38. Levi Olan, "A Sermon for Un-Believers," Feb. 13, 1949, WFAA Radio, transcript.

39. Reference is to HUC professor Richard Rubenstein. Steven T. Katz, ed., *Jewish Philosophers,* pp. 223–28; Meyer, *Response to Modernity,* pp. 360–61.

40. Olan, "Religion and the Social Problem," Apr. 10, 1949, WFAA Radio, transcript.

41. Ruth Andres, interview with author, Hot Springs, Ark., Nov. 15, 1997.

42. Ibid.

43. Liz Olan Hirsch, interview with author, Dallas, Aug. 2, 1997.

44. "Autobiography," p. 7; "Olan Oral History," part 1, Dallas Library.

45. Samuel G. Messer (1911–77) played the bad guys in *The Silver Chalice, The Big Combo, The Law and Jack Wade,* and *The Desperate Hours.* He was a palace character in *The Court Jester.* His most acclaimed role was in *The Lincoln Conspiracy.* Ephraim Katz, *The Film Encyclopedia,* p. 939.

46. Turner interview.

47. "Olan Oral History," part 1, Dallas Library; Levi Olan, oral history conducted by Hortense Sanger, Aug. 5, 1972, tape and transcript, Temple Emanu-El Archives, Dallas.

48. "Olan Oral History," part 1, Dallas Library.

49. James Street, "Dazzling Dallas," *Holiday,* Mar., 1953, pp. 102–19.

50. Derro Evans, "Rabbi Levi Olan: A Conversation," *Sunday Magazine, Dallas Times Herald,* Oct. 11, 1970; Street, "Dazzling Dallas," pp. 102–19.

51. Olan, oral history with Sanger; Nelson Glueck (1903–71) delivered an inaugural prayer for John F. Kennedy and was the subject of a cover story in *Time,* Dec. 13, 1963.

52. Stanley Marcus interview.

53. Street, "Dazzling Dallas," p. 109.

54. "Olan Oral History," part 1, Dallas Library.

55. Olan often played tennis with J. B. "Tiste" Adoue, 1938 Davis Cup team captain and Dallas mayor from 1951–53. Joe Jacobs, telephone interview, Oct. 4, 1997.

56. "Olan Oral History," part 1, Dallas Library

57. "Autobiography," p. 8.

58. Levi Olan, in introduction to *Medicine for a Sick World.*

59. Gerald J. Klein, "The Lefkowitz Years, 1920–1955: A memoir and an attempt to contribute to the historical record," the 1990 Rabbi Levi A. Olan Lecture, Mar. 9, 1990, Dallas, Texas.

60. Jacobs interview.

61. "Autobiography," p. 9; "Olan Oral History," part 1, Dallas Library.

62. Michael V. Hazel, "The Critic Club: Sixty Years of Quiet Leadership," *Legacies: A History Journal for Dallas and North Central Texas* 2 (fall, 1990): 9–17; "Autobiographical Sketch of William H. Greenburg," Mar. 29, 1948, Critic Club Collection, A6354, Dallas Historical Society; Payne, *Big D,* p. 29.

63. Annual Reports, 1949, 1950, Temple Emanu-El Archives, Dallas.

64. "Autobiography," p. 9.

65. Joseph Rosenstein, interview with author, Dallas, Nov. 6, 1997.

66. Olan, oral history with Sanger.

67. Turner interview.

68. "Autobiography," p. 9.

69. David Olan, telephone interview, New York, Jan. 26, 1998.

70. Levi A. Olan, "Philanthropy and the Modern World," address to Hogg Foundation for Mental Health, Jan. 28, 1965, pp. 2, 10, Levi A. Olan papers, Bridwell Library, Perkins School of Theology, Southern Methodist University, Dallas.

71. Turner interview.

72. Levi Olan, "The President's Message to the 79th Annual Convention of the CCAR," June 17, 1968, passim.

73. "Olan Oral History," part 1, Dallas Library.

74. Zan T. Holmes, telephone interview, Aug. 21, 1997.

75. Paul Boller, conversations with author, Fort Worth, Nov. 4–10, 1997.

76. Albert Outler, eulogy, Oct. 19, 1984, tape, collection of Gerald Klein.

77. Smith, "How Business Failed Dallas," p. 161.

78. Outler eulogy; Zan Holmes interview.

79. Schubert Ogden, telephone interview, Rollinsville, Col., Sept. 19, 1997.

80. Decherd Turner, "In Memoriam: Levi Olan. . . ." *HRC Notes,* no. 11, Harry Ransom Humanities Research Center, University of Texas, Austin.

81. *Day in the Life of Lon Tinkle,* pp. 39–40; Lillian Moore Bradshaw, *Friends of the Dallas Public Library: The First Forty Years,* pp. 1–2; Larry Grove, *Dallas Public Library: The First 75 Years,* p. 65.

82. John O. Beaty, *The Iron Curtain Over America,* passim. The book includes supportive quotes from Rabbi Elmer Berger (pp. 38–39), whom Olan despised.

83. "Professor John Beaty," *Facts* 7 (Feb.–Mar., 1952): 1–4.

84. Rabbi S. Andhil Fineberg, national investigator for the American Jewish Committee (hereafter AJC), assisted the ad hoc committee. AJC papers, unpublished history, Dallas office, AJC.

85. Winifred Weiss and Charles S. Proctor, *Umphrey Lee: A Biography,* p. 178.

86. "Professor," *Facts,* pp. 1–4.

87. AJC papers, unpublished history.

88. Boller, *Memoirs of an Obscure Professor,* pp. 1–34.

89. Ibid.; Boller interview, Nov. 4, 1997; Weiss, *Umphrey Lee: A Biography,* pp. 180–85; "The Friendly Professor," *Time,* Apr. 12, 1954, pp. 57–58; The seven clergy were Robert E. Goodrich, First Methodist; Luther Holcomb, Lakewood Baptist; Jasper Manton, Trinity Presbyterian; Dean Gerald Moore, St. Matthews Episcopal; Tom Shipp, Lovers Lane Methodist; Arthur Swartz, Central Congregational; and W. A. Welsh, East Dallas Christian, according to *Dallas Times Herald,* Feb. 25, 1954, Beaty file, Dallas Temple Emanu-El Archives.

90. Ogden interview.

91. Boller, "Memoirs of an Obscure Professor," pp. 25–27; Boller interviews.

92. Grove, *Dallas Public Library,* pp. 76–81; "George Leighton Dahl: An Oral History Interview," Dallas Public Library, Oct. 6, 1978.

93. Jerry Bywaters, *Seventy-Five Years of Art in Dallas: The History of the Dallas Art Association of the Dallas Museum of Fine Arts,* pp. 35–37.

94. Payne, *Big D,* pp. 283–86.

95. Levi Olan, "Communism and the Biblical Tradition," Apr. 1, 1962, WFAA Radio, tape, Levi A. Olan papers, Bridwell Library, SMU, Dallas.

96. Sisterhood of Temple Emanu-El, Dallas, Texas, "A Significant Year for Significant Books 25th Anniversary," Feb. 4, 1981; note card featuring Psalm 150 and tapestry by Ben Shahn (1898–1969); Olan papers, box 808, Bridwell Library, SMU; *Dallas Times Herald,* Oct. 10, 1976, p. 21.

97. Street, "Dazzling Dallas," p. 112; Payne, *Big D,* p. 252; Levi Olan, *Maturity in an Immature World,* p. 266.

98. Olan, "Communism and the Biblical Tradition," April 1, 1962, WFAA Radio, transcript.

99. Levi Olan, "From Birmingham to Memphis," Apr. 28, 1968, tape, Olan papers, Bridwell Library, SMU; Payne, *Big D,* pp. 301–302; Glenn M. Linden, *Desegregating Schools in Dallas: Four Decades in Federal Courts,* passim.

100. "Sanctuary Rededication Service, Oct. 5, 1990," Olan, box 31, Temple Emanu-El Archives, Dallas.

101. Cristol, *A Light on the Prairie,* p. 186.

102. AJC papers; David Olan interview.

103. Caesar Clark, telephone interview, Aug. 21, 1997.

104. *Dallas Times Herald,* Jan. 2, 3, 4, 5, 1963.; *Dallas Express,* Jan. 5, 12, 1963.

105. Yvonne Ewell, telephone interview, Oct. 3, 1997.

106. Rhoads Terrace files, Temple Emanu-El Archives, Dallas; Rhoads Terrace folder, Texas/Dallas History and Archives Division, Dallas Public Library.

107. *DMN*, Dec. 5, 1965, Feb. 2, 1966.

108. Bemporad, *A Rational Faith,* pp. 107–24.

109. Levi Olan, *Prophetic Faith and the Secular Age,* p. ix.

110. Sandra Lubarsky and David Ray Griffin, *Jewish Theology and Process Thought,* pp. 1–34, 89–94.

111. "Best Things," *Dallas Observer,* Oct. 15, 1987.

Bibliography

ARCHIVAL MATERIALS

American Jewish Archives (AJA), Jacob Rader Marcus Center, Cincinnati. Congregation Beth Israel Collection, Houston. Ephraim Frisch Papers (EFP). Levi Arthur Olan Papers (LAO). David Philipson Papers. Hyman Judah Schachtel Papers. Lewis Wolsey Papers (LWP).

Barker Texas History Center, Center for American History (CAH), University of Texas, Austin. Henry Cohen Papers (HCP). Maurice Faber, vertical file. William Clifford Hogg Papers. Sam Perl Papers. Texas Jewish Historical Society Collection (TJHS).

Bloom, Leona G. and David, Southwest Jewish Archives, University of Arizona, Tucson. Floyd Fierman Papers.

B'nai B'rith Archives, Washington, D.C. Mexico Bureau Collection (MBCBB).

Bridwell Library, Perkins School of Theology, Southern Methodist University, Dallas. Levi Arthur Olan Papers and Tapes.

Catholic Archives of Texas. Clergy Collection.

Chicago Jewish Archives, Spertus Institute of Jewish Studies. David Rosenbaum Papers. South Shore Temple Collection.

Congregation Beth-El Archives, Fort Worth.

Congregation Beth El, Tyler. Minutes books, memorabilia, videotaped oral histories.

Congregation Beth Israel Archives, Houston.

Dallas Historical Society. Critic Club Collection.

Dallas Public Library, Texas/Dallas History and Archives Division.

Fort Worth Jewish Archives, Jewish Federation of Fort Worth and Tarrant County.

Fort Worth Public Library, Genealogy and Local History Department.

Houston Metropolitan Research Center, Houston Public Library. Henry Barnston Papers. Hyman Judah Schachtel Papers.

[Sadie] Klau Library, Hebrew Union College, Cincinnati.

Rosenberg Library, Galveston and Texas History Center. Rabbi Henry Cohen Manuscript Collection and subject file. Monsignor James Martin Kirwin subject file.

National Archives. Supervising Inspector, Immigration Service, October 14, 1913. File 52809/73.

San Antonio Public Library, Texana/Genealogy Collection.

Sixth Floor Museum at Dealey Plaza, Dallas. Kennedy Memorial Collection.

Tyrrell Historical Library, Archives and Special Collections, Beaumont.

University of Texas at Arlington. Special Collections Division, *Fort Worth Star-Telegram* Archives.

Weisberg Library, Temple Emanu-El, Dallas. Levi Olan, Radio Transcripts, 1949–68.

ARTICLES, BOOKS, AND ACADEMIC PAPERS

Alexander, Charles C. *Crusade for Conformity: The Ku Klux Klan in Texas, 1920–1930.* Houston: Texas Gulf Coast Historical Association, 1962.

——. *The Ku Klux Klan in the Southwest.* Lexington: University of Kentucky Press, 1965.

Backal, Alicia Gojman de. *Memorias de un Desafio: Los Primeros Pasos de B'nai B'rith en Mexico.* Mexico: B'nai B'rith, 1993.

Baker, Eugene W. *Nothing Better Than This: The Biography of James Huckins, First Baptist Missionary to Texas.* Waco: Baylor University Press, 1985.

Bauman, Mark K, and Arnold Shankman. "The Rabbi as Ethnic Broker: The Case of David Marx." *Journal of American Ethnic History* 2 (spring, 1983): 51–68.

Beaty, John, *The Iron Curtain Over America.* Dallas: Wilkinson, 1951.

Bemporad, Jack, ed. *A Rational Faith: Essays in Honor of Levi A. Olan.* New York: Ktav, 1977.

Bentley, Max. "The KKK in Texas," *McClures,* May, 1924, pp. 11–21.

Betts, Vicki. *Smith County Texas in the Civil War.* Tyler: Smith County Historical Society, 1978.

Block, W. T. "A Brief History of the Early Beaumont Jewish Community." *Texas Gulf Historical and Biographical Record* 20 (November, 1984): 42–54.

Block, W. T. "From Cotton Bales to Black Gold: A History of the Pioneer Wiess Families of Southeast Texas." *Texas Gulf Historical and Biographcal Record* 8 (November, 1972): 39–60.

Boller, Paul F., Jr. *Memoirs of an Obscure Professor.* Fort Worth: Texas Christian University Press, 1992.

Bradshaw, Lillian Moore. *Friends of the Dallas Public Library: The First Forty Years.* Dallas: Friends of the Dallas Public Library, 1991.

Breen, Helen Goldstien, *History of Temple Emanuel: Its First Hundred Years.* Beaumont: privately published, 1995. Booklet.

Bregstone, Philip. *Chicago and Its Jews: A Cultural History.* Chicago: Privately published, 1933.

Brenner, Anita. "Making Mexico Jew Conscious." *Nation,* September 9, 1931, pp. 252–55.

Bristow Edward J. *Prostitution and Prejudice: The Jewish Fight Against White Slavery 1870–1939.* New York: Schocken, 1983.

Brown, Norman D. *Hood, Bonnet, and Little Brown Jug: Texas Politics, 1921–1928.* College Station: Texas A&M University Press, 1984.

Brownstein, Bobby. "The Battle of the 'Basic Principles,' Congregation Beth Israel and the Anti-Zionist Revolt in American Reform Judaism." Master's thesis. University of Houston, 1991.

Bywaters, Jerry. *Seventy-five Years of Art in Dallas: The History of the Dallas Art Association of the Dallas Museum of Fine Arts.* Dallas: Dallas Museum of Fine Arts, 1978.

Carleton, Don E. *Red Scare! Right-wing Hysteria, Fifties Fanaticism and Their Legacy in Texas.* Austin: Texas Monthly Press, 1985.

Cartwright, Gary. *Galveston: A History of the Island.* New York: Atheneum, 1991.

Chalmers, David M. *Hooded Americanism: The First Century of the Ku Klux Klan, 1865–1965.* Garden City, N.Y.: Doubleday, 1965.

Chyet, Stanley F., ed. *Lives and Voices: A Collection of American Jewish Memoirs.* Philadelphia: Jewish Publication Society of America, 1972.

Cohen, Anne Nathan, *Centenary History of Congregation Beth Israel of Houston, Texas 1854–1954.* Houston: Privately published, 1954.

Cole, Thomas R. *No Color Is My Kind: The Life of Eldrewey Stearns and the Integration of Houston.* Austin: University of Texas Press, 1997.

Connor, Seymour V. *Texas: A History.* New York: Thomas Y. Crowell, 1971.

Cristol, Gerry. *A Light in the Prairie: Temple Emanu-El of Dallas, 1872–1997.* Fort Worth: Texas Christian University Press, 1998.

Curran, Thomas J. *Xenophobia and Immigration, 1820–1930.* Boston: T. Wayne, 1975.

Cutler, Irving. *Jews of Chicago: From Shtetl to Suburb.* Urbana: University of Illinois, 1996.

Day in the Life of Lon Tinkle. Dallas: Friends of the Dallas Public Library, Southern Methodist University Press, 1981.

Diner, Hasia. *A Time for Gathering: The Second Migration, 1820–1880.* Baltimore: Johns Hopkins University Press, 1992.

Dinnerstein, Leonard. *The Leo Frank Case.* Athens: University of Georgia Press, 1987.

Dreyfus, A. Stanley, ed. *Henry Cohen, Messenger of the Lord.* New York: Bloch, 1963.

East, Lorecia. *History and Progress of Jefferson County.* Dallas: Royal, 1961.

Eichhorn, David Max. *Evangelizing the American Jew.* Middle Village, N.Y.: Jonathan David, 1978.

Encyclopaedia Judaica. Jerusalem: Keter, 1972.

Ephraim Katz. *The Film Encyclopedia.* New York: Harper Perennial, 1994.

Evans, Eli. *The Provincials: A Personal History of Jews in the South.* New York: Simon and Schuster, 1973, reprinted 1997.

Fehrenbach, T. R. *Lone Star: A History of Texas and the Texans.* New York: Macmillan, 1968.

———. *The San Antonio Story: A Pictorial and Entertaining Commentary on the*

Growth and Development of San Antonio, Texas. San Antonio: Continental Heritage Press, 1978.

Feingold, Henry L. *A Time for Searching: Entering the Mainstream, 1920–1945.* Baltimore: Johns Hopkins University Press, 1992.

Ferber, Edna. *Giant.* New York: Grosset and Dunlap, 1952.

Fierman, Floyd S. "Insights and Hindsights of Some El Paso Jewish Families." *El Paso Jewish Historical Review* 1 (Spring, 1983): 1–268.

Fisch, Louise Ann. *All Rise: Reynaldo G. Garza, The First Mexican-American Federal Judge.* College Station: Texas A&M University Press, 1996.

Fisher, Lewis F. *Saving San Antonio: The Precarious Preservation of a Heritage.* Lubbock: Texas Tech University Press, 1996

Flemmons, Jerry. *Amon: The Life of Amon Carter, Sr., of Texas.* Austin: Jenkins, 1978.

Fox, G. George. *Abraham Lincoln's Religion: Sources of the Great Emancipator's Religious Inspiration.* New York: Exposition Press, 1959.

———. *An American Jew Speaks.* Chicago: Falcon Press, 1946.

———. *Judaism, Christianity and the Modern Social Ideals.* Fort Worth: Monitor, 1919.

———. "Why the State and the Church Should Require Health Certificates Before Marriage." In *The New Chivalry—Health.* Nashville: Benson Printing, 1915, pp. 159–64.

"Friendly Professor," *Time,* April 12, 1954, pp. 57–58;

Frisch, Ephraim. "The Book and the People of the Book," *American Scholar* 14 (fall, 1945): 435–46.

———. *An Historical Survey of Jewish Philanthropy from the Earliest Times to the Nineteenth Century.* New York: Cooper Square, 1924, reprinted 1969.

———, ed. *Hebrew Union College Annual.* 1904.

Garis, Roy L. *Immigration Restriction: A Study of the Opposition to and Regulation of Immigration into the United States.* New York: Macmillan, 1927.

Gebet Ordnung der Synagogen Gemeinde zu Allenstein. Allenstein, Germany: University of Harich, 1877.

Gitlitz, David M. *Secrecy and Deceit: The Religion of the Crypto-Jews.* Philadelphia: Jewish Publication Society of America, 1997.

Glanz, Rudolf. "Vanguard to the Russians: The Poseners in America." *Yivo Annual of Jewish Social Science* 18 (1983): 1–38.

Glatstein, Jerome, and Charles Rutstein. *History of Congregation Anshe Emeth [Pine Bluff, Ark.] 100th Anniversary.* Privately published, 1967.

Glazer, Simon. *The Jews of Iowa: A Complete History and Accurate Account of Their Religious, Social Economical and Educational Progress in This State.* Des Moines: Koch Brothers Printing, 1904.

Glover, Robert, and Linda Brown Cross. *Tyler and Smith County, Texas: An Historical Survey.* Tyler: Smith County Historical Society, 1976.

Golden Anniversary, 1900–1950: A History of Congregation Temple Emanuel, Golden Jubilee. Beaumont: Temple Emanuel, 1950.

Goldenstein, Raphael. *History and Activities of Congregation Anshe-Emeth, Pine Bluff, Ark., 1867–1917.* Publication of the congregation, 1917.

Goodman, Fanny Sattinger. "In the Beginning: The Jewish Community of El Paso, Texas." 23 pages. 1970.

Greater Houston Section National Council of Jewish Women. *Yesterday, Today and Tomorrow.* Houston: R. Printing, undated.

Green, Alan S. *If God Were King: The Times and Words of Rabbi Alan S. Green.* Cleveland: Temple Emanu El, 1988.

Greenberg, Mark I. "Becoming Southern: The Jews of Savannah, Georgia, 1830–70." *American Jewish History* 86 (March, 1998): 55–76.

Greene, Casey Edward. "Apostles of Hate: The Ku Klux Klan in and Near Houston Texas, 1920–1982." Master's thesis. University of Houston, Clear Lake, 1995.

Greenstein, Howard R. *Turning Point: Zionism and Reform Judaism.* Chico, Calif.: Scholars Press, 1981.

Grove, Larry. *Dallas Public Library: The First Seventy-five Years.* Dallas: Dallas Public Library, 1977.

Haley, James L. *Texas: From Spindletop Through World War II.* New York: St. Martin's Press, 1993.

Harris, Larry A. *Pancho Villa: Strong Man of the Revolution.* Silver City, N.M.: High-Lonesome Books, 1989.

Hartog, Jan de. *The Hospital.* New York: Atheneum, 1964.

Haynes, Robert. *A Night of Violence: The Houston Riot of 1917.* Baton Rouge: Louisiana State University Press, 1976.

Hazel, Michael V. "The Critic Club, Sixty Years of Quiet Leadership." *Legacies: A History Journal for Dallas and North Central Texas* 2 (fall, 1990): 9–17.

Held, John A. *Religion, a Factor in Building Texas.* San Antonio: Naylor, 1940.

Heller, James G. *Isaac Mayer Wise: His Life, Work, and Thought.* New York: Union of American Hebrew Congregations Press, 1965.

Henderson, Richard B. *Maury Maverick: A Political Biography.* Austin: University of Texas Press, 1970.

History of Waller County, Texas. Waco: Waller County Historical Survey Committee, 1973.

Holmes, Ann Hitchcock. *Joy Unconfined: Robert Joy in Houston, a Portrait of Fifty Years.* Houston: San Jacinto Museum of History Association, 1986.

Horn, Stanley F. *Invisible Empire: The Story of the Ku Klux Klan, 1866–1871.* Second edition. Montclair, N.J.: Patterson Smith, 1969.

Hurley, Marvin. *Decisive Years for Houston.* Houston: Houston Chamber of Commerce, 1966.

Hyman, Harold M. *Oleander Odyssey.* College Station: Texas A&M University Press, 1990.

Inselberg, Lee Bradley. "Changing Worlds: Jewish Women in Lubbock, Texas." Master's thesis. Texas Tech University, 1982.

Jacobs, Louis. *The Jewish Religion: A Companion.* New York: Oxford University Press, 1995.

Jewish Encyclopedia. New York and London: Funk and Wagnalls, 1901–1906.

"Jewish Texans." San Antonio: University of Texas, Institute of Texan Cultures, 1974. Booklet. 28 pages.

Johnson, Frank W., and Eugene C. Barker, *A History of Texas and the Texans,* vols. 1–3. Chicago and New York: American Historical Society, 1914.

Johnston, Marguerite Barnes. *Houston, the Unknown City, 1836–1946.* College Station: Texas A&M University Press, 1991.

Joseph, Harriett Denise. "Temple Beth-El, 1931–1981." In *Studies in Brownsville History,* ed. Milo Kearney. Edinburg, Tex.: Pan American University, 1986, pp. 230–44.

———, and Sondra Shands. "Sam Perl: Mr. Friendship and Mr. Temple Beth-El of Brownsville, Texas." *Locus* 5 (spring, 1993): 145–62.

Journal of the Senate, State of Texas, Second Called Session Thirty-fifth Legislature, Convened in the City of Austin, August 1, 1917, and Adjourned Without Day August 30. Austin, 1917.

Kaganoff, Nathan, and Melvin Urofsky. *Turn to the South: Essays on Southern Jewry.* Charlottesville: American Jewish Historical Society and University Press of Virginia, 1979.

Kallison, Frances. "100 Years of Jewry in San Antonio." Master's thesis. Trinity University, San Antonio, 1977.

Karff, Samuel, ed. *Hebrew Union College–Jewish Institute of Religion at One Hundred Years.* Cincinnati: Hebrew Union College Press, 1976.

Kessler, James Lee. "B.O.I.: A History of Congregation B'nai Israel, Galveston, Texas." Doctoral dissertation. Hebrew Union College, 1988.

———. "A Study of the Split of Congregation Beth Israel, Houston, Texas, 1942–44." Manuscript. Hebrew Union College, 1971. AJA.

Kingston, Mike, ed. *Texas Almanac and State Industrial Guide.* Dallas: *Dallas Morning News,* 1993.

Kohlberg, Ernst. *Letters of Ernst Kohlberg: 1875–1877.* Translated by Walter L. Kohlberg. El Paso: Texas Western Press, 1973.

Kolsky, Thomas A. *Jews Against Zionism: The American Council for Judaism, 1942–1948.* Philadelphia: Temple University Press, 1990.

Krause, Corinne Azen. "The Jews in Mexico: A History with Special Emphasis on the Period from 1857 to 1930." Ph.D. dissertation. University of Pittsburgh, 1970.

———. "Mexico—Another Promised Land? A Review of Projects for Jewish Colonization in Mexico: 1881–1925." *American Jewish Historical Quarterly* 61 (June, 1972): 325–41.

Kroutter, Thomas E., Jr. "The Ku Klux Klan in Jefferson County Texas, 1921–1924." Master's thesis. Lamar University, Beaumont, 1972.

Lefever, Alan J. *Fighting the Good Fight: The Life and Work of Benajah Harvey Carroll.* Austin: Eakin Press, 1994.

Lefkowitz, David. *Medicine for a Sick World.* Dallas: Southern Methodist University Press. 1952.

LeMaster, Carolyn Gray. *A Corner of the Tapestry: A History of the Jewish Experience in Arkansas, 1820s–1990s.* Little Rock: University of Arkansas Press, 1994.

Lester, Paul. *The Great Galveston Disaster.* Philadelphia: Globe Bible Publishing, 1900.

Linden, Glenn M. *Desegregating Schools in Dallas.* Dallas: Three Forks Press, 1995.

Linsley, Judith Walker, and Ellen Walker Rienstra. *Beaumont, a Chronicle of Promise: An Illustrated History.* Woodland Hills, Calif.: Windsor, 1982.

Lomax, John A., and Alan Lomax. *Best Loved American Folksongs.* New York: Grosset and Dunlap, 1947.

Lubarsky, Sandra B., and David Ray Griffin. *Jewish Theology and Process Thought.* Albany: State University of New York Press, 1996.

Maas, Elaine H. *The Jews of Houston: An Ethnographic Study.* New York: AMS Press, 1989.

Malone, Bobbie. *Rabbi Max Heller: Reformer, Zionist, Southerner, 1860–1929.* Tuscaloosa: University of Alabama Press, 1997.

Mangan, Frank. *El Paso in Pictures.* El Paso: Mangan Books, 1971.

Marcus, Jacob Rader, and Abraham J. Peck. *The American Rabbinate: A Century of Continuity and Change, 1883–1983.* Hoboken: Ktav, 1983.

Marinbach, Bernard. *Galveston: Ellis Island of the West.* Albany: State University of New York Press, 1983.

Martinez, Pete. "A History of Tyler Masonic Lodge No. 1233." *Chronicles of Smith County Texas* 35 (summer, 1996): 22–27.

McComb, David G. *Galveston: A History.* Austin: University of Texas Press, 1986.

———. *Houston: A History.* Austin: University of Texas Press, 1981.

Meites, Hyman L. *History of the Jews of Chicago.* Chicago: Chicago Jewish Historical Society and Wellington Publishing, 1924.

Mensing, Raymond C., Jr. "A Papal Delegate in Texas: The Visit of His Eminence Cardinal Satolli." *East Texas Historical Journal* 20 (fall, 1982): 18–27.

Meyer, Michael A. *Response to Modernity: A History of the Reform Movement in Judaism.* Oxford: Oxford University Press, 1988.

Meyers Lexicon. Leipzig: Biographische Institut, 1929.

Miller, Ray. *Ray Miller's Houston.* Houston: Cordovan Press, 1982.

Moore, James T. *Through Fire and Flood: The Catholic Church in Frontier Texas, 1836–1900.* College Station: Texas A&M University Press, 1992.

Moses, Jay Henry. "Henry A. Henry: The Life and Work of an American Rabbi, 1849–1864." Rabbinical dissertation. Hebrew Union College, 1997.

Nalle, Ouida Ferguson. *The Fergusons of Texas or Two Governors for the Price of One: A Biography of James Edward Ferguson and his wife, Miriam Amanda Ferguson, Ex-governors of the State of Texas.* San Antonio: Naylor, 1946.

Nathan, Anne, and Harry I. Cohen. *The Man Who Stayed in Texas: The Life of Rabbi Henry Cohen.* York, Pa.: Whittlesey House, McGraw-Hill, 1941.

Norton, Wesley. "Negro Trail-Driver, Jean Spence Perrault, and His Beaumont Descendants." *Texas Gulf Historical and Biographical Record* 19 (November, 1983): 35–50.

Noveck, Simon. *Milton Steinberg: Portrait of a Rabbi.* New York: Ktav, 1978.

Olan, Levi A. *Maturity in an Immature World.* New York: Ktav, 1984.

———. *Prophetic Faith and the Secular Age.* New York: Ktav, 1982.

Ornish, Natalie. *Pioneer Jewish Texans.* Dallas: Texas Heritage Press, 1989.

Ousley, Clarence, ed. *Galveston in 1900.* Atlanta: William Chase, 1900.

Paddock, B. Buckley. *History of Texas: Fort Worth and the Texas Northwest Edition.* Chicago: Lewis, 1922.

Paulissen, May Nelson, and Carl Randall McQueary. *Miriam: The Southern Belle Who Became the First Woman Governor of Texas.* Austin: Eakin Press, 1995.

Payne, Darwin. *Big D: Triumphs and Troubles of an American Supercity in the 20th Century.* Dallas: Three Forks Press, 1994.

Petit, Don R. *Threshold of Tomorrow: The Great Society: The Inauguration of Lyndon Baines Johnson, 36th President of the United States.* Washington, D.C.: 1965 Presidential Inaugural Committee, January 20, 1965.

Peyton, Green [Wertenbaker]. *San Antonio, City in the Sun.* New York: Whittlesey House, McGraw-Hill, 1946.

Pirtle, Caleb, III. *Fort Worth: The Civilized West.* Tulsa: Continental Heritage Press, 1980.

Podet, Mordecai. *Pioneer Jews of Waco.* Waco: Privately published, 1986.

Porterfield, Nolen. *The Last Cavalier: The Life and Times of John A. Lomax, 1867–1948.* Urbana: University of Illinois Press, 1996.

Postal, Bernard, and Lionel Koppman. *American Jewish Landmarks,* 2nd ed. Vol. 2, *The South and Southwest.* New York: Fleet Press, 1979.

Preuss, Karl. "Personality, Politics, and the Price of Justice: Rabbi Ephraim Frisch and the San Antonio Police Raid of 1937." *American Jewish History* 85 (September, 1997): 263–88.

"Quaint Customs and Methods of the Ku Klux Klan." *Literary Digest,* August 5, 1922, pp. 44–52.

Rabinowitz, Stanley. *The Assembly: A Century of Life in the Adas Israel Hebrew Congregtion of Washington, D.C.* Hoboken: Ktav, 1993.

Raphael, Marc Lee. *Abba Hillel Silver: A Profile in American Judaism.* New York: Holmes and Meier, 1989.

Rips, Geoffrey. "Living History: Emma Tenayuca Tells Her Story." *Texas Observer,* October 28, 1983, pp. 1–7, 11.

Ritz, David. "Inside the Jewish Establishment." *D: The Magazine of Dallas,* November, 1975, pp. 50–55, 108–16.

Rochlin, Harriet, and Fred Rochlin. *Pioneer Jews: A New Life in the Far West.* Boston: Houghton Mifflin, 1984.

Rosen, Evelyn Rosing. "Martin Zielonka: Rabbi and Civic Leader in El Paso." *El Paso Jewish Historical Review* 1 (September, 1982): 5–12.

Rosenberg, Stuart. *The Jewish Community in Rochester, 1843–1925.* New York: American Jewish Historical Society, 1954.

Rosenwald, Lessing. "Reply to Zionism." *Life,* June 28, 1943, p. 11.

Rosinger, Samuel. *My Life and My Message.* Beaumont: Privately published, 1958.

Rosten, Leo. *The Joys of Yiddish.* New York: McGraw Hill, 1968.

Rutherford, Bruce. *The Impeachment of Jim Ferguson.* Austin: Eakin Press, 1983.

Sachar, Howard. *History of the Jews in America.* New York: Alfred A. Knopf, 1992.

Schachtel, Hyman Judah. *How to Meet the Challenge of Life and Death.* Houston: Privately published, undated.

———. *The Real Enjoyment of Living.* New York: Dutton, 1954.

———. *The Shadowed Valley.* New York: Knopf, 1962.

———. "Varieties of Preachers and Preaching." Lectures, January 20–23, 1964. In *Aspects of Jewish Homiletics,* vol. 7, ed. Eugene Mihaly. Cincinnati: Hebrew Union College, 1964.

Schlam, Helena Frenkil. "The Early Jews of Houston." Master's thesis. Ohio State University, 1971.

Schmier, Louis. *Reflections of Southern Jewry: The Letters of Charles Wessolowsky, 1878–1879.* Macon, Ga.: Mercer University Press, 1982.

Schrecker, Ellen W. *No Ivory Tower: McCarthyism and the Universities.* New York: Oxford University Press, 1986.

Selcer, Richard F. *Hell's Half Acre.* Fort Worth: Texas Christian University Press, 1991.

Sender, Alexander. *Hatarat N'darim* [The Redemption of Vows]. Vilna and Jerusalem, 1880.

Shargel, Baila Round. *Lost Love: The Untold Story of Henrietta Szold.* Philadelphia: Jewish Publication Society of America, 1997.

Shelton, Beth Anne et al. *Houston: Growth and Decline in a Sunbelt Boomtown.* Philadelphia: Temple University Press, 1989.

Shilo-Cohen, Nutrit, ed. *Bezalel: 1906–1929.* Jerusalem: Israel Museum, 1983.

Sibley, Marilyn McAdams. *George W. Brackenridge: Maverick Philanthropist.* Austin: University of Texas Press, 1973.

Smallwood, James M., *Will Rogers' Weekly Articles.* Vol. 2, *The Coolidge Years: 1925–1927.* Stillwater: Oklahoma State University, 1980.

"Smith County Religious Denominations." *Chronicles of Smith County Texas* 31 (summer, 1992): 26.

Smith, Jesse Guy. *Heroes of the Saddle Bags: A History of Christian Denominations in the Republic of Texas.* San Antonio: Naylor, 1951.

Smith, Richard Austin. "How Business Failed Dallas." *Fortune,* July, 1964, pp. 156–63, 211–16.

Spindler, Frank MacD. "Concerning Hempstead and Waller County." *Southwestern Historical Quarterly* 59 (April, 1956): 454–72.

St. John, Robert. *Jews, Justice and Judaism.* Garden City, N.Y.: Doubleday, 1969.

Steen, Ralph W. "The Ferguson War on the University of Texas." *Southwestern Social Science Quarterly* 35 (March, 1955): 356–62.

Steven T. Katz, ed. *Jewish Philosophers.* New York: Bloch, 1975.

"Storm Over Zion." *Time,* January, 17, 1944, pp. 38–40.

Stratton, Florence. *Story of Beaumont.* Houston: Hercules Printing and Book, 1925.

Street, James. "Dazzling Dallas." *Holiday,* March, 1953, pp. 102–10.

Temple Shaaray Tefila. "Conclusion of 150th Anniversary and Dedication of Our New Torah." May 21, 1995. New York. Booklet.

Teter, Donald L., and Gertrude M. Teter, eds. *Texas Jewish Burials.* Texas Jewish Historical Society, 1997.

Tunick, Irve. "An America Ballad," *The Eternal Light,* NBC Television, July 4, 1948. Transcript.

Tyler, Ron, ed. *New Handbook of Texas,* vols. 1–6. Austin: Texas State Historical Association, 1996.

Universal Jewish Encyclopedia. New York: UJE, 1943.

Vinson, Robert E. "The University Crosses the Bar." *Southwestern Historical Quarterly* 43 (January, 1940): 281–94.

Vorspan, Albert. *Giants of Justice.* New York: Union of American Hebrew Congregations, 1960.

———, and Eugene Lipman. *Justice and Judaism: The Work of Social Action.* New York: Union of American Hebrew Congregations, 1956.

Wade, Wyn Craig. *The Fiery Cross: The Ku Klux Klan in America.* New York: Simon and Schuster, 1987,

Waldron, Webb. "First Citizen of Texas." *Reader's Digest,* February, 1939, pp. 97–98. Reprinted from *Rotarian,* February, 1939.

Weinbaum, Eleanor Perlstein. *Shalom America.* Burnet, Tex.: Nortex, 1981.

Weiner, Hollace Ava. "The Mixers: The Role of Rabbis Deep in the Heart of Texas." *American Jewish History* 85 (September, 1997): 289–332.

Weiss, Winifred, and Charles S. Proctor, *Umphrey Lee: A Biography.* Nashville: Abingdon Press, 1971

Winegarten, Ruthe, and Cathy Schechter, *Deep in the Heart: The Lives and Legends of Texas Jews, a Photographic History.* Austin: Eakin Press, 1990.

Wolf, Simon. *The American Jew As Patriot, Soldier and Citizen.* Philadelphia: Levytype, 1895.

Wolfe, Jack. *A Century of Iowa Jewry: As Complete a History As Could Be Obtained of Iowa Jewry from 1833 through 1940.* Des Moines: Iowa Printing and Supply, 1941.

Zielonka, Martin. "El Sabado: A Spanish American Jewish Periodical." *Publications of the American Jewish Historical Society* 23 (1915): 129–35.

———. "Francisco Rivas," *Publications of the American Jewish Historical Society* 35 (1939): 219–25.

———. Microfilm No. 46. "Material from Martin Zielonka Collection." AJA.

———. Microfilm No. 484. "Sermons, lectures and newspaper clippings dealing with his career, material on Mexico City Jewish community, and necrologies. El Paso, Texas. 1900–38." AJA.

———. Microfilm No. 600–600B. "Correspondence and Reports, Mexican Bureau, B'nai B'rith, 1921–33." AJA.

TAPE-RECORDED INTERVIEWS AND WEB SITES

"Armand Spitz." Internet Web site http://www.griffithobs.org/IPSArmand.

Bass, Adelle Isaacson, and Lorraine Solomon Moss. Interview with author. Chicago, November 6, 1995. Tape.

"Congregation Shaareth Israel, Lubbock, Texas." Internet Web site http://uahc.org/congs/tx/ tx002.

Davis, Robert A. "Virtual Restoration of Small-town Synagogues in Texas." Internet Web site http://www.neosoft.com/~TJHS/identity.html.

Garza, Reynaldo. Interview with author. Brownsville, February 10, 1997. Tape.

Goldsmith, Allen. Interview with author. San Antonio, April 4, 1997. Tape.

Goodman, Frances Perl. Interview with author. San Antonio, August 9, 1996. Tape.

Goodman, Leonard Sr. Interview with author. El Paso, April 9, 1994. Tape.

Kahn, Robert I. "Oral Memoirs." Houston, May 30, 1977. Cassette C-10, American Jewish Archives.

———. Interview with Louis Marchiafava. Houston, August 6, 1975. Transcript. Texas Jewish Historical Society Collection. Center for American History.

Kallison, Frances. Interview with author. San Antonio, January 7, 1996. Tape.

Marcus, Jacob Rader. Interview with author. Cincinnati, December 13, 1992. Tape and transcript.

Maverick, Maury Jr. Interview with author. San Antonio, April 4, 1997. Tape.

Olan, Levi A. Interview with Hortense Sanger. Dallas, August 5, 1972. Tape and transcript. Dorothy M. and Henry S. Jacobus Temple Emanu-El Archives, Dallas.

Schachtel, Barbara. Interviews with author. Houston, March 3, 7, 1997. Tape.

Turner, Decherd, and Margaret Ann Turner. Interview with author. Austin, August 14, 1997. Tape.

Weil, Marion. Interview with author. Fort Worth, July 31, 1994. Tape.

PERIODICALS AND ANNUALS

Alcalde. Austin: University of Texas Ex-Students Association, 1916–18.

American Hebrew, New York, 1915–18.

American Israelite, 1859–1908.

American Jewish Year Book. Philadelphia: Jewish Publication Society of America, 1899–1997. Annual.

Austin American, 1916–17.

Beaumont Enterprise, 1910–65.

Brenham [Texas] Daily Banner, 1873–75.

Brownsville Herald, 1926–80.

Cactus. Austin: University of Texas Student Publications, Inc., 1916–50. Annual.

Central Conference of American Rabbis Yearbook. Cincinnati: Bloch, 1899–1997. Annual.

Chicago Sun-Times, 1922–60.

Congress [Philadelphia] Weekly, 1942–43.

Dallas Daily [and Weekly] Herald, 1874–84.

Dallas Express, 1963.

Dallas Morning News, 1917–18, 1949–84.

Dallas Times Herald, 1949–84.

Die Deborah, Cincinnati, 1873–1900.

El Paso Times, 1898–1934.

Fort Worth Star-Telegram, 1910–22, 1986–97.

Galveston Daily News, 1900–24.

Galveston Tribune, 1900–24.

Hebrew Union College Journal, 1896–1903.

Hebrew Union College Monthly, 1914–35.

Jewish [Fort Worth] Monitor. Klau Library microfilm reels: April 1–September 30, 1915; March 28, 1919–October 18, 1920; November, 1926–December, 1929 (incomplete); April 12, 1930. Center for American History, Austin, microfilm reels: June 20, 1919–October 25, 1929.

Jewish [San Antonio] Record, 1927–38.

Kallah Yearbook: An Annual Convention of Texas Rabbis. 1927–36. Publisher and location vary.

Lubbock Avalanche Journal, 1939–79.

New York Times, 1918–57.

Occident, 1853–80.

Reform [Chicago] Advocate, 1910–22.

San Antonio Express, 1923–42.

San Antonio Light, 1923–42.

Sentinel [Chicago], 1922–60.

Texas [Houston] Jewish Herald/Jewish Herald-Voice, 1914–18, 1941–43.

Tyler Courier Journal, 1910, 1916, 1934.

Tyler Daily Courier Times, September, 1934.

Western States Jewish Historical Quarterly/Western States Jewish History, 1967–97.

Woodville [Mississippi] Republican, 1885–88.

Index

Pages containing illustrations appear in italics.